ZULU

ZULU

Queen Victoria's Most Famous Little War

W.B. BARTLETT

The
History
Press

To Pete – a true friend

First published 2010

The History Press
The Mill, Brimscombe Port
Stroud, Gloucestershire, GL5 2QG
www.thehistorypress.co.uk

British Library Cataloguing in Publication Data.
A catalogue record for this book is available from the British Library.

ISBN 978 0 7524 5543 3

Typesetting and origination by The History Press
Printed in Great Britain
Manufacturing managed by Jellyfish Print Solutions Ltd

CONTENTS

INTRODUCTION

The Anglo-Zulu War has not always gripped the imagination in the way that it does now. However, recent decades have seen a veritable surge in interest. It is tempting to speculate that the increased profile of the conflict arose from the same two factors that first stimulated my own interest. Hollywood played its part; the film *Zulu* (1964) gripped the imagination when it was first released and continues to do so. Despite its glaring historical inaccuracies (the drunken Hitch, the pompous upper-class Bromhead and the singing of *Men of Harlech* by the gallant defenders for example), it works magnificently as what it is supposed to be: an epic movie, not a historically accurate documentary.

There was for me though another seminal event at around the same time: the publication of the equally grand *The Washing of the Spears*, written by Donald Morris and first published in 1965. This remains a vividly written work of history and, although contemporary commentators may question some of its factual content, there can be no disputing the richness of the narrative which does full justice to the depth of the drama it is based on.

Recently there has been a remarkable increase in activity and this has taken research to an altogether higher level. There have been some prolific researchers who have undertaken a great deal of work, adding to knowledge of the Anglo-Zulu War immensely. It is always dangerous to mention individuals by name but the debt that students of the Anglo-Zulu War owe to people such as Ian Knight, Ian Castle, Dr Adrian Greaves, Professor John Laband and many others is immense and I acknowledge from the outset that without them this book could not have been written. Importantly, they have introduced a sense of balance, which has in some ways led to the antithesis of the heroic image portrayed in the Hollywood take on the Zulu story.

War is always an emotive subject. Although many aspects of it are distressing, many of us are also fascinated by it because it often provides, in addition to vivid drama, examples of courage under fire, perseverance against insuperable odds and tactical skill. In this book I have tried to recognise these qualities where they exist but also acknowledge that for each virtue there is an opposite vice. That is an immutable result of our human failings. I do not, at this remove, intend to judge harshly the actions of men from either side in battle, who must often have been terrified out of their wits. I have never been directly involved in a war and can barely imagine how awful one must be for a protagonist.

However, that exemption of judgement does not extend to the political arena. There were a number of mistakes that were made which led to the war being fought in the first place. Most (though not all) came from the British side. Of course, the paradigms of the ruling classes in South Africa (then a region rather than a country) were often very different than our own. But it is important to point out that there were a number of people at the time, even on the British side, who felt that the war was misguided and morally unjustifiable. I do not intend to let politicians off the hook as easily as I will soldiers in battle.

Neither would it be right to let military strategists, as opposed to the common soldier, escape judgement; it was their decisions that shaped the course of the war. More accurately 'wars', perhaps, for there were two invasions, the first of which was dramatically repulsed by an unexpected Zulu triumph. Strategic failings on either side were both apparent and decisive in determining the course of events.

I am particularly interested in the role of Lord Chelmsford. Of course, a commander in the field is usually the dominant figure, certainly in terms of shaping the strategy, but the Anglo-Zulu War was a conflict that exposed Chelmsford to the whole gamut of emotions in a way that is rarely the case. This in part was because Chelmsford's great reserves of energy meant that he was often right in the thick of the action. The war took over Chelmsford's life, so much so that he wanted to be involved in even the most mundane of details. And, in turn, the war would be the decisive factor in establishing his own reputation.

He also played an important part in the events that led up to the war in the first place. He therefore deserves examination at both the political and the military level. He is a complex character; a bumbling oaf would seem to be the prevailing assessment in some quarters. However, an assessment of his performance in the war is not that simple and, although I will certainly not be painting him as a military genius, it is important that we recognise the lessons he learned along the way as well as how his strategy was shaped by events.

It is vital to ask ourselves why the Anglo-Zulu War has such a hold on modern imaginations as opposed to other Victorian-era conflicts. There are some obvious reasons concerning its dramatic nature – the defence of Rorke's Drift, the bloodbath of Isandlwana and the death of the Prince Imperial, for example. But there were other striking events from other wars of the time that have been, in comparison, long forgotten.

I think it is because the war asks some very clear questions, in particular about post-colonial views of the colonial era. The two sides cannot have been more different; although it was not completely a case of guns against spears, there was certainly a massive difference in the armament of the two sides. This suggested to those in command that the result of the war should be a foregone conclusion.

Perhaps there is a guilt element involved; it is hard to escape the conclusion that the war was impossible to justify in moral terms. There were unmistakable racial undertones too and, in the race-conscious era in which we live, this touches a nerve. And it was indeed a slaughter in the end, with thousands of Zulu lives lost through battlefield wounds, disease and hunger brought about by draconian scorched-earth policies.

Whatever the reason, that the fascination in the Anglo-Zulu War is as strong as ever is self-evident. For example, a vibrant Anglo-Zulu War Historical Society continues to thrive; I also acknowledge my debt to the research undertaken by its members as well as other associations with a keen interest in the conflict. They have helped to provide a much better understanding of the course of events.

The story which follows attempts to explore what it was like for all those caught up in it, drawing on contemporary research as well as the large number of eye-witness accounts that have survived. It is important to return to the basic story minus its trappings from time to time and, therefore, I have attempted to look in particular at the accounts of those who were there at the time in the narrative.

There is no doubting the richness of the drama that is provided by the war but there is also no mistaking its tragic nature either. It was a conflict that brought to an abrupt end the rise of a great nation that came out of nowhere. But it was also in its own way a clash that pointed towards the demise of another great empire that would, within much less than a century, find its own place in the world radically changed. It was a situation that Victoria, empress and ruler of a third of the globe, could never have envisaged. She too played her part in events and, in one of the strangest interviews that can be imagined, met the defeated Zulu king Cetshwayo in England after the war. Perhaps even at the time she realised that this might become the most famous of her so-called 'Little Wars'.

MAPS

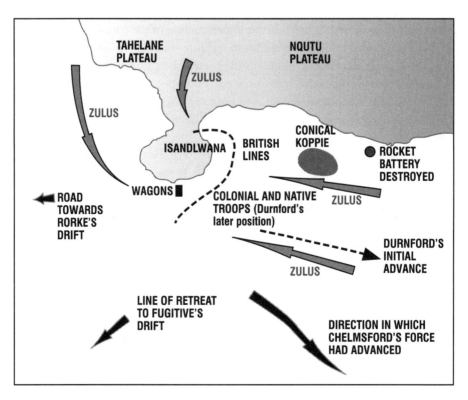

Outline plan of Isandlwana

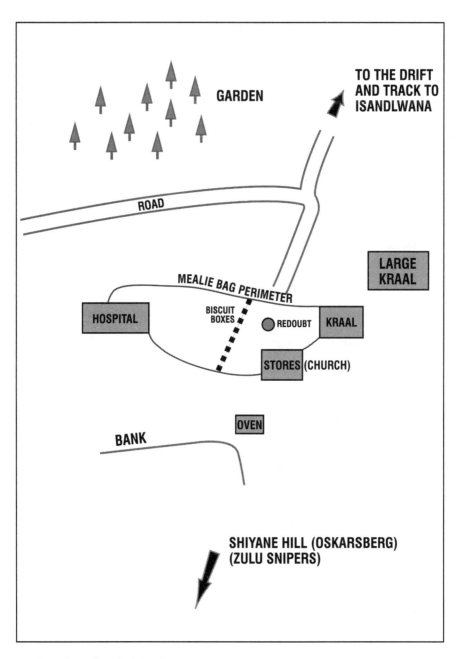

Outline plan of Rorke's Drift

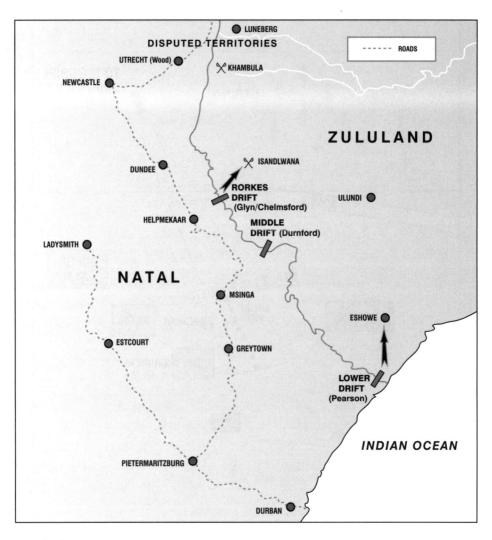

The first invasion

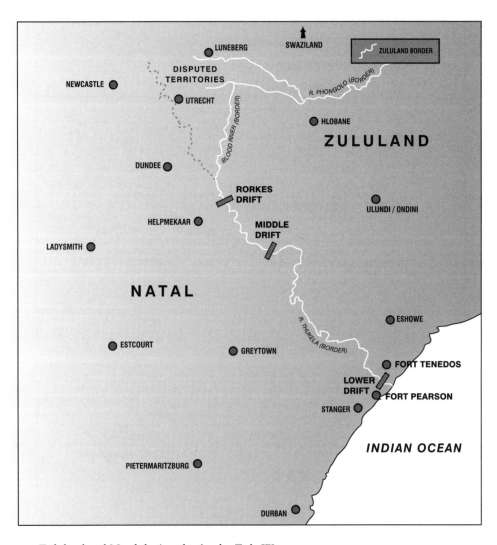

Zululand and Natal during the Anglo-Zulu War

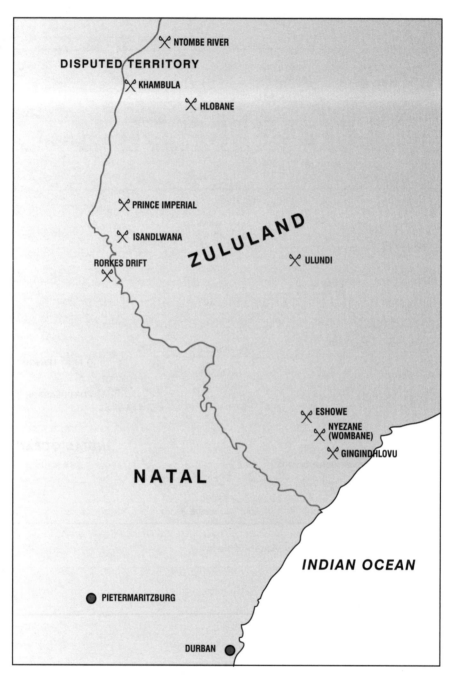

Battlefields of the Anglo–Zulu War

one

A CLASH OF EMPIRES

The Rise of the Zulus

For millennia, Africa – with the exception of the regions in the north – was an almost completely unknown entity to Europeans. Then in the fifteenth century a great age of exploration began most famously when Columbus journeyed west in search of a route to the riches of the Orient. It was a brave move, a leap into the dark, but there were others equally bold who looked for a route the other way round, travelling to the east. They too had little idea where they were going or what they would find when they got there. The only route possible, they soon found, was to travel far to the south for thousands of miles before then heading east into an ocean that was entirely new to them.

One of these valiant explorers was a Portuguese mariner by the name of Vasco da Gama. He made his way down the coast of Africa and then, in simplistic landlubber terms, turned left. He turned the corner and started to make his way north, up the eastern coast of the continent. It was on Christmas Day 1497 that he spied a previously unknown land. It did not offer an easy harbour anywhere so he was unable to land. However, in honour of the festival of the nativity he called it Natalia. Thus was Natal introduced to Europe.

At the same time, unknown to Vasco da Gama or anyone else in Europe, a group of black tribes were journeying south down the eastern side of Africa. They were Bantu people, hunter-gatherers, and in their own way they themselves were empire-builders as much as the Portuguese, Spanish, Dutch or British were. Their tactics were somewhat different from the Europeans, progressing by land rather than sea. So too was the stage of technological development that they had reached. But they also wanted land, though more for survival than mere exploitation.

The Bantu people eventually stopped in the south-eastern corner of Africa, almost as far as they could go. The Europeans, in the meantime, had shown little interest in the country there. It was harsh terrain with little attraction for mercenary-minded adventurers other than as a staging-post on the long voyage east to much richer climes. It was not until well into the seventeenth century that a European settlement was established anywhere in the region and then it was at Cape Town, in the far south-west corner of Africa. Its sole use was as a place for ships to stop on the journeys to and from India and the Far East. It was a remote settlement, of interest only to extreme adventurers or ne'er-do-wells; every bit a place on the frontiers of civilisation and, indeed, at the very edge of the world.

The hinterland beyond this tiny corner these Europeans largely left untouched. It was a place where savage tribes lived: dangerous, barbaric and uncivilised, as they saw it. Therefore the two groups, a tiny number of whites on the coast and a mass of black tribes everywhere else, largely lived in ignorance of each other. Just occasionally a ship would be wrecked on the treacherous coastline of Natal and a small group of survivors would be swallowed up by the tribes living in the area. Apart from this, there was no contact at all.

The Europeans were therefore initially largely unaware of the rise of a major new power in the region which took place at the end of the eighteenth century. The Zulus were a minor clan of no major importance until the emergence of an extraordinary leader by the name of Shaka. Like many other great warriors – Alexander or Genghis Khan, for example – his upbringing had been difficult. His mother Nandi was a proud and spirited woman, the daughter of a chief, and his father Senzangakhona was a prominent if feckless Zulu who was destined to be chief of the tribe. Unfortunately, his father and mother were not married to each other and his conception was an accident.

It was a great humiliation in Bantu society to be born out of wedlock and Nandi and her son were subject to scorn and abuse during Shaka's formative years. Senzangakhona grudgingly married Nandi but threw her out a few years later. Shaka and his mother therefore suffered the bitter taste of rejection and his subsequent adolescence was extremely unpleasant. The boys whom he grew up with teased him mercilessly, in particular remarking on his underdeveloped genitalia. As such, he reached maturity with a burning desire to succeed and a passionate hatred of those who had made his early years such a misery. They were to suffer for it.

Nandi and Shaka later found sanctuary with another tribe, the Mthethwa, after being effectively thrown out by their own people. The Mthethwa were at least a rising power and their chief, Dingiswayo, was an astute leader. However, no special status was afforded Shaka or his mother despite their prominent background and the young man's sense of resentment continued to grow.

Dingiswayo in many ways looked after them well and Shaka grew in stature, both in a physical and a metaphorical sense. He became an outstanding military tactician and introduced a number of innovations including the development of a regimental system which would later form the basis of the Zulu military organisation. When he eventually had enough men under his command, the regiments – known as *amabutho* – were formed of men of similar ages who therefore bonded strongly together. His tactics were also a revelation in Bantu warfare, previously a formalised affair with normally limited casualties. Shaka introduced a different concept into warcraft, that of attempting to obliterate your enemy.

Shaka became a prominent warrior in one of the Mthethwa regiments, the iziCwe. He developed a reputation for both his strength and ingenuity, and, although the stories told of him may have lost nothing in the telling, there seems to have been more than a grain of truth in them. Eventually, a reconciliation of sorts with Senzangakhona, his natural father, was achieved and Shaka was recognised as the heir to the Zulu chiefdom. When his father died, Shaka's half-brother, Sigujana, attempted to grab the throne for himself. He died a painful death as a result (though Shaka himself avoided killing him in person as this would result in a severe stigma in Bantu society). Shaka had introduced himself to the wider world.

When Shaka took over as leader of the Zulus, his inheritance was a mediocre one. There were just a few thousand members of his tribe and they had no great heritage to look back on. His first task was to take over the military organisation of his warriors, allocating them into regiments. Crucially, he also decided that the assegai should no longer be a throwing weapon, but used for stabbing at close range instead. He also ordered his soldiers to remove their sandals to help them move more quickly – not an easy option in the broken terrain that characterised Zululand. To help them to adapt to this change, he ordered his warriors to dance barefoot on a carpet of thorns. Drums beat out a rhythmic pulse; any man who was not dancing in time to the music was executed.

Shaka also changed the tribe's battle tactics, building on what he had already learned when fighting for Dingiswayo. His warriors were given specific roles in the battle formation, which was organised in four sections: the chest, the loins and two horns. The chest led the attack, launching itself in a headlong assault, whilst the horns deployed either side in an encircling movement. They would then surround the enemy whilst the loins hung back in reserve (the men here were supposed to look away from the fighting in case they became overexcited and rushed to join in). When an attack was launched there would be no mercy shown. It was a very different approach to what had previously been seen in local warfare and it was often devastating.

Shaka and his men started to conquer all before them. In a further move to maintain discipline, Shaka decreed that his warriors would no longer be able to marry without his permission. They would in effect be married to his army and would only be allowed to take a wife when he gave permission for a whole regiment to do so. This was a privilege he did not grant lightly.

Women were similarly organised in *amabutho* though not for the purposes of fighting, but rather to organise them for mass marriages when the king did give a group of his warriors' permission to marry. They had a crucial role in Zulu society, as they were required to tend the crops (looking after the herds and hunting being a man's job). When they were married, the family of these women would each receive a dowry (*ilobolo*), inevitably in the form of cattle.

But these changes were not possible without the strong arm of the king. Shaka was cruel and ruthless, as a result of which he made many enemies. Amongst them was his half-brother, Dingane. Blood-relationships were no bar to a violent death; in fact, if a man felt threatened because of them then a gruesome end was more likely. Living in fear as a result of Shaka's violent temper, and feeling that it was only a matter of time before they too died a horrible death, some of those threatened decided to take matters into their own hands.

On 23 September 1828 Shaka was holding court, dressed for a delegation of emissaries that, annoyingly, was late. When they arrived, the angered chief laid into them, berating them for their poor punctuality. Then, out of nowhere, the mood changed. The hour was late and it was dark. The army was away and there were therefore few guards around the king. From the shadows assassins emerged, armed with assegais, the short, stabbing-spear that Shaka had introduced. They thrust at him repeatedly and Shaka fell, dying, to the ground. As his life ebbed away, he could see Dingane standing over him. Realising that there were just seconds remaining before the spark of life was extinguished, Shaka made a poignant peroration: 'The whole land will be white with the stars, and it will be overrun with swallows.'[1]

Perhaps there were those who thought even at the time that this ominous, if cryptic, prediction referred to a development that had occurred in the last years of Shaka's reign. In 1824, a small group of white men, British adventurers, had put ashore at a place that became known as Port Natal with the intention to stay there, unlike previous visitors to the region. Nevertheless, they were respectfulness personified in their actions and approached Shaka reverentially to ask for his permission to do so. They were granted it and the first hesitant steps in the colonisation of Natal began; the swallows had taken nest in Shaka's kingdom.

Shaka generally treated the tiny group of white men well. Dingane, however, proved less accommodating. He did not trust them but he did not seem to trust many of his own people either. The opening days of the new reign were characterised by a bloodbath as a number of prominent potential opponents were ruthlessly removed – his own brothers included. Only one individual of note survived, another son of Senzangakhona called Mpande, a simple-minded man who seemed to provide no threat and was allowed to live. It was a significant blunder on Dingane's part.

But then a major threat started to emerge from further afield. The whites, Dingane came to realise, were not one homogeneous grouping. The Boers, Dutch settlers in southern Africa, were a different breed than the British and, when the latter abandoned slavery and attempted to impose other changes on the Boer way of life, the former started to look for somewhere else to live.

The hinterland of the continent was still barely known by the Europeans and large numbers of Boer settlers set out in their wagons, leaving the Cape colony and British rule to try and find somewhere else to live. In what became known as the Great Trek, hundreds of families set out looking for a Promised Land. There was no initial unanimity about their ultimate destination, but a number of them had heard that Natal was a fecund and promising land, and it was towards here that some of the great wagon trains began to head.

Leading them was a man of rare talent, a Boer by the name of Piet Retief. Arriving in Natal, these trekkers first of all approached Port Natal, now renamed after its first governor Benjamin D'Urban. The people of Durban were still in an isolated outpost and further settlement in Natal had not taken root; representatives of the British government had shown no interest whatsoever in formally establishing a colony there. The Boers were a welcome addition to the settlers and were therefore greeted warmly.

However, they stayed there at Dingane's sufferance and it was from him that Retief and his followers really needed to obtain permission to remain. The Zulu king was terrified at the prospect, perceiving the Boers, who were good horsemen and excellent marksmen, as a great threat. They had not long before won a stunning victory against the Matabele tribes further west at a place called Vegkop. Hugely outnumbered, they had nevertheless massacred their enemy thanks to their firepower. Dingane would have heard of this one-sided triumph and was very nervous as a result.

Dingane wanted access to a supply of guns for his own people but the Boers, unsurprisingly, were unwilling to co-operate. They continued to negotiate with the king for lands to settle but they sustained their advance too despite the lack of any formal approval from Dingane. In an attempt to impress the chief, Retief decided to journey to his capital with a large delegation. It was a blatant attempt to intimidate but it was also a fatal miscalculation.

At the beginning of February 1838, the Boer delegation arrived at the king's dwelling. There were seventy-one of them. They were arrogant towards the Zulus, which only served to further anger the king and make him more unpredictable. On the morning of 6 February, the delegation made ready to leave. Entering the central enclosure of Dingane's capital they were first of all deprived of their firearms – a normal precautionary measure. Their suspicions not aroused, they sat themselves down before Dingane.

A dance started with hundreds of warriors moving around the delegation. They moved forward in an aggressive fashion but it was all part of the act, or so it was thought. But then Dingane suddenly rose to his feet and shouted a terrifying injunction: 'kill the wizards!' There was a fierce struggle but it was a one-sided fight. The unarmed Boers were overwhelmed, then one by one they were executed. In a cruel refinement, Retief was one of the last to die, having been forced to witness the slaughter of his own son.

This was only the beginning of the killing. Hundreds of Boer wagons were spread out across the veldt in isolated pockets. Dingane now sent his armies out to obliterate them. They were far away and received no word of the fate that had befallen Retief. They were therefore unprepared when, on the night of 17 February, the impis fell on them. The killing lasted for days. As the settlers became aware that they were under attack, some managed to organise themselves and fight off the enemy. However, when the spears of the Zulus had finally been washed, over 500 of the trekkers were dead, including a disproportionate number of women and children.

These events seared themselves into the souls of the Boers. A village that grew up on the site of one of the massacres later was simply called *Weenen* – 'weeping'. However, the Boers were not the only ones to suffer. The British settlers at Durban unwisely allied themselves with the Boers and their small expeditionary force was annihilated. Then the Zulus marched on Durban and sacked it for a week. Fortunately there was a ship in harbour at the time that managed to evacuate some of the citizens, for to stay ashore was a death sentence.

Dingane's crushing of the threat invited terrible retribution that would not be long in coming. The British were first to react: in December 1838 a party of Highland infantry landed at Durban to enforce the peace. The British then sought to stop the Boers from attacking the Zulus, not wanting further disturbance in what had now formally become a colony. They were too late.

On 15 December 1838, the Boer commando that had set out from the hinterland with the aim of avenging Piet Retief set up camp by the River Ncome. Under their leader Andries Pretorius, they had formed their sixty-four wagons into a fortified camp, a laager. It was a formidable position: the river was very deep on one side, precluding any approach from that direction. There was a deep ditch in front of the camp, ruling out an assault from there too, meaning that any attack would be funnelled into a very narrow channel.

At dawn on 16 December, a Zulu attack was launched in overwhelming force. However, their vastly superior numbers counted for nothing. The concentrated gunfire of the Boers, supported by several cannon, brought the warriors down in their droves. Then, with the impi on the point of exhaustion, Pretorius unleashed his cavalry. The victory turned into a massacre. The Boer triumph at what became known as Blood River assumed iconic status, which it retained into the modern era.

In the aftermath of the war, various important changes occurred. The Zulus were in future to inhabit only the lands to the north of the Thukela River, with the area to the south to be the British colony of Natal. The Boers created their own state further inland with a capital established at Pietermaritzburg. The Zulus, in the meantime, turned on each other. A number decamped south and moved into Natal. Those that remained moved to fight each other, with two factions emerging: one supporting Dingane, the other the supposed simpleton, Mpande.

The Boers sensed an opportunity and moved to support Mpande, whom they thought they could easily manipulate. A climactic battle was fought soon after, which Dingane lost. He was forced to flee to the Swazis in the north. The Boers took as their prize 1,000 Zulu children who effectively became slaves. They also took another chunk of Zululand for settlement. The price of Mpande's victory was high but the cost of Dingane's defeat even higher, for he was soon murdered.

The reign of Mpande was defined for many years by peace and stability. But then, in 1856, a bitter succession dispute began – a fork in the road that led at last to the Anglo-Zulu War. Shaka and Dingane had both failed to leave a natural heir but Mpande, who enjoyed the comforts of his harem,[2] if anything succeeded too well in this respect. His firstborn was a son named Cetshwayo and he was named heir. However, Mpande took a number of other wives and regretted his decision to nominate Cetshwayo when another favourite son appeared.

The rival's name was Mbulazi and, when armed conflict with his brother became unavoidable, he sought the help of the whites from over the Thukela in Natal. Only a small group came to his aid, led by John Dunn. Dunn was a fascinating character, who could hold his own in conversation with an English lord and was a connoisseur of good wines, yet would eventually become so comfortable with Zulu life that he would happily take a number of wives in keeping with their polygamous lifestyle. But on this occasion, it would turn out he had backed the wrong horse.

Cetshwayo moved his army towards that of Mbulazi, having a huge numerical advantage. The two forces met by the mouth of the Thukela River, near the spot where it flowed into the vastness of the Indian Ocean, which was much swollen by heavy rains. The battle resulted in a decisive victory for Cetshwayo in which Mbulazi was killed along with thousands of his followers, including large numbers of women and children; there was no such thing as a 'non-combatant' in this battle. Dunn managed to escape by means of a small boat that a friend had brought across the river to help him. The Battle of Ndondakusuka, as it was known, was the bloodiest ever fought in Zulu history.

Cetshwayo built a settlement to commemorate his triumph at a place called Gingindhlovu. Relations with Mpande were still strained. Another son, Mkhungo, fled to Natal where he found sanctuary with an ambitious colonial official, Theophilus Shepstone. Shepstone was considered by a few (especially himself) to be a man of great talent. He saw in Mkhungo an opportunity to intervene in Zulu affairs to his own advantage.

The presence of Mkhungo in Natal led to the only real scare in the colony between Dingane's massacre of the Boers in 1838 and the outbreak of the Anglo-Zulu War in 1879. In 1861, rumours were rife that Cetshwayo was about to attack and at one stage the alarm seemed so real that a bona fide panic broke out and it was believed that a Zulu army was actually in the country. It turned out that this was completely untrue and nothing came of it.

Mpande initially refused to recognise the result of Ndondakusuka, decisive and irreversible though it was. However, his people were not with him. They saw in Cetshwayo a certain strength that they admired and a hint at least of the greatness that Shaka had once enjoyed. Eventually Mpande had no choice but to accept the verdict of the battlefield and reluctantly he recognised his firstborn once more as his heir.

Cetshwayo then let nature take its course. Mpande lived for sixteen years after Ndondakusuka before dying, a corpulent caricature who had to be wheeled around in a cart because he was too obese to walk. Cetshwayo then took his place on the throne. Mpande owed his station to the help of the Boers; Cetshwayo now sought the approval of the British to reinforce his authority, who were happy to oblige.

Theophilus Shepstone, now Secretary of Colonial Affairs and one of the most powerful British officials in southern Africa, offered to crown Cetshwayo but only if he agreed to rule in line with British expectations. At the subsequent coronation tension was high, with some of Cetshwayo's entourage extremely suspicious of Shepstone's intentions; it was even rumoured that Mbulazi was not dead at all and was in fact with Shepstone to be crowned instead of Cetshwayo. This of course was wrong. The 'coronation' would go ahead but Shepstone would nevertheless take full advantage of it for his own purposes.

On 1 September 1873 Shepstone placed the crown on Cetshwayo's head. It was not much of an ornament, a cheap, tacky object made of tinsel, much as one would expect to see in a pantomime. It was an appropriate indication of the level of respect that Shepstone had for the Zulu crown. Even the king was well aware of just how tawdry a spectacle Shepstone was creating with his cheap props; many spectators, it was suggested, believed that the ceremony was both 'trifling and ridiculous'.[3]

In return for the bauble he handed over, Shepstone demanded a high price. He presented a series of demands to Cetshwayo, laying out his expectations for how he should reign. These mainly concerned the sanctity of life within Zululand. Previous Zulu kings had had absolute power of life and death over their subjects.

It was something that sat uncomfortably with British sensibilities and Shepstone attempted to put a stop to the arbitrary execution of subjects.

The list of rules that Cetshwayo allegedly agreed to comply with included the injunction 'that the indiscriminate shedding of blood shall cease in the land'. Further stipulations were that no Zulu should be condemned without having an open trial and that they should have a right of appeal to the king. Minor offences, which had previously been capital crimes, would be given lesser penalties in the future. There would also be less use of witch doctors, something that was very much a feature of everyday life. Shepstone thought that this condition in particular would be hard to comply with in the near future.[4]

And in this respect at least he was right, for Zululand was at a different stage of its evolution than the British Empire was. Some apologists for the Zulus such as Francis Colenso, daughter of the Bishop of Natal, pointed out that it was only a few centuries since supposed 'witches' were being burned at the stake in their thousands in Europe, and to expect the Zulus to change their ways overnight was totally unrealistic.[5]

Nevertheless, Shepstone was delighted with the profile he had gained from being the kingmaker in Zululand. Once the private ceremony in which Cetshwayo had become king was over, he was led out to meet his people. And so, Shepstone said, 'he, who a few moments before had been but a minor and a Prince, had now become a man and a King'.[6] The inference, of course, was that it was Shepstone who was responsible for both levels of transformation. It was a position he seemed to enjoy greatly.

Shepstone returned to his politicking in the British colonies in southern Africa; Cetshwayo got on with the business of governing his people. It was a difficult challenge for him. The Zulus were living on past glories; they were a warrior people who had fought no major war against anyone but themselves for decades. They basked in the great days of Shaka but those days were long in the past. The new king had high expectations to live up to.

Hopes were high amongst his people. Cetshwayo was a striking figure of a man, about 6ft in height with a strong presence. He possessed an air of regality, not something that all previous Zulu kings could claim. But his coronation had also created expectations amongst the British which would be hard to live up to. Certainly, supporters of the British cause were quick to claim that the British had placed Cetshwayo on his throne and that he was obliged to comply with Shepstone's caveats as if they were terms and conditions that must be complied with if he wished to carry on ruling.[7]

Some of the British saw the coronation ceremony in a very different light than Cetshwayo and believed that he would do exactly as he was told. This was a gross mistake. Any king of Zululand who wished to keep his position could not afford to be perceived as a mere puppet. Rather than lessening the chances of misunderstandings, the terms of the coronation ceremony instead strengthened the possibility of one occurring. It was a ceremony that, in the few contemplative moments Cetshwayo had to himself six years later, he surely came to regret.

But when Cetshwayo's reign began there was no imminent sense of crisis. There had been no conflict between the British and the Zulus for forty years. The Zulu king saw the British as a powerbroker against the Boers who were threatening chunks of Zulu territory in the Transvaal, which was still an independent Boer state. However, the political landscape was about to change dramatically, with ultimately catastrophic results for the Zulu nation. In the form of a seemingly harmless coronation ceremony, the first unwitting steps to war had already been taken.

two

THE SCENE IS SET

The Road to War

There were several key protagonists on the British side who played a part in the build-up to war. Shepstone, for one, performed a key role alongside Sir Bartle Frere, the High Commissioner for Southern Africa and Sir Henry Bulwer, Lieutenant-Governor of Natal, for example. But the man who, more than any other, would become forever associated with the Anglo-Zulu War was Frederic Thesiger, soon to become the second Baron Chelmsford.

Thesiger was born on 31 May 1827. He came from a noble family, his father being the first Baron Chelmsford. Yet the dynasty had only recently come into prominence. John Thesiger, born in 1722, emigrated to Britain from Dresden – one of the many who made the migration following the accession of the Hanoverians to the throne. John Thesiger became secretary to a prominent states-man, the second Marquess of Rockingham. Later, Frederic's father, also Frederic, entered the House of Commons as a Tory Member of Parliament, and in 1844 became solicitor-general. The family fortune was assured – a situation confirmed when, in 1858, Frederic senior became Lord High Chancellor of England.

Frederic Thesiger was therefore born into money, as his attendance at Eton as a scholar shows. But to an extent this impression was misleading, for he was not from the ranks of the super-rich and adequate financing would always be a problem for him. In 1844, Thesiger purchased a commission as second-lieutenant in the Rifle Brigade, the buying of a commission then being the conventional way to become an officer – military ability had next to nothing to do with such a move. The year after, he moved on to the Grenadier Guards in which he was eventually promoted to captain in 1850.

After a spell in Ireland, Thesiger joined his battalion on active service in the Crimea in 1855. The war there was something of an aberration. It is an irony that during Queen Victoria's reign the British army was in action virtually every year, yet between the history-making battle at Waterloo in 1815 and the outbreak of the First World War in 1914, the Crimean War was the only major war that was fought by Britain against a European enemy. That led to a certain mentality with regards to military matters. The British army still marched and fought with its blood-scarlet uniforms and its tactics were honed against barely organised enemies whose arms were, in most cases, very basic. The military establishment was conservative, slow to change and in many ways stuck in the past.

Britain had a huge and still-developing empire. Her interests were in the main outside of Europe. In Europe itself she sought merely to hold the balance of power so that the continent stayed in some kind of equilibrium. Military entanglements with other European powers were certainly frowned upon as a matter of policy; such a state of affairs would have been a tacit admission that this policy of balance that Britain sought as a way of avoiding war had failed.

India was undoubtedly the jewel in the imperial crown and Thesiger was to spend many years there, serving from 1858 to 1874. Apart from a short stint in a war in Abyssinia in 1868, his career mainly involved a variety of administrative posts. During his time in India some crucial contacts were made, especially with Sir Henry Edward Bartle Frere who was for a time Governor of Bombay. The empire was a network of contacts and acquaintances that often followed each other around, sometimes accidentally, more often as a loosely defined form of patronage. It was an era when who you knew was often far more important than what you knew.

Thesiger's decision to stay in India was in part because he was not excessively well off. To be an officer in the British army was a major financial drain and India was a much cheaper place to live in style than Britain. Whilst he was in the sub-continent Thesiger married Adria Fanny in 1867 and four sons followed, one of whom became Viceroy of India in 1916 and eventually third Baron Chelmsford. Thesiger was very much a product of the Raj, with its racially superior attitudes and condescending views of other cultures, which frequently revealed themselves during the Anglo-Zulu War.

In 1874 Thesiger returned to Britain where he took up several short-term staff appointments, but by 1877 he was seeking a return to India, money issues again being the most likely reason. However, in 1878 he was posted to southern Africa (Frere had arrived there the year before) where he brought a brief war being waged against tribes on the eastern Cape frontier to a satisfactory conclusion. In that year too he became a Knight Commander of the Bath, an illustrious honour reflecting his popularity in some elevated circles; the queen would prove an especially useful ally in times of trouble.

Thesiger's performance in the Anglo-Zulu War (by which time he had become Lord Chelmsford), especially at its outset, has coloured opinions to the exclusion of a fair assessment of some of his personal qualities. He displayed tremendous reserves of energy, thinking nothing of riding many miles in a day to explore the territory in which he was campaigning. Yet in its own way, this was evidence of a weakness, an inability to delegate effectively, that was to manifest itself on many occasions. He was a general who became far too heavily involved in minutiae to the exclusion of the big picture of well thought-out military strategy. And, at key times in the forthcoming campaign, he would be absent on scouting expeditions when his presence with his main force was urgently needed.

Thesiger's leadership has frequently been derided based on some of the setbacks he suffered during the Anglo-Zulu War. Yet he was not completely incompetent. He would, however, make one fatal mistake in the war which undermined everything else: he would underestimate his enemy. He allowed his own prejudices concerning the superiority of the British over other 'savage' cultures to colour his military judgement with, from his perspective, catastrophic results. His crucial error was to assume that all African tribes fought in the same manner. Such, he would find out, was far from the case.

He had other failings which contributed to his misfortunes. Around him he would place a small clique of officers that he relied on in the absence of a properly manned and organised general staff. In the process he displayed another key weakness: an inability to judge his officers effectively. His choice of Major John Crealock, a pompous, sometimes obnoxious character with a short fuse, as his main military adviser in the field was particularly damaging. But, that said, Thesiger was an extremely popular man with many of his men. A big bear of a man, with a face hidden beneath a thick, bushy beard, many overlooked his faults as a strategist in deference to his personal qualities.

Despite this, when faced with accountability for the disasters that occurred at the beginning of the looming war, he was quick to look for scapegoats to take the blame. Whilst seemingly able to attract supporters, at the same time he was not slow to pass the buck to others when matters went awry. He would, in the process, understandably antagonise those who were associated with those he tried to blame.

In 1879, Thesiger's was a record undisturbed by much in the way of military action, apart from his time in Abyssinia, yet in many ways it was typical of the class-orientated nature of the British army of the time. The purchasing of commissions meant that there was little prospect of anyone with talent rising to a senior command unless he also had money. However, the British army was changing, although the process was painfully slow. Under Edward Cardwell, Secretary of State for War between 1868 and 1874, some much-needed improvements had been implemented. But even then the results were not wholly successful. Some unfortunate side effects would reveal themselves during the Anglo-Zulu War.

The reforms Cardwell introduced were not universally popular and alienated many traditionalists in the military establishment. Several important changes were implemented with the aim of saving money as well as improving the army. The introduction of short service in 1870, where soldiers signed up for six years and then spent a further six in the reserve, brought many young men into the army and also gave the British establishment access to a much larger source of reserve manpower on which to call in times of stress.

However, this infusion of young blood was not without its problems. Some commanders – and Thesiger was one of them – were to bemoan the raw green-horns they were given as soldiers as a result. Complaints about untrained young soldiers were consistent enough during the Anglo-Zulu War to imply that there was a real problem.

Cardwell also introduced brigade districts in Britain to which two sister battalions would be affiliated. The theory was that one would be at home whilst the other was abroad. Although superficially an excellent idea, in practice so many campaigns were fought overseas that in many cases both were away at once. By 1879, eighty-two battalions were abroad and only fifty-nine at home. This imbalance was due to what has often been called Queen Victoria's 'Little Wars', which resulted in military entanglements across the globe from New Zealand to Canada, from the Gold Coast to Afghanistan. It stretched the British armed forces to the limit and occasionally beyond.

In conjunction with this reformed organisation of regiments, the purchasing of military commissions was abolished – a move that outraged many who had bought their way up the ladder. Nevertheless, this did not stop the British army from remaining an essentially conservative institution. This resistance to change was reinforced by the commander-in-chief of the British army, the Duke of Cambridge, who was very much of the old school. He too would remain a useful ally of Thesiger during the troubles that lay ahead (for a time at least), which reflected the fact that they were both, by nature, conservatives.

Thesiger arrived in southern Africa with the Ninth Frontier War well under way, where Colonel Glyn's 1st Battalion of the 24th Regiment played a prominent role in the fighting. The tribes who were their enemy had routinely melted away rather than face the British army. Their strategy played a significant part in Thesiger's future thinking, as he reasoned that other African armies would fight in the same fashion. The major problem against the Zulus, he believed, was getting them to fight. Once a battle was in progress there could, in his view, only be one winner.

Thesiger was only the military half of what would be a double-act bent on expansion in southern Africa. The chief political figure driving the move to war was the High Commissioner for South Africa, Sir Bartle Frere (though the role of Theophilus Shepstone should not be understated either). Frere had adopted the policy of Confederation, by which a block of friendly colonies in southern Africa would protect British interests there, in the process becoming little more than satellite states. Powerful independent entities like Zululand were an obstacle to this strategy and therefore had to be eliminated. This is where Thesiger, fresh from his triumphs in the Frontier War, came in.

Confederation was not a completely new phenomenon. The system tried in Canada gave individual states a degree of autonomy under the arrangement although they were expected to act in accordance with British interests. A similar system could work in southern Africa. The administrators of these Confederation states came from the ranks of colonists, as did the men for the militias which formed the bulk of their armed forces, helpfully relieving the pressure on overstretched battalions of the regular army. Frere was the local architect who planned to implement Confederation in southern Africa. The discovery of diamonds in the region in the recent past did nothing to discourage the development of this policy. Before, the area had been seen as nothing save a potential drain on resources; now the opportunity to reap the harvest of previously unknown natural resources made it much more attractive.

Frere had only arrived in Cape Town in 1877, but the idea that Africa offered the British Empire unexploited potential was already in his mind. He had said as much in a speech he had given at the inauguration of the African section of the Society of Arts on 30 January 1874. Frere's reputation was made during his service in India and an impressive statue of him still stands proudly in the gardens by the Victoria Embankment in London. An information board next to it describes him as 'an enlightened 19th Century administrator'. It is an interpretation that those who suffered from his supposedly enlightened policies in southern Africa, especially the Zulus whose country would ultimately be torn asunder by the British, would bitterly dispute.

His first target though had not been native tribes in the area but a Boer republic in the Transvaal. The ostensible excuse for British intervention there was that the small but independent state was teetering on the verge of bankruptcy (this followed the annexation of the Boer Orange Free State in 1871; again, the discovery of diamonds there four years earlier may not have been entirely unconnected with this move to expand the empire). Despite the presence of goldmines in the Transvaal, there was just £1 left in the state treasury.[1] An unstable Transvaal, it was argued, would inevitably impact on neighbouring British colonies and could not, therefore, be accepted.

The Transvaal Boers had been involved in skirmishes with some of the neighbouring native kingdoms, especially the Zulus with whom they had had such a chequered history. Frere felt that the economic crisis and the border disputes that had occurred there introduced an unacceptable level of instability into the region and, as such, he intervened. He moved in and annexed the state. For the time being, the Boers felt powerless to resist. This was a situation, however, that would not last. But the Confederation juggernaut in southern Africa was now truly under way.

Sir Theophilus Shepstone was in London when he heard reports that a Boer force had been defeated by the Zulus. He had already been doing what he could to present the case for war against Cetshwayo, which he thought was inevitable. He received instructions from the British government that he was to annex Transvaal as long as the Boer settlers consented (though war against the Zulus was to be discouraged). On returning to southern Africa, Frere subtly amended this to annexation without any conditions.

The Boers had been encroaching on Zulu lands for some time. Cetshwayo, his patience exhausted, gathered together an army of 30,000 men and moved towards the Transvaal border. Shepstone, now back in Africa, hurried ahead of him and the deeply worried Boers agreed to British rule. Shepstone sent a message to Cetshwayo and the attack was called off. Some of the Zulus later suggested that Shepstone had encouraged their king to threaten the state so that he could take it for his own sovereign. Cetshwayo, however, tried to see the good in the situation; at least now the Boers might be easier to control, he thought. In the aftermath of the annexation he wrote that he was 'glad to know that the Transvaal is now English ground; perhaps now there may be rest'.[2] It was a statement made with touching and tragic naivety.

In the border disputes that had marked the situation in the Transvaal, the British had historically tended to side with the Zulus. However, now that they were the owners of the state, their view changed and they did a complete about-turn. There was undoubtedly room for confusion as to what was going on with regards to the frontier. Over a process of decades, Boers who had originally escaped from the British colonies in southern Africa had progressively expanded their territories. They had initially been well received by Mpande but levels of Zulu resentment had increased in proportion to Boer landholdings. It was difficult to define a border in this rugged, mountainous land and angry Zulus had started to resist further Boer encroachment. It was a situation compounded by the Zulus' limited appreciation of what treaties that ceded land to the settlers actually meant in practice.

Zulu hostility due to the border dispute that Frere had inherited fuelled his belief that they were a threat towards British interests in southern Africa. They were therefore a prime target for Confederation. It was a fear fed by several flare-ups with other local tribes such as those in the Cape and the Pedi further north, who had recently defeated the Boers. Frere was a man who believed implicitly in the moral superiority of Western 'civilisation' and nothing could be allowed to stand in the way of its march towards dominance in the region.

There were a number of advantages that Frere foresaw as a result of a war with the Zulus. It would, of course, remove a powerful potential antagonist, but it would also both ingratiate the British to the Boers and emphasise to dissentient elements in the Transvaal the pointlessness of resisting their new masters. It would give Natal more freedom to manage African affairs and would send an exemplary message to any other tribes that dared resist British expansionism. All these were strong practical reasons but whether or not any would morally justify a war is a completely different matter.

Shepstone had outlined his own line of thinking in a dispatch he composed on 5 January 1878. To his mind, Zulu society was constructed solely with war in mind: 'the Zulu constitution is essentially military; every man is a soldier ...' The absence of war in recent times had in fact generated significant tensions; in his view 'the question is, what is to be done with this pent up and still accumulating power?'

The answer, of course, was that there must be a war to release this stored-up aggressive energy. Cetshwayo, Shepstone argued, was powerless to resist the tide. However, Shepstone also felt that most of the king's people did not desire a war with the British in Natal. He further postulated that many of them were unhappy with Cetshwayo's rule and would welcome, as he himself described it, a 'revolution' that would depose the king.[3]

This was far from the truth. There were no doubt disaffected parties in Zululand, but many of them had long since left the country, seeking safety in Natal in particular. But the enthusiasm with which the Zulus would fight in the upcoming conflict provided the strongest evidence possible that this conclusion was erroneous. It is hard to ignore the perception that Shepstone himself knew this when he said it and was merely searching for an argument for war.

Although there may be a temptation to see the Anglo-Zulu War as a clash between races, to do so would be a gross oversimplification. The huge majority of Natal residents were black; the government statistics produced in *The Blue Book* for Natal in 1879 show that there were 26,654 Europeans, 16,999 Indians and 319,935 Africans.[4] The vast majority of Africans either supported the British against the Zulus or stayed out of it; many Natal residents were families of refugees from Zululand and had little time for Cetshwayo. In fact, the size of the population in many ways underscored the stability that had been a feature of Natal in recent times; in the early years of the 1840s the highest estimate of the total population was 42,000.[5]

The natives in the colony either lived in 'locations' set aside for them or worked on lands farmed by settlers. They were still organised in clans, each under their own chief. Most of them still formed part of a regimental system, arranged along the same lines as those of Cetshwayo's army, though they had not fought in earnest for some time and their fighting skills were rusty. However, they provided a significant reservoir of manpower for the British to tap to provide logistical support.

Frere was confident that British arms would emerge triumphant in any conflict. British forces were not numerous in the region as London did not see it as a colonial priority but Frere believed that the troops' superior armament would be decisive. The British soldier relied on modern rifles, usable at long range, whereas a Zulu warrior was armed with a short stabbing spear, the assegai, only of use at close quarters.[6] Many Zulus did have firearms but they were largely of old design and the marksmanship of their owners was not good. One man who faced them, Captain William Molyneux, felt that the British army would have been in much more trouble if the Zulus had stuck to assegais instead of trying to use firearms.[7]

That said, it was estimated that there were up to 20,000 firearms in Zululand in 1879, though only 500 of them were relatively modern breech-loaders.[8] But the short-range stabbing assegai was the main weapon of choice even though the throwing version was also still in use. A number of warriors also carried heavy wooden clubs, knobkerries, vicious looking with nodules carved out at the end to increase their braining power.

Frere, despite his coterie of Confederates, had experienced opposition from other quarters. The Lieutenant-Governor of Natal, Sir Henry Bulwer, was quite content with the state of relations with the Zulu state which had been almost entirely peaceful in recent years. Therefore, he was at best a reluctant supporter of the plan to go to war with Cetshwayo; his opposition to the war would increase as it progressed. He now offered to be an arbitrator in the dispute over the lands bordering the Transvaal and Zululand. Frere could hardly refuse and Cetshwayo was happy enough to agree. A Boundary Commission was duly established.

The Commission met in March 1878, close to a crossing point into Zululand known as Rorke's Drift. It would take several months to work through the evidence. A number of Zulu and Boer witnesses were called to present their respective cases. At the end of the deliberations, the result was exactly the opposite of what Frere wanted: a decision broadly in support of the Zulu case. Although this was kept secret for a while, some got an inkling of it: the *Natal Witness*, a colonial newspaper, was one, expressing the view that 'the Border Commission have brought their labours to a close, and we think it very probable that more harm than good will result from the costly comedy'.[9]

One of the Commissioners, Lieutenant Colonel Anthony Durnford, felt that they had acted fairly; he hoped their decisions would be respected. This would not be the case, and Durnford and many others would suffer tragic personal consequences. The Commission, also including a prominent lawyer Michael Galwey and John Shepstone, brother of Sir Theophilus, nevertheless had performed its task conscientiously. Frere, whose arguments for war had been seriously damaged by its decision, used his influence to keep the result secret for the time being.

Frere had apparently decided that a war was by now virtually unavoidable. As early as April 1878, he was writing to the British naval chief in the region, Commodore Sullivan, requesting him to remain in Natal as 'it appeared almost certain that serious complications must shortly arise with the Zulu tribe … which will necessitate active operations'.[10] But now, after the Commission's unhelpful conscientiousness, another cause for war was needed. A border violation helpfully provided it. Close to Rorke's Drift on the Zulu side of the Mzinyathi River lived a Zulu chieftain, Sihayo kaXongo. Two of his wives were involved in affairs and fled to Natal with their lovers. They remained close to the border, a humiliating reminder that they had cuckolded Sihayo and caused a slur on his honour.

Sihayo himself was, on the surface, a picture of restraint. He refused to openly involve himself in any ill-advised action that would compromise his position or that of Cetshwayo with the authorities in Natal. However, when he was away at oNdini (known to the British as Ulundi), Cetshwayo's capital, his sons decided to seek reparation on his account. In two separate raids a few days apart, they crossed the border into Natal, seized the errant wives, brought them back to Zululand and executed them.

Such incidents occurred from time to time, normally without leading to war. A similar situation a couple of years previously had merely led to an exchange of letters between Bulwer and Cetshwayo.[11] Despite this past restraint, Frere formulated demands that those responsible for this infringement of Natal's sovereignty should be handed over to the colonial authorities. It was a request that Sihayo could not accede to without a major loss of face, jeopardising his own position with his people in the process.

The cross-border raids by Sihayo's sons were badly timed for Cetshwayo, happening in July 1878 just as the Boundary Commission (as yet unknown to him) had decided substantially in his favour. There was a small group of Border Police close at hand when these raids took place. They did not intervene, though they did consider doing so. However, such an intervention would have been suicidal. Accounts spoke of about 300 Zulus present in the second raid, some of which were on horseback, armed with guns.

The Border Police were hugely outnumbered but, in some ways, an attack on them would have helped Frere as he would need little more justification to launch a retaliatory strike against the Zulus. Despite them escaping unscathed, these events had still helped to provide a ready-made excuse to intervene. Settler sentiment was outraged. The *Natal Witness* correspondent thundered: 'I should think, after this, the Zulus must be put down with a strong hand; if not, we had better all clear out of this part of the country as soon as possible.'[12]

There were other incidents too. Further north, in those disputed lands bordering Zululand and the Transvaal, lived a client chieftain of Cetshwayo's, Mbilini.

He was not a Zulu but a Swazi, who had been forced to leave his homeland when he lost out in a succession dispute there. He was an excellent fighter with a penchant for guerrilla warfare. He led a raid near Luneberg killing many German settlers, and took a number of cattle away with him. This gave Frere another opportunity to portray the Zulus as a threat. The attack, given Mbilini's close relations with him, was a major embarrassment for Cetshwayo at a time when he could ill-afford it. Although the king distanced himself from Mbilini, further damage had been done to his reputation.

As well as Frere, Cetshwayo had other opponents pressing for war with the Zulus. For years missionaries had been trying to further their cause in Zululand. They had not been especially successful. Frustrated by their failure to make progress, and blaming the Zulu king for it, the missionaries withdrew. Many of them were implacable enemies of Cetshwayo as a result of their frustrated efforts.

Not everybody sided with the missionaries though. Most famously, John Colenso, Bishop of Natal, was vociferous in his opposition to the war that now seemed increasingly likely. Despite his position in the Church of England hierarchy, he was a non-conformist with strongly held opinions and he vigorously argued against the hawkish views of the missionaries, a position in which he was prominently supported by Anthony Durnford, who was soon to make his mark on the battlefield.

On the other hand, despite Bulwer's reticence, there was no doubt that in Natal there was real concern about the possibility of a Zulu attack on the colony. A huge stone laager was begun at 'Fort Pine', halfway between Dundee and Helpmekaar; it was a formidable fortification that would have proved a massive obstacle to any Zulu impi, although it was not completed when war finally broke out. Some of the colonists saw the Zulus as European-haters and, even though the same individuals admitted that their aggression was being fed by white arms traders, they thought that action was needed.

By early July, Thesiger was writing to Sir Theophilus Shepstone that he felt that the Zulus were fully ready for action but that his own forces were far from being so. He argued that a number of local volunteers and native levies were needed to support the regular troops at hand. However, he could not embark on more war-like steps until there had been a final resolution of the boundary dispute regarding the lands on the frontiers of the Transvaal – the ultimate outcome was still officially under review. He hoped that the Boundary Commissioners might soon throw some light on a situation that was, to him, rather foggy.[13]

He revealed more of his strategy to the same correspondent soon afterwards. If there was to be a fight then the outcome must be as decisive as possible. In his view, 'half measures do not answer with natives – they must be thoroughly crushed to make them believe in our superiority'. He continued by saying that he would strive to demonstrate to the Zulus how 'hopelessly inferior' they were to his forces in terms of their fighting power regardless of any numerical advantage that they might have [14]

The language that Thesiger employed in this latter correspondence with Shepstone is critically important. Here is a commander who is convinced that the fighting power available to him was overwhelmingly superior. In many ways he was right, as the upcoming war would demonstrate painfully on a number of occasions. Yet this was also the vocabulary of a man so convinced that he held all the winning cards that he was in great danger of appearing complacent. There is, it has been said, a thin dividing line between supreme confidence and arrogance, and Thesiger was in peril of crossing it.

Having started to work at the politics of the war, Thesiger then set his mind to his detailed military strategy. His initial plan was to overwhelm the Zulus using a multi-pronged attack. He wrote to Bulwer on 24 August with his strategy for what he called the 'Invasion of Zululand; or Defence of the Natal and Transvaal Colony from Invasion by the Zulus', the latter part of the statement again being disingenuous as there was little sign that Cetshwayo was preparing to make such raids. [15]

Here again Thesiger was playing the politician, but he had a lot of convincing to do. There had been occasional small-scale problems in the recent past but these had not led to any significant clash of arms since the days of Dingane in 1837, when the late Zulu king had raided Natal. So desperate was Thesiger to garner support for his dubious venture that he could not avoid mentioning the raid of over four decades ago in another dispatch to Lord Stanley, the British Secretary of State for War. [16] The present machinery of defence was, in his view, 'almost hopeless' in Natal. Despite this, Stanley remained unconvinced, responding to his requests for help, on 18 October, with the news that no help in terms of extra troops would be forthcoming from England unless it was 'indispensable', though special service officers would be made available. He was, in best civil service tradition, also asked to 'keep down expense of transport as much as possible'. [17]

Thesiger was at this stage on his best behaviour with Bulwer. Over time, their relationship would deteriorate until it reached a point of no return, but now he politely outlined his plan of action to him. He was considering five main lines of advance. The first was on the coast, by moving from Durban up to the mouth of the Thukela River from where he could then menace the south-east of the Zulu kingdom. Then, to the west of this, he could move troops up from Fort Buckingham to Middle Drift. The third route was up from Ladysmith to Rorke's Drift, which would enable him to move troops into the centre of Zululand from the south.

The fourth and fifth routes would enable him to move on the far west and north-west of Cetshwayo's realm, via the Blood River and Phongolo River respectively. Against a European enemy, it was a plan that made little sense, especially when Thesiger's army was at a vast numerical disadvantage. But this was no European enemy and an attack from several directions was not without some strategic merits. It would keep Cetshwayo guessing and possibly split his forces. It would help lessen Thesiger's logistical problems too; he suspected that maintaining an army of this size in the terrain through which they must pass would be a nightmare and, in this respect, he would be absolutely right.

Yet there were some serious weaknesses in the approach too. Five columns was too many, making the approach too complex and beyond the resources available. Thesiger himself would recognise this quickly enough and reduce the number of attacking columns to three. But most problematically of all, to be successful the strategy required excellent co-ordination of the forces in an era where communication was difficult and where the nature of the terrain made it even more so. It was on this rock that the stratagem would, in practice, founder.

The composition of the army was also a cause for concern. Thesiger had some imperial infantry available to him and some guns from the Royal Artillery (though they were light 7-pounder mountain guns with limited striking power). However, he was seriously handicapped by the absence of any regular cavalry except for the Imperial Mounted Infantry (IMI), who were volunteers from the regular infantry who had been retrained as horsemen. Apart from them he would have to rely on local volunteer cavalry, both colonial and native, to bridge this significant gap. He would also use some sailors and marines who were locally available to augment the coastal column (designated Column Number 1).

Where Thesiger particularly needed Bulwer's help was with recruitment in Natal. He needed to enlist both colonials and natives, organise them with officers and equipment, arrange rendezvous points for them to assemble at and allocate any recruits to his columns. This would take time, something he did not feel that he had too much of. It would not be easy to get support from the colonial authorities either. Thesiger's predecessor, Sir Arthur Cunynghame, was recalled in part because he could not get agreement from colonial officials to command both regular and local forces in the field.[18]

He already had plans for what he would do with these forces. The dismounted portion of the Natal Volunteers, colonial recruits, could be used to garrison Pietermaritzburg and Durban, freeing up imperial troops for the invasion campaign. This was sensible as it was one thing to ask for colonial volunteers to assist in the defence of Natal, but there was a good deal of sentiment in the colony against using them for aggressive action in Zululand. There were also legal barriers that meant they could not be forced to operate outside of Natal, so they could not be conscripted into taking part in an offensive action against the Zulus.

However, Thesiger needed the mounted volunteers in Zululand, not Natal. He suggested forming them into two regiments of 200 men each, to be spread across the three columns at the mouth of the Thukela, at Middle Drift and at Rorke's Drift. The Natal Mounted Police, a standing body that had existed for only five years, could also be used and attached to one of the columns. The Natal Native Contingent (NNC) could be divided into three commands, each under white officers. The Contingent was formed at the instigation of Colonel Anthony Durnford of the Royal Engineers, who wrote to Thesiger proposing the formation of an army of native recruits with five regiments of infantry and five troops of cavalry.

Durnford had worked it all out in some detail, estimating that it would cost £28,667 to keep this force in the field for a year.[19] Recruiting these natives would not only augment his forces but would also lessen the possibility of rebellious elements in the colony rising up against their colonial masters. However, recruiting these men was one thing; using them quite another. The white officers and NCOs charged with their leadership, as a general rule, cared little for their men and thought them not worth the effort. They treated them on the whole extremely shabbily.

Yet in one respect Thesiger was quite enlightened. Although his attitudes would today be considered paternalistic to the point of being patronising, he did at least make an effort. Regulations were issued as to how to deal with the native soldier, one phrase in particular having a surprisingly open-minded ring about it: 'never use epithets of contempt such as niggers, kafirs etc. Call them "abantu" (people), "amadoda" (men) or "amabuti" (soldiers).' Despite these laudable injunctions the levies were treated little better than third-class citizens and the language he discouraged was used frequently in some of the eye-witness accounts that were written after the war.

One of the more vivid accounts of the Anglo-Zulu War was written some years after the event by George Hamilton-Browne, Commandant of the First Battalion of the 3rd Regiment of the NNC. Thesiger's injunctions to be respectful of native soldiers were clearly long forgotten by Hamilton-Browne when he committed his thoughts to print. The language he uses is, to a modern mind, jarring in the extreme. Equally as unsettling was the way in which he held such a low opinion of the men under his command, rating their lives as being of little worth.

Hamilton-Browne was more a story-teller than a historian and there are places in some of his writings which suggest that he was not above embellishing a tale in the interests of improving the quality of the read. That said, he was a first-hand witness of some of the great events of the war and as such deserves a fair hearing. He was in command of ten companies in his battalion but only three of them, the isiGqoza, were considered by him to be good fighting material.

These three companies of the isiGqoza were composed of Zulus who had supported Mbulazi in his war against Cetshwayo and, forced to flee after the disastrous reverse at Ndondakusuka, had since settled near Weenen, led by another son of Mpande, Mkhungo, considered by some to be a possible replacement for Cetshwayo but well past his prime now. These were the kind of auxiliary troops that the British wanted. Thesiger hoped to raise 15,000 natives for the Natal Native Contingent by the measures he took, many of whom were closely related to the Zulus though some had left Zululand decades before and lost much of their martial prowess as a result.

Thesiger also thought that another 400 mounted colonials could be recruited. However, action needed to be taken to confirm that this was not an unrealistic expectation and some of his colonial or imperial officers were instructed 'to feel the pulse' of the colony. Of course, a certain standard was required of recruits: they must be good riders and competent shots. All of these men needed to be equipped too, not just with weapons but with camp equipment, entrenching tools and other accoutrements. It was no small challenge for Thesiger to meet.

Yet the recruitment of men in Natal created its own problems. The men's contracts defined their role as being defensive, to protect the borders of the colony, and they had the explicit right to refuse to operate outside of it. There were several occasions when they threatened this but it was no 'mutiny', merely a case of those involved acting within their rights. They would also have the full support of Sir Henry Bulwer in the process. In the event, most of the men would go along voluntarily. The Maritzburg Rifles were one example: when the decision about crossing the border was put to a meeting of about seventy of them all but one voted affirmatively.[20]

Thesiger spelt out his plans 'should the invasion of Zululand be decided upon' in a letter to Colonel Stanley in London on 14 September 1878. He also presented his case for imperial troops in this document. In addition, he required staff officers, as well as officers to command the various volunteer corps. He currently had two battalions of the 24th (2nd Warwickshire Regiment) available to him which he would use as the main fighting force of the Central Column (Number 3), which would spearhead the attack. The 1st Battalion had been in southern Africa since early 1875 and had fought several campaigns against natives in the region since.

The 2nd Battalion had only been in southern Africa since February 1878 and although they had been involved in action since their arrival, the 1st Battalion was the one with more combat experience in recent times. The 2nd Battalion's presence was a bonus. With the Ninth Frontier War over, their primary reason for being in southern Africa had gone. It was likely, especially with a difficult war in Afghanistan looming, that they would be moved on soon. For Thesiger, time was therefore of the essence in utilising them whilst they were still there.

Yet the native opposition in the Cape in 1878 proved an inadequate benchmark for the war against the Zulus. The conflict there was against Xhosa tribes, the Gaika and Galeka people in particular, very different opponents from the Zulus. In all, just one soldier was killed in action from both battalions combined, though significantly, thirty-nine expired from disease.[21] Thesiger commended both battalions for their service in the campaigns and for their part many of his men seemed to like and respect him. It was easy to do so in many ways: he had a generally pleasant manner and his energy and zeal were important motivational qualities in a leader. His strategic failings were not, as yet, apparent.

The 24th were good soldiers, experienced and toughened to southern African conditions. Their attitude in the recent wars in the region had been first class. Many of them now wore bushy beards, grown under the searing African sun, their uniforms patched up as well as they were able – a move made necessary by the wear and tear of campaigning in this tough country. They had a distinguished history with one black spot on it: a disaster experienced in India a few decades before at a place called Chilianwala – when the invasion of Zululand at last began the officers drank a toast that they might have better luck this time.

Thesiger presumably did not think he had made out a convincing enough case for imperial reinforcements for, just two weeks later, he wrote another much more detailed argument to Stanley.[22] He explained that he believed a Zulu attack to be far more likely than it ever had been in recent memory. In the past, he suggested, the Zulus had managed to play off one party, the British, against another, the Boers. However, the annexation of the Transvaal had removed that counterbalance. Incredibly he thought that this must lead to a Zulu attack, 'although Cetshwayo himself has apparently been slow to recognise it'.

Thesiger then was taking credit for being a mind reader whose instincts were so finely tuned that he knew the king's deepest thoughts better than Cetshwayo himself. He suggested that Zulu warriors were still inspired by tales of Dingane's raids into Natal in 1837, but in reality few colonists recalled the massacres at Weenen and other places four decades before.

Cetshwayo's Zulus helpfully continued to offer minor provocations. There was a road constructed to the Middle Drift halfway along the Thukela between its mouth and the mission station at Rorke's Drift. It had been built by Sir Garnet Wolseley when he had been Governor of Natal in 1875. In September 1878 two surveyors had been out inspecting it when they were seized by Zulus and manhandled, in some versions being stripped naked to add to the humiliation, though they were eventually released unharmed. Regardless of the possible military uses of the road, given its strategic position, it was an act that could easily be portrayed as an affront to British dignity and another avoidable provocation.

Laying it on thickly, Thesiger explained in his letter to Stanley that Natal was singularly poorly prepared to resist a cross-border raid should one be launched. He pointed out that the Zulus had recently made claims and encroachments of a threatening nature, yet this referred to either the territorial disputes in remote areas in the north-west and Mbilini's raid there or to the minor incidents in Natal itself with Sihayo's sons which were far from threats of all-out invasion. However, it was easy to see how they might be presented as such.

If a war was to start, it was important for Thesiger to consider not just invasion but also the defence of Natal against expected Zulu counter-raids on the colony. He felt that Natal's defences could best be considered as covering three separate regions, the main road from Durban to the mouth of the Thukela, the region from Pietermaritzburg to the middle Thukela and the third from Ladysmith to Rorke's Drift. Each zone extended to a depth of around 60 miles inside the Natal border and in total they covered a width of around 100 miles from the Thukela mouth to Rorke's Drift.

Thesiger believed that the Zulus could attack with an army of perhaps 40,000 warriors. To defend against it, he proposed a front line on the border itself composed of the Natal Native Contingents. Behind them, the Natal Mounted Police could form a second line of defence. The final lines, protecting the towns of Durban, Greytown and Ladysmith, would be composed of British infantry. In other words, the lines of defence might cynically be regarded as being arranged in order of expendability.

The problem of troop numbers was a constant headache. On 1 October 1878 Thesiger wrote to his trusted lieutenant, Colonel 'Evelyn' Wood[23] on the subject of sparing troops for the defence of the town of Luneberg, where there were many German settlers, no doubt disturbed after Mbilini's raids. He hoped that Colonel Hugh Rowlands, who was leading a desultory campaign against the Pedi to the north, would be able to offer troops when it was over but this particular operation seemed to be taking much longer than expected. In the meantime, he wondered, could Wood see if a volunteer force could be raised by the Germans themselves?

The letter to Wood was full of practical concerns. Wood's horse had died; could Wood think of a place that might be safe for the animals in the event of an outbreak of horse sickness to which the region was prone? Did the Germans have enough weapons to defend themselves? Might the Boers be persuaded to join in the war against their traditional foe, the Zulus? Could the town of Utrecht defend itself against a 'rush' from the Zulus (who, Thesiger said, seemed to be getting suspicious of British intentions)?

Luneberg would remain a problem. To protect it, Wood would later take troops from Utrecht and Newcastle, an action that Thesiger likened to the action of an Irishman who, thinking his sheet was too short, cut a piece off the bottom and sewed it on the top. Thesiger also had information that the good residents of Luneberg, as well as being concerned for their safety, were also very happy to make a profit out of any looming conflict by charging extortionate prices to the British for supplies.

Thesiger was fortunate to have Wood as part of his command structure. The two men knew each other well as Wood had served under Thesiger in the Frontier War. Wood was ideally suited to the role intended for him, being capable of operating very effectively and aggressively on his own initiative. He would be operating in what was the 'disputed territory' bordering the Transvaal, which was an unforgiving, demanding terrain particularly characterised by table-topped mountains which were ideal for an aggressive Zulu enemy to wage guerrilla warfare from; real frontier country in other words.

Rowlands' campaign became a problem for Thesiger. The war against the Pedi was lasting far too long (their king, Sekukuni, had been wily, taking advantage of the fastnesses of the mountains in the region to escape the overwhelming force of imperial troops) and needed to be brought to a close even if a decisive victory had not yet been attained. Further, the weather was about to change for the worse and campaigning would therefore be brought to a halt. Zululand was now to take priority. The war there, Thesiger reckoned, would take eight months – then they could get back to the Pedi.

Thesiger continued to put his plans in place. No one could fault his energy; he was, he said himself, a man who liked to see the country and he toured the roads in Natal towards the border with Zululand to see which offered the best military possibilities. Based on this surveillance, he decided to make Greytown his main supply base.

He also considered the position of the natives inside Natal itself in the event of a war. There were two major spots inside the colony where the natives were situated in large concentrations: at the Msinga and Thukela 'locations', as their allocated territories were known. However, Thesiger noted that they had not been instructed what to do if a Zulu raid was to occur. He believed that the natives were well disposed towards the colony and were quite prepared to fight for it if asked to. Nevertheless, many said openly that 'the English do not trust them' – an astute observation as it happened.[24]

Thesiger adopted some highly dubious measures as the war loomed closer to encourage more local volunteers to enlist. Such volunteers would be given large grants of land, over 6,000 acres, if they joined and helped put down the 'rebellion'. This was extraordinary; Thesiger had no authority to make such promises and was already acting as if he was lord of the manor. And there was no 'rebellion': Zululand was sovereign territory and there was no insurgence in Natal. Given these fatal flaws, it was perhaps not a surprise when in the final analysis no grants of land were forthcoming.

Steps also needed to be taken to close the borders which were very porous. Orders were to be issued that no natives were to cross over from Natal into Zululand and any travelling the other way were to be taken prisoner. And arrangements were to be made to employ native spies to glean information.

This was much needed; it would turn out that far too little was known about Zululand and the shortage of good quality information would lead ultimately to one major disaster and several significant defeats.

Thesiger considered that when the British invaded Zululand a number of Zulus would come across to his side for protection. He claimed that Cetshwayo was 'most unpopular', a rare piece of fiction as a generalised statement. Once the British launched their attack, in Thesiger's opinion, a rebellion against Cetshwayo was likely.

If such a rebellion did occur, Thesiger continued, then arrangements should be made to deal with any Zulus who might opt to come over to the British. They should of course be well treated, fed and rewarded for fleeing the supposed tyranny of the Zulu king. Potential chieftains who might defect, such as Hamu in the north of Zululand (in Wood's sphere of operations), should be approached to encourage them to change sides at the earliest opportunity.

As the build-up to war continued, Thesiger's preparations were interrupted by some sad personal news. His father, the First Baron Chelmsford, had died on 5 October 1878. It meant that the commander-in-chief had inherited the title and from now on would be known as 'Chelmsford'. Chelmsford wrote to Wood, whom he considered a friend as well as a subordinate commander, that the news had been a dreadful shock. The late baron's constitution had been strong and Chelmsford had left England with every expectation that he would return after the campaign to find him hale and hearty.

Chelmsford also had other problems. In the same letter, he confessed that 'our Transport Department here has entirely broken down'. This was a disaster. Every army marches on its stomach of course, but the invasion of Zululand posed a particularly difficult logistical problem. Enormous numbers of oxen would be needed to move the stores upon which the British soldier was almost entirely dependent. Chelmsford had taken steps to introduce new officers to help in the process. The commissariat, he said, were 'rabid' about the changes but that could not be helped. A complete breakdown in the supply chain appeared imminent and decisive action was needed.[25]

The Commissary-General, Edward Strickland, was about the only person in the field that Chelmsford felt he could rely upon as far as the commissariat was concerned. Chelmsford believed he had no option but to take a close personal interest in the running of the department. There were admittedly few people he could rely on and he had asked for specialists to be sent out from England to fill the gaps. However, this action is also indicative of a man who was far too slow to delegate.

Wood's column posed some particular challenges for Chelmsford. He had great trust in Wood as a commander but was finding it difficult to provide sufficient local natives to support him. As war loomed nearer, he had managed to find 2,000 natives for each of the columns at the mouth of the Thukela and Rorke's Drift (1 and 3 respectively). Another defensive force, composed of colonial and natives forces, would be based at Middle Drift under Colonel Anthony Durnford. Durnford's men were to take up defensive duties to protect Natal whilst Rowlands' in the far north were to form a reserve, again as a defensive unit.

Chelmsford could not provide any natives for Wood though. He wrote to Wood in November 1878 that he wanted to but 'I could not get them for you out of this colony [i.e. Natal] without an immense deal of correspondence and of pressure on the part of the High Commissioner, which I am anxious to avoid ...'[26] This hinted at increasing resistance from Bulwer in Natal, who was very protective of his colonial and native recruits and did not want them used in aggressive actions in a war with which he was increasingly uncomfortable.

Wood was instead encouraged to raise his own native forces. Chelmsford also made further suggestions about recruiting amongst the local Boers. He felt that this might have political as well as military benefits by aligning Dutch interests with British ones. However, it would not be an easy task. Wood had met with Andries Pretorius, one of the Boer leaders, but was greeted with stony silence from Pretorius' companions. The Boer response to these overtures was blunt:

> we have sworn an oath to be true to Messrs Kruger and Joubert, who went to England to see your Government, and will not move till we hear the answer to our delegation, and we will not help you to till the Transvaal is given back to us.[27]

In the meantime, Hamu (also known as 'Oham') must be told to decide if he was for the British or against them. Chelmsford had said that he could not contemplate any neutrals inside the borders of Zululand. Chelmsford was to give authority that Hamu and any other chiefs were to be allowed to keep their land after the war provided they co-operated during it, even if they were forced to temporarily abandon it during any conflict.

He was also working out further details of how to use the native troops he had recruited. He had no plans to issue them all with guns: every section of ten men would be under the command of a senior native and he alone would be so armed. For the rest, assegais and a shield would have to do; it was, after all, these basic weapons that the majority of the Zulus fought with. This was not just a question of the number of guns available; many in Natal were opposed to the thought of natives being armed this way as they were afraid the weapons might be used against them rather than the Zulus.

It was also felt by Chelmsford that the native troops would be of little use in the front line of a defensive position and would be better suited to either scouting duties or assisting in the pursuit of a beaten enemy. He clearly did not think much of their fighting abilities and perhaps this negative attitude transmitted itself to the levies. Yet it is also true that when, within a couple of weeks of the invasion, native troops unwittingly found themselves close to the front line, his reservations were amply confirmed.

Chelmsford had moved the Natal Mounted Police up towards the border as early as November 1879, where they would be stationed at Helpmekaar. The small settlement, little more than a hamlet, was to be the advanced depot for supplies en route to the front. It was perched high up in the hills at an altitude of 5,000ft. This was both an attraction and a problem. Attacks of horse sickness were much less common at high altitude, hence the suitability of Helpmekaar as a supply depot. From the hills here one could see for scores of miles; on a clear day the steep scarp of the Drakensberg, 100 miles to the west, could be seen, whilst below the hills in which the settlement stood lay Zululand itself.

If Helpmekaar was a fine place to guard against horse sickness, the down-side was its frequently awful weather. This could switch from scorching heat to ominous black skies in a moment. Hailstones of huge dimension frequently fell from leaden clouds, some so large that they dented corrugated tin roofs and it was not unknown for snow to carpet the ground in winter. This was definitely something of a 'hardship posting'. One of those who stayed there, the war correspondent Norris-Newman, wrote that 'the cold during the night was intense and we all suffered for the want of sufficient blankets'.[28] Helpmekaar literally means 'help one another' – the troops stationed there soon found out why such an injunction was necessary.

The Natal Mounted Police's horses were discourteously ungrateful regarding the thought that had been given to their health. They arrived at night in pouring rain which had left the surrounding terrain like a paddy field. When they were put out to graze the next morning, most of the horses promptly ran away. Of seventy-two beasts, sixty ran off. Some were not recovered for months, eventually being picked up a hundred miles away.

This was a major problem for Chelmsford and more immediately the commander of the Mounted Police, Major John Dartnell. Dartnell was a useful man to have around; he had already seen service in the Indian Mutiny. He had retired to Natal in 1869 but had been requested by the colony's government to form the Mounted Police. His men would be crucial in the forthcoming campaign in the absence of regular cavalry.

By the end of November, Chelmsford had had some good news. The War Office in London had assented to send two battalions of regular troops and two companies of Royal Engineers to supplement the forces he already had with him, plus drafts for the regiments already in southern Africa. This amounted to 1,948 infantry and 240 engineers.[29] They would soon be needed. On 30 November,

Colonel Richard Glyn led his 1st/24th Regiment out of their headquarters at Pietermaritzburg. The battalion's band led them out, proudly marching towards Helpmekaar. The colonel's wife and daughters watched on as he, as notional commander of Number 3 Column, moved towards his appointment with destiny. A week's uncomfortable trudging through appalling weather followed, with pouring rain turning the dirt tracks into rivers of mud before they arrived close to the borders of Zululand.

In the meantime, pressure was being put on Cetshwayo by Frere to summon his great council to hear the findings of the Boundary Commissioners. They were to come to a meeting to be held in early December near the Lower Thukela Drift. However, there would be other matters to discuss there. As Chelmsford noted, this was 'in connection with certain outrages committed lately on our Border by those for whose good behaviour the Zulu King is responsible'.[30] In the event, these extra provisions would prove very useful for anyone who wished to start a war and needed a good excuse for it.

The most crucial of the extra conditions that Frere, aided by Chelmsford, planned to impose was a requirement that Cetshwayo disband his army. This was not only an unwarranted intrusion into the affairs of a sovereign state; it was also a fundamental assault on the traditional Zulu way of life. The king was also to be deprived of the right to decide when his people could marry, another interference with Zulu custom. Yet if the king was to refuse these demands, so Chelmsford told Lord Stanley, then an invasion of Zululand was unavoidable.

Chelmsford also informed Stanley that he was trying to raise more troops locally. Approaches to persuade the Swazi to join in on the British side had been rebuffed for the time being. He was prepared to offer money or arms to buy their support but any land transfer to them was out of the question. But Chelmsford was not unduly concerned at their reluctance as he thought that the first British victory would soon see them rushing to join his cause.

As December 1878 arrived, there were other things to worry Chelmsford. Rowlands offered to resign, despondent at his lack of progress, but Chelmsford would not hear of this. He admitted in a letter to Sir Theophilus Shepstone, who was Secretary for Native Affairs in the Transvaal, that Rowlands was not an ideal commander as he spent too much time in his tent and 'a commander must ride about and see the country himself' – something that he himself certainly did. He also criticised Rowlands' tactics in the recent war.

He confessed that 'as an independent commander he is no doubt a failure' and so he would not put him in that position again. Yet his major reason for discouraging the resignation from being confirmed was that it would be a professional mistake for Rowlands. This summed up as eloquently as possible Chelmsford's limitations as a commander. Career considerations of individual officers should not have come into the equation – the primary consideration was the well-being of the army and its ultimate chances of success. Chelmsford's attitude typified the shortcomings of the British army of the time and demonstrated why reform was urgently needed.[31]

An alternative view of Rowlands was offered by Major Redvers Buller, who would be Wood's key commander on the western borders of Zululand. He had served in the desultory campaign led by Rowlands and said of him that he was 'quite useless, he cannot make up his mind to do anything, sitting on his behind in his position'.[32] Buller despised Rowland's lack of aggression and longed to work with Wood again – a wish that would soon be fulfilled.

The unhelpful findings of the Boundary Commission could not be hushed up much longer. Chelmsford told Wood on 10 December that the Boers in the Transvaal should prepare themselves for bad news though they would be allowed to carry on occupying their farms in return for a rent paid to the Zulus instead of, as they currently did, to the Transvaal government.

The climax of the Commissioners' deliberations on the border territories was due to be announced at the Lower Drift near the mouth of the Thukela on 11 December. The delegations met underneath the welcome shade of a clump of fig trees where a makeshift canvas canopy had been draped over the branches to give more protection from the searing heat. By the river, at the bottom of a hill crowned with a hostelry, Smith's Hotel, the future of the Zulu nation was about to be decided.

The Zulu delegation numbered less than fifty but included in their number were some of the most prominent men in Zululand. However, they were not there to negotiate; that could be done by their king alone in consultation with his council. They were there to listen and report. Ironically, the most prominent man with them was John Dunn, one-time enemy of Cetshwayo, now one of his most trusted advisers. He held a great deal of land in Zululand but was also paid by the government of Natal as their representative there. He was very much a man with a foot in both camps; he had many wives and also traded items, including guns, to the Zulus. When war broke out, he would find it very hard indeed given his divided loyalties.

Bartle Frere was represented by the Honourable C. Brownlee and John Shepstone, Secretary of Native Affairs. Brownlee, an experienced administrator, was no friend of Cetshwayo and was convinced of the need for war every bit as much as Frere.[33] To give the scene a slightly more martial air, a detachment of British sailors and marines stood around. Cetshwayo's delegation sat patiently and listened as the results of the arbitration were read out. As the conclusions were announced, they murmured in approval. Most of the decisions were going in their favour and they felt a growing sense of satisfaction. British justice perhaps was much fairer than they had assumed it to be.

With the Commission's conclusions finally revealed, and the disputed lands confirmed as belonging mostly to the Zulus, Cetshwayo's delegation felt a mixture of relief and contentment at their fairness. Lunch was served, roast beef washed down with sugar-water, a favourite of the Zulus. They had no written language of their own but were adept at remembering the details of long speeches. Talking over the findings, the delegation was no doubt well pleased. It appeared that Cetshwayo was to be the recipient of good news.

However, the drama was not yet over. A dispatch had been sent from Frere and this was read to the Zulus after lunch. Those feelings of satisfaction quickly started to evaporate. The High Commissioner demanded that Mbilini and Sihayo's sons should be handed over. This demand would be very difficult to comply with, though might have been possible, and indeed there were some amongst the Zulus who believed that they should be given over to the British.

What was a complete impossibility was what then followed. Cetshwayo, claimed the dispatch, had acted like a tyrant and that had to stop. He had an arbitrary power of life and death over his subjects and that was not acceptable. To this assault on the king's character, a listening *induna* fairly asked, 'have the Zulus complained?' Then, the *pièce de résistance*: the Zulu military system, the core of the Zulu culture, was to be dismantled within the next thirty days or else military action would be taken to destroy it. Even later historians who were broadly supportive of Chelmsford in the war that now loomed concede that this made war close to a foregone conclusion.[34]

This left little chance of a diplomatic resolution but the reality, of course, was that diplomacy was not on Frere's agenda. What was needed was a resolution of the Zulu problem and the elimination of the military threat that they posed. The demands could not be met without Cetshwayo's effective capitulation. But Confederation must be developed at all costs and this could only be achieved by demolishing the Zulu way of life. By the stroke of a pen, Frere had committed his country to war, a situation that neither the authorities in London nor their representative in Natal wished for.

Cetshwayo eventually sent back a reply to these extraordinary demands, though it was not published until after the invasion of Zululand had taken place. With perfectly dignified logic, the king asked the question:

> why does the Governor of Natal speak to me about my laws? Do I go to Natal and dictate to him about his laws … Go back and tell the white men this, and let them hear it well. The Governor of Natal and I are equal. He is the Governor of Natal and I am the governor here.[35]

It was a well-worded response from a man who desperately wanted to avoid a war he knew would be a disaster for his people. Yet his opponents over the

Thukela were not interested in rhetoric, only the submission of Cetshwayo unconditionally to their demands.

The king could expect no help from the British government, several weeks away in terms of communication. The nearest long-distance telegraph station to Britain was in Madeira and messages would have to be taken by ship there before they could then be forwarded to London; in good weather this meant a sixteen-day delay between sending a message from southern Africa and its arrival back in England.

Within a few months of the war's outbreak the telegraph would be extended to the Cape, but before then the lack of a prompt mode of communication would be distinctly advantageous to those who wished to put an end to Zulu power. By the time British officials back in the mother country heard about the ultimatum, it would have already expired and the war would be under way. London had bigger fish to fry, such as the war in Afghanistan, and did not want a conflict in southern Africa. The affairs of Zululand were an unwelcome distraction. They would do what they could to stop a war there but they were to be deprived of the opportunity to intervene.

The inbuilt time delay gave Frere and Chelmsford the opportunity that they needed to commit the British government to a war that they would have done much to avoid. As an example of these time lags, the popular weekly publication, the *Illustrated London News*, carried news from Cape Town, dated 17 December 1878, that 'every preparation for war continues to be carried on'. It reported this on 11 January 1879, the very day that the invasion of Zululand took place.

Even as Frere's unfeasible demands were read out, his willing lieutenant, Frederic Thesiger, Second Baron Chelmsford (and now seemingly prospective Resident in a conquered Zululand, a position he was provisionally offered when Wood turned it down), put the finishing touches to his plans of execution.

In contrast, the Zulu delegation made its way despondently back to Ulundi with the news; they were under no illusions as to the magnitude of the threat facing them. Frere, in the meantime, sat back contentedly admiring his handiwork. Everything was working splendidly. He probably reasoned well enough that many Zulus might die and with them a way of life, though no doubt he hoped with every ounce of his Christian spirit that needless bloodshed might be avoided. That, after all, would be the 'civilised' thing to do.

But he did not perhaps reckon on the shedding of European blood that would flow from his actions; that was not at all what was required or anticipated. However, the die was cast and a war – short, sharp, brutal and decisive – was now imminent. Pleased with the way that his plans were developing, the 'enlightened 19th Century administrator' now waited to see what would happen next.

three

A MORAL VICTORY?

The Invasion Begins

As the hands on the clock moved inexorably towards zero hour, Chelmsford used the final minutes to position the last pieces on the military chessboard. Not for a second did he think that Cetshwayo would comply with the terms of the ultimatum. He threw himself enthusiastically into the last stages of planning, knowing that he would soon be at war. Militarily he did not foresee any difficulties, except that he was afraid the Zulus would not offer themselves helpfully up for slaughter in a set-piece battle. Ironically, the Zulus very much hoped for a major confrontation themselves, though they wanted the British forces to fight them man-to-man rather than hiding themselves away behind prepared positions.

Both British and Zulu commanders were being a little naive if they expected their opponents to play into their hands. No military general with a modicum of intelligence would do such a thing. However, Chelmsford was in the main relaxed about the military campaign that now appeared unavoidable. Far more of a headache for him was the ongoing challenge of sorting out the difficult logistical challenges that the invasion of Zululand would pose.

As 1878 drew to a close, the British columns started to assemble. Just at the wrong time for them, the weather changed. There had been several years of near-drought conditions in Zululand and Natal but now the heavens opened. For troops who were living in tents, it made for a very uncomfortable and damp beginning to the campaign. But it was known that the rainy season was approaching and indeed this was welcomed; swollen rivers would make it much harder for the Zulus to raid into Natal using anything other than known fords, which would all be closely guarded. Chelmsford was most afraid that the Zulus would avoid his army, skirt round behind them and raid the colony whilst his back was turned, so he did all he could to keep this from happening. In this respect, at least, the weather would help.

What was slightly less welcome was the effect that the dreadful weather of that summer season would have on his own army. By late December, the Natal press was reporting that:

> it is feared the rains will retard operations. Ox wagons are apt to stand still when rain is pouring down, and roads are deep in mud. Many days of endless rain and never ending reports of flooded or impassable rivers have made the exact period of our departure uncertain.[1]

Chelmsford himself noted in a letter to Stanley that the weather made it impossible to 'encamp a force without shelter of some kind'.[2] This was an interesting observation; within two months this is exactly what they would be doing.

The timing of the invasion was inopportune for another reason, which Chelmsford should have already realised. Every year in January the Zulu warriors amassed at the king's capital for the ritual known as the First Fruits ceremony. Chelmsford was invading Zululand at the very time that virtually every warrior in the country was due to assemble in one place. In terms of Cetshwayo assembling his men to resist an invasion, ordinarily a major logistical feat, little more needed to be done. They were already due to meet up and all that was required was to tell them to arrive along with their best weapons.

Chelmsford's plan was, after some reflection, to be based on a three-pronged assault rather than the five columns he had initially planned to be on the offensive; the other two would now be kept back for defensive purposes. He could not launch an attack until the ultimatum expired. An invasion would be initiated by the refusal of the Zulus to hand over Sihayo's sons, to pay the large fine of 500 cattle that had been imposed on Cetshwayo for their offences and to disband their armies. As no one seriously expected these things to happen, the tactics for a war were finalised assuming that it would go ahead.

Each column would consist of two regular battalions of infantry and an artillery battery. There would also be a unit of auxiliary infantry and a number of irregular cavalry troops. The reserve columns would be smaller than this; Chelmsford did not have the luxury of large numbers of spare men to keep back as a contingency.

Chelmsford put pen to paper and wrote to the commanders of his three attacking columns. First in line was Colonel Pearson, in command of the column waiting to attack in the east of Zululand. He would cross over from the southern bank of the Thukela River. The key thing for his column was, first of all, to establish a strong line of communication with the troops when they were ferried over on the ponts that had been put in place. Chelmsford told Pearson that some reinforcements were on their way from England and that a company of engineers would be sent to his column as soon as they arrived.

He would not, however, be sending any cavalry reinforcements yet. Apart from being in short supply, the terrain through which Pearson's men had to pass would be hard on the health of the horses. The initial destination for the column would be the abandoned Norwegian mission station at Eshowe, 40 miles or four tough marches away. Once he got there he was to assemble strong fortifications around it and use Eshowe as an advanced base.

Pearson would be supported by a reserve column under Colonel Durnford. Although subordinated to Pearson, Chelmsford wanted Durnford to act fairly independently at first. Initially his force would guard the crossing at Middle Drift but might later move down to Lower Drift and cross over behind Pearson. This plan of action would soon be amended, in keeping with Chelmsford's reputation for changing his mind.

Chelmsford instructed Pearson that he was not to seek a confrontation with the Zulus but instead adopt a passive defensive approach by which he would fight only if forced to. Mounted scouts should be sent out by day to see if any hostile forces were massing close to the column prior to an attack. Pearson was also to make free use of spies.

The big challenge involved in making Chelmsford's strategy work was co-ordinating the three offensive forces. They were all to move into Zululand at the same time. Once the armies were on the move, full use was to be made of the Border Police who, in the absence of regular cavalry, would act as couriers for messengers between the three armies. They would move to and fro, in theory providing lateral communication between the forces as they reached deeper into Zululand.[3]

A letter to Wood at the head of his more independent column was penned the following day. Chelmsford told Wood that Frere did not wish the army to go on the offensive unless forced to once they crossed into Zululand (as if the Zulus would meekly put down their arms when their sovereignty was ignored). Wood was told to make wide-ranging reconnaissance but that 'Sir Bartle Frere and I are both anxious not to lay open the troops of the charge of unnecessarily bringing on hostilities' and to this end reliable officers should be deployed who were likely to be sensitive to the situation.

Part of the reason for this caution was to encourage Zulus who did not wish to fight to come over to the British side. If any gave themselves up, they should be sent to the rear as soon as possible and an officer dedicated to them was to look after them. A copy of Pearson's instructions was also given to Wood so that he could have an insight into Chelmsford's thinking. Some reinforcements would be sent to Wood too: a party of engineers if they arrived in time and a group of Basuto horsemen – 500 were hoped for – would also be dispatched. The latter would be useful in maintaining communication with other columns.[4]

That just left the Central Column under Colonel Richard Glyn. This was to be the main invasion force but the chain of command here would be confused as Chelmsford would journey with this column and, to all intents and purposes, would be in command rather than Glyn. This force would cross over into Zululand at Rorke's Drift. Two ponts, flat-bottomed ferries, were to be put in place before the end of December in case the river itself became too swollen for the men to cross unassisted.

From Rorke's Drift a direct road ran on to Ulundi but the going would not be easy. The first stream beyond Rorke's Drift was 9 miles into Zululand. There would also be wood here for fuel but further on it would be in shorter supply. As the column would need to communicate with both the left and right columns of Wood and Pearson, it would have more Mounted Infantry than the other forces.

The Central Column would be accompanied by the only official correspondent with the expedition – a situation that showed both how unprepared the wider world was for the outbreak of war in Zululand and also how relatively unimportant it initially was. He was Charles Norris-Newman ('Noggs') of the *London Standard*, who happened to be in the region at the time. He went up to see the troops as they prepared for war but was keen to ensure that he was able to get back for his Christmas dinner in Pietermaritzburg. As he returned through thick fog up to the front, he noticed how quiet the farms he passed were. He later found out that this was because the farmers there had rented out their wagons to the invasion force in return for large sums of money.

Norris-Newman spent most of his time before the invasion with the Natal Native Contingent and soon felt like one of their adopted officers. He enjoyed their hospitality and the sense of excitement that was palpably building as the date set for the start of the war loomed closer. The lowlight of these days, however, was undoubtedly the awful weather, torrential rain at one stage causing flash floods that washed out the camp.

By 29 December, Chelmsford was certain that Cetshwayo was not going to comply with the ultimatum. He sent a message to Sir Henry Bulwer in which the eagerness of the men for a fight was eloquently expressed: 'I found all here in good health and spirits and very pleased at the prospect of going across the border.'[5] He wrote soon after to Pearson that he should advance to Eshowe as rapidly as possible once the ultimatum had passed to prevent the mission station from being burned and made unusable. Once he got there with his wagons, they were to be offloaded as quickly as possible and sent back to Natal for more supplies. The mission station was to be crammed with as many provisions as it could hold. Sailors from HMS *Active* were to accompany the column.

At Eshowe the column was to halt, as it was anticipated that it would move more rapidly than the other two offensive columns. As well as lateral communication with the other columns, telegraph messages were also to be sent daily to the base established at Fort Pearson by the Lower Drift at the mouth of the Thukela.[6] A memorandum was sent to all troops regarding their behaviour when the war began. It promulgated good intentions that would not long survive the first clash of arms:

> officers commanding columns are requested to have it clearly explained to the native portion of the force under their command that any native convicted of wilfully killing a woman or child or a wounded man, will render himself liable to be hanged. No huts in Zululand are to be burnt except under the special orders of the officer commanding the column – Any soldier, European or native, transgressing this order will render himself liable to a flogging.

Soon soldiers would forget the injunction against killing wounded natives and clouds of acrid smoke would be blotting out the sun from the huts that had been set alight. There are no records that tell of anyone being flogged or hanged for these actions. But by then Chelmsford had realised that the 'civilised ideals' he wished to employ in what he supposed would be a military walkover were hopelessly out of place. His chivalric policies were predicated on an assumption of comfortable British victories, in the aftermath of which he could afford to be magnanimous. These expectations would soon prove to be very optimistic.

By 4 January 1879, Chelmsford had moved forward to Helpmekaar. The small settlement had expanded dramatically now it was a military base but conditions there had been difficult. Those there for Christmas had enjoyed a most un-festive period with thick mists and drenching downpours characterising the weather. Helpmekaar became an unpleasant, sodden quagmire. With Chelmsford's arrival, an inspection was called which made the men buck up their ideas in order to look their best for the commander-in-chief.

The day after his arrival, Chelmsford attended a church parade. There he repeated a previously made promise that any volunteer who wished to be given farmland in Zululand after the war would be generously provided for. It was a tempting gesture, though Chelmsford had far exceeded his authority in making it.

He was not adept at playing local politics. His cavalry were all local volunteers who were contracted for the invasion of Zululand and by the terms of their contracts were supposed to have a say in the appointment of their commanding officer. The man they accepted as their leader was Major John Dartnell but when, shortly before the invasion, John Russell of the 12th Lancers arrived in southern Africa, Chelmsford appointed him to the command of the cavalry in his stead.

The cavalry refused point-blank to accept him. This was well within the rights given them by their contracts. Chelmsford eventually managed to smooth the problem out. He promoted Dartnell to a position of cavalry adviser and then prevailed on him to convince the cavalry to accept Russell. The plan worked but only for a short while as, once in action, it became clear that Russell was simply not up to the job. This suggested that Chelmsford was not the best judge of men, a perception that would be reinforced by other decisions he made.

As the time ran down until the deadline expired, Chelmsford became even more bullish than Frere about the need for war. Cetshwayo sent a number of messengers to Chelmsford in an effort to negotiate but he insisted in his letters to Frere that these men were just spies. However, the Zulu king was desperate to avoid the looming war which he believed would be a disaster for his people. He protested his innocence and his willingness to live in peace with his neighbours in Natal. But he did not comply with the terms of the ultimatum which would have effectively been an admission of his subservience to the colonial authorities and an end to the Zulu way of life.

Advance units of British and colonial troops started moving towards Rorke's Drift in dribs and drabs. The volunteers had been the first to arrive, setting up camp on the slopes of a hill overlooking the drift called the Biggarsberg. Companies of the 24th Regiment would join them soon after. They had been maintaining a degree of fitness by being taken out for runs or by participation in impromptu cricket matches. But it was not long before the first death of the war occurred. Trooper Arthur Dixon was in a small volunteer unit, the Newcastle Mounted Rifles. They had moved up to the banks of the Buffalo which in the humid heat proved a tempting spot to bathe. Dixon, a non-swimmer, was one of those who availed himself of the opportunity; however, he got out of his depth and drowned.

Chelmsford visited Rorke's Drift on 9 January. Here he inspected the mission station near the banks of the river. It had once been the store of a trader, James Rorke, from which the drift got its name; the Zulus called it *kwa Jimu*, 'Jim's Place'. It was overlooked to the rear by a towering hill, Shiyane ('eyebrow'), recently renamed Oskarberg by the current resident Otto Witt in honour of his Swedish king and also the missionaries' patron saint Oscar.

Rorke had been a larger-than-life character. Local legend asserted that he had committed suicide in 1875 when his supplies of gin ran out. Aware that the native tribes sometimes used body parts in their magic rituals, he had insisted that he be buried under a yard of concrete. Following his death, his widow had been left penniless and had therefore sold the property to Witt.

Witt may have been a missionary but he was also a tough negotiator. When the British army commandeered his home he haggled a good price with Chelmsford as compensation and a sum of £14 a month for the lease of the property was agreed (until his death in 1875 Rorke had been paying just over £3 a month for it). However, the contract was never signed; by the time it was ready for signature, the mission station was a charred ruin.

The day before Chelmsford arrived the ponts had appeared at Rorke's Drift. They were in pieces and needed to be assembled *in situ*. They were to be erected by a party of Royal Engineers, who started the job at once. Later that day, a group of Zulus was seen on the far side of the river but any excitement quickly evaporated when it became clear they were one of Wood's units scouting far ahead of his column. They had made a 30-mile trip through Zululand since leaving Wood and had been well received on their journey with not a hint of trouble en route.

Norris-Newman was there to witness events in the build-up to the invasion. The presence of what were described as signal fires across the river from Rorke's Drift suggested that the Zulus were watching the column as it advanced. He also noted that every time a new body of troops advanced to the drift, smoke would go up from a homestead on the same side of the water. Thinking not unreasonably that they were being spied on, Captain Shepstone of the NNC had surrounded it and taken the male inhabitants prisoner, sending them back to Helpmekaar. They were the first official prisoners taken in the Anglo-Zulu War.[7]

On 10 January, Chelmsford wrote to Frere that he was going to move his camp up to Rorke's Drift ready for the crossing over into Zululand. He was disappointed that Wood had contacted him with the unwelcome news that the Boers, rather than offering to join him as irregulars, had instead chosen to move further away from the likely conflict zone. As far as Chelmsford was concerned, if they were now raided by the Zulus it was largely their own fault for refusing to help. Chelmsford hoped that Theophilus Shepstone would take up residence in Utrecht close to where the Boers were concentrated; he seemed to be fairly popular with them and might have been able to induce some of them to join the war.

In the meantime, even before the invasion had begun, the oxen – regarded by Chelmsford as the Achilles heel of his invasion forces – had already started to die off. He hoped that he would be able to replenish his depleted stocks by confiscating others from the Zulus. He was also upset that reinforcements had not been sent from England earlier as he felt the shortage of troops to guard his lines of communication very keenly.

Critical information had started to come in about the Zulus' likely tactics. Chelmsford's spymaster was Francis Fynn, a magistrate in the Msinga Division on the west bank of the Buffalo River. His real usefulness emanated from the fact that he had grown up amongst the Zulus – his father had been one of the first white settlers in Natal – and he knew more about them than most other white men. He also had an invaluable network of connections inside the Zulu kingdom. He later wrote:

it was planned for this column to proceed northwards to central Zululand. I pointed out that the Zulu plan to descend the Mangeni Valley of the Hlazakazi Mountain and there shelter until Number 3 Column had moved forward sufficiently to enable the Zulu army to creep round from the Mangeni Valley, up the Buffalo River and close in upon them.[8]

If Fynn's spies were indeed saying that the Zulu plan was to creep up behind the advancing British force and cut them off from the rear, then the news should have been taken very seriously by the British high command. It would have suggested a more cautious approach from Chelmsford than that which he actually adopted. It would also have implied a greater degree of sophistication in Zulu tactics than that of simply offering their warriors up as cannon fodder for the British columns. It is a dangerous mistake to underestimate an enemy and Chelmsford was already beginning to make it.

Certainly there was one white man in Zululand who suspected that this would be a difficult war. John Dunn had taken the precaution of moving his family south across the Thukela and into Natal. He brought with him a number of retainers. He knew that he could not remain neutral in the war and given the colour of his skin there was only one side he could opt for.

Dunn was now in his mid-forties, described by Norris-Newman as:

> of medium height, strongly built … and has all the appearance of being just what he is, a thoroughly seasoned colonist. His manner is inclined to be abrupt, and at times he is absent-minded, as even while his eyes seem intent on your face, his thoughts appear to be elsewhere.[9]

Now he found himself caught in the middle of a very awkward and difficult situation in which he personally stood to lose much.

On 11 January 1879, the war officially began which cannot have come as a surprise to anyone locally but would have been a major disappointment to the authorities in London. There had been no acceptance of the ultimatum terms by Cetshwayo, as indeed was always likely to be the case. Wood had already pushed into remote corners of Zululand even before the conflict started in earnest. But on 11 January, both Glyn/Chelmsford and Pearson began their respective moves into Zululand, about 75 miles apart.

Despite his misgivings, Chelmsford still had a sizeable force available to him, although he was short in some areas, especially cavalry. In all, he had 17,929 men of which 5,476 were regular British soldiers, with 1,508 colonial horsemen; 9,035 were local African troops and 1,910 were conductors for the wagon trains, so important in supporting the rest of the men logistically.

The main thrust would come from Number 3 Column where from the outset the command structure was confused. Chelmsford's Chief of Staff, Major John Crealock, was often at his lordship's side. A bumptious, spiteful man whose tongue was far sharper than his insight, Crealock's appointment was a major mistake on Chelmsford's part. Crealock was particularly damning of his fellow officers. He regularly corresponded with Major-General Sir Archibald Alison, in charge of intelligence at the War Office back in Britain, and in his private letters to him he made no bones about his low opinion of some of his colleagues.

He was particularly harsh on both Major Cornelius Clery, Glyn's principal staff officer, and on Glyn himself. In one letter he wrote that 'Clery is out here with Colonel Glyn and high time too; do not expect anything from the latter. He is purely a regimental officer with no idea beyond it.'[10] Chelmsford and Crealock developed military strategy between them and kept Glyn, the notional column commander, in the dark; his main function seemed to be in detailing the guards to look after the camp. Such lack of clarity would soon become very useful to certain parties.

The British invasion of Zululand began when reveille was sounded at Rorke's Drift at 2 a.m. on the 11th. At that unearthly hour the weather was fine but that would change by the time the river began to be forded in earnest a couple of hours later. By then there was a heavy drizzle, a damp pall hanging over proceedings. Despite being January, summer in southern Africa, it was a cold morning. The buglers sounded out reveille and everywhere in the cramped camp grumpy soldiers rubbed the dust of sleep from their eyes, stretched aching muscles and pulled themselves groggily to their feet. Artillerymen watched over the crossing, their guns ready to start blazing at the first sign of opposition from the far bank.

Rather appropriately given later events, there was a false alarm when someone thought they saw some Zulus on the far bank and the men readied themselves for a fight; night-time alarums were something of a feature of the war to come. The whole camp, including Chelmsford and his staff, stood to battle stations and was not impressed when it turned out that there was no enemy waiting to greet them.

It was the cavalry who made the first move into Zululand here, though the first man across — so he claimed — was Norris-Newman who accompanied them.[11] They took off their equipment and put it on the pont to keep it dry whilst they themselves swam their horses across. The 3rd Battalion of the Natal Native Contingent began to cross almost at the same time. The river was deep, up to their necks in places, and the current was strong, tugging at their feet and legs at a rate of 6 knots — there was no pont crossing for them. They formed human chains to enable them to cross the river safely. They made a murmuring noise as they went, like a swarm of bees; this was to frighten off any enemies, including any crocodiles that might be in the vicinity.

The situation was not helped by the stony river bed which made it difficult for those crossing to get a grip; they were thankful for a small island in the middle of the river. Hamilton-Browne with his battalion of the NNC was grateful for his strong and experienced horse, a veteran campaigner from New Zealand who got him safely across. With frank honesty, he said that he had no idea how many, if any, of his men were lost because no one had ever bothered to draw up accurate records of how many had joined up in the first place. It was a revealing insight into both the inadequate administration affecting aspects of the campaign and also how little value was attached to the lives of the native troops.[12]

The two battalions of the 24th Regiment crossed over on the ponts. They had suffered the indignity of having their possessions searched for alcohol before crossing; there could be no risk of having any of the soldiers incapacitated in enemy territory from excessive affection for such substances. Some of them had looted the liquor store during the night and had to be deprived of their ill-gotten gains. Once across, they formed into a square, dressed in their magnificent scarlet tunics, many of them no doubt somewhat tattered by now. It was when they were established on the far bank that the tedious and problematic task of ferrying the bulky wagons across began.

The raid on the liquor store evidenced an ongoing issue. Problems with alcohol were rife in the army. The *Natal Witness* correspondent noted from Utrecht, in Colonel Wood's sphere, that 'drunkenness is very prevalent here at present. Men are being tried by court-martial and flogged nearly every day.' The worst incident took place at Durban where the 99th Regiment were landed after having apparently gone a day without food. Finding little open in the evening when they arrived, many ended up in the pubs of the town.

Here they drank local hooch, Natal rum, which had a devastating effect on them. The *Natal Witness* noted that there were 'about eighty young soldiers lying in West Street, totally insensible from liquor obtained from our local canteens'. It reported that 200 men were incapable of walking back to the camp. It was subsequently claimed that three soldiers actually died as a result of their intoxication. The reporter sagely noted that not much attention had been paid to their demise, which would not have been the case had they died in battle.[13] Given this background, the seriousness with which the British army took the problem of alcohol is quite understandable.

Nor was this incident particularly out of the ordinary. Artilleryman Lieutenant Henry Curling, who served in the Ninth Frontier War of the previous year, recorded an incident where men were so drunk that they had been ferried off in a cart as they were incapable of moving under their own steam.[14] Yet the same correspondent hinted at the reasons why: wartime might be exciting and for men like Curling it presented a chance for rapid promotion in an otherwise very static military hierarchy, but in between times campaigning often involved extended periods of boredom, unappealing rations, uncomfortable long months of sleeping under canvas and plenty of other reasons for the common soldier to seek solace and distraction in a bottle of 'Cape Mist' gin.

It was not until the afternoon that the whole force was across and ready to advance. By then the cold and damp of early morn had given way to a searing, scorching sunny day where wet clothes quickly dried and men soon began to bake. The Zulus did not attempt to prevent the crossings and not a shot had been fired when the army crossed. Many in the invasion force had expected a fight and saw this as a sign that the campaign might be rather straightforward. As one local correspondent noted: 'crossing the river at this point, without any resistance, is a moral victory as if a battle had been fought and won.'[15] Another man there, Captain Hallam Parr, on Colonel Glyn's staff, spoke to some passing Boers who pointed out a prominent hill in the distance. They told him they thought the Zulus called it Isandlwana.[16]

The column was only half across when Chelmsford had taken himself off on a ride north to meet up with Wood, some miles off. It was useful for him to have face-to-face discussions with his most trusted lieutenant, but it was also rather symptomatic of his cavalier attitude that he should do so before his men were safely installed in Zululand. He was certainly a commander who liked to acquaint himself with the country through which he was to march but in the process he took a number of risks. It was a policy tinged with danger and it would soon have spectacular adverse results.

By the time that night fell with its dramatic suddenness, the column at Rorke's Drift was safely across and the men prepared themselves to turn in, save those tasked with picket duty who were to watch out for surprise attacks during the dark hours. Hamilton-Browne looked around him and was not impressed at what he saw. Field regulations decreed that camps should be laagered at night but no one had taken any notice of them – a state of affairs that Norris-Newman remarked on too.[17] It was clearly thought to be too difficult and time consuming for men who were not experienced in undertaking what was a complex manoeuvre.

Some of those with the column wrote home about the invasion that had begun. One of them was Private Owen Ellis of the 1st/24th, who wrote that things were under way and there might be a fight soon but they did not have supplies for more than seventeen days and they all expected to be at Cetshwayo's 'Grand Kraals', as he called Ulundi, in about a week's time. Sadly for him, this was wrong by about six months and Private Ellis, and many others with him, would never see Ulundi.[18]

During his discussions with Wood, Chelmsford was already looking forward to the post-war settlement, as if the battle was already won. He asked Wood to be Resident of Zululand when the country had been successfully subsumed into the British Confederation in southern Africa – an offer that Wood refused. They talked for two hours before Chelmsford took himself back with a strong escort to the column advancing from Rorke's Drift.

En route, they raided several homesteads and took off the cattle, making a mockery of the claim that they were fighting not the Zulu people but just their king. This was just a small-scale reflection of what Wood had been doing already; by now he and his men had already taken 7,000 cattle and sold them for a handsome profit, little if any of which found its way down to the common soldier.

Many of the border regions had already been decimated. Cattle had been driven off to safer pastures by the Zulus, to places hopefully away from the rapacious eyes of the British army. A few warriors stayed to keep a watch over the British movements but most converged on Ulundi in their regiments. Here the main army would assemble and prepare for war. This involved a number of traditional purification rituals which the warriors used to prepare themselves for battle.

Chelmsford had his own plans for the border regions. To counteract the risk of raids into Natal, he aimed to create a buffer zone inside Zululand itself. His initial objective was to neutralise any potential opponents there, hopefully by persuading them to side with the British voluntarily but, if not, by the use of overwhelming force.

In theory, Cetshwayo had over 40,000 men at his disposal giving him a huge numerical advantage over the British forces. However, the king was no fool and recognised that the enemy would have the benefit of more advanced weaponry. He realised too that the invaders could not be resisted on all fronts. His scouts would watch closely and see which of the British forces appeared to be strongest and then he would focus Zulu resistance against this main threat.

Sihayo's settlement at Sokexe lay just a few miles from Rorke's Drift and it was likely to be the first target of any attack. After all, he (or more accurately his sons) had provided the initial excuse for the war. Just a day after crossing at Rorke's Drift, the first significant attack of the Anglo-Zulu War was launched here. Many of Sihayo's men – including the *induna* himself – were at Ulundi with the gathering armies. But some had stayed behind and a fight was imminent.

It started when Chelmsford noticed some cattle being driven into the hills close by Sihayo's homestead. Chelmsford deployed four companies of the 1st/24th Regiment and one company of the 3rd Regiment of the Natal Native Contingent for the attack. The NNC had been formed into three regiments for the invasion but the commandant of the 3rd, Rupert Lonsdale, was incapacitated after a heavy fall from his horse not long before and they were led into battle in this first action by Major Wilsone Black, 'borrowed' from the 24th Regiment of the imperial army.[19]

The Zulus took up position in some rocky hills, which were full of caves that provided splendid cover, and began shooting, largely inaccurately, at the invaders.

They sang war chants that echoed around the amphitheatre-like walls of the valley. As the redcoats and colonials advanced, a deep voice cried out from the Zulu ranks asking why the soldiers were there. In response, Captain Duncombe, interpreter to Commandant 'Maori' Hamilton-Browne, replied that they were there by the orders of the Great White Queen. As Her Majesty, or indeed her government, had no idea that the two nations of Britain and Zululand were even at war, this was something of a fib. [20]

Both the NNC and the regulars went into action, scrambling up the jagged cliffs. Some of the Zulus were armed with firearms, but they were old-fashioned and ineffective pieces that did little damage. However, the NNC did not perform well, many of them diving for cover when the firing began. Just one part of the native forces fought gamely, the isiGqoza who were highly regarded by Hamilton-Browne.

One of the NNC officers, Lieutenant Henry Harford, was made of sterner stuff. He had stormed a cave single-handed, a precarious step which was made all the more risky because his revolver was not working. He had bluffed his way through magnificently, persuading the Zulus inside to surrender (he spoke the language having previously lived in Natal) and leading his captives back to the British ranks.

Harford was a special service officer (an officer in the regular army who had obtained special permission to take leave of his regiment to take part in the war with the forces in action). He was an adjutant in the 99th Regiment but he had effectively resigned his post to participate in the war. On his arrival, Chelmsford had appointed him staff officer to Commandant Lonsdale. [21]

Harford allegedly inspired a moment of rare comedy during the engagement. He was a keen entomologist, a man much liked by his comrades. There was therefore widespread concern when he was seen on his knees during the battle as if shot. However, there was equal amusement when it transpired that he had spotted a rare beetle and was merely on his haunches picking it up whilst bullets whistled around his ears. [22]

Perhaps inspired by Harford's bravado, the British and friendly native forces now pushed on in a series of rushes. They probed each cave that they found, firing inside and clearing them of Zulus. The enemy were pushed out of the area and Sihayo's homestead was set ablaze, though all other huts were left untouched. Chelmsford noted with satisfaction that not one wounded enemy was killed, neither were any women or children. A number of Zulu defenders were captured whilst others managed to clamber up the rocky cliffs and escape to eventually join up with Cetshwayo's main impis.

Another moment of light relief occurred in the battle. Major Black of the 24th moved forward to encourage the men into the fray. Hostile Zulus resisted by, amongst other things, throwing down rocks on the ascending enemy. One hit Black in a rather delicate and sensitive part of his body and he went down in agony. Black, a Gaelic speaker, let forth a terrifying tirade which of course few others could understand. Those around him could barely contain themselves as the major came to terms with an injury that, as Hamilton-Browne said, 'he could not show to anyone but the doctor'.[23]

Lieutenant-Colonel Russell was ordered ahead down the road to probe further. His men were fired upon by about sixty Zulus, though their shooting was again erratic and no one was hurt. In firing back, about ten Zulus were killed, including one of Sihayo's sons. Overall, Chelmsford reckoned about thirty of the enemy were slain in the engagement for the loss of three of his own native troops. In addition, about 400 cattle, thirty horses and ponies and a number of sheep and goats had been taken.[24] Official records suggested that sixty-seven Zulus were killed in the action.[25]

It was a very satisfactory start to the military campaign, though Chelmsford was magnanimous enough to admit that the enemy had fought bravely. Lieutenant Harford's view was that he hoped the army would meet up with Cetshwayo's impis soon, as 'we shall give him a tremendous thrashing he won't ever forget'.[26] Confidence was high; far too high as it turned out.

There had been some hints at problems ahead when a group of carbineers found themselves being charged by a group of Zulus. They fixed bayonets, ready to fight off the enemy. It was only when the 'Zulus' threw up their hands in a sign of submission at the last moment that it was realised that they were not the enemy at all but a party of NNC who, fearful of meeting the enemy, had taken off their distinguishing red headbands.

Hamilton-Browne was brutally dismissive of the performance of his NNC men during the battle. The officers had Martini-Henrys issued to them but only fifty were issued to the rank and file between the best part of a thousand men. For this the commandant was thankful, as he said that the gun was not to be used by a 'duffer' and the rest of the battalion were in more danger of being shot by them than the enemy was. This being the case, it might have been a nice idea to have given them some proper training in how to use them beforehand.

Some old muskets had also been issued to the NNC warriors. Thankfully, Hamilton-Browne noted, most of them were not fired because they were not loaded properly and refused to go off as a result. With only five rounds per man, it would not take long anyway before the bullets they had had all been fired off. However, when they had first gone into action any enthusiasm that the NNC had shown for fighting in most cases quickly evaporated.[27]

Chelmsford told Frere that he hoped the news of the victory 'may have a salutary effect in Zululand and either bring down a large force to attack us or else produce a revolution in the country'. He wanted a quick and absolute resolution to the war; his wishes for a decisive action were to be granted, though with unforeseen results. Soon after the battle he visited two wounded Zulus in the field hospital. As soon as they were recovered he planned to let them go; with everything going to plan, it was easy to be generous in victory. Even at the time some of his officers thought he was being too lenient.[28]

Chelmsford had other problems to worry him. The recent awful weather had left the country in a terrible state. Working parties would need to be deployed to do what they could to repair the roads, which were littered with wheel-shattering rocks in some places and cloying bogs in others. He had planned to haul each wagon with sixteen oxen but now thought this was insufficient and planned to increase this to twenty per vehicle. This was not easy as losses of oxen had already been great and the campaign had barely begun. Thunderstorms were a daily occurrence and the rain continued to lash down in torrents, but despite this the morale of the troops was excellent.[29]

Supplies, nevertheless, were becoming an even greater problem than Chelmsford had anticipated. On 13 January he had moved back from the front line to inspect the stores and was far from impressed at what he had found. In fact, he found nothing there when there should have been stores in place for a month's campaigning. He noted that the sole representative of the Commissariat Department at Rorke's Drift was Commissary Dalton and, in Chelmsford's view, he was 'too young to take the weight of responsibility that a column represents, although I am sure he would do well under another'.[30]

Chelmsford urged Commissary-General Strickland to resolve the problem. More men were needed to organise the stores and Strickland should at all costs avoid the shame that would result if the column had to stop short of its destination due to a shortage of supplies. To his credit, Chelmsford showed commendable energy trying to resolve the supply issue. The challenge involved should not be underestimated. He had in total 12,500 men to think about, each with daily rations of at least 1lb of meat, 1½lb of bread (or biscuits as an alternative), plus fresh vegetables and fruit. Organising this lot in the circumstances cannot have been easy.

Another problem soon emerged to create an additional headache for Chelmsford. Colonel Durnford was a soldier (actually an engineer) with an unfortunate blemish on his record which he wished to erase. In 1873 there had been an incident in Natal when a local chieftain, Langalibalele, who lived in the foothills of the Drakensberg Mountains, tried to escape with his people to a new life beyond the clutches of the British Empire.

Langalibalele's 'crime' had been to fail to register some guns that had been given to his people in part-payment for some work they had done in the nearby diamond fields. Whilst this was an offence under local law, he had not been involved in any violent acts nor had he even threatened to become so embroiled; he said that he did not register the guns because when he had done so before they came back damaged.

His subsequent 'crime' was to try and move his people out of Natal into another country, which was in legal terms no offence at all (a fact which was recognised when the trial after his ultimate capture was held unusually under native rather than colonial law, as under the latter he had committed no crime). Repression of southern African tribes did not start with the Anglo-Zulu War.

A force of two companies of regular infantry, 150 local volunteers and 2,000 African levies was assembled with Durnford appointed chief of staff. Two mobile forces were created to stop Langalibalele escaping across the mountains. Durnford was given command of one of these, a small unit with fifty-five Natal volunteers and twenty-five mounted natives.

It was Durnford's first field command but there had been problems from the outset. As the force set out, its baggage train wandered off in the night with ammunition and supplies, and had to be rounded up again, as a result of which the cohesion of the small column broke down. As the morning of 3 November 1873 broke, the native levies had to share their supplies with everyone else. They then started to scramble up the steep scarp of the Drakensberg, during which process several men dropped out with exhaustion.

Men fell from their horses on the perilous path, including Durnford. He fell 50 yards, cracked several ribs and dislocated a shoulder but was determined to carry on. They pushed on and camped out that night. At about 6.30 a.m. on the 4th, Durnford spotted a party of the rebels herding cattle. He moved on them but, at this stage, there was no fighting, just a parley as Durnford outlined the government's terms for Langalibalele and his people to hand themselves in.

The rebels soon after started to drift towards Durnford's position at Bushman's Pass, but they had a sullen attitude and the atmosphere was tense. Durnford's men started to feel threatened and began to back off. As they retreated, a shot was fired. Durnford's natives broke and fled. More shots were fired, though fortunately not that many as the rebels did not have much ammunition. Several men were killed.

During the skirmish, a spear pierced Durnford's arm, leaving it unusable ever after. Although it was far from a military disaster, his command had fled the field and it was not a positive outcome for him personally, especially with the loss of the use of his arm. He had been determined not to fire the first shot in the scuffle and from then on he was known as 'Don't Fire Durnford', an unfair sobriquet as his decision not to do so was fully in accord with his orders.[31] Despite the personal setback, Langalibalele was eventually brought to book and, after a farce of a trial, was imprisoned on Robben Island, later the 'home' for many years of Africa's greatest modern hero, Nelson Mandela.

But of Durnford's personal bravery there was no doubt. Despite being paralysed for life in one arm by his wounds, he had insisted on returning to the field against medical advice. His men had cheered him when he did so. Here was a man who knew only too well how dangerous the thrust of an assegai could be and he longed for the chance to avenge the damage done to him both physically and to his reputation.

Now Durnford was determined to restore his prestige; he was an acquaintance of the famous General Charles Gordon (of Khartoum fame) and appeared to be of a similar reckless ilk. Although an engineer by profession, Durnford had aspirations to be a dashing cavalry leader. With a thick, drooping walrus moustache he also dressed in a way that was calculated to attract attention. With a wide-brimmed hat, carrying a revolver and hunting knife, with his boots and spurs, Durnford – in his own words – described himself as 'very like a stage brigand'.

Durnford had powerful allies in Natal. He was a close friend of Bishop Colenso of Natal, or more pertinently his daughter Frances (known to her close friends as 'Nel'). Durnford had married young but the relationship had not worked, tainted by tragedy with lost children. Durnford found spiritual consolation – though given the morals of the time it was unlikely to be more than this – in Nel, understanding and sympathetic but unattainable. The two were deeply devoted to each other.

Durnford's force, composed of volunteers and natives, was posted at Middle Drift. He was proud of his men and they in turn were proud to serve with him. At his side was Sergeant-Major Simon Kambule from the Edendale Horse, whose father, Elijah, had died in battle in the skirmish with Langalibalele. Durnford now received unsubstantiated rumours that the Zulus were moving in force on the other side of the River Thukela and he proposed to cross over to face them. By so doing, he was actively flouting Chelmsford's orders and demonstrating that the spirit of the maverick was alive and well in him.

When Chelmsford got wind of his plans, he was uncharacteristically furious. He sent an irate countermand which arrived in Durnford's camp at 2 a.m. on the morning of the 14th, stopping the advance in its tracks. Chelmsford's message was as plain as it could be: 'Unless you carry out the instructions I give you, it will be my unpleasant duty to relieve you from your command and to substitute another officer for the command of Number 2 Column.'

He proceeded to lay down the law. He would allow a commanding officer to exercise discretion if acting separately in an enemy's country, but ignoring Chelmsford's orders on this occasion was reckless. The rumours of Zulu movements were little more than hearsay and Durnford could effectively be setting out on a wild goose chase. Chelmsford ended with the phrase: 'I trust you will understand this plain speaking and not give me any further occasion to write in a style which is distasteful to me.'[32]

For all Chelmsford's flaws as a military commander, the rebuke was entirely justified. Durnford's men played an important part in the plans for the campaign that he had mapped out and could not be allowed to change military direction on a whim. His actions also left Natal exposed to a Zulu raid. Above all though, it suggested serious problems with Durnford's judgement, a suspicion that would be tragically confirmed within the next week or so.

The news was better from Wood. On 11 January, the first official day of the war, he had seized about 2,000 cattle from the Zulus, which had a great impact on the level of supplies available locally. He soon after seized more from another local chieftain, Seketwayo, which he said would be returned if he sided with the British in the war. There had been an incident when Captain Barton had been sent with the Dutchman Piet Uys to disarm a petty chieftain named Niboosa. In the clash that followed seven Zulus were killed.

Wood then made a long reconnaissance, finding the land through which he passed largely deserted. The roads, however, were also appalling here. It was a problem that continued to exercise Chelmsford too. He did not think a rapid march on Ulundi was possible as the supply trains could not possibly keep pace with the army in such conditions.[33] A steady advance was the aim, possibly taking hostages en route to Ulundi as guarantees for good behaviour. He was soon confiding to Frere that he did not think it would be a matter of more than a few days before Cetshwayo would be brought to terms.

Given the nature of the terrain, Chelmsford told Wood,[34] the first move would be to 'Isanblana hill' where they would find wood and water. From here, he would push out into the nearby forests and clear them. He had ordered Pearson in the east not to go beyond Eshowe but would later ask him to move laterally. By joining forces, he hoped to force Cetshwayo to move his forces together, giving him a major provisioning headache.

Chelmsford had ridden ahead of his main force on 16 January and had arrived at the hill of Isandlwana that day. Rising to a height of 4,371ft above sea level, it towered above the plains to the east, though there were other hills to the north and south of a similar height. But it was its strange shape that gave it its most prominent aspect. Rising sharply with sides that were close to perpendicular as they reached the higher parts of the slopes, it gave all who saw it the appearance of a sphinx lying lazily in the sun. This was, some remarked, a strange omen as this was also the regimental badge of the 24th Regiment.

However, it was not the hill that probably attracted Chelmsford's attention first off. He had sent Russell scouting off to the east and what he had found there had been disturbing. The ground in front, though a flat plain from a distance, was bisected by large dried-up watercourses, *dongas*, sometimes 20ft deep and twice as wide. Such terrain would be a nightmare for the wagons to move through. But the die was cast; Chelmsford – with inadequate intelligence – had committed himself to a difficult route towards Ulundi and would have to stick to it.

As he made his way to Isandlwana, there was an incident which spoke volumes about the attitude of those in command of the British forces. A depot had been established for firewood en route. It was guarded by a group of soldiers under the command of Major William Dunbar. Its position was appalling, close to rocks with thick thorn bushes up to its edge. It was perfectly placed for a surprise attack from Zulu raiding parties.

Dunbar quite sensibly asked for permission to move the camp to the other side of a nearby stream. However, Chelmsford's pompous alter ego Crealock quickly became irate and unpardonably shouted that 'if Major Dunbar was afraid to stay here, we would send someone who was not'. Dunbar, incensed at this slur on his character, resigned on the spot. It was all that Chelmsford could do to get him to withdraw his resignation (which was just as well for Dunbar, who would eventually rise to command the regiment). If Chelmsford does not emerge from the Anglo-Zulu War very well, it must also be said that he was not well served by some of his senior staff.[35]

By 19 January, Chelmsford was writing to Durnford, whose men had now moved close to the border near Rorke's Drift, that he was planning to move his forces up the following day to 'Insalwana Hill'. He ordered Durnford to bring his men across the river at Rorke's Drift and prepare himself for imminent action against two chieftains, the 'Matyanas'; their role in events would prove to be a crucial one. An attack from the Zulus was expected, or perhaps more accurately hoped for, soon. Norris-Newman noted that an attack was anticipated that night, though it never materialised.[36]

Durnford's journey across country to Rorke's Drift from the region of Middle Drift shortly before had been quite epic. Much of it had taken place at night, men leading the horses, lanterns at their head, with a wagon train that was spread out over a distance of 5 miles. They stopped from time to time and killed some of their cattle for food; the smell of the freshly roasted meat created a pleasant and almost enchanting aroma. Durnford loved camp life.

The force was something of a hotchpotch. Durnford had about 250 horsemen but, apart from a few officers, all of them were black. A number of his native troops were refugees from Zululand to Natal some years before. Here they had taken up the ways of the colonists, including their dress and even their Christian religion. They had in many cases volunteered enthusiastically for Durnford's command. Particularly prominent amongst them was the splendid Edendale Horse who would prove their qualities in the next few days. Yet for all their enthusiasm and effectiveness, the colonial government only saw fit to pay them at half the rate given to their white equivalents.[37]

Chelmsford's march on 20 January went largely without a hitch. Apart from one nasty swampy area on the route there were few bad places. It was a relief; during the march the line of wagons had at times been very extended, spread out over miles, and the terrain they had crossed had been awful. Trooper Clarke of the Natal Mounted Police later told how he was 'one of the left flank skirmishers and never have I ridden over such appalling country. At no time was I in sight of the column which stretched for miles.'

Given the long, drawn-out wagon train, it was just as well that the Zulus had not attacked whilst it was in transit. Nevertheless, part of the 2nd/24th Regiment was forced to stop short of the camp as their oxen were exhausted but everyone else arrived. That same afternoon, at around 1 p.m., Chelmsford led a reconnoitring mission to a Zulu stronghold about 12 miles away.

The ground before the camp was tough, corrugated with deep dried-up river courses, though Chelmsford thought that wagons would be able to negotiate them well enough. However, he found few signs of Zulus or cattle. His reconnaissance force climbed a hill from which they could see for miles. There were a few homesteads and an occasional sighting of a woman far off running away with bundles on her head, but that was it.

Some of the few locals remaining said that everyone else had gone to join the king at Ulundi, others that they were hiding in the bush. Chelmsford had sent Commandant Lonsdale out with his two battalions of the Native Contingent with orders to scout around in the Malakata Hills to the south. He hoped that he would soon know for certain whether or not there were Zulus around. He would have proof in a surprising and rather unwelcome manner.

The reporter from the *Natal Witness* present with the column mused as to why no Zulu warriors had been seen. He opined that it was because they had seen what Chelmsford's army could do at Sihayo's settlement; indeed that was what one of the Zulus still left in the area had told him. The reporter told his readers that 'this amount of fear does not look very much like the wonderful prowess of the Zulus, of which we have heard so much in Natal. I imagine they are very much like other natives – very great at bragging, but easily depressed and panic-stricken by any sudden reverse.'[38]

There had been reports from a Mr Fannin of a large force in the bush but Chelmsford felt that 'Mr Fannin like a good many other Natal officials is an alarmist and, not being able to appreciate what an enemy can do and what he cannot do, sees danger when there really is none'. The commander-in-chief might have done well to take a bit more notice of him.[39] This letter, sent off to Frere on the eve of a cataclysmic action, gives an insight into a man who was not anticipating any serious danger and was overconfident that, should a serious position arise, he had more than enough resources to deal with it.

Chelmsford closed his report to Sir Bartle Frere from 'Insalwana' with a few prescient thoughts. He was convinced that if Natal was to be safe from future raiding from the Zulus, then both sides of the Buffalo and Thukela rivers must be held by those friendly to British interests. The ultimate aim, he mused with Frere, was that Zululand should be 'parcelled out into small divisions under small chiefs'. It was the policy that would ultimately be adopted and, whilst it might have been good for Natal, it was definitely the opposite for Zululand and the Zulu people.

Unfortunately for Chelmsford, Cetshwayo's people had no intention of allowing themselves to be steamrollered without a fight. They were a proud people with a warrior tradition. Cetshwayo, realising that the British were set on a battle, had called his soldiers together to join him at his chief residence at Ulundi for the First Fruits ceremony.

The threat of war had not united everyone in Zululand. Some thought that the sons of Sihayo should have been handed over as commanded by the terms of the ultimatum; several thought that Sihayo was not a true Zulu and should be surrendered if necessary (though as he was a favourite of Cetshwayo this was not likely to happen). Cetshwayo wished to be conciliatory and this probably led to the fact that the British forces were unopposed when they started their crossing into Zululand. However, he had now been forced to concede that war was inevitable.

The divisions within Zululand, it seems, came mainly from the council of the king and not his warriors, who were spoiling for a scrap. There were rumours that all the young men were to be enslaved whilst the women would be concubines for the redcoats. The invasion of the British forces had merely served to make them angrier than ever and they were humiliated by the way that Chelmsford had probed deeper into Zululand without any real resistance.

The impis had undergone their ritual preparation for battle. A great black bull had been brought into the midst of the king's capital and there, cruelly taunted, had been slaughtered. Mock battles had been fought with barely mock savagery. Then this huge army of Cetshwayo's finest had marched the 15 miles to the ancestral burial grounds of the king's ancestors, there to invoke the aid of the spirits of the departed on their endeavours.

Prayers were offered up to their ancestors and they slept a night in the moonlit valley to soak up the martial spirit of those who had gone before but who still kept a watchful eye on the Zulu nation. Cattle were ceremonially butchered, their blood spilling out into the sacred earth as a sacrificial offering. During the pre-dawn hours the lowing of the cattle was taken as a sign that the great spirits had given their approval to the warriors.

That only left the witch doctors to practise their protective magic on behalf of the army. A number of sacred substances were collected: herbs, roots, the flesh of warrior-animals like lions and body parts of the enemy (during the savage war that was about to follow some of the slain would have these removed; they were considered powerful magic by Zulu warriors).

This unappetising cocktail was used to doctor the army who were fed with it. In a final act of ritual, each of the warriors would be given an emetic. They would then vomit into huge 6ft-deep pits. Some of the soldiers, wise to what was coming, would only pretend to drink the noxious substance, but elders were looking for this and beat such miscreants until they did what was required of them. The pits, once filled with this collective vomit, would be covered over to hide them from any enemy who wished to find them and use them as part of a destructive magic ritual of their own against the Zulus. This was probably not something that Chelmsford had in mind.

The great black bull was then cut into tiny slivers and blessed with magic powder. The army paraded past the elders and the small scraps of bull flesh were thrown amongst them. These were caught and then sucked, not eaten, and the pieces passed on to a comrade. Any piece that fell to the ground was left. Then the army marched past its leaders, who sprinkled the men with a specially pre-pared substance, flicked over them with the tail of a wildebeest.

By 17 January, the Zulus were ready to meet with the enemy. In contrast to the British column, the Zulus were able to move very fast, with the capacity to nimbly cross country that was well known to them, though on this occasion they travelled slowly, wishing to conserve their energies for the battle that was imminent. They needed food to sustain them, about 120 cattle a day. Feeding a force this size was not easy. Cattle would be taken with them but, especially if an operation was extended, supplies would soon run out. This would put an enormous strain on the local economy in which they were campaigning.

They were enthusiastic about the challenge ahead. Cetshwayo's orders rang in their ears: throw the invaders back over the Buffalo and eat up the red soldiers. At their head was one of the king's ablest military commanders, Ntshingwayo kaMahole. In his sixties, Ntshingwayo was a wily fox, a shrewd tactician and a capable commander. He made no concessions to his age, marching alongside the men, unlike some of the other *indunas* who chose to travel on horseback.

For the first two days out of Ulundi they covered barely 10 miles in each march. There were mainly men with the impis but not exclusively; a number of boys, the *udibi*, accompanied them carrying cooking pots and sleeping mats. They also had small assegais of their own which they would use amongst other things to finish off a wounded enemy after battle. These would soon be put to good use.

The two armies were now, though still a fair distance apart, moving on a collision course. The Zulus were not unaware of this and as they closed in the impi divided. The two halves stayed within visual range of each other but about 4 miles apart. Scouts moved ahead of the main force, some of them mounted. In the distance they could see, about 20 miles off, the distinctive shape of Isipesi Hill, which had formed the eastern limit of Russell's reconnaissance a couple of days earlier.

Late in the afternoon, the day that Chelmsford set up camp at Isandlwana, the impis did so at Isipesi. From its summit they could see tiny white dots on the hill in the distance – the British army's tents in their loosely laid out camp. For his part, Chelmsford had no idea whatsoever where the Zulu army was. The Zulus had called in the local chieftain Matshana, who lived to the south and whom Chelmsford thought might be 'turned' to the British side. This transpired to be a rather optimistic assessment.

It was not entirely clear whose side Matshana was really on and many of the Zulu *indunas* did not trust him. Whilst many Zulus had fled to Natal for refuge over the years, Matshana had gone the other way, having fallen foul of John Shepstone in a domestic dispute in the colony. But it was said that he missed Natal and would like to return. So Matshana was called over by the Zulu commanders to Isipesi Hill to see if it could be determined whether he was for Cetshwayo or against him.

Ironically, that very day Chelmsford too had been looking for Matshana but had done so without success. Having rebuked Durnford for nearly being lured out on a wild-goose chase, he had allowed himself to be tempted out on one of his own. When Chelmsford returned to the camp, he may have noted – though he did not comment on – the fact that it was laid out in a sprawling fashion. There was no sign of a laager, the defensive formation which the Boers routinely adopted when campaigning against the Zulus. Clearly it was either felt that there would be no Zulu attack or, if there was, then a laager would not be needed.

There had in fact been some debate over the suitability of the site chosen for the camp. Major Clery, Colonel Glyn's principal staff officer, had chosen it, in the company of George Mansel, in command of the Natal Mounted Police contingent there. Mansel did not like it one bit. It was overlooked by other hills to the north. However, he was overruled and had then been made responsible for posting mounted pickets to take up sentry duty at strategic points around the camp.

But his differences of opinion with Clery were not yet at an end. The major complained that the *vedettes* were positioned too far out and, although Mansel maintained that they were where they needed to be because of the nature of the broken ground around the camp, he was again overruled. It was not long before one of his men saw a Zulu in the distance. He gave chase and caught up with the elderly Zulu. Brought into the camp for questioning, he told his interrogator that a large impi was on its way from Ulundi.

Later in the day, Sub-Inspector Phillips had complained to Crealock, Chelmsford's chief lieutenant, that the rear of the camp was inadequately protected. Chelmsford overheard the conversation and intervened, telling Crealock to 'tell the police officer my troops will do all the attacking but, even if the enemy does venture to attack, the hill he complains about will serve to protect our rear'.[40]

Others too were unconvinced by the site of the camp. Major William Dunbar from the 2nd/24th was one of them, Lieutenant Teignmouth Melvill of the 1st/

24th another. One described it 'as defenceless as an English village and with the air of a racecourse on a public holiday'. Chelmsford and Crealock remained unconcerned. They only expected to be there for a couple of days before moving on and anyway they did not expect much resistance from the Zulus. Norris-Newman noted that 'not a single step was taken in any way to defend our new position in case of a night or day attack from the enemy, either by forming the waggons [sic] into a laager or by erecting a shelter trench around it'.[41]

It was not until late on that day that the remaining delayed wagons hauled into the camp. It was probable that on the morrow many of them would have to go back to Rorke's Drift to pick up more supplies. When they arrived, they found a site with 300 bell tents erected and about 4,500 men waiting for the next move.

Chelmsford, all action, had already decided what that next move should be. Having failed to secure the defection of Matshana, he now sought to bring him to book with a show of force. There would be a large reconnaissance to the south-east of the camp the next day. This would involve half the men in the column.

The backbone of this force would be 1,600 of the Natal Native Contingent led by Lonsdale, though some of Chelmsford's officers would accompany the foray. The men had been told to take a day's rations with them, but believing that they would be back in the camp at nightfall, many had chosen not to do so. However, the countryside through which they would travel was some of the toughest in Zululand, protected with thick thorn and scrub and torn with great ravines gouged out of the rock. It would be a much tougher assignment than many had anticipated. Lieutenant Harford subsequently noted ruefully that he only took a few biscuits with him as he expected to be back that evening; as it happened it would be another fifty-six hours before he ate again.[42]

There were still some Zulus in the area. Cattle were confiscated from some of them, intelligence beaten from others. Two young warriors were caught and pummelled for information. They said they had left the main impi earlier that day. When asked where it was, they pointed to Isipesi Hill, a version of events confirmed by other villagers. It seems that little was done with this very accurate information.

There were other clues to be had too. Hamilton-Browne was with Lonsdale at the head of his battalion. They captured a number of cattle and goats as they advanced from the settlements that were scattered across the area. Hamilton-Browne returned a few of the goats that they had taken to a young girl. He then questioned her. Where was the king's army, he enquired? She pointed over to the north-east and added further that they planned to attack the invading column in two days' time. This was yet another piece of information to help form a comprehensive picture but unfortunately no one joined up the dots to get a complete synopsis of the situation.[43]

Further to the east, Major John Dartnell was also in charge of part of the reconnaissance mission. He had with him a force of mounted police and other mounted colonial troops. Throughout the day they had seen pockets of Zulus in the vicinity, though frustratingly they were not prepared merely to stand around and let themselves be attacked by the horsemen. Like will-o'-the-wisps they kept disappearing from one spot and then turning up in another in a different direction.

Dartnell's force had been under constant watch by Zulu sentries, who had summoned hundreds of warriors from Isipesi. By late morning on 21 January the two forces were in contact. The first exchanges were desultory (in fact non-existent), Dartnell unwilling to engage with his troops and the Zulus standing off at a distance of about half a mile. Then the Zulus disappeared, as if swallowed up by the earth. It was very difficult for the British officers to gauge exactly how many of the enemy were in the area.

By late afternoon the British and colonial forces were at the end of a flat-topped plateau on Hlazakazi Mountain. It was decided that now was the right time to take the cattle captured during the day back into camp, some 7 miles away. The task was given to Captain Orlando Murray and Lieutenant Pritchard, along with two companies of the NNC. They could also report back to Chelmsford with information.

Dartnell sent a force forward to scout what now appeared to be an empty hill. However, as they reached it, it was suddenly alive with Zulus who had concealed themselves effortlessly in the scrub. One of the men there, Trooper Symons, noted that suddenly:

> [There] rose a long line of black warriors advancing at the double in short intervals of skirmishing order. It was a magnificent spectacle, and no British regiment could excel in keeping their distances in skirmishing at the double. They uttered no sound. On reaching the brow of a hill their centre halted, while the flank came on, thus forming the noted horns of the Zulu impi.[44]

Despite these threatening manoeuvres, the Zulus fired no shots, but their general demeanour was enough to drive the horsemen back. They eventually made contact with the NNC. Dartnell considered that the situation was serious enough to ignore the orders Chelmsford had given him and stay where he was rather than return to Isandlwana. He prepared to spend the night in the open whilst a few riders were dispatched to the camp to tell Chelmsford what was happening.

Norris-Newman recorded that 'loud, deep, and frequent was the grumbling among some of the officers of the Natal Native Contingent at having to bivouac out there, tired, and without blankets, food, or forage'. Amongst them were Lieutenants Avery and Holcroft who, unwilling to put up with the situation, rode back to Isandlwana without being given permission to do so. It was a fatal move on their part; within twenty-four hours they would both be dead.[45]

It had been a frustrating day for Chelmsford. A local chieftain, Gamdana, had earlier come in to surrender to him. Although on the surface this was good news, it was clear that many of his young warriors had fled, probably to join up with the main Zulu impis. The firearms he surrendered were old, of limited utility and probably the more modern weapons he possessed had gone with the young warriors. Perhaps to ingratiate himself with Chelmsford, who saw through the surrender to the real situation underlying it, Gamdana passed on the information that a large impi was on its way with the aim of eating Chelmsford's column up.

Chelmsford did not seem unduly impressed with this news. Gamdana, having had a great opportunity to spy out the poorly defended camp, departed. Chelmsford then set out to reconnoitre the Nqutu Plateau to the north of Isandlwana. He was there when, at around 4 p.m., the riders from Dartnell came up and told him that they had encountered a large body of the enemy, which Dartnell proposed to attack next morning. Chelmsford at once responded, authorising him to do so. These orders were sent to him post-haste along with food for his hungry men.

Chelmsford rode up to the high point of the ridge from where he had a great vantage point. To the south he could see Hlazakazi Mountain where Dartnell waited for the next day and the chance to attack. To the east, he could see Isipesi Hill. However, he could see no sign of a large impi in the vicinity. But there were some hostile Zulus around for Lieutenant Milne, Chelmsford's staff officer, saw them. He picked out about fourteen mounted scouts watching them. Outlying pickets had also been involved in a small skirmish with a few Zulus in which shots had been fired and some of the enemy, it was believed, had been killed.

Putting these isolated bits of evidence together, there was good reason to believe that a significant army might be on its way to attack Chelmsford. And this was exactly what he wanted. An assault by the Zulus on his force would expose them to the withering fire of his soldiers and their quick-firing Martini-Henry rifles. Chelmsford returned to Isandlwana, satisfied with the way things were going.

Whilst he was out, the senior officer in camp was Lieutenant-Colonel Henry Pulleine, recently appointed commanding officer of the 1st/24th. Pulleine was an efficient administrator but a man with no combat experience, his last post having been garrison commander at Pietermaritzburg. An affable man who most people liked, there was no reason to think his lack of combat experience would be an issue. Everyone assumed any attack by the Zulus would be obligingly directed at Chelmsford with his main strike force. Little did Pulleine know that he was about to lose not just his innocence of combat operations but also his life. The carefully laid plans of Chelmsford were about to be rendered horrifyingly obsolete.

four

THE DAY OF THE DEAD MOON

The Zulu Victory at Isandlwana

On 27 January 1879, a telegram was dispatched by Lord Chelmsford to Colonel F.A. Stanley, the Secretary of State for War in Disraeli's Cabinet back in London. The news it contained was dramatic, shocking and unprecedented. It must have given Stanley a bad dose of indigestion, for it was clear that a war that he did not want and that he barely knew had begun had already started to go wrong within days of its commencement.

The tidings, which would not reach London for several weeks because of the lack of a direct telegraph link, were so awful that it meant the hands of Stanley and the administration he served in were tied, for a catastrophe had occurred of such magnitude that national pride dictated that it must be avenged. It was not just a question of a dented ego either; the British Empire existed in significant part because of its reputation as a great power, which had to be protected at all costs. A reputation, once lost, is almost impossible to recover. It was noticeable that within a short time British soldiers facing the Pondo tribes nearby were remarking that they were getting much more 'cheeky' as a result of the reverse that had descended on Chelmsford.[1]

Chelmsford's message got straight to the point: 'I regret to have to report a very disastrous engagement which took place on the 22nd instant between the Zulus and a portion of No 3 Column left to guard a camp about 10 miles in front of Rorke's Drift.'[2] Details followed of a setback of unfathomable proportions: how the Zulus had attacked the camp at Isandlwana in overwhelming numbers, how 'gallant resistance' had followed but had all been in vain. The camp was taken with all the supplies, ammunition and transport that were such an integral part of Chelmsford's invasion plans. Apart from anything else, it meant that the invasion itself was on the backburner.

The loss of life had been of nightmare proportions. Chelmsford reckoned that about thirty officers and about 500 rank-and-file soldiers and NCOs of the imperial army had been slaughtered, along with twenty-one officers and seventy NCOs of the colonial forces (he either had no idea how many black levies had also died, though hundreds would be a decent if imprecise estimate, or he did not think they were worth bothering about too much). Only a handful of imperial soldiers managed to escape.

The language used in this missive was similar to that which Chelmsford had used in a dispatch to Sir Bartle Frere sent four days earlier.[3] However, then he had gone into considerably more detail in his communication to his close confidant. He did not know exactly what had gone wrong but he concluded that:

> the camp had been defended with the utmost gallantry, but the soldiers had been beaten by much heavier numbers. Several officers and men have, I am happy to say, escaped but by far the larger proportion died at their posts and their bodies were found on our arrival in the camp.

So did Chelmsford break the news of a terrible defeat to a largely incredulous world. After all, he himself had expected a straightforward campaign. Unfortunately for him, the Zulus had most inconsiderately failed to walk into the trap he had laid for them – or so it seemed.

But, in fact, as details started to emerge, it turned out that the problem lay not so much in Chelmsford's overall strategy, which postulated a Zulu attack on a prepared position where the superior firepower of the British and colonial army could be used to maximum effect, but in its execution. In a letter to Wood the previous November, Chelmsford had remarked that 'I am inclined to think that the first experience of the power of the Martini-Henrys will be such a surprise to the Zulus that they will not be formidable after the first effort'. It now turned out that the Zulus were not quite the pushover he had expected them to be.

The story that would unfold was one of poor organisation, ineffective co-ordination and downright complacency in the ranks of Chelmsford's army. In fact, it spoke of a series of blunders arising from quite appalling amateurism, much of it, it must be said, to be found in Chelmsford's own command structure. Before the end of the inevitable inquests that followed, one or two careers would be in serious trouble. Chelmsford would be at the very top of the list. Problems had begun even before war had started with inadequate information. Chelmsford had written to Colonel Rowlands on 6 January that the Zulus were dividing their forces, just as he wanted them to. In fact, this was exactly the opposite of the true situation: Cetshwayo was waiting to see where the main British threat would come from to concentrate his forces there. Further evidence of Chelmsford's misanalysis was provided on 8 January when he wrote to the Duke of Cambridge that Zululand was in a state of confusion pending the invasion.[4]

The newspapers and periodicals in Britain had contained quite a bit of war news already that year. An examination of the early 1879 issues of the *Illustrated London News* shows that nearly every reference to conflicts overseas, and certainly every picture, related to the ongoing conflict in Afghanistan. The first detailed reference in the periodical to the Anglo–Zulu War was an editorial on 1 February 1879, which recognised that the war had probably started. The editor did not blame Cetshwayo for it but the colonists in Natal by a combination 'of suspicion, of fear, of greed'.

He also suggested that the annexation of the Transvaal was injudicious, that Frere's governorship had raised a lot of questions and that southern Africa would likely offer little advantage to the British government or people. In future, he opined, the colonists should fight their own wars and not rely on British troops to do so. The week after, on 8 February, the first pictures appeared in the periodical but news of Isandlwana, seventeen days in the past by the time of publication, had still not arrived.

When it did, it caught the British press on the hop. The account included in the *Illustrated London News* of 15 February was a dry, factual resume of the battle from Chelmsford's reports, betraying the fact that there were no journalists *in situ* to add more detail. That of 22 February showed how the wind had changed; the front page featured a picture of an intimidating looking Cetshwayo and more details of the battle, along with news that the paper was sending the famous war artist Melton Prior to create pictures for a now hungry readership. The war was now very hot news indeed.

Few disasters arise from one single factor or malfunction. They are usually a result of a chain reaction of interconnected events. Isandlwana was no different, but there was one factor above all others that led to the looming catastrophe and it flowed straight from the top, from Chelmsford in person: a complete underestimation of the enemy. Hubris above all else led to the deaths of hundreds of imperial infantry and their colonial and native allies.

But also to blame was the quality of Chelmsford's enemy. The Zulus might be hugely outgunned but they had much larger numbers available to them. This in itself meant little on its own; what was significant was the fact that the warriors were brave, tough and had well-honed tactics to call on. They also, the evidence suggested, had a far better general than the British forces did.

The sequence of events that led up to the shattering defeat of Isandlwana was started unwittingly by Dartnell when he sent his message to Chelmsford on the evening of 21 January, intimating that he intended to attack the enemy he could see nearby when it was daylight. This exceeded his orders and as time went on and he had received no confirmatory message from Chelmsford, he sent out another messenger, Lieutenant Davey, to ensure that the commander-in-chief approved of his action. It would be a harrowing journey for Davey, as it got dark long before he arrived back at camp and he had little to light his way through enemy territory.

Meanwhile, with the onset of darkness Dartnell began to doubt the wisdom of his decision. The NNC had been led up onto a small plateau for the night, a position that offered a degree of protection. They were formed into a square, believed to be the best means of defence when faced with a native enemy who had much greater numbers as the fire of the troops could then be concentrated.

The enemy was camped on the hill opposite and was making no attempt to hide their presence. Campfires were being lit without a thought as to concealment. This was probably a psychological ploy for as the night advanced the number of fires grew. It was clear within hours that there were large numbers of Zulus close by. They shouted taunts at the colonial troops (mostly, in fact, natives from the NNC), mainly describing what they would do to their wives or daughters if they captured them.

It soon became apparent that this impi was a much bigger threat than originally thought. Neither had Dartnell's officers reassured him much. Many of them had come from Isandlwana without their rifles, which they thought too heavy to carry on a mere scouting expedition; it was an action that spoke volumes for the regard in which they held their foe. Now they grabbed those that were with the already under-armed NNC, making them even more nervous than they had been at the outset.

This was indeed the last thing that the NNC needed. In the main treated dismissively by their officers and isolated in an exposed position miles away from the main British camp, their morale was already low. When, through the shadowy darkness, one of the sentries heard a rustle nearby he assumed it was the enemy creeping up for a surprise attack. When he gave the alarm all hell broke loose. The NNC fired their guns and banged their shields in traditional native fashion; the racket was heard at Isandlwana 10 miles away. The square, formed for their protection, soon dissolved as terrified NNC warriors ran to and fro and discipline collapsed completely.

It was a false alarm, to be followed by another later in the night. Order was restored but the men were clearly on edge and in no mood for a fight in the morning. The chaos that reigned was well summed up by the example of Commandant Hamilton-Browne who, exhausted, soon fell into a deep sleep when night fell. As a result he dropped his revolver. When the alarms came he could not find it again. When he was disturbed for the second time, he ordered the Zulu warriors in his NNC battalion to fire on any men who tried to run off into the night.

In the meantime, Dartnell had received confirmation from Chelmsford that he was at liberty to attack in the morning. However, Dartnell no longer felt confident in doing so. Another message was therefore sent back to Isandlwana. It would have a decisive impact; it informed Chelmsford that he would need help for the attack, asking for two or three companies of imperial infantry to be dispatched to his aid.

The messenger carrying this request arrived at Isandlwana at 1.30 a.m. He went first of all to Major Clery, who took the message on to Colonel Glyn, the man technically in charge of the column. Who was actually in charge of it became clear when Glyn ordered it taken at once to Chelmsford. It arrived in Chelmsford's tent, according to Lieutenant Milne, at about two o'clock.

The problems of an unclear chain of command within the camp were eventually to come home to roost for Glyn in particular. Major Clery, his chief aide, and Crealock, Chelmsford's equivalent, were both outspoken characters who, to compound potential problems, appear to have loathed each other. Crealock did not have a good word to say for Glyn either. Now key decisions were about to be made in which Glyn would have next to no part; all the evidence suggests that every important decision was taken by the commander-in-chief with little or no reference to the theoretical commander of Number 3 Column. It would not stop Chelmsford and his staff later suggesting that a significant part of the responsibility for the looming catastrophe rested with Glyn.

Chelmsford's reaction was rapid. He decided to assemble no less than six companies of imperial infantry along with four 7-pounder guns and a number of NNC troops to go to Dartnell's aid. Chelmsford would later, in self-defence, assert that:

> the two native battalions [with Dartnell] were very raw and the colonial troops with Dartnell had never been under fire – I felt certain therefore that they could not be expected either to attack any large force of the enemy, or to retire from in front of it with any chance of success.

This may be revisionism or perhaps Chelmsford had suspected all along that Dartnell's men were not up to the challenge. In any event, Dartnell's message had changed everything. Whereas a few hours before he had been content to send Dartnell into battle unaided, now Chelmsford rushed to help him. Given the large number of men he took with him, it appears that Chelmsford believed a significant impi, perhaps the main army, was about to attack Dartnell. It did not appear to cross his mind in anything but a superficial way that the camp might be attacked whilst he was away.

If it was indeed the main impi close to Dartnell, it was in exactly the place that Chelmsford's information, provided by Francis Fynn earlier, suggested it would be. Fynn, who had lived in Zululand for years and spoke the local language fluently, had been seconded to Chelmsford's staff, or more accurately commandeered by him. He had established a fledgling spy network in Zululand. Information had come via this that the Zulus planned to let the British forces advance into Zululand and then slip behind them into Natal when their back was turned. The presence of the Zulu army close to Dartnell and near the border appeared to confirm the likelihood of a move on Natal by Cetshwayo's warriors.

It is tempting to wonder, speculative though such a thought must be, whether this may have been disinformation sown deliberately to lure Chelmsford away from the camp. Little did Chelmsford know that the main body of the enemy was not to the south-east, but to the north-east, hidden in the Ngwebeni Valley just a few miles away from Isandlwana. By his decision to march to the south-east he had left the back door to the camp wide open.

Chelmsford sent out orders reacting to the changed situation. A rider, young Lieutenant Horace Smith-Dorrien, was dispatched to Rorke's Drift to tell Durnford to bring his men in Number 2 Column up to Isandlwana. Chelmsford's own men were to march with no reserve ammunition. The wagons at Isandlwana had been due to travel to Rorke's Drift in the morning, to later return with more supplies. They were now to stay where they were for the time being.

The camp was not formed in a proper defensive position. Normally, so it was claimed, a laager would have been formed with the wagons acting as makeshift parapets. Additionally, entrenchments would have been built around the camp but the rocky ground prevented this. Chelmsford felt that the imminent dispatch of the wagons back to Rorke's Drift meant that a laager should not be formed; he felt confident that an enemy army would be seen coming from miles off. Chelmsford would later suggest it was Glyn's responsibility as column commander to fortify the camp. This does not ring true in the least: Glyn had earlier suggested fortifying positions at the camps at both Helpmekaar and Rorke's Drift and had been overruled by Chelmsford and his staff.[5]

Others noticed the poorly prepared defences of the camp at Isandlwana too, though hindsight as always would be a wonderful gift in this respect. Norris-Newman reported that 'not a single step was taken in any way to defend our new position in case of a night or day attack from the enemy, either by forming the waggons [sic] into a laager or by erecting a shelter trench around it'. He did note that a small stone wall was built on two sides of the camp though he was not clear that this had been for any defensive purpose.[6]

It was about 4.30 a.m., daybreak, when the column began to march out of Isandlwana. The sun's first rays were painting the sky a vivid, blood-hued scarlet whilst in the hollows the mist hung wispily around, though it would burn off later in the day. Only one company of the 2nd/24th was left in camp, under the command of Lieutenant Charlie Pope. The battalion's band had been due to stay behind too but at the last moment they were conscripted as stretcher-bearers, still a role that military bandsmen in the British army play in the early twenty-first century. Five companies of the 1st Battalion made up the bulk of the regular forces left in camp. As they left, men of the 2nd Battalion jokingly offered their condolences to those they were leaving behind who were presumably going to miss out on the action.[7]

Progress for Chelmsford's force as they moved away from the illusory safety of the camp was slow, especially for the artillery; the rutted, unforgiving tracks formed corrugated, rock-hard barriers that seriously impeded the progress of the guns which had to be lowered into some of the *dongas* with drag-ropes. It turned into a hot day with barely a whisper of wind. It took three and a half hours to arrive at Dartnell's position – not a bad rate of progress given recent journeys but one requiring immense effort on the part of beast and man alike. Chelmsford, somewhat typically, had ridden on ahead with an escort of just a dozen men. One of them was Milne who wrote that when they arrived 'the enemy had retired from their former position and was not in sight'.[8] No one had a clue where they had gone.

It has become customary to assume that the Battle of Isandlwana happened almost as an accident when the hidden main Zulu army was stumbled upon by a British scout. However, this does insufficient credit to the Zulu strategists, particularly Ntshingwayo, who appear to have set up a decoy opposite Dartnell to split the British forces. Rather than the Zulus playing into the hands of the British as Chelmsford had hoped, the situation was in fact precisely the other way round.

Not that this was yet clear to Chelmsford. Whilst he thought about his next move, his foremost confidant, Crealock, sketched out a watercolour (he was a skilled artist and would later contribute sketches to the *Illustrated London News*). The main body of troops would not arrive until an hour and a half after Chelmsford and his tiny retinue. Just as they hove into a view, a large party of Zulus was seen to the east. More then appeared to the north. In total, it appeared that several thousand of the enemy were nearby.

This must have been exactly what Chelmsford hoped for. It looked to him as if the main impi was about to attack. It was in a strong position, protected by steep, rugged hills a thousand feet high. The cavalry were sent to outflank them. Chelmsford sent instructions to Glyn telling him to dispatch Russell, in charge of the Imperial Mounted Infantry, to the west of a hill known as Magogo. Chelmsford later countermanded this without even bothering to tell Glyn. Any idea that Glyn had any real part to play in the operations of the column was patently a myth.

Chelmsford pushed his men forward but it was not easy. The terrain was awful and the column quickly became fragmented. Chelmsford often found himself far in advance of the infantry. Even more frustratingly, the Zulus they were chasing refused to stand still, disappearing from time to time only to reappear somewhere else soon after. One man with the force, Captain Hallam Parr, aide-de-camp to Glyn, later noted that 'the morning was spent in endeavouring to get to close quarters with an enemy who could, and did, avoid us at his pleasure'.[9] It was a perfect, if succinct, description of what was happening.

After about three hours of this fruitless chasing around, Chelmsford decided to stop. He now switched his attention to the far more mundane subject of deciding where the next camp should be. The guns had not managed to keep up with the main British force and the army was scattered across several miles. In short, his force was dotted around all over the place in just about as bad a defensive position as it could be. Lieutenant-Colonel Arthur Harness, in charge of the battery, was ordered to stay put a few miles behind the main force at the Mangeni Falls. They would later be joined by Chelmsford's main force. However, it was not long before significant news reached them there.

Lieutenant Smith-Dorrien had arrived back at Durnford's camp at Rorke's Drift at around 6 a.m. (just when Chelmsford was catching up with Dartnell) only to find that Durnford was not there. The man in charge of the NNC in his absence, George Shepstone, immediately took it on himself to order all his troops to prepare to move off. A messenger was sent out in the meantime to try and find Durnford who was out foraging. He caught up with Durnford after about half an hour's riding, who was ecstatic at the news. The chance of a good scrap and possible redemption for Bushman's Pass seemed at hand.

When he arrived back at his camp at Rorke's Drift, Durnford was delighted to see Shepstone had used his initiative in preparing to move up to Isandlwana. The two men were old acquaintances: George, son of Sir Theophilus, had been at Bushman's Pass too. Raring to go and disobeying field regulations, Durnford galloped his horsemen, 250 of them, on to Isandlwana as fast as they could travel, leaving a dangerously isolated and vulnerable baggage train travelling on slowly behind them.

Smith-Dorrien, in the meantime, went the other way to the mission station at Rorke's Drift. Here he picked up some ammunition for his revolver having ridden through the night with it unloaded. Although there was not much to spare, he managed to beg, steal and borrow eleven cartridges from Lieutenant Gonville Bromhead of B Company of the 2nd/24th, who provided the small garrison there. Bromhead probably thought he personally was unlikely to need them in the near future. It was a decision to which Smith-Dorrien later owed his life in what would become the most remarkable day of a distinguished military career. After a brief sojourn at the mission station, he set off back towards Isandlwana.

The camp at Isandlwana had a major blind spot, being overlooked to the north by the Nqutu Plateau. Several scouts had been sent out to search the area first thing in the morning of 22 January. Some had been posted on the Nqutu the day before but Major Clery had complained that they were too far out from the camp – a significant and possibly fatal blunder on his part. The furthest group of the few scouts sent out was now 6½ miles away from the camp. So good were the Zulus at concealment, and so perfect the ground for hiding them away, that they were within half a mile of 20,000 warriors without having a clue that they were there.

The camp was now in the hands of Lieutenant-Colonel Henry Pulleine, recently arrived and with no previous combat experience to call on. But then again, at this stage there seemed no reason to think he would need any. Even if he did need to fight, he had the men of the 1st/24th to call on. They knew the country well and there were no better troops to have at a commander's disposal than these battle-hardened soldiers.

In addition to the men of the 24th, some mounted men, two guns and at least two companies of the 3rd NNC were also in camp. Although exact numbers would give a false degree of accuracy (the companies of redcoats may not have been at full strength), Pulleine had over 1,500 men to protect the camp, which would have been considered more than adequate by most observers.

However, the camp seemed more dispersed than ever now that half the men had gone, leaving the tents behind them. It covered a frontage of two-thirds of a mile on the eastern slopes of the sphinx hill of Isandlwana. It undoubtedly looked pretty and neat, but as a defensive position it was suspect. In the meantime, as the sun rose higher in the sky, with Chelmsford and his men long gone and well out of sight, two troopers, William Barker and the splendidly named Villiers Caesar Hawkins, were in an advanced scouting position when they saw a body of men coming towards them. They thought at first it was perhaps a party of Russell's IMI but then realised they were coming from the wrong direction. All of a sudden it became clear that it was hundreds of hostile Zulus coming right at them.

Barker and Hawkins rode back to report to the next line of scouts but they were not at first believed. Then another trooper came riding into camp, frantic and breathless. He was Trooper Whitelaw and he had been half a mile away from the Ngwebeni Valley. Now he told an incredulous audience that thousands of Zulus were headed for the camp. It was 7.30 a.m. and it was promising to be a memorable day. Pulleine, receiving this information from his advanced screen of scouts, started to realise that being in command could be a stressful experience.

Soon after, large numbers of Zulus appeared on the Nqutu Plateau. A small force of cavalry made their way gingerly up there to see if they could find what was wrong. But by the time they arrived most of the Zulus had disappeared again, taking advantage of the broken ground. The cavalry opened fire on those they could see but there were few of the enemy left in sight. Although Pulleine knew that there were Zulus around, he did not know how many or what their intentions were.

Just who these Zulus were is a matter for debate. Those who had been seen in the hills may have been the right wing in the traditional Zulu battle formation, seeking out a good position from which to launch their attack, though according to Zulus interviewed later no attack was planned until the following day. It was about 0830 and the first shots in the Battle of Isandlwana had been fired, from a distance and with no obvious sign yet that an all-out attack on the camp was imminent. Messengers were nevertheless dispatched to Chelmsford. They caught up with him between 0900 and 0930. He had confidently written to Sir Bartle Frere on 11 January that he would ensure he did not advance leaving a large enemy force at his back, but this was precisely what he had done.[10]

What is not unclear is Chelmsford's reaction to the news. The note reporting the Zulu advance on the camp was given to Clery who handed it straight to Chelmsford, Glyn again being bypassed. Chelmsford handed it back to Clery without comment. Clery asked if any action was to be taken on it. Chelmsford replied dismissively that 'there is nothing to be done on that'. Clery later recalled that all was not well with the high command and there were tangible tensions. He said 'the fact is that, whether from overwork, or other causes, the General has got rather irritable since we knew him, and particularly touchy about suggestions being made to him'.[11] Hamilton-Browne would find this out for himself later the same day.

Back at Isandlwana, the firing on the plateau was hidden from most men in the camp and it was still unclear to the majority what was actually happening up in the hills. Pulleine had been far from expansive in his dispatch to Chelmsford about what the situation was, unaware himself of what was taking place. There was no mention of numbers or firing (when he wrote the note there had been none; it seems that the messenger to Chelmsford had added that detail verbally).

In the camp bugles sounded and the men were ordered to fall in. Zulus continued to appear and disappear, much to the bafflement of Pulleine and his fellow officers. These included Lieutenant John Chard, a Royal Engineer who had been left at Rorke's Drift with a view to organising a defensive position to guard the ponts[12] and had come up to the camp to clarify his orders. He would leave the camp to return to the drift soon after but would see thousands more Zulus before the day was out.

Whilst at Isandlwana, Chard had spotted large parties of Zulus with a telescope he had borrowed and believed they were headed for the drift, so he thought he should return there to warn the soldiers who were in the mission station – it did not occur to him or anyone else that they might instead be threatening the rear of the camp at Isandlwana.

On the way back to Rorke's Drift, he met Durnford's cavalry charging on to Isandlwana. Chard told Durnford of the Zulus on the Nqutu Plateau. Durnford acknowledged the message and asked Chard to tell Major Russell, in charge of his rocket battery, to push on for Isandlwana as quickly as possible. Nevertheless, although there were clearly large numbers of Zulus in the vicinity, there was still no sign of a full-scale attack on the camp; most of the warriors seen earlier had now faded out of sight. Durnford trotted in to the Isandlwana camp soon after with his 250 cavalry and made his way to Pulleine's tent. When he arrived everything seemed calm and the earlier sightings of Zulu warriors did not, it seemed, presage an attack.

Something of a conundrum then manifested itself. It transpired that Durnford was senior to Pulleine and therefore nominally in command. It was no doubt disappointing to Pulleine to be deprived of the chance to lead men into battle for the first time. However, Durnford quickly put Pulleine's mind at rest, saying that he had no intention of staying in camp for long.

But again there was a problem. Chelmsford had sent orders to Durnford telling him to make his way to the camp. He had left none whatsoever telling him what to do when he got there. It turned out to be a fatal oversight. Even with orders to follow, Durnford might well have disobeyed them (recent experience suggested as much). With none to follow, there was a strong probability that his actions might be aggressive to the point of rashness.

Pulleine, however, was clear of his own orders if a battle was to begin: 'to defend the camp'. He briefed Durnford on the strange events of the day so far and told him politely but firmly that he would not be joining him in any offensive action. Durnford did not seem unduly perturbed but settled down to a hurried breakfast, merely asking Pulleine to send troops in support if he later needed assistance.

After the initial sighting of the Zulus, who had now largely disappeared, there was absolutely no sign of concern. The men were stood to and eating a delayed breakfast. Lieutenant Curling of the Royal Artillery had been involved in the conflict with natives in the Ninth Frontier War the year before and, 'having in the last war often seen equally large bodies of the enemy, never dreamed they would come on'.[13] The reference to 'seeing' the enemy had something of an ironic ring about it. Curling had poor eyesight and according to Colonel Wood, who had served with him in the Frontier War, had failed to fire on a body of the enemy at close range for the simple reason that he did not see them.[14]

Chelmsford, 10 miles off, was also unperturbed. Following the arrival of the messenger from Isandlwana, he had sent Milne to the top of a hill at around 0940 to see if he could see anything unusual in the camp with the aid of his telescope. Despite watching for an hour, he saw nothing to cause him anxiety. In particular, the tents were still erect. Standing orders decreed that if the camp was to be attacked they should be struck; therefore everyone looking from a distance assumed that no attack was taking place. At that precise moment, they were correct in their analysis.

Reassured, Chelmsford helped himself to a bite to eat. He was in fact largely on his own, again with an escort of about a dozen people in an area where there were hundreds of Zulus. He then made his way back to the Mangeni Falls but took a different route without informing anyone else. For around an hour at this crucial time Chelmsford effectively disappeared.

Durnford, back in the camp, was frustrated at the lack of clear information on the Zulus in the area. The problem was that much of the terrain in front of Isandlwana was effectively 'dead ground', concealed from his view. The plateau to the north was also very well hidden from Isandlwana. Durnford could not understand where the Zulus had gone and believed they might be moving on Chelmsford.

His fears appeared to be confirmed when his scouts reported back that the Zulus appeared to be retiring. He therefore decided to lead his men eastwards, towards Chelmsford, arguing in justification that he was going to intercept an attack against the rear of the advancing part of the column. It was a disastrous misanalysis of the situation; the Zulus were doing anything but retiring. Yet there is surviving evidence that Durnford was not alone in thinking that the Zulus were moving off. The diary of Lieutenant Pope, who would not survive the day, was later found. In it he noted that Zulus were retiring everywhere when Durnford galloped off and the men back in camp stood down for dinner.[15] The misconception that the Zulus were pulling back was also confirmed by Lieutenant Cochrane, one of the few surviving officers, at the later inquiry into the battle.[16]

Durnford asked for two companies of the 24th to accompany him on an offensive move against the Zulus. Pulleine again objected, insisting that his orders were to protect the camp. Durnford eventually gave in, with Lieutenant Melvill particularly annoyed at his attitude; it must have been galling for imperial officers to be ordered around by a man leading colonial troops. However, Durnford reiterated that if Pulleine saw his men in trouble then he must send reinforcements to his aid. But although there may have been tension between Pulleine and Durnford, according to the only likely witness to the conversation to survive the battle, Lieutenant Cochrane, a special service officer who was accompanying Durnford, there were 'no high words of any kind'.[17]

Durnford then set out with his horsemen or, more accurately, he set out with some of them. One troop had been sent back to escort his wagon train (still not arrived) into the camp. Two more troops (fifty men in each) were up on the plateau helping to look for Zulus. The rest now rode off with Durnford, along with the rocket battery, slow moving and vulnerable against a fleet-footed enemy. It was now around 1130.

Durnford set out across the corrugated plain, as his men made their way cautiously through the maze of *dongas* before the camp, still unable to see any large bodies of Zulus in the area. The two troops that had made their way up to the top of the Nqutu Plateau fanned out, one led by Lieutenant J.A. Roberts, the other by Lieutenant Charles Raw. It was hard going up there, the ground strewn with rocks, boulders, scrub. They spotted Zulus in the distance, just small groups moving away from them. They gave chase until they were perhaps 4 miles from the camp.

Raw's account of what happened next is interesting. Traditionally the main Zulu impi was discovered by accident, sitting patiently and quietly in the Ngwebeni Valley.[18] But this does not gel with Raw's version. Instead, he said that the main Zulu force all of a sudden appeared from behind a hill 'where they had evidently been waiting'.[19] It was, according to his evidence, part of a pre-arranged trap.

With the troop was Captain George Shepstone. Alongside him was Sergeant-Major Nyanda, who described how all of a sudden a Zulu army of 15,000 men sprung up. Another account, that of Acting Commissary Officer J.H. Hamer, also at Shepstone's side, gave a version of events that tallies very closely with the 'traditional' account and is probably its source. He was riding with Shepstone when 'we tried to capture some cattle. They disappeared over a ridge, and on coming up we saw the Zulus, like ants in front of us, in perfect order as quiet as mice and stretched across in an even line. We estimated those we saw at 12,000.'[20]

It was not an auspicious day for the Zulus to fight. It was a day of the 'dead moon' (the day before the new moon rose) and this was considered to be an ominous time for a battle. The Zulus had planned to rest up for the day here and then launch an attack on the morrow. Yet there was now no doubt with the main impi discovered that a battle would be fought at once. Raw and the men with him started to conduct a fighting retreat whilst Shepstone and Hamer dug their spurs into the side of their horses and galloped off towards the camp as quickly as they could go. A vast wave of Zulu warriors chased after them as they went.

Back down on the plain Major Russell was doing his best to keep up with Durnford. His rocket battery was very exposed. The rocket was an extremely inefficient weapon whose greatest impact seemed to be the noise it made as it flew through the air; this was believed to have a dramatic psychological impact on a 'savage' enemy. However, it was not at all accurate and the damage it caused on impact, unless there was a direct hit, was minimal.

Russell, advancing across the plain, was now in the shadow of the Nqutu Plateau and could not see up on to its summit. Although he could hear firing he had no idea what was happening up above. He was also out of sight of Durnford who was much in advance of him and hidden by the hills. His mules would not be capable of moving up the steep slope on to the plateau where the firing was coming from so he ordered his men to unload their gear and climb up on foot. He himself was on horseback and managed to ride to the top. The sound of firing was getting heavier and he needed to see what was happening on the hidden plateau.

As he was almost at the top of the path, a horrifying sight met his eyes: a swarm of Zulu warriors headed towards him. He turned his steed around and started to descend. The rest of his men, seeing too late what was happening, erected the rocket tube as quickly as they could but only one rocket was sent up, causing virtually no damage at all. The Zulus, a number of whom were armed with rifles, took aim and fired at the battery. Three of the eight gunners were killed at once and Russell too fell, mortally wounded. The native troops with the rocket battery, terrified at the Zulus who were coming to gobble them up, mostly turned tail and fled as fast as they could.

Durnford was unaware of all this. He was some way in front of the battery when he heard the firing to his rear. However, other British scouts had seen only too well what was happening and desperately chased after him to warn him of the impending threat of a huge Zulu army descending on him. Durnford was taken aback when they caught up and refused to believe the situation was as extreme as had been painted. His response was to claim that 'the enemy can't surround us, and if they do, we will cut our way through them'.[21]

Whilst Durnford was debating his next move, thousands of Zulu warriors appeared. They were less than a mile away from him, coming on in lines 'about ten or twelve deep'.[22] Unfortunately for him he had only 100 men with him, far too few to fight off this huge army moving towards him. A steady retreat back towards the camp was the best that he could hope for.

It was a fighting withdrawal, taking advantage of the *dongas* and gullies that bisected the ground. His men fired steadily, performing creditably against an enemy that outnumbered them hugely, but the Zulus, with their numerical advantage, moved out to their left in an attempt to outflank Durnford's men. One of those falling back, Lieutenant Harry Davies, who was in command of the Edendale Horse, came across survivors from the rocket battery. He picked them up and escorted them back towards the camp.

As Durnford moved back towards Isandlwana, he came across another survivor of the rocket battery, Private Johnson of the 24th Regiment, who had been seconded to help Russell. Durnford asked him what had become of Russell and the battery. Johnson told him the battery had been destroyed and Russell shot. Durnford told the dismounted soldier that he had better go back and fetch him, then left him to his fate – a foolish, even vindictive move from a man whose dreams of glory were unravelling before his eyes.

Durnford retreated further. Just over a mile out from the camp, he came across a particularly deep *donga*, the Nyogane, where he decided to make a stand. Some of the other mounted soldiers left behind in the camp, men from a number of units such as the Natal Carbineers, the Newcastle Mounted Rifles and the Buffalo Border Guard, were already there. Durnford's men deployed in line alongside them and started to fire at the Zulus, taking a withering toll of the mass advancing towards them.

In the camp itself, the sight of the Zulus swarming like angry bees across the plateau and the distant plain stirred Pulleine to respond. The six imperial companies got ready for action and the two guns prepared to fire at the enemy. The only front-line imperial officer on the firing line to survive the approaching cataclysm, Lieutenant Henry Curling (in charge of the guns before being replaced mid-battle by Major Stuart Smith who returned to the camp from Chelmsford's force), later recalled that the companies of the 1st/24th were well under strength, with only about fifty men in each. Just where the rest were is a matter of ongoing debate, although they might have been getting the camp ready to move to catch up with Chelmsford when the sudden Zulu attack took them unawares.

Pulleine was faced with a difficult situation. His men were widely dispersed where their firepower could not be concentrated for maximum effect. The companies of regular infantry were to be drawn up in a dangerously extended firing line with C Company of the 1st/24th under Captain Reginald Younghusband kept back in reserve. But these were seasoned soldiers and good shots and their fire was extracting a heavy toll from the enemy.

However, both Pulleine and Durnford were at a major disadvantage compared to the Zulus. The terrain around the British camp effectively hid the size of the threat from view until it was too late. Pulleine could not see what was going on atop the Nqutu Plateau; neither did he have a very good view to his front. Durnford too could not initially see the size of the Zulu force until it was on top of him. The hills to the north screened the Zulus from the plains below, which meant that the British commanders on the spot were almost fighting blind. Their reactions were piecemeal and unco-ordinated, and could only delay the oncoming tide, not turn it back indefinitely.

The guns began firing when the Zulus moved into range. Shells began to explode amongst their advancing, massed ranks. One well-directed salvo completely destroyed a hut in which a number of Zulus were sheltering. Earlier in the battle, in response to the initial threat now several hours old, E Company had climbed a hill to the north of the camp, the Tahelane Spur, and began to fire from their stock of seventy bullets per man into the huge impi. Yet there were so many Zulus that the loss of men to this fire was almost incidental and the offensive waves swept onwards unperturbed.

Lieutenant Cavaye, in charge of E Company, had seen a number of Zulus disappear behind a ridge, from which they threatened to outflank him. He ordered Lieutenant Edward Dyson to take a party of soldiers 500 yards to the left to counteract the threat. The thin red line became still thinner. However, that early threat had seemed to come to nothing. Unknown to anyone, the Zulus he had seen were making their way to the rear of the hill of Isandlwana. In fact, after the early alarms the most common feeling seemed to be that a threat no longer existed and everyone's guard dropped as a result. Now it was clear that it had re-emerged.

It was not long before firing broke out at many points of the compass, but given the dispersed dispositions of the troops and the broken ground it was difficult to have an overall picture of what was happening. There was, perhaps because of this, still no sense of crisis. A transport officer, Captain Essex, continued writing letters in his tent, seemingly unaware that a major fight was under way. When he did hear firing, he picked up his revolver and went to see what the matter was. He did not take his sword with him, 'as I thought nothing of the matter and expected to be back in half an hour to complete my letters'.[23]

Essex rode up the hill to the left of the camp and, in his own words, took it upon himself to direct the men's firing. On top of the plateau the Zulus were firing back but their marksmanship was erratic. They moved closer to the British troops here, taking advantage of the rocks for cover. They appeared to be moving to the left of Essex and the soldiers in an attempt to outflank them.

Lieutenant Nevill Coghill, injured in an accidental fall on the 20th when out on a reconnaissance with Chelmsford, issued an order that Colonel Glyn's tent be struck even as the camp was about to be attacked by thousands of Zulus. Still, as battle commenced, Coghill was providing evidence of his close affection for Colonel Glyn, with whose family he had billeted for a while.

A charming man, Coghill – who until very recently had been an aide to Sir Bartle Frere and had only rejoined the 1st/24th on 9 January – was a great favourite with all who knew him, Colonel Glyn more than most. The colonel was surrounded by women at home, with a domineering wife and four daughters. He loved male company, which perhaps explained his obsession with hunting (jackals rather than foxes, the latter being absent from southern Africa) and he had taken Coghill to his heart almost as if he were his son. Now, as the Zulu hordes attacked, Coghill was thinking of Glyn.

In the meantime, a number of the Natal Native Horse (NNH) had made it back to camp, where they joined Cavaye's men in firing at the Zulus. It was now that a realisation of his exposed situation dawned on Pulleine. He sent Lieutenant Melvill up to Cavaye to tell him to retreat closer to the camp. Similar orders were sent to Captain William Mostyn in charge of F Company, fighting alongside Cavaye. They beat a steady but nervous retreat back towards the firing line where they fell in alongside Younghusband's C Company.

Zulus now started to pour down the ridge to the north of the camp as well as from the plains in front of it. It was, according to Smith-Dorrien, about midday when the Zulus started to come down from the hills above the camp. Pulleine was further distracted by the untimely orders of Chelmsford, received via a rider, telling him to break camp and catch him up. Pulleine replied with the message that there is 'heavy firing to left of our camp. Cannot move camp at present'. He was still, though, not fully aware of how exposed his situation was.

The messenger was Captain Alan Gardner of the 14th Hussars, who had arrived between twelve and one o'clock when a great deal of firing in front of the camp was evident.[24] He carried with him instructions to break camp and bring forward provisions and forage for the next seven days. Given the state of affairs on the battlefield, nothing could have been more inappropriate than this message. Gardner would be very lucky; he would be one of the few officers present to survive the slaughter that was moving closer by the minute.

Out in front, Durnford's men had been fighting staunchly from the protection of the Nyogane *donga*. This ensured that few of them had been hit. Durnford, in his element now, exposed himself to the enemy's fire, heedless to the risk that entailed. However, his men had been in action longer than any other and they were starting to run low on ammunition. Durnford, with his useless hand, could not load his gun easily so one of his men helped him. He then returned to the fight, seemingly enjoying every second of it.

It was, in his eyes, no doubt heroic but some of those nearby were not impressed. One of those close at hand, Lieutenant Alfred Henderson of the Basuto troop, later wrote: 'If I had known what sort of man Durnford was, I don't think I would have gone with him. He was close to me during the fight and he lost his head altogether; in fact I don't think he knew what to do.'[25]

Durnford's men took a heavy toll of the enemy but then, in the wider scheme of things, such losses could be afforded. The Zulus merely filtered further to their left in an attempt to outflank Durnford (the warriors here were from the uVe Regiment, the youngest in the army, and were therefore presumably amongst the fittest of them all). But even then they were still being held at bay by the shattering volleys emerging from the *donga*, which meant they could only rush forward in small bursts.

In the heat of battle, problems in the British supply lines became apparent. Durnford had sent some of his men back to collect more ammunition. Native troops tended to fire at a far greater rate than imperial soldiers and their ammunition would have been in short supply relatively quickly as a result. Durnford's errand runners could not find their own wagons (their wagon train arrived in the camp in the midst of the battle, and by the time it turned up it was too late to make a difference) so went instead to an ammunition wagon 'belonging' to the imperial infantry. The quartermaster refused point blank to issue any of their supply to them. The despondent messengers returned empty-handed to Durnford from a camp where there were 400,000 rounds of ammunition going spare.

The imperial companies were starting to run low too, especially E company which had been the first to start firing from Tahelane. Supplies of ammunition started to emerge but it was difficult to keep up with the demand given the fact that there was a significant gap between the firing line and the ammunition wagons. Then Quartermaster Edward Bloomfield, in charge of the 2nd/24th's ammunition, was shot dead alongside his wagon, which only made a difficult situation worse.

Captain Essex had also made his way back to camp to pick up more ammunition. He grabbed what he could in terms of bullets and made his way back towards E Company, in the process conscripting anyone he could find, including bandsmen and cooks to help him.

Others witnessed problems with the supply line. Horace Smith-Dorrien had approached Bloomfield for more ammunition and was told that he could not have it for he was not a soldier in the 2nd/24th for whom he was the quartermaster. Smith-Dorrien snapped back at him 'hang it all, you don't want a requisition now do you?'[26] There was also much debate subsequently about how easy the ammunition boxes were to open. They were of very stout construction and the lid was screwed down.

Some would later claim that difficulties in opening the boxes slowed down the ammunition supply, perhaps fatally. It is one of those grey areas much debated by historians and the consensus now is that there should not have been a problem.[27] However, it is interesting that two months later, on 26 March, Chelmsford issued orders that all reserve boxes must have the screw taken out and a screwdriver should be kept handy just in case this had not been done. It is tempting to speculate that this very detailed order was made because a specific problem had been experienced in the recent past.

Whatever the problems with the ammunition flow, the companies in the firing line were extracting a fearful toll from the Zulus. The Martini-Henry was the most advanced firearm of its day, capable of firing quickly and accurately. Still, the Zulus advanced but were shot down in their droves. Eventually their progress was halted; it was too much even for the heroic Zulus and they took shelter in dead ground not far in front of the British lines. Here they found good cover. The grass, fertilised by the exorbitant rainfall of that summer, was 3ft high in places and it was hard for the British to find a target once the Zulus had gone to ground.

Horace Smith-Dorrien looked on, still relatively unconcerned. The British soldiers were no raw recruits but battle-tried experienced soldiers who made every shot count. There was no sign of panic in their lines but a perfect discipline and a confidence that they would still yet have the upper hand. A Zulu warrior by the name of uMhoti, from the uKhandempemvu Regiment, was in the force trying to break through the screen of bullets and later admitted that 'we crouched down and dare not advance'.[28]

With the centre stalled, a Zulu hero emerged, a sub-chief by the name of Mkhosana kaMvundlana. He came down into the dead ground, berating the warriors for hiding themselves away. He succeeded in getting the men to return to the attack but Mkhosana paid the supreme price for this – he was shot down just as the impetus was about to return to the Zulu charge.

Mkhosana was an officer in the uKhandempemvu Regiment, but the impact of his bravery touched others too. To their left were the iNgombamakhosi (known as 'the humblers of kings'), fierce rivals. Inter-regimental rivalry was very common amongst the Zulu ranks. Now, the leader of the iNgombama-khosi, Sikizane kaNomageje, taunted his men, asking them why they were lying down when the uKhandempemvu were charging towards the British lines.

This intervention came at a critical time. The flanks of the British position were already starting to come under huge pressure and, along the line, imperial companies as well as Durnford's men (the two forces being isolated from each other) were starting to run short of bullets. Durnford's problem was becoming acute. His men had been blazing away from the *donga* and holding a pivotal posi-tion in the line.

The situation was made worse by the position of the NNC, who were now close to the front line. They were not cut out for fighting like this. They were poorly led by their officers and in many cases not even properly armed. Now, as they saw thousands of angry Zulus charging towards them, they turned and fled. It was a disastrous development; Captain Essex, one of only five offic-ers present to survive the looming slaughter, noted that 'those of the Native Contingent who had remained in action, rushed past us in the utmost disorder, thus laying open the right and rear of the 24th, the enemy dashing forward in the most rapid manner'.[29]

The right and rear was also dangerously exposed to parties of Zulus who had worked their way round to the back of Isandlwana. There were insufficient reserves left to guard against them. Allied to the advance of the Zulu left, the end was already a foregone conclusion. The two guns were able to fire just two more rounds before they were deluged by the ocean of warriors. The gunners attached their weapons to the limbers in an attempt to escape but a number were quickly stabbed and killed by Zulu assegais. The Zulus had, in any case, been getting wise to the artillery. When they saw the gunners stand aside as the guns were about to fire, they ducked for cover and avoided the worst of its effects as a result.

With the ammunition situation becoming extremely serious, Durnford decided to withdraw. Durnford's retreat had a disastrous effect as it left the right wing and in particular G Company hanging in the air. For the Zulu left wing, opposite them, the decisive moment had come. They were outflanking the British right just as Durnford's men were running short of ammunition and retreating and they sensed that victory was imminent. Their spirits soared and they started to charge towards the British lines.

The renewed vigour in the Zulu charge now swept them towards the thin red line left hanging by Durnford's retreat like a tsunami. It crashed home with its full force. The line slowly began to disintegrate. Shortages in ammunition did not help but more would only have extended the fight and not changed its outcome.[30]

The firing line was some distance in front of the tents, perhaps a mile. The only hope now was to move back on the camp and form a tighter defensive position and also get closer to the ammunition wagons. A frantic bugle call summoned the retreat and the infantry did their best to comply, but it was too late. The Zulus saw the retreat, sensed its import, rose up and chased the back-tracking soldiers. It was not over yet, and the 24th in particular would carry on the struggle against insuperable odds, but a crisis point had been reached.

G Company under Charlie Pope was the most immediately exposed. Thousands of Zulus streamed into the abandoned Nyogane *donga*. To Pope's right, Durnford's scratch force of his own men plus other irregulars was rushing up the slope, chased by large numbers of ecstatic Zulus. Their sudden retreat exposed Pope and his men to the full force of the Zulu attack.

In reality, the end was now a mathematical certainty given the overwhelming disparity in numbers, but the men of Pope's company would go down fighting. The iNgombamakhosi were opposite and rushed on them oblivious to the bullet storm which continued to assail them. In this part of the line, G Company was in small knots of isolated men, overwhelmed by an irresistible torrent of a determined enemy.

Durnford's scratch force arrived back at the camp and dismounted from their horses. According to a Zulu eyewitness:

> they never succeeded in getting on them again. They made a stand, and prevented our entering the camp, but things were getting very mixed and confused; what with the smoke, dust, and intermingling of mounted men, footmen, Zulus, and natives, it was difficult to tell who was mounted and who was not.[31]

The battle had been raging at full intensity for perhaps ninety minutes. One of the small band of survivors gave a detailed account of the timings of the action which Norris-Newman quoted, and although as in many such cases there may be a margin for error in the chronology, it is a useful indication. The eyewitness told how the cattle had been brought into camp at 1030, how Durnford had arrived at 1100 and how by 1230 the Zulus were in a line about 3 miles long, effectively surrounding the camp and breaking into the rear of it. By 1300 the Union Flag in front of the command tent had been torn asunder and there were already many apparent signs of panic.[32] This survivor fled the scene and, as he did, saw Durnford already surrounded and men hammering desperately to break into ammunition boxes for more bullets.

The smoke from rifle fire hung like a pall over the camp. Zulu warriors yelled out their blood-freezing cries of *uSuthu* as they sensed the imminence of victory. Further to the left of the line (as the British looked at it), clusters of soldiers from the 24th fought bravely but hopelessly on, increasingly isolated pockets of resistance in the path of the overpowering tidal wave. They too would disappear beneath the flood though they would die hard and take a huge number of the enemy with them. Towards the end even nature joined in, with a partial eclipse of the sun adding a mystical tinge to the slaughter.

Though the fighting continued, the emphasis had changed. For those British soldiers still left alive, it was now a matter of escape or dying bravely rather than victory. Most of those who would survive the battle had left earlier, before the road to Rorke's Drift was closed when Zulu forces poured round the rear of Isandlwana. Essex returned to the camp where he bumped into Durnford. Durnford tried to organise some men for a last stand but Essex headed off.

The survivors are of little use in explaining the course of the fight after they left; they did not witness the end. But the evidence of where bodies were found and of Zulu eyewitnesses suggests that most of the imperial soldiers of the 24th continued to fight on against impossible odds, in large batches at first, inevitably whittled down and then finally overwhelmed when their ammunition ran out. They had no chance of escape and it seems likely that, even if they had one, they would in the main rather have stayed and died alongside their fellow soldiers.

Lieutenant Melvill galloped out of the camp with the queen's colour of the 1st/24th. It was later claimed that he was ordered to do so but no evidence has been uncovered to confirm that this was indeed the case. He started to spur his way out of the camp through the enemy hordes. Other isolated individuals grabbed a horse if they could and tried to make their way to freedom. In a turn of poetic justice, one of them was Private Johnson, abandoned to his fate by Durnford just an hour or two before. Johnson would survive; Durnford would not.

Lieutenant Colonel Henry Pulleine, it appears, was spared the terrible sight of the battle's end. Coghill would later tell several others before he lost his own life that Pulleine had been shot in the battle. The position in which his body was later found would suggest that he was close to the front line before it finally broke. It was a small mercy at least that he did not see the slaughter that was now imminent.

Panic was abroad in the camp. Interpreter J.F. Brickhill reckoned that 'the Zulus, for the last 300 yards, did not fire 25 shots, but came on with the steady determination of walking down the camp by force of numbers. I consider that they were 30 to 1 of us … [then] they came on with an overwhelming rush.' Brickhill looked around him and saw that men were already trying to escape from the looming massacre.[33]

The camp was now a sea of Zulus, stabbing mercilessly at any living object in their path. Assegais were buried deep in the bodies of British and colonial soldiers. Animals, mules, horses and dogs were not immune either. The stench of death started to hang heavy, accompanied by the smell of fear. Knots of soldiers still fought on, at the start at least in fairly large groups, determined to sell their lives dearly. One man, Lieutenant Godwin-Austen, made an impression on his enemy because of the monocle he wore. He had wounded the warrior attacking him twice but then a thrown spear struck him down. As he tried to pull it out, a Zulu warrior ran forward and pushed it in deeper.

Durnford, whatever his lack of tactical judgement, died bravely. He could easily have made a bid to escape but opted deliberately not to do so, perhaps seeking the martyr's vindication that his associate, General Charles Gordon, would ultimately achieve. Despite suggestions that would be made in some quarters that he was deserted by most of his men, others vehemently denied this was the case. Inspector George Mansel insisted that Durnford's men fell in their scores round him; it was the 'regulars' who tried to flee.

Such suggestions owe as much to colonial sensitivities as they do to accuracy; the colonial press were keen to play up their own men against suggestions of ineptitude by some British observers and this inevitably led to some jaundiced perceptions. The positions in which large clumps of dead soldiers were later found, and the thick piles of Zulu slain around them, suggest that a desperate and valiant though hopeless last stand was fought involving ever-smaller groups of the 24th and does not support Mansel's slurs against the imperial infantry in the least. Numbers in this case are hard to argue with; of 20 officers and 567 privates from the 24th involved in the battle, there were two survivors.[34]

The point-scoring though was not all on one side. Lieutenant Curling later wrote that 'you will see all sorts of accounts in the papers and no end of lies. Most of those who escaped were volunteers and native contingent officers who tell any number of lies.' Most but not all. There were five officers who survived from the regular army and Curling was one of them.[35] This is not to imply any criticism of his personal actions, but merely to suggest that those who remained alive owed their survival to luck more than anything else, regardless of whether they were colonials or not.

The last large-scale resistance in the camp came from Younghusband's men on the left of the line. They were pushed back to the upper slopes of Isandlwana, where eventually they were trapped by the sheer cliffs behind them. They blazed away with their rifles until their ammunition ran out. Younghusband resolved on one last gesture. His orders could not be heard in the din but one look at his face told all. Their bayonets thrust forward, they charged headlong down the hill to die a soldier's death. It was perhaps one of Younghusband's company who was last to die. Legend has it that he made his way to a high-up cave where he proceeded to shoot any Zulu who got close. Eventually, a body of Zulus advanced on the cave and, firing in en masse, ended his life.

Those who were present from the Zulu side also spoke of a fierce though doomed defence on the part of the trapped British soldiers. They fired on until their ammunition ran out, officers turning to their revolvers when the rifle fire had stopped. Then they formed themselves up in lines, back to back, bayonets splayed, ready to take down their enemy with them. In the end, a number of the Zulus took to throwing their assegais to finish them off.[36]

One of the Zulu warriors there, Mehlokazulu, a son of Sihayo, related that as the battle started to increase in intensity the British soldiers, initially strung out, started to bunch together. At the end, cavalry, minus their horses, and infantry were mixed up. They put up a desperate resistance but were overwhelmed. As Mehlokazulu later looked over the dead bodies, he noticed one of them with his arm in a sling and a big moustache. Durnford lay here surrounded by his dead carbineers, having found the glory in death that he had craved so much in life.[37]

The process of ritual disembowelment was then acted out; in fact, it seems that it was witnessed even whilst some of the survivors were still trying to flee the camp.[38] This was not an act of gratuitous mutilation but a way of releasing a warrior's spirit; if it was not done then it was believed that the body of the man who had slain him would swell along with the corpse. The NNC were regarded as traitors and some of their corpses were decapitated. For a few powerful enemies, body parts were removed to be used for potent magic at a later stage.

A particularly savage fate awaited the drummer boys who were in camp. These were typically boys of around 14 years of age. Some were allegedly hung up by the chin on meat-hooks in the camp and then had their throats cut. One of them was even identified, Joseph McEwan from Dover, aged 14. When British soldiers saw the devastation wreaked in the camp later, all magnanimous thoughts towards their enemy soon evaporated.[39]

Another man whose end was recorded by his Zulu foes was a sailor, Signalman William Aynsley. He was Lieutenant Milne's personal servant and, whilst his master was busy on a wild goose chase a few miles off, he fought for his life heroically. Trapped against a wagon, he fought so fiercely with his cutlass and did such execution that one of his assailants was forced to creep up behind him under the vehicle and stab him with his assegai through the spokes of the wheel.[40]

Other stories emerged of some of the heroes who stayed behind to die. Sergeant-Major Kambule of the Edendale Horse came across an ammunition wagon being watched over by one of the drummers. He would not let Kambule have any of the ammunition, saying that he was responsible for watching over it for the 24th. Kambule did not push the point but offered the boy a lift on his horse. The drummer seemed almost offended by the suggestion and proudly held his ground. Kambule left him to his fate, respecting his decision to die like a man.

For those who had managed to break out of the Zulu noose, a horrific 6-mile-long race for life now began. They headed in the main for the Buffalo River, some on foot (mostly doomed to die), and some on horseback (Essex reckoned that every white man who survived was mounted). For most, this was the only way out once the road to Rorke's Drift had been cut off. The countryside they had to cross was awful, making it easier for a fleet-footed Zulu warrior to run across it than to ride a horse over it. There were rocks, ravines, bogs and, at the end of it all, sheer precipices on the edge of the river. It was a dash for survival. As Hallam Parr graphically put it: 'on the English side there were but few winners'.[41]

One Zulu-speaking survivor watched in horror as his comrade was stabbed by a Zulu who jumped out of the bushes as he fled, saying *'uya ngapi umlungu?'* ('where do you think you are going white man?')[42] The Zulu flung his assegai at the fleeing soldier who fell to the ground. The warrior then pulled the blade out and thrust it into his victim's heart.

Other Zulus watching were not impressed at the actions of those who fled. One, Luke Sofikasho Zungu, said (much later in 1935) that 'I saw quite a lot of white men escape on horseback, soon after we attacked ... They were cowards to leave their brothers behind'.[43] The Zulus chased after the fleeing enemy, their blood up. They hacked at them with assegais from left, right and centre.

Zungu also noticed the actions of other British soldiers which were rather different:

> I saw a line of soldiers near the tents who were in a line shoulder to shoulder and I was afraid to go and attack them as they had chucked away their guns which were broken by using them as clubs and were standing with those small spears that they carried at their sides. I saw them like a fence holding hands against the attackers.[44]

Their guns had been shattered by being smashed so hard against those who were coming at them with their assegais, a graphic image of a terrible battle, almost from a time gone past. Understandably, in the horror of it all some tried to flee the slaughterhouse whilst others steeled their nerves in the face of what all would have known by now was certain, savage death. The 24th Regiment went down gloriously, their heroism even making its mark on their foe. But Zulu witnesses wrote of men who averted their eyes as a Zulu moved in for the *coup de grâce*, understandably trying to shut out the inevitable end.

The screams of the dying merged harrowingly with the otherworldly howls of injured and crazed horses. Another of those trying to escape, Horace Smith-Dorrien, had borrowed a mount, a 'broken-kneed old crock'.[45] Looking round and seeing the camp surrounded, he and most others fleeing headed towards the point where the Zulus seemed to be in the smallest numbers. He had to use his revolver regularly to keep the Zulus off, though with only eleven bullets he also had to be prudent in doing so.

Curling was another of those fleeing, with a few of his gunner comrades. He looked on in horror as wounded men cried out for help, knowing the fate that inevitably awaited any man who could not outpace the Zulus, but it was all he could do to save his own life. Another escapee was Captain Essex, who recalled that he had:

> thank God, a very good horse, and a sure footed one, but I saw many poor fellows roll over, their horses stumbling over the rocky ground. It was now a race for dear life. The Zulus kept up with us on both sides, being able to run down the steep rocky ground quite as fast as a horse could travel.[46]

Once the road to Rorke's Drift had been closed off by the right wing of the Zulus, who came round from behind the hill of Isandlwana, the only way out was across brutal terrain to a crossing which later became known as Fugitives Drift. Smith-Dorrien was one of those who made it to the rocky bluffs overlooking it. He halted briefly at the edge of the river when he reached it, stopped by a soldier who asked for help in applying a tourniquet to staunch the bleeding from his wound.

As he did so, Major Smith of the artillery suddenly appeared and shouted that the Zulus were right on top of them. Smith was bleeding heavily and was very pale. Large numbers of Zulus threw themselves on them. They speared and killed Smith-Dorrien's gallant steed along with Smith and a wounded soldier with him. Smith-Dorrien jumped into the river and miraculously landed cleanly in it. He swam across – in itself quite a feat as the river was, in his words, a roaring torrent – only to be chased by a group of Zulus who had crossed into Natal.

It was now that the remainder of the eleven bullets he had cadged that morning saved him. Whenever one of the chasing Zulus got too close Smith-Dorrien shot at him. After several miles they gave up; perhaps the young officer benefited from a hereditary advantage as his brother was a renowned middle-distance runner.[47] The relieved lieutenant then walked the 20 miles to Helpmekaar, where he spent the night in command of one side of the laagers that had been erected there.

He would go on to witness the last time the British redcoat was ever worn in battle, he would take part in the famous Battle of Ondurman, when the last ever cavalry charge of the British army in a battle took place, he would be in command of British troops on the spot where Britain and France nearly went to war over the so-called Fashoda Incident. He would also be a general in the trenches of the First World War, taking part in the Battle of Ypres. This was certainly an eventful career, but nothing compared with this long, harrowing day at Isandlwana.

James Brickhill, an interpreter, was another fortunate survivor. His account of the terrible journey to Fugitives Drift is the most powerful of them all:

> No path, no track, boulders everywhere. On we went, borne now into some dry torrent bed, now weaving our way amongst trees of stunted growth, so that unless you made the best use of your eyes you were in constant danger of colliding against some tree or finding yourself unhorsed at the bottom of some ravine. Our way was already strewn with shields, assegais, blankets, hats, clothing of all descriptions, guns, ammunition belts, saddles which horses had managed to kick off, revolvers and belts and I don't know what not. Whilst our stampede was composed of mules with and without pack saddles, oxen, horses in all stages of equipment and flying men all strangely intermingled – man and beast apparently all infected with the danger that surrounded us.[48]

Smith-Dorrien made an interesting point about the survivors. All the officers that survived the battle (five of them) were wearing blue coats. No one in a red jacket lived. Cetshwayo had apparently told his armies to concentrate on the redcoats, for they were soldiers rather than civilians. His warriors had complied literally with this advice.[49]

A heroic end awaited Melvill and Coghill. They too made it to the river, Melvill finding the cased colour of the regiment an awkward burden in the scrub. He refused to let go of it, however, like a centurion guarding the eagle of the legion, a prize worth more than life itself. But he lost his horse in the river. Coghill was already across. He had not left the camp with Melvill and was seen by Smith-Dorrien about half a mile in front of him.[50] Now Coghill, seeing the plight of both his comrade and the colour, swam his horse back towards him, only to have the horse shot from under him.

Coghill, barely able to walk, was now doomed. Melvill was clinging from a rock midstream along with a colonial man, Lieutenant Higginson. In the roaring torrent, he lost hold of the colour but managed to make it to the far bank. Melvill did his best to help Coghill when they both made it to the Natal side of the river, whilst Higginson ran off to try and find horses. Higginson scrambled uphill, exhausted and almost spent. Fortunately for him, he bumped into Trooper William Barton of the Natal Carbineers.

Barton gave him his horse and asked Higginson to wait at the top of the slope for him. But Higginson's nerve had gone and he promptly rode off. Both Melvill and Coghill had revolvers and managed to keep the Zulus at bay for about half a mile, but then they slumped to the ground exhausted and were overwhelmed and slain by the chasing Zulus.

The Zulus also saw Barton and chased after him. Higginson, thinking Barton was dead, told the retreating horsemen of Lieutenant Raw when they caught him up that he had found the horse wandering loose. Swapping the horse for a Basuto pony, Higginson then galloped off to Helpmekaar. Raw, fortunately for Barton, moved back towards Fugitives Drift and found Barton, who had been running for his life for 3 miles, keeping off his pursuers with his revolver. Barton was recommended for the Victoria Cross but the proposal of Colonel Evelyn Wood, made some months after the event, was turned down.

Others were also luckier than Coghill and Melvill. As they escaped over Fugitives Drift, survivors saw the Natal side was swarming with Zulus. However, the Edendale Horse had managed to emerge from the battle more or less intact and had kept their discipline splendidly. A few well-placed volleys dispersed the Zulus and allowed many more men to escape than would otherwise have been the case. This was a creditable performance from men whose salary levels suggested they were only worth half as much as their white counterparts. It was thanks in part to them that a significant proportion of the fifty-five Europeans who escaped alive managed to do so. But their ammunition was soon expended and they too were forced to move off.

Of course it was a terrible death for all those trapped in this vast encirclement by the Zulu army. Even those who survived would be haunted by the terror they felt for the rest of their days. Edward Evans was in the Mounted Infantry and was one of the few to escape with his life.

Writing home shortly afterwards, he said:

> You know nothing of the horrors of war and if I was to write from now till Christmas, I could never explain half what I have seen or how I was saved. Myself and two more comrades rode our horses through the centre of their line of fire and hundreds of guns pointing at us; but I can assure you it was a ride for life. Many of our noble heroes that escaped from the hands of the enemy lost their lives in crossing the Buffalo River. Thank God for learning me to swim. My horse fell in the water and both of us went down together and both swam out again – but a very hard struggle. I had to let go my rifle and ammunition and everything I had.[51]

As all this was going on, Hamilton-Browne was headed back to the camp across the plain on the orders of Chelmsford, ostensibly to help pack the camp up and allow Pulleine and the men left behind at Isandlwana to rejoin the main force. Hamilton-Browne knew there were some Zulus around at least and did not fancy the thought of his men being left to fend for themselves in a battle situation. According to his later memoirs, he nearly fell off his horse when given his orders, wondering to himself, 'are we all mad or what?'

Hamilton-Browne, though, had no choice in the matter and duly set off. By about 1230 he was able to see the camp in the far distance. A couple of hours before, he had captured an isolated Zulu warrior who told him exactly where the main Zulu impi was. He had immediately sent a messenger to Chelmsford with the news. No action was taken on it.

The rider he now dispatched arrived at Chelmsford's camp at about 1300. He looked for the general but no one at first knew where he was. The rider met up with Lieutenant-Colonel Russell, in charge of the cavalry. All Russell could do was tell him where he had last seen Chelmsford hours ago at breakfast.[52] Another rider met up with Russell soon after. He too was unable to find the general. A crucial battle was under way and Chelmsford had gone AWOL.

Hamilton-Browne's timing was, for him and his NNC troops, fortuitous. By the time he got closer to the camp the battle was already in motion. A few minutes earlier and he and his soldiers would have been wiped out. Now he could see from the distance that a major scrap was in progress. Whiffs of smoke suggested cannon fire and then he saw a large shadow on the hill above the camp. There were no clouds and a horrifying truth dawned on him; he was witnessing a huge Zulu army attacking Isandlwana.

As the NNC battalion he was leading had moved closer to the camp his men had got increasingly nervous. They too could see what was happening. The pace of the march noticeably slowed, much to Hamilton-Browne's anger. He sent his isiGqoza Zulus to the back with orders to hurry anyone up who appeared to be dawdling. As they got closer he could see that the fight was in full swing. A message had been sent back to Chelmsford's HQ saying that the camp was still holding its own. At 1300 this still appeared to be the case, but it all changed very quickly.

It was about 1330 when Hamilton-Browne believed the defence collapsed. He saw a swarm of cattle charging panic-stricken into the rear of the camp, behind which were hordes of Zulus. It was this, combined with a determined attack from the front, which resulted in the defences being overwhelmed, he thought.

Hamilton-Browne was certainly a man who gave the impression that he was fired up by a thirst for glory, but he knew that to carry on moving forward now would be tantamount to suicide. Wisely, he chose to form his men into large groups, with the white officers on foot and hidden in the middle. Then they retreated slowly until they were far enough away to stop and await reinforcements from Chelmsford with his part of the column.

In the meantime, as Hamilton-Browne's messenger hurried east, he told groups of British soldiers that he met what was happening. Some of them began to turn round and head back towards Isandlwana. The guns, accompanied by Major Wilsone Black, had not gone half a mile in this direction when Chelmsford's aide, Major Gosset, intercepted them and immediately turned them back round again. Gosset point-blank refuted tales of the attack as idle gossip; it was, after all, not at all what his lordship was expecting so it could not be right.

Black was livid. He got as close as he could to disobeying orders without risking a court martial and stood where he was. Then he sent his own messenger off looking for the strangely absent Chelmsford. Many of those in his part of the column were, however, already starting to suspect something was wrong. Close by, Lieutenant Harford peered towards Isandlwana in the far distance. He could only see two tents standing and they looked as if they had been scorched.[53] Others were taking lunch at the new camp of Mangeni when the distant sound of gunfire was heard. This was at about 1230. Soon after, at around 1245, Chelmsford arrived back at the camp. This was just as well, as Crealock himself later admitted that at this time 'our whereabouts was not exactly known'.[54]

What of Chelmsford whilst all this had been happening? Out on the plains, safely out of sight of the Zulus, Hamilton-Browne had looked on incredulously as the Zulus pushed home their attack. Increasingly frantic, he sent a final message back for the general: 'For God's sake come back, the camp is surrounded, and things I fear are going badly.'[55] So frenzied was he that he did not even write the message down for his messenger but gave it to him verbally. Underneath his breath, he cursed Chelmsford's staff who had so misjudged the situation, though he was always quick to defend the general himself. Before leading his men on the march back to camp, he asked Crealock what his orders were if they met any hostile Zulus on the way. Crealock replied: 'Oh, just brush them aside and go on.'[56] Given the host before him, this was a pipe dream.

Although timings at any great event are often suspect, Crealock confirmed that 'not a suspicion had crossed my mind that the camp was in danger, neither did anything occur to make me think of such a thing until about 1.15'.[57] However, it began to be clear that something significant was going on around the camp. Norris-Newman had been with Chelmsford when they were watching a large mass of Zulus about 10 miles away, the time being about 1230. They soon after interrogated a group of Zulu prisoners who had been brought in. They told Chelmsford that a large army had been dispatched by Cetshwayo and that their arrival was imminent. Then came the distant but unmistakable sound of the guns from the direction of the camp. Nerves started to jangle.[58]

There was a nearby hill which gave a distant view of Isandlwana, about 10 miles distant. Chelmsford and his staff galloped up it as quickly as they could. Milne once more trained his telescope on the camp but the tents still stood erect so he assumed that everything was still in order. As they rode back down, another rider came in, Lieutenant Parsons, the messenger Black had sent. He asked if the guns should continue back towards the camp. Chelmsford replied with a peremptory 'no'; the guns were to rejoin Colonel Glyn at once.

Eventually Chelmsford decided that he perhaps ought to find out what was going on after all. There had been some skirmishing in the hills around him during the morning (Norris-Newman was close at hand to see this; fortunately he had left the camp with the NNC the day before), in which perhaps 100 Zulus lost their lives, but all in all Chelmsford was frustrated that he had not got to grips with the main army of his foe, who had a frustrating habit of disappearing and reappearing at will. At some time, he decided to head back for the camp at Isandlwana to see for himself what was happening.

Norris-Newman had already set off for Isandlwana along with some of the NNC. Chelmsford followed on in a separate party. As usual, he did not take many men with him. Hamilton-Browne, nearest to the camp, had continued to send messages to Russell offering to attack the Zulus from the rear if he would support. It was probably just as well that Russell ignored what was effectively an invitation to jointly commit suicide.

At around 3.30 p.m. Chelmsford met up with Hamilton-Browne. Hamilton-Browne told him what he had witnessed, struggling to contain his anger even though he was speaking to a superior officer. Chelmsford, unable to comprehend, listened in bewildered silence, unwilling to accept the inevitable. His initial reaction was to snap at Hamilton-Browne and insist that he was wrong – an insight into Chelmsford's faults which show that he would not accept any information that was contrary to his expectations. He then ordered him to march back towards Isandlwana. It was yet another example of poor leadership on a day that had been liberally supplied with illustrations of such shortcomings.

Confirmation of the terrible tidings was about to arrive in the most extraordinary way. Earlier in the day Commandant Rupert Lonsdale had ridden back towards the camp to pick up rations. The heat of the day had drained him and he fell into a half-slumber as his horse led him back towards Isandlwana. Eventually he reached the edge of the camp where he saw the welcoming sight of a redcoat. It took a few moments for Lonsdale to be jolted from his daydream. The redcoat soldier had a black face. It took a matter of seconds to work out what had happened; Lonsdale turned his tired horse rapidly about and rode for his life. His story was all the confirmation that was needed.

It was just before 4 p.m. when Lonsdale met Chelmsford.[59] The bewildered general listened as the true import of the news sank home with a thud like that of an assegai. He muttered quietly 'but I left over 1,000 men to guard the camp'. It was now clear that he had miscalculated disastrously. Whilst he had been out picnicking, he had got the battle he wanted, the fight in the open, the Martini-Henry and the bayonet against the assegai. Unbelievably, the assegai had won.

Chelmsford's plans were in tatters. His reputation might very soon be in the same state. In a statement he later sent to the Duke of Cambridge in response to questions about Isandlwana, he said: 'I had received no report whatever previous to Commandant Lonsdale reporting that the camp was in the hands of the enemy, that led me to suppose that an action was going on near the camp.'[60] This does not fit very comfortably with Hamilton-Browne's assertions that several messages had been sent to him saying exactly that.

Major Gosset was sent to the temporary camp where Colonel Glyn and what was now the surviving portion of the 24th were stopped. Doing his best to conceal his inner turmoil, he calmly told Glyn that the Zulus had got into the camp at Isandlwana and that his men were to start off back there as quickly as possible.[61]

Now there was nothing for Chelmsford to do but to gather up his men and fight his way back into the wreckage of the camp – a metaphor for Chelmsford's military strategy. Everything had been turned on its head in this nightmare of incredible proportions. Everything had been lost: supplies, wagons, ammunition, and most of all 850 imperial and colonial soldiers and perhaps 500 black allies. The *Natal Mercury* noted soon after that the losses sustained by Natal natives since the start of the war amounted to 482, most of them at Isandlwana. With poignant irony, the largest losses from amongst the natives had been sustained by those staying in Weenen County, the scene of dreadful Zulu massacres against the whites four decades previously.[62]

The most graphic analysis of the battle's outcome perhaps comes from the 24th Regiment's official history, which said:

> there were no 'wounded' or 'missing', only 'killed'. From the 1st Battalion the twenty-fourth lost sixteen officers and 407 NCOs and men, including RSM Gapp, QMS Leitch, five other staff sergeants and five colour sergeants. Of the 2nd Battalion there perished five officers and 127 other ranks, including Bandmaster Ballard and QMS Davis. It was a worse blow than Chilianwala; even 1914–1918 was not to produce such another casualty list.[63]

Worse than the bloodbaths of the trenches of the First World War – what more telling comparator could there be? It was also far worse proportionately than any battle in the Crimean War, as the colonial secretary of the day, Sir Michael Hicks-Beach, pointed out.[64] But one point needs to be made forcefully: although Isandlwana was a disaster for the British, it was one they had brought upon themselves. They had decided to use strong-arm tactics against a sovereign state that had offered them no provocation. They were the aggressor and they were defeated. The Zulus only saw this battle as a disaster because of the huge losses they themselves suffered and not, of course, because of its outcome. For them it was a great if ultimately pyrrhic victory.

In retrospect, Isandlwana was an even harsher blow for the Zulus than it was for the British. Heavy Zulu losses had been sustained; along with other engagements fought elsewhere at more or less the same time, several thousand Zulus were dead and they would be hard to replace. In contrast, the British infantry could be. In fact, the scale of their defeat inevitably meant that the British, with all their massive resources, would now fight the war to the death. Any chances that the Zulus ever had (and they had always been close to nil) of escaping from the war with their power even partially intact had now gone. As would be said of an incident in a later war, all that the Zulus had done by their victory was to disturb a sleeping giant.

five

NOWHERE TO GO

The Epic Tale of Rorke's Drift

Lieutenant John Rouse Marriot Chard rode back discontentedly to the ramshackle post at Rorke's Drift. He had delivered a small party of engineers to the camp at Isandlwana and received his orders. It is probable he was not happy. He had been told to return to Rorke's Drift and supervise the ponts there. That meant effectively he had nothing to do as the ponts were fully operational. He had only been in southern Africa for three weeks, having shipped out from Gravesend in England on 2 December 1878. Since his arrival, he had been further delayed by a dreadful journey through the rains to Rorke's Drift. Now it looked like he was going to miss out on all the glory of the campaign in Zululand. This was not at all what he expected.

He had not had a distinguished career, but as he was still young, only just 31 years of age, he had time to make up for this. He had struggled to pass his exams at the Royal Military Academy at Woolwich, a place where he was mainly remembered for his poor record of punctuality. Finally commissioned in 1868, he had spent two tours of duty in Bermuda and Malta and then held a number of minor posts in England. There was nothing on his career résumé to suggest that he would be anything save a competent engineer. He was, in short, an unlikely hero. Yet within twenty-four hours his life would be changed forever. In contrast, the small batch of engineers he had left behind at Isandlwana would be dead. Such were the fates of war.

No less unlikely a hero was Lieutenant Gonville Bromhead from B Company of the 2nd/24th, whose men provided most of the garrison at Rorke's Drift. The son of a baronet who had fought at Waterloo, he did at least come from a military family. He had become a lieutenant in October 1871. Bromhead was a shy man who did not seem to enjoy the fame that was soon to be his in abundance. This led to a number of so-called superior officers thinking that he was not particularly bright – a perception probably fuelled by his deafness. However, this is not fair on him. An excellent sportsman and very adept at that great English pastime, cricket, he was very popular with his men. Those amongst higher-ranking officers who regarded him as something of a 'duffer' would often have been well advised to look at themselves first.

The men of B Company were not happy either. Placed in charged of the stores depot at Rorke's Drift, their replacements – a company expected from the 1st/24th led by Captain Rainforth – were long overdue. In the meantime, their mates with Number 3 Column were marching to glory in Zululand. They had little to do either, except lull around in the searing heat of the African summer and kill time until they at last marched off to join their comrades across the river. It is likely that there was a good deal of dissatisfaction and grumbling going on at Rorke's Drift.

No longer was Rorke's Drift a mission station. As well as a stores depot, it also served as a temporary hospital. The Reverend Witt's house had been adapted for the purpose. It was, when you looked at it, a strange building: a number of rooms had doors that only opened to the outside rather than into each other. No one thought much of it at the time but it would later become a matter of life and death for those inside.

Thirty-five patients were in the hospital, though not all of them were bedridden. One of the more serious cases, Sergeant Maxfield, delirious with fever, had been assigned the Rev. Witt's bed. The others had to make do with wooden pallets propped up on bricks. Nearly all the patients were hospitalised because of disease or accidents; only three NNC members in the hospital had suffered battle wounds.

Rorke's Drift was under the command of Major Spalding, who was becoming increasingly irritated by Rainforth's late arrival. In fact, Rainforth's company had endured an appalling journey to Helpmekaar, assaulted not by hostile Zulus but incessant rain. They had now arrived at Helpmekaar where they had met up with another company of the 1st/24th. They were planning to move to Rorke's Drift later that day, though Spalding had no idea that this was the case.

Spalding had sent several written orders to Helpmekaar but had received no reply. Now he decided to go there himself and see what on earth was happening. Almost as an afterthought, before setting off he remembered that he needed someone to take command of the post in his absence. Consulting the Army List, which noted such things, he saw that Chard was senior to Bromhead in terms of when he had received his lieutenancy. Chard, therefore, would take command. However, it was a mere formality. As he told Chard: 'I see you are senior, so you will be in charge, although, of course, nothing will happen, and I shall be back again this evening, early.'[1]

And so Spalding rode off, away from his chance of glory. Chard decided to return to his tent and write some letters home. Although he had seen Zulus above the camp at Isandlwana hours earlier, he had clearly decided that nothing would come of it (though he had informed Spalding of the fact, which meant that this was an odd time for the commanding officer to disappear). In the meantime, a small party of soldiers from the drift had made their way up to the summit of the Shiyane hill behind the mission station. Led by the popular, youthful-looking Colour Sergeant Frank Bourne, they were there at midday when they heard artillery fire from Isandlwana, some miles off. Though they strained to see what was happening, the plain below the sphinx-like hill was obscured from view.

Others heard firing from far off across the river as the afternoon advanced. Watchers from the Oskarberg hill above Rorke's Drift soon worked out where it came from. A Zulu force was approaching, composed of elements from four regiments, most of whom had played little part in the battle at Isandlwana except in harrowing some of those attempting to escape. They crossed the river 4 miles down from the drift. The river was, as Chelmsford had hoped, in flood but this did nothing to deter them from passing over, mostly unharmed, into Natal. The spot where they came across, a craggy fissure in the rocks of the Mzinyathi River, was forded with ease. They crossed in a leisurely fashion by linking arms and then stopped to take snuff on the Natal shore.

The men of Prince Dabulamanzi (Cetshwayo's half-brother) were frustrated that their spears had not been washed in the glorious victory just won. Their intention now was not to invade Natal – there were only about 4,000 of them – but to raid the border region, even though crossing into Natal was against Cetshwayo's orders.[2] The Zulus, like their British counterparts, had a regimental system and they were not amused that all the glory had been won by regiments of younger men at Isandlwana. They quickly fanned out from the river, coming across a number of fortunately abandoned farms and setting them ablaze. However, the lure of what appeared to be an undermanned garrison at Rorke's Drift was irresistible.

Chard was relaxing in his tent by the river when, at around 3.30 p.m., he saw two riders approaching. These were, it turned out, two survivors from the massacre at Isandlwana, Lieutenants Adendorff and Vane from the Natal Native Horse. They told him the unbelievable news of the loss of the camp. At almost the same time, a messenger arrived for Chard, sent from Bromhead. News had come in from a few of the surviving officers who had escaped the slaughter; Gardner had written notes to both Rorke's Drift and Helpmekaar confirming the desperate tidings.[3] Chard quickly made his way back to the mission station.

The two NNH men rode off, Adendorff saying that he would stay and fight (not every historian believes that he did). Chard presciently had a water cart filled from the river, which his small detachment hauled back to the mission station. Vane and Adendorff suggested that the camp should be evacuated as quickly as possible. This advice was ignored, which was just as well; with a much faster Zulu army close at hand and thirty-five hospitalised men to think about, this would have meant certain death.

It was at this point that a largely forgotten hero of Rorke's Drift made his entrance. Commissary James Langley Dalton was a man in his mid-forties with a huge bushy beard so beloved of middle-aged Victorian gentlemen. He had joined the 85th (Shropshire) Regiment in 1849. During his twenty-two years of service in the army he had participated in several frontier disputes in southern Africa, gaining valuable experience in the process. He left the army in 1871 and then settled in southern Africa. He volunteered for service in the Ninth Frontier War in 1877, where he caught the eye of Colonel Glyn, being the only civilian to be mentioned in dispatches. Observing the conversations, he offered the advice that they should stand and fight until Spalding returned with reinforcements. His advice was accepted, though Vane was sent on to Helpmekaar to tell Spalding what was happening.

Chard was quick to acknowledge the wisdom of Dalton's advice and he later pointed out the part that the commissary officer subsequently played in the defence. He would write in his detailed report, prepared specifically for Queen Victoria, that his 'energy, intelligence and gallantry were of the greatest service to us … and I am sure that Bromhead would unite in saying with me that I can not sufficiently thank him for his service'. It was a view confirmed by the queen's secretary after Chard later met her at Balmoral; from what he had said the secretary thought Dalton was 'quite as much (if not more) the presiding genius there'.[4]

Fortunately there were literally tons of materials for creating an impromptu defensive structure at hand and some steps had already been taken to fortify the position. Lieutenant Harford recalled that when the invasion commenced the position had already been entrenched[5] and further described the position as a 'fort'.[6] In addition, a guest of Rev. Witt's, a fellow Swede by the name of August Hammar, wrote in his journal for 6 January that 'we have put rocks around the outside of the house' and also noted that the house and store had been prepared to resist a Zulu attack.[7] Now, in addition to the work that had already been done, heavy 200lb mealie bags, and biscuit and meat boxes weighing a hundredweight, were used to create a stronger wall. It was not a classic material to work with but it proved very effective.

The mission was in a far from perfect position for a defence, being overlooked by hills from which sharpshooters could fire into the camp. However, it did have some advantages. In particular, on the north side there was a 5ft-high natural rocky ledge. On top of this, a 4ft-high wall of mealie bags was hurriedly constructed, making it very difficult for any assailant to get over. Whatever defences had already been erected were clearly not felt to be sufficient to repulse a deter-mined Zulu attack.

Fortunately, there were enough men to construct a barricade quickly: nearly 100 regular soldiers and 300 NNC men were at hand. As this was a supplies depot en route to Zululand, there would also be plenty of ammunition to go around. Although not perfect, to say, as Hallam Parr did, that 'a worse position could hardly be imagined'[8] is a long way from the truth, particularly given the armament of the enemy.

Other matters needed to be hastily attended to as well. The house/hospital was not designed for a battle. There were few openings in its walls to fire from, so loopholes were hurriedly smashed out in them. The doors were barricaded too, the fact that they in so many cases opened to the exterior suddenly becoming a major failing. The hospital was clearly a major weak point in the British lines and it would not be long before the Zulus identified it as one.

At about this time, Rev. Witt breathlessly galloped in from the Oskarberg over-looking the drift. He had seen the threat moving inexorably towards his mission station and decided that his place was with his family, who were in an isolated farmstead a few miles off. Taking a very sick officer with him, he galloped off.[9]

He said he watched the battle develop from a distance. Much of his property was about to be destroyed, which would later lead him to launch an unsuccessful claim for compensation of £600 against the British government. His co-watcher from the hill earlier on, Rev. George Smith, decided to join him. Unfortunately, by the time he did so both his horse and his native groom had disappeared.

Smith later became part of the Rorke's Drift legend. Sir Garnet Wolseley, who would be commander-in-chief of the army in southern Africa when the war ended, heard that Smith encouraged the defenders with cries of 'Don't swear boys and shoot them!' A rather more prosaic version told by Adendorff was that Smith had heard one of the defenders using somewhat industrial language and asked him 'please, my good man, stop that cussing. We may shortly have to answer for our sins.' The brief but decisive reply came 'all right mister, you do the praying and I will send the black Bastards to Hell as fast as I can'.[10]

By 4 p.m. the barricade had been completed. The position appeared to be strong but events were about to change radically for the worse. Chard went down to the ponts; the detachment there had not yet come back to the mission station. As he was hurrying them up, a party of Natal Native Horse rode in from Isandlwana and agreed to try and hold the Zulus up at the drift. It was around 4.20 p.m. when the first of the enemy approached the river. There was an out-break of firing and the Zulus closed in on the mission station.

The sight was too much for the NNH who decided to retreat, fleeing past the mission station. As they did so, the Natal Native Contingent inside the mealie bag walls suddenly panicked. As one, they jumped over the walls and ran off.

They were followed by their own white officers, not trying to stop them but rather joining them. The regular soldiers were incensed and started to fire at them. One of the fleeing NCOs, Corporal Anderson, fell dead. It is supremely ironic that the first British combatant to die at Rorke's Drift was deliberately shot by his own side. Chard was contemptuous of the NNC's actions but felt that their desertion made little difference to the defence. He was more disparaging of the officers than their men, especially Captain Stephenson at their head, though he did at least acknowledge that they had done valuable service in preparing the post for the defence.

This was a dreadful blow as a perimeter designed to be defended by 400 combatants now had to be manned by 100. There were some biscuit boxes as yet unused (in fact, by this time the parapet was only the height of two biscuit boxes) and Chard, thinking on his feet, ordered that they should be employed to build an internal wall between the hospital and the store (which was normally Witt's church). It would have made sense to have evacuated the hospital and defended a smaller parameter inside this newly erected wall, but Chard did not do so, perhaps thinking he did not have time.

Colour Sergeant Bourne was given the task of organising the handing out of ammunition. At least the small area to defend helped to ensure that there would be no extended supply lines as there had been at Isandlwana. In fact, the battle that was about to be fought was exactly the one that Chelmsford had wanted: massed Zulu ranks against compact lines of infantry armed with Martini-Henrys.

Bourne had been instructed to take out a few men in a skirmishing line in front of the walls but when the size of the threat became apparent they were quickly back inside the perimeter. The first shots of the battle proper were fired at around 4.30 p.m., when the Zulus launched a rush against the south wall. Nearby at the hospital, the walking wounded inside the cramped building had been issued with rifles. Everyone knew that there would be no non-combatants in this fight.

Private Hitch, on the roof, watched in horrified fascination as about 600 Zulus deployed in the classic 'horns' formation to attack. Some of the attackers spotted him and let off a couple of shots in his direction, which missed. Hitch, firing back, noticed that the Zulus were mobilising in a disciplined manner, vastly different from what he been used to in previous battles against native African opponents.

From a range of about 400 yards the first volley spewed out and a number of the attackers fell. There was some cover for the Zulus as they tried to rush closer (the defenders had not had time to clear the scrub around the post) but the accuracy of the defenders started to improve. A number of the Zulus, nevertheless, got to within 50 yards of the mission station, where they managed to find cover behind some conveniently sited boulders.

The Zulus also found cover of sorts behind a 5ft-high garden wall near the buildings. However, here they were still exposed to crossfire. Others found refuge in bushes, in dried-up stream beds and behind the ovens scattered outside the buildings. This first attack being repulsed, the Zulus then charged against the north wall. Here, where the defenders looked down from high above their attackers, the toll on the Zulus was greater. They were forced back with the bodies of scores of their comrades lying dead, dying or wounded close to the mealie-bag walls.

Sheer numbers and bravery began to tell. Seemingly oblivious to the hailstorm of bullets, the rushes continued. The defenders did not have time to stop and load after they had fired so were forced to use their bayonets. This was a fearsome weapon in its own right and the Zulus were well aware of its stopping power. They were again forced back. The accuracy of some of the defenders was impressive. One man, Private James Dunbar, shot down a chieftain he had spotted atop a white horse. With his next six shots he reputedly hit another six Zulus.

These were, though, just the first skirmishes. The main Zulu army had come round under the cover of the Oskarberg and now got ready for a full attack. Some of them, armed with rifles, a number of which may well have been taken from fallen British soldiers at Isandlwana, climbed up the slopes to begin an enthusiastic but largely inaccurate assault against the mission station; they were only 300 yards away and it was inevitable that some shots would hit home from this range.

By around 6 p.m. the daylight had begun to fade. Night comes quickly here and it would have been dark shortly afterwards. However, there would be no reduction in the level of hostilities. Dabulamanzi instructed his men to launch simultaneous attacks against the north and south walls, putting immense pressure on the British lines. The redcoats fired back, Dalton in particular being noted for the accuracy of his shooting. He moved up and down the walls encouraging the other men around him to stay cool.

The Zulus attempted to grab hold of rifle muzzles when they appeared over the walls. Then a shot rang out and went right through Dalton's shoulder. The commissary officer calmly handled his rifle to Chard before collapsing. Surgeon Reynolds rushed to his aid and dressed the wound. Within minutes, a patched-up Dalton was back in the fight.

In the meantime, Reynolds, in addition to his surgical duties, regularly took supplies of ammunition up to the hospital. One of his patients, Corporal Schiess, had put himself in the front line. His medical problems were minor (huge blisters) but they did hamper his mobility. Irritated beyond measure by a group of Zulus who had deposited themselves at the base of the mealie-bag wall, he climbed up on top of the parapet to fire downwards. As he did so he found himself face to face with the muzzle of an enemy firearm.

Incredibly the bullet missed and went straight through his hat. Schiess bayoneted the warrior, shot a second and bayoneted a third. But despite such gallantry the defenders were increasingly stretched. Now and again a Zulu sniper would bring down one of the small number of British soldiers and the intensity of the attacks threatened to overwhelm the defence. Some Zulus nearly succeeded in breaking over the south wall. In a brief lull, Chard and Bromhead conferred. They were in danger of losing the battle and no one doubted what that would mean.

The only option they felt they had was to retreat behind the inner barrier that had been erected at the last minute. This they quickly did but it created further problems. It meant that those left in the hospital – twenty-four bedridden patients and six able-bodied men – would have to look after themselves. The Zulus were quick to take advantage and seized the abandoned positions. From their new location, Chard, Bromhead and their men tried to keep the Zulus away from the hospital but it was very difficult to do so.

The Zulus were elated as they saw the defenders abandon their first line of defence and surged forward against the exposed hospital. They hacked at the doors to the rooms with their broad-bladed assegais. Those inside realised it was only a matter of time before the doors gave way. They were now on their own if they wished to survive. Their situation was about to deteriorate still further. Zulu warriors threw brands of fire on to the straw roof. It was damp because of the recent heavy rains but it did not take long before the roof was smouldering and acrid smoke started to fill the claustrophobic rooms inside the hospital.

Privates Hook and Cole were defending one of the corner rooms. With the pressure building up to an unbearable level, Cole's nerves failed him. The oppressive and suffocating atmosphere was too much. He opened the door, rushed out into the throng of Zulus outside and was at once speared to death. Another man, Private Beckett, also ran out. He was speared and badly wounded but managed to break through into the scrub around the hospital. However, although he managed to crawl away in the night, he was found dying of his wounds the next morning.

Hook was now in the room on his own. Using his bayonet as a makeshift pick, he managed to dig a hole through the thin plaster walls into the next room, where he found three more defenders. Whilst Hook kept guard over the hole he had made, his new roommates, copying his example, began to dig another hole into the room next to them. The fighting in this confined space was desperate. At one stage Hook was struck in the helmet with an assegai. It took the sting out of the spear-strike but still left him with a nasty scar on his head.

As a final escape route to the outside world was being devised, Hook was busier than ever. Scores of Zulus were in the building now. Each one who tried to enter the room that Hook was in through the hole he had made was bayoneted. The body of the slain warrior would be pulled out and the process would be repeated again and again.

The way to freedom was a window, high up in the wall. It was too small for a man to get through so the frame was smashed out. The escapees would have to jump from the window and dash, as well as hospitalised patients could, across 40 yards of open ground to the British lines. If they stayed where they were, only death awaited. Bitter hand-to-hand fighting raged throughout the confused interior of the hospital now, as British soldiers shot Zulus at point-blank range whilst assegais probed in the smoky blackness trying to strike down a foe.

To compound the difficulties of the patients in the hospital, the Zulus were close to the window on the outside of the building. Chard, seeing the danger the escapees were in, asked for volunteers to help them across. Private Hitch and Corporal Allen both offered to do so, despite the fact that both were already wounded. Hitch had been shot through the shoulder by a Zulu at close range; he later had thirty-nine pieces of broken bone removed from the wound. Now he and Allen made their way across the open ground, their way aided by covering fire from the British soldiers manning the parapets.

Some armchair commentators, from the safety of their cosy clubs and homes, suggested even at the time that the heroism of those at Rorke's Drift was overplayed and that the men had no option but to fight. This view is not only patronising, it is also plain wrong. Men like Hook, Hitch and Allen could easily have abandoned their comrades to their fate but made conscious decisions not to do so, endangering themselves in the process. This was indeed a heroic action.

Despite their bravery, one wounded patient, Trooper Hunter of the Natal Mounted Police, was killed as he crawled on all fours across the open ground. Hunter had been dazed and unsure of which direction he should move in. His hesitation proved fatal. Seeing this happen, the defenders on the parapets were so incensed a shattering volley ripped out from their lines, in turn killing the Zulu who had slain him.

The flames were now taking hold of the hospital after two hours of heavy and terrifying fighting. Sergeant Maxfield, delirious in his bed, had had to be abandoned and his fleeing companions could only watch in horror as he was speared to death where he lay. Private Adams was another who stayed where he was and therefore died. Of the other patients who were left to a terrible fate, one of them was a wounded native whose body was later found in the burned-out wreck of the hospital.

Some were luckier. Gunner Howard was still inside when the roof partially collapsed. In the confusion that immediately followed he managed to dash outside into the darkness where he safely found cover. One man, Private Waters, hid himself in a wardrobe. He was not found by the Zulus and managed to sneak out in the darkness, hidden underneath one of Rev. Witt's coats which he had taken with him, to be rescued the next morning. Life and death relied now more than anything on plain old-fashioned luck.

Fred Hitch did what he could to help the would-be escapees but the effect of his wounds now became overwhelming. Tired and thirsty, he collapsed. Before lapsing into unconsciousness, one of his comrades asked him if he should save a bullet for him if the mission station was overwhelmed. Hitch declined the offer, reasoning that a Zulu assegai might as well finish him off.

Chard later regretted that the men in the hospital had not taken earlier action to open a communication channel inside the building; he said that he had instructed them to do so at the outset but in the heat of battle this had not been done. He also regretted that the four engineers he had taken up to Isandlwana earlier on were not still around, as they would have been most useful.

Chard, Bromhead and their men now had nowhere else to go. After fighting for hours they were tired and thirsty. The Martini-Henrys became hot after extended use and men rapped rags, gleaned from anywhere including ripped-off pieces of their uniforms, around the barrels. The rifle had a kick too and after a time shoulders became bruised and sore. There were accounts from the morning after the battle of soldiers holding the rifles away from their bodies before firing them. In close-quarter actions such as this, there was little need to take aim. In order to relieve the discomfort, men would change the shoulder they used for firing from time to time.

But it was not only the British soldiers who had problems. Dabulamanzi had taken a chance by launching an attack against a prepared position and Cetshwayo would not be happy that he had done so. To call off the fight with so many lives lost and the mission station untaken would be a bitter pill to swallow. Therefore, despite the serious losses his army had already sustained, he could not contemplate withdrawal. He was trapped by his own plan and could not give up the fight without a massive loss of face.

His men were tired and thirsty too. They had suffered heavy losses and setting the hospital ablaze had only worsened their situation. The blazing building illuminated them as they attacked during the hours of darkness, making them perfect targets. Despite this, Dabulamanzi now ordered that the roof of the storehouse (the converted church) be set ablaze too.

Chard realised what he was planning. To counteract the move he planned to utilise some mealie bags that had not yet been used. He gave orders to Assistant Commissary Walter Dunne to supervise the building of a massive redoubt. Dunne was another who played a hero's role, directing his men as they built it, exposed to enemy fire all the time but miraculously avoiding being hit.

At some stage in the battle, one of the sentries swore that he could see redcoats in the distance. Even the Zulus, perhaps unnerved by the evident change in mood, stopped fighting for a while. But no one came and after a while the fighting resumed. The sentry, nevertheless, had not been hallucinating. Major Spalding had been close to Helpmekaar at around 3.30 p.m. when the reason for his mission was suddenly made null and void by the sight of the two companies he was looking for marching towards him. Spalding, relieved, turned round and led them towards Rorke's Drift. On his way down the steep road, he had bumped into the fugitives from the mission station who had told him of both the disaster that had befallen the column at Isandlwana and also the then imminent attack on his post.

Spalding, alarmed at this news, rode on ahead. From a vantage point in the hills he could see the flames rising from Rorke's Drift. Then a large group of Zulu warriors appeared not far in front of him and started to array themselves in their traditional battle formation. Spalding was isolated, accompanied only by a Mr Dickson from the Buffalo Border Guard. They turned their horses around and raced back towards the troops, about a mile behind them.

When he safely arrived back, Spalding was told that Zulu scouting parties had been seen in the hills above. He decided to retreat back to Helpmekaar. This made perfect sense in the light of the information that was then available. The British army had already suffered a massive defeat and now there was every reason to believe, given the smoke from Rorke's Drift, that his own much smaller command had suffered the same fate. He led his men back to help with the defence of Helpmekaar. Unknown to him of course, he had just missed another chance of glory.

This must have happened before sundown, some hours before. Spalding had probably been within 2 miles of Rorke's Drift but it had become clear to the defenders that they were still on their own. The Zulus continued to attack the storehouse. Corporal Francis Attwood of the Army Service Corps did sterling service shooting every Zulu who tried to set fire to the roof. But the British were still being forced back, yard by yard. They had, up until now, held a walled cattle enclosure at the far end of the storehouse but they were forced to abandon it.

The redoubt, however, was completed. It was a formidable position. It had elevated steps which would give the British soldiers an excellent raised field of fire against the Zulus. There was only one narrow entrance to the impromptu fort so access for the enemy would be extremely difficult. Several well-aimed volleys spewed out from this new position and took a heavy toll on the Zulus. They had themselves fought bravely for hours against a tenacious enemy and their morale was starting to suffer.

By midnight the intensity and frequency of the attacks was beginning to diminish. As they did, so the British got bolder – born of desperate thirst. Chard could see the water cart he had ordered to be brought up from the river, from what must have seemed like a lifetime ago, and led a small party in a dash over open ground to bring it across to the walls. The plan worked. Although the water cart could not, of course, be lifted over the walls, a makeshift hose was used to bring water inside the parapets, much to the relief of the dry-throated defenders.

The night ebbed away and the British woke, bleary-eyed, from what must have seemed like a nightmare to a new dawn. Daylight brought with it a stunning and wonderful discovery: the Zulus had gone. After a while, Chard cautiously sent out a scouting party to eliminate any Zulu snipers and kill any of the enemy who were wounded – Chelmsford's instructions not to do so now suddenly forgotten.

One man had had an amazing escape. Chard's wagon driver, a native from the Cape Colony, had hidden away in a cave in the Oskarberg when the attack started. Before long he had company: Zulu snipers firing down on the mission station. He even saw one sniper being shot dead by a well-aimed response from down below. Despite having snipers in the cave for several hours, no one noticed him.

Waters too, the hospital patient who had hidden in the wardrobe for a while before rushing out into the night when it got dark, also had an amazing escape. He had tried to make his way back into the mission station but instead found himself close to a party of Zulus. He had blacked himself up and incredibly had not been noticed. In the morning, he made himself known to the British when the Zulus had started to leave. He came within an inch of losing his life as a result. Seeing his black face, one of the defenders was about to shoot. Just in time, Waters shouted out and told him who he was.

It was now time to tidy up. As the defenders of Rorke's Drift walked around the post to confirm the results of their night's work, they found the bodies of 351 dead Zulus. Of the 139 British and colonial troops at the mission station, fifteen were dead and another two would die of their wounds. A further ten had been wounded. Yet these losses were low when compared to what might have happened. The relative lightness of the casualty list (which included several men killed in the hospital because they were too infirm to escape) in many ways justified Chelmsford's initial belief that the Zulu army should prove no match for his own men if the latter were in a prepared position.

The soldiers put themselves to the job of clearing up the mess, burying the dead and reflecting on a miraculous escape. There was still the odd enemy in the vicinity. One Zulu had hidden himself away and fired on the British soldiers as they got close. Then, shouting insults, he ran off. The men fired at him but missed. Chard, with good grace, reported that 'I am glad to say the plucky fellow got off'.[11]

The British patrols looked at the Zulu dead with a mixture of horror and fascination. Many of them wore head-rings – the sign of a married man in Zulu society. This showed they were men of middle age, in line with the regiments who had fought at Rorke's Drift. Some of the bullet wounds were gruesome, one man looking as if his head had been split open with an axe. Despite the fact that the battle seemed to be over, there were still risks. One of the defenders, Trooper Lugg, was suddenly attacked by a warrior who was hidden away. The Zulu tried to shoot him with a musket but the gun misfired and Lugg managed to kill him with a hunting knife.

Hook was also out patrolling. He was walking down a little stream near the drift when he saw a Zulu, apparently dead but strangely bleeding from the leg. This did not make sense to Hook but yet did not stop him carrying on past the 'corpse'. As he moved past the warrior, suddenly his rifle butt was seized. Hook managed to pull the butt away and then brought it crashing down on the head of his attacker. Hook subsequently finished him off.

At about 7 a.m. there was a shock when suddenly the Zulus reappeared in the hills. They did not stay for long, sitting down and taking snuff at a safe distance. Then they got up and left, heading for the drift and the relative safety of Zululand. The battle for Rorke's Drift was over. It had not been one long action but a series of rushes, frantic hand-to-hand fighting followed by brief lulls, over a period of twelve hours. But against huge numerical odds, Chard's gallant force had survived.

In terms of the strategic direction of the war, Rorke's Drift changed nothing; from this perspective the battle was famous but irrelevant. Yet paradoxically, in its own way, it was vital. Its major impact was on morale, both of the army and, perhaps even more importantly, of the British people. No war can be fought without the political will to wage it. Now a legend had been created, one that would have a crucial effect. The British public reacted enthusiastically to another epic in the annals of Victorian military history to put alongside incidents such as the Thin Red Line at the Battle of Balaclava and the Relief of Lucknow in the Indian Mutiny. Lord Chelmsford too was to quickly see that the battle would give him an opportunity to save his own political skin.

Over time, of course, the legends have grown stronger. The movie version of *Zulu* did more than most to strengthen them. There was the legend of the brandy-swilling Private Hook as one example. Ironically, he was a teetotaller for fifteen years before the battle, a paid-up member of the League of Victorian Virtue, part of the abstinence movement. Nevertheless, on the morning after the battle he stood in line for a tot of rum, explaining to the surprised orderly serving it that he felt such a special occasion demanded it. But this was an exception to his general rule. Hook was, in fact, highly regarded and soon after the battle became 'batman' to Major Black of the 2nd/24th.[12]

The power of legend was quickly recognised as a potent weapon by none other than Lord Chelmsford. He needed to salvage something from what had been for him a disastrous start to the campaign and he would soon come to see

Rorke's Drift as a saving grace. But not straightaway, for he needed to recover his nerve.

The night before, 22 January 1879, had been the longest of his life. As he marched his tired army back across the plain towards the camp they had left in such high spirits just twelve hours before, Chelmsford reflected on how a body of soldiers over 1,000 strong, including hundreds of trained imperial soldiers, had been bested by a native impi. His invasion plans were in tatters and he would have to go back to the drawing board.

Of course, that was if he and the rest of the column survived. He had no idea whether or not the Zulu army was now going to attack him. If they did then it would be a desperate fight, particularly as there were no reserves of ammunition to call on, having decided to leave them at the camp. Chelmsford, all energy, prided himself on his ability to make a snap decision and stick with it. Being a decisive decision-maker of course had its merits. However, it helped no end if those snap decisions subsequently turned out to be right.

Once it was clear that the camp had fallen on that previous afternoon, Chelmsford had turned the surviving part of the column quickly around towards it. The regular infantry, despite their tiredness, set off at a breakneck speed, so much so that the Natal Native Contingent had to trot to keep up. A scouting party went ahead, led by Captain Scott of the Carbineers, and reported large numbers of Zulus in the camp. As Chelmsford's men got closer, many could be seen moving away, some manoeuvring wagons into the hills. Then the tents started to disappear too, their material cut up for use by the Zulus.

The Imperial Mounted Infantry naturally got close to the camp quicker than the infantry did. They reported back that the camp was in the total possession of the Zulus, 'who were like bees in the camp, and all along the plains and the foothills, and on the hills, they were swarming'.[13] Major Clery, close at hand, watched on as Chelmsford took it all in, stony-faced, gloomy but determined. The commander-in-chief gave a short speech, telling it how it was, warts and all, but explaining that there was no option but to fight their way into the camp. He told them that they would have to 'fight for their lives'.

About 2 miles away from the camp, four shapes were seen in the gloom. Mounted troops were sent to investigate and the shapes disappeared behind a rock. They were fired at. One was hit and the others were taken prisoner, running out into the open with their hands above their heads. It was only then discovered that they were NNC survivors from the battle who had hidden themselves away until the British returned.

The sun was starting to dip below the hills now. The column, or at least its remnants, marched determinedly towards the wreckage of the camp, guns in the centre, ready to pound the enemy. As they reached a point about half a mile from the tents, they began to stumble over Zulu dead. Horses reared, refusing to step over the corpses, which had to be pulled out of the way by the gunners so that their mounts would move on.

Those there thought they could see barricades across the road back to Rorke's Drift made of captured British wagons. They also thought they could hear the sounds of Zulus hitting their shields with their assegais. It appeared that they would have to fight their way back in and in their current position there was no guarantee of success.

Major Wilsone Black of the 2nd/24th was given the unenviable task of leading his men up a hill near the camp. In the darkness, it might have been tantamount to a suicide mission but Black was grimly determined to do his bit. His commands were to the point and indicative of someone not in the mood for any compromise: 'no firing boys, give them the cold steel'. As the main force moved towards the unmistakable peak they had left in such high spirits just that morning, 'the grotesque and large shadow of Isandlwana' at last could be glimpsed through the gloom.[14]

Hamilton-Browne was towards the fore with the NNC. Behind them, British regulars marched with bayonets fixed, not just to take on any Zulus who were left, but also to stop the NNC from running away. From a distance of about 600 yards, twenty rounds were loosed into the camp by the artillery. Then four companies of the 2nd/24th stormed forward, bayonets levelled, ready to avenge their fallen comrades. But there were few left on whom to avenge themselves. The Zulus had gone. The camp, or what was left of it, was back in British hands. The deep *dongas*, however, were hard to spot in the dark and many men tumbled into them. An army stumbling around in the dark was an apt metaphor for what had happened.

About half a dozen Zulus, drunk on looted liquor, were found staggering around. They were immediately bayoneted. This was a symbolic moment, when Chelmsford's chivalrous best intentions went out of the window. From now on there would be few prisoners. Chelmsford patrolled the perimeter of the camp, once re-established, paternally, making sure that sentries were posted in abundance. Only once did he lose his rag, berating a Native Contingent NCO for not knowing where his men were, only to humbly apologise to him soon afterwards.

There was no moon that night and it was very dark, which was just as well for the horrors of what might otherwise have been seen would have haunted a man for the rest of his days. Men woke up after a fitful sleep to find they had literally been lying in blood. Some also remembered the smell; one who was there described it as being like the aroma of sweet potatoes that had gone off. Lieutenant Harford noticed a strong smell too and thought it was the smashed-up contents of a Royal Army Medical Corps wagon.[15] Most of all, there was the stench of death which registered itself permanently on the senses of all who experienced the nightmare. It was a scene of dreadful proportions, the most gruesome bivouac perhaps ever endured by a British army. One man there, Sergeant Warren of the Artillery, noted that 'you could not move a foot either way without treading on dead bodies'.[16]

Strangely there were others many miles off who thought that something was wrong. Colonel Wood reckoned he was about 50 miles away from Isandlwana that night but, after night had fallen, he and his staff heard the far-off sound of guns. When some of his officers asked his opinion of what it suggested, his response was: 'guns after dark indicated, I apprehended, an unfavourable situation.'[17]

It was a terrible night for those who lived through it at Isandlwana. Captain Hallam Parr was one such. He believed that the Zulus were only waiting for the onset of dawn, their favourite time for an attack, to come and finish them off. The night started off pitch black but at about 1 a.m. the clouds cleared and a brilliant array of stars patchily lit up the field of death. Parr dozed, like many of his comrades no doubt, but fitfully. From time to time he heard the quiet voices of men nearby talking, unable to sleep, afraid of the dawn. All around in the hills Zulu campfires burned through the gloom, adding to the horror and terror of it all.

Understandably, this terrible reverse cast a huge shadow over the survivors. One of them, Private Francis Ward of the 2nd/24th, much regretted his decision to join up. Ward had been under the influence of drink when he enlisted. Now, on the field of death, he must have been particularly haunted by the error of his ways. On his safe return to Natal he wrote to his aunt telling her that a good friend from his village back in Wales, Tom Jones, 'Aunt Betsy's son', was dead. Bemoaning the 'terrible calamity' that had befallen the column, he ended with the pensive words: 'I wish I had listened to your advice and give up the drink. I would not be where I am at present ...'[18]

During the night there was an alarm. Such alarms were a regular feature of the war but, given the circumstances, this one must have been especially terrifying. There was, Parr noted, 'a rush of naked feet and the rattle of assegais and shields, and the clatter of accoutrements and rifles of the men in the ranks as they rose from the ground and then a confused volley'.[19] It was, fortunately for Parr and his companions, a false alarm. Some of the native levies had heard a noise near the camp and, panicking, had rushed back towards the regulars. It was their 'naked feet' that could be heard. Chelmsford deputed some men of the 24th to keep watch over the NNC for the rest of the night with orders to bayonet any man who tried to run off.

Chelmsford wisely decided to depart with the men long before dawn so the terrors of the massacre might be hidden from them. Parr was given the task of handing out the limited rations that were left to help the ragtag column make it back to Natal. In the distance a fire was seen lighting the sky above Rorke's Drift. Chelmsford decided to preserve his remaining ammunition supplies in case a fight was necessary to get back across the river. However, if he had looked around the camp he would have found plenty of provisions left; the Zulus had seemingly not been very efficient in their looting. Hamilton-Browne, for one, did so and managed to stock up with bully beef from remaining provisions. He also managed to obtain a bottle of port and brandy, which were much appreciated given the situation.

He looked around the camp to see whether any of his personal possessions were still there. The sight that met him would live with him for the rest of his days. Slaughtered men were everywhere but everything else appeared to have died with them. Mules were slain in their harnesses, oxen in their spans; dogs had been butchered amongst the tents. The dead soldiers were often in small knots, some of them back-to-back, evidence of a determined but doomed last stand played out dozens of times. Dead Zulus lay scattered liberally amongst them too, as often as not bayoneted rather than shot. This was an ancient form of warfare, brutal and almost primeval in its intensity.

Just inside the door of his tent, Hamilton-Browne found his old white setter dog, slain like the rest. Next to the tent his two horses had been butchered along with his groom. As the sun started to illuminate the scene, he could see further ahead and noted large numbers of dead in front of the camp, both British/colonial and Zulu. Despite the carnage they had caused, he felt a sneaking admiration for an enemy who had come on through a hailstorm of bullets, regardless of their heavy losses.

He heard the bugle sound the advance and prepared himself to leave. As he rode towards the remnants of the column, he pulled his horse up sharp. He had stumbled across the body of Colonel Pulleine. There was no time or means to do anything for him, so Hamilton-Browne gave him one last salute and then rode off.[20] He was not a moment too soon; by the time he arrived back at the column most of it was already starting to move off.

Others too saw ghastly sights when they looked around the camp. Harford found that nothing remained of his possessions but between his tent and that of Lonsdale, who had been placed next to him, were the bodies of two disembowelled and mutilated artillerymen. He also came across two dead drivers with their faces blackened as if they had been trying to disguise themselves in a vain effort to escape.[21]

Some men ransacked what was left in the camp in an attempt to assuage their growing hunger pangs. Harford was intensely annoyed that Lieutenant Newnham Davis, part of the IMI, helped himself to a 2lb tin of bully beef and scoffed the lot without a thought of sharing it with anyone else.

As they moved away from this scene of carnage, the retreating army passed close to a Zulu house, previously deserted but now with a number of men and women inside. Milne, who generally seemed by nature a mild-mannered man, thought to himself that they must have been involved in the fight and that it was a shame there was not time to stop and kill them all. Revenge was at the top of most men's agendas.

The march was not long into its stride across broken and hilly ground when a large group of Zulu warriors appeared. However, they did not seem in the mood for a fight. Only one Zulu tried to egg his comrades on to the attack and then, failing to do so, charged the British lines single-handedly. A ragged volley rang out and he fell dead. Mansel was bringing up the rear with his Mounted Police when a body of about 2,000 Zulus suddenly appeared about 300 yards away. There were tense moments as the two forces faced up to each other but neither side wanted another fight. There would be no other corpses added to the abattoir of Isandlwana.

The hearts of the men retreating in ignominy after just a few days campaigning were heavy, their thoughts full of memories of those they had lost and their fears prey to the terrible sights they had seen. Amongst it all, they felt something else too for their enemy: horror, hatred even in many cases, but also a grudging admiration. As one staff officer later noted: 'in the future the Zulu army will command the amount of precaution and respect which is necessary before it can be conquered.' It was a pity from the British perspective that they had had to lose hundreds of their comrades to find these truths out.[22]

The situation in Helpmekaar had also been fraught during the night of 22 January. The pitiful handful of men that had survived the wreckage of the camp at Isandlwana had largely headed here. Captain Essex had been the senior officer in Helpmekaar and he had taken charge. But with Spalding and the two columns on their way to Rorke's Drift, he would be hard pressed to call the small force he was notionally in command of an army. At one stage, he had just twenty-eight guns to call on, including some local farmers who had made their way in for protection.

Helpmekaar had always been a small, insignificant hamlet. For a few weeks it had been transformed into a bustling way-station through which supplies and men were shipped to the front. Now it had reverted to type, a minor, exposed settlement perched high up in the hills. There were, in fact, just a few tin shacks there and Essex improvised a defensive position around these as best he could. A laager was made using the three wagons available interspersed with sacks of mealie bags – another Rorke's Drift. Again he did not start from scratch as there is strong evidence that Helpmekaar had been at least partly fortified some time before.[23]

He also had another problem. A few mounted colonial officers and soldiers had turned up but they did not stay for long. Their horses gave them the chance to flee for their lives, which several of them did. To encourage the others to stay, so to speak, Essex deprived them of their steeds. Amongst those who fled from Helpmekaar were two men whose conduct was already suspect. Lieutenant Higginson had been with Coghill and Melvill when they had got free of the Buffalo River. He had found a horse for himself but never went back to see if the two men he had left needed help.

The other was Captain William Stephenson whose men of the Natal Native Contingent had fled pell-mell from Rorke's Drift. Stephenson would suffer the dubious 'honour' of being named as a deserter by none other than Lieutenant Chard in both his official report and, later, his more detailed account for Queen Victoria. After this double desertion at Helpmekaar, he was dishonourably discharged from the service.

At about 9 p.m. Major Spalding returned with his two companies of the 24th. This bucked up spirits somewhat but it was still a terrifying night. Whilst it might be better to face up to the Zulus with two companies rather than twenty-eight men, everyone was very conscious that six companies had been wiped out earlier that day. Zulus had already been spotted above the road on the way up to Helpmekaar and the small force defending it was full of anxiety about their own fate. But as the next day broke, a foggy morning at Helpmekaar, there was not a Zulu in sight.

By dawn the feared Zulu onslaught had not materialised, not at Rorke's Drift, not at Isandlwana nor at Helpmekaar. Chelmsford moved back across the river he had crossed with such high hopes just twelve days before. It was about 8 a.m. when Chard saw Chelmsford's column approaching. It was a relief in more ways than one for he now knew that at least the column had not been completely destroyed. At first he was not sure it was the column he could see for most of them appeared to have black faces and he feared that those wearing red jackets could be Zulus who had pulled them off slaughtered British soldiers. But it at last became clear that these were indeed British soldiers along with many native levies.

A white flag was improvised to let the column know that the mission station was still in friendly hands. Mounted troops galloped ahead of the column and reached the beleaguered garrison to many hearty cheers. Chelmsford arrived soon after and emotionally thanked the men for their defence. The emotion was two-edged. He may have hoped to find more survivors from the camp at the drift but it was now obvious that this hope was in vain. Other parts of Chelmsford's surviving force moved in, to be greeted by the welcome sight of commissariat officers Dunne and Dalton doling out generous rations of biscuits to the famished soldiers.

Chard washed his face in a muddy puddle and a soldier, Private Bush, his face covered in blood, gave him a dirty towel with which to wipe it. Chard accepted it with gratitude. How important after all were the stains of mud and dirt after surviving all this? Bush had been shot in the nose by a bullet that had also killed

Private Cole. Chard and Bromhead sat down exhausted. Someone had found an intact bottle of beer in a wagon. The two officers who had fought so gallantly happily shared it, an unbreakable bond now formed between them.

Much has been made of the heroism of the British soldiers, but the Zulus too fought magnificently and many of them made the ultimate sacrifice in the defence of their land and their way of life. Across Zululand, the bereaved would mourn the dead. Amazingly, a white man, Cornelius Vijn, a trader, was still in Zululand and witnessed such scenes.[24] He told of people wailing, rolling across the ground and never quietening down. The mourning lasted for a fortnight. The most poignant comment came from Cetshwayo himself. When the remnants of the Tulwana Regiment returned to Ulundi and paraded before him, he asked 'why don't the rest come in?'[25] An assegai, he said, had been thrust into the heart of Zululand.

For a Zulu involved in the battles at Isandlwana and Rorke's Drift, the prospects of survival were not encouraging; of the 25,000 Zulus involved in both perhaps 10 per cent were now dead. To be anything other than slightly wounded also equated to a death sentence. A man, if he were lucky, might drag himself off home, there to die a long, painful death with nothing save native medicines to help him survive. More often he would be finished off by his own comrades or, if not them, by British and NNC patrols. At Rorke's Drift about fifty bloodstained shields had been found down by the river; possibly they had been used as makeshift stretchers for Zulus to drag wounded comrades down to the waters and then give them the relatively merciful release of a death by drowning.

For the British, Rorke's Drift had been an epic, yet even at the time some mean-spirited individuals downplayed the heroism of the defenders. Chard and Bromhead particularly aroused envy in some of their fellow officers. Major Clery, that irascible counterpart to the noxious Crealock, noted that both Bromhead and Chard were of what he called a very dull class, altogether uninteresting. He still seemed to rate flair, however misguided and disastrous, above organisation and calmness under fire.

Perhaps here too was another insight into the flaws of the British command in southern Africa. Qualities such as stoicism and organisation seemed commonplace when compared to flair and dynamism. The model of Gilbert and Sullivan's British major-general (literally, as it happened) was Sir Garnet Wolseley: flamboyant, outspoken, hard to ignore, and soon to be back in Zululand. In some ways Chelmsford was of his ilk too. He lacked his strategic brilliance for sure and he had more of a common touch with the ordinary soldier about him, but Chelmsford was all energy and action.

The problem was that these qualities were not always connected to a rational thought process. What did Chelmsford do when he heard at two o'clock in the morning that the Zulus were 10 miles away from the camp at Isandlwana? He marched his way towards them, leaving all his spare ammunition behind and no clear orders for how the camp was to be defended when he had gone. In contrast, Chard, Bromhead and Dalton had used the short space of time they had to engineer a strong defensive position with the raw materials at hand.

The command at Rorke's Drift had displayed dogged determination at the mission station, allied to a good deal of commonsense and organisational skill. Chelmsford, on the other hand, had displayed huge reserves of energy that some might have mistaken for flair. The end result was that most of the defenders at Rorke's Drift had survived whilst half of Chelmsford's column had been wiped out. Chard, Bromhead and Dalton might not have displayed the characteristics of a stereotypical hero, but it does not take a great deal of thought to conclude whose men were served best.

The personal heroism of these men should not be understated. Bromhead was one of seven men who took part in a hand-to-hand defence of a particularly exposed part of the line. Of the six with him, two were killed and four wounded, he alone escaping unscathed. This was no picnic for Bromhead. At one stage he was nearly stabbed in the back by a Zulu assegai and was only saved by the quick thinking of Fred Hitch, who made to shoot at the assailant with what was in fact an empty rifle. Not knowing this, the Zulu had quickly jumped out of the laager.

Of the fight at Rorke's Drift itself, Clery noted that 'as a matter of fact they all stayed there for there was nowhere else to go'.[26] Whilst it was undoubtedly true that the only option they really had was to fight where they were, and Clery did at least have the grace to accept that the common soldiers had fought with great determination, by downplaying the credit to both Bromhead and Chard and the efforts of their men Clery had shown himself up in a poor light.

That said, it is worth considering, without in any way underestimating their achievement, whether or not the odds were really stacked against the defenders at Rorke's Drift. In terms of absolute numbers, there was no question, but consider the wider facts. Seventeen men died or were mortally wounded on the British side during the battle. Of these, eight were from the hospital, dreadfully exposed once hundreds of potential defenders had fled just as battle was about to commence. One fatality was shot by his own side whilst running off. Of the remaining eight some died of gunshot wounds.

Of the wounded, only a handful were injured by an assegai and most of them not seriously (though Private Beckett is an exception as he was mortally wounded). In other words, the deaths or injuries caused by close-quarter action were small which suggests just how great the technological advantage enjoyed by the British army against their enemy was. It was not just the rifles that gave the British an advantage either; Hitch for one noted how the Zulus seemed to be unwilling to come to grips with a soldier armed with a bayonet.[27] This being the case, the triumph at Rorke's Drift was not so much a glorious victory against the odds but rather served as a demonstration of how pointless and avoidable the British catastrophe at Isandlwana had been.

But that is easy to say from a safe distance. Those in command at the drift – Chard, Bromhead and the largely unsung Dalton – had performed magnificently under immense pressure. Just because the men had no option but to fight did not mean there was a guarantee that they would fight well or intelligently. They had all done their part, coolly and unflappably. Further, it was an epic that others, particularly the commander-in-chief, smelt a whiff of redemption in. Not only had the defenders of Rorke's Drift saved themselves, they might also have helped to save Lord Chelmsford too.

1 Fort Pearson, overlooking the Thukela River (all pictures taken from editions of the *Illustrated London News* published between November 1878 and November 1879).

2 The *Dublin Castle*, a troopship used to ferry reinforcements to the war.

3 An imposing-looking King Cetshwayo.

4 Lieutenant-General Lord Chelmsford, commander-in-chief of the British forces.

5 A wagon-train making laborious progress towards the front.

6 Reinforcements set out for southern Africa.

7 Mounted volunteers from Natal prepare to set out for war.

8 *Right*: Lieutenant John Chard.

9 *Left*: Dabulamanzi, the half-brother of King Cetshwayo, who led the fateful attack on Rorke's Drift.

10 *Right*: Lieutenant Gonville Bromhead, the hero of Rorke's Drift.

11 Lieutenant Neville Coghill, killed during the retreat from Isandlwana.

12 Lieutenant Teignmouth Melvill, killed at Isandlwana and later awarded the Victoria Cross.

13 The grave of Melvill and Coghill close to Rorke's Drift.

14 Cetshwayo's cooks at work.

15 Collecting the hut tax from natives resident in the British colonies.

16 A humorous contemporary sketch showing the reaction of the untrained ear to the music of bagpipes.

17 The naval contingent prepares to repel the Zulu army at Gingindhlovu.

18 *Below*: The rough sea conditions at Port Durnford caused Sir Garnet Wolseley no end of trouble when he tried to land.

19 Lieutenant-Colonel Durnford, killed at
Isandlwana and afterwards a potential scapegoat
for the disaster that befell the British army.

20 The British army, including the Naval Brigade,
march to the relief of Eshowe.

21 The 91st Regiment leaves Durban for the front.

22 Sketches of the
mission station at Eshowe.

23 *Below:* The inside of
the uncomfortable fort at
Helpmekaar.

24 The British army encamped as it moves in Zululand.

25 A Gatling gun being prepared for practice at Fort Pearson – this was the first time that a form of machine gun had been used by the British army in battle.

26 Another disaster for the British: the daring Zulu attack on the Ntombe.

27 William Beresford's dramatic encounter with a Zulu near Ulundi.

28 Zulus attacking a laager during the Anglo-Zulu War.

29 The death of Lieutenant
Frith on the march to Ulundi.

30 Lieutenant Chard receiving
his VC.

31 The small homestead in Zululand where the great-nephew of Napoleon Bonaparte met his end.

32 The body of the Prince Imperial being carried on a gun-carriage in Zululand.

33 Ambassadors from Cetshwayo vainly try to sue for peace.

34 Archibald Forbes rides post-haste from Ulundi with news of the decisive British victory there.

35 Ulundi goes up in flames as the British exact retribution.

six

UNDER SIEGE

The March to Eshowe

The epic events at Isandlwana and Rorke's Drift overshadowed another significant battle fought some 60 miles to the east at approximately the same time. Chelmsford's grand strategy called for three offensive columns and, whilst that under Wood in the west of Zululand was to be given something approaching a free hand, the column that was to march up from the mouth of the Thukela was integrally linked to the progress of the Central Column.

Colonel Charles Pearson was to march his men up the coast to an old mission station at Eshowe and set up an advanced base there. Eshowe had been abandoned by the missionaries, to whom it had been home until a couple of years previously. The missionaries in Zululand had been concentrated in this part of the country. One of their local converts had then been murdered and, although Cetshwayo disclaimed all knowledge of the act, relations were strained. With the missionaries now gone, no one was even sure how much of the mission station was left.

Pearson, on arrival at Eshowe, was to wait until Durnford, in conjunction with the Central Column, had marched into Zululand, with Wood pushing his way over from the far west. The only problem with the plan was that within a few days of it being put into action Durnford was dead, along with over a thousand others from the British forces.

The fatal weakness with this strategy, as would soon become apparent, was that it relied on everything going to plan for all the columns. If something was to go amiss with the progress of the Central Column in particular then Pearson would be badly exposed in enemy territory. But everyone assumed that everything would work out as planned and so there was absolutely nothing to worry about. This proved to be a short-lived hope which did not long survive 22 January. Such has been the fate of many a master plan over the ages.

Pearson, in command of Number 1 Column, was well known to many of the soldiers he led. Until the outbreak of the war he had been in command of the 2nd Battalion, 3rd Regiment (known as 'the Buffs'), which was now one of the core elements of the force. He would also have use of the 99th (Duke of Edinburgh's) Regiment, giving him fourteen companies of imperial troops, about 1,460 infantrymen in total.

In addition, he would have the services of two 7-pounders and a rocket battery, a company of Royal Engineers, a Naval Brigade with a further two 7-pounders, two more rocket tubes and a Gatling gun, a squadron of Imperial Mounted Infantry and five mounted volunteer corps. Two battalions of the Natal Native Contingent (over 2,000 men) would also form part of the column. In total, this was over 4,000 men with their horses – a substantial force. This, however, posed its own problems as keeping these men supplied would be a major logistical headache.

The drift at the mouth of the Thukela, the Lower Drift, had been long regarded as a critical strategic position, standing at the gateway to Natal. Several crucial battles had been fought here over the years. Now its importance was emphasised by the construction of a strong defensive position, sycophantically named Fort Pearson. Part of the Naval Brigade was to be stationed there, along with two 7-pounders, a rocket tube and a Gatling gun.

Standing on top of a hill that dominated the drift, being surrounded by ramparts thrown up from the deep ditches dug around it, in location if not architectural design, it looked almost like a medieval castle. On several sides the approach to Fort Pearson was sheer. In summary, it was as close to an impregnable position as one was likely to get when considering the arms available to the Zulus.

Getting across the river would, however, be a challenge. It was both wide and swollen by the heavy rains. There were also other problems arising from its location in what was effectively a sub-tropical zone. A pont needed to be constructed and this was no easy feat. In the process several men fell overboard and were lost. They may have drowned or alternatively they could have been taken by some of the many crocodiles that populated the area.[1]

Fort Pearson was a sound base from which the column could set out, but the route which they planned to follow suggested both how poor British intelligence was and also how badly the enemy were being underestimated by the high command. It would travel through thick bush and scrub along poor roads that would leave the column dangerously extended. This would be ideal for an ambush by the Zulus. There was an alternative route closer to the coast. It would be wrong to say it was easy, but it was certainly less risky. At the time, however, the British command did not think the risk unduly high or it would not have adopted the course it did. That assessment too would change after the catastrophe at Isandlwana.

By the time the ultimatum expired, Pearson's column was still not ready to move. The roads locally had been badly affected by the torrential rains and some of the transport wagons had not yet arrived, nor indeed had some of the men. On 11 January, a group of Zulus had been seen watching things rather too closely from across the river, but a few well-placed shells from Fort Pearson quickly drove them off.

It was on 12 January, the day after the ultimatum expired, that the first British troops crossed the Thukela. A company of the Buffs was first over and secured a crossing point for the rest of the column. Although the crossings started at dawn, it was not until well into the following day that all the men were across. This was just the start. The huge baggage train then needed to be ferried over too. Eventually, late on 16 January, Pearson was ready to march. Five days just to get everything in position spoke eloquently of the logistical challenge that loomed. This was not an army travelling light.

They were being watched as they set off too. Not just by Zulu scouts waiting to see where the column would head, but also by tourists, come to see the army off from places like Durban. It was a surreal sight, made even more so by the presence of two cannon, ready for action, in front of the hotel by the drift.

It is difficult to appreciate quite how significant an undertaking the provisioning of this army was. Wagons in Zululand carried on average about 3,000lb of provisions (on better roads in other regions it would be over twice that). The ox-wagons were 18ft long. Most problematic, though, were the number of beasts pulling them – sixteen were required to pull each wagon. To be able to function properly, an ox needed to spend eight hours a day grazing and eight hours resting, digesting its food. This left a maximum of eight hours to work (and the oxen would certainly need a breather in between times too) and meant that, at most, the column could hope to travel 10 miles in a day.

Once the men had started to cross, Pearson ordered scouting parties to be sent out. One of them journeyed to a nearby abandoned mission station called St Andrews. In doing so, they surprised a small party of Zulus. Two were taken prisoner, one of whom asked the not unreasonable question 'what do you redjackets want?' From another larger body seen shortly afterwards, a further eleven captives were taken. Eight of those taken were subsequently let go, the others being taken to the British camp for questioning.

One of those seized was rather roughly treated. When he was knocked down, he proudly twirled his assailant's moustache and told him that he might have taken him prisoner but – pointing towards the hills as he said so – there were plenty of his comrades waiting for the redcoats. Scouting parties that were sent out later were less successful in taking prisoners. However, a number of Zulus were spotted in the distance and, most noticeably of all, signal fires were being lit on distant hilltops. Pearson was clearly being watched.

Within the camp there were some of the problems of discipline often found at the time amongst the rank-and-file. The 99th Regiment under Lieutenant-Colonel Welman had recently arrived. Barrels of rum had been ferried across the river. One of Welman's NCOs became suspicious at the behaviour of some of the men and sure enough found some soldiers had surreptitiously been helping themselves. Those caught were charged and found guilty. They could have been flogged, a punishment then banned in peacetime but still allowed in times of war. Instead, they were consigned to guard the lines of communication for the duration of the war – a punishment that might have in fact been far more dangerous.

Captain Warren Wynne of the Royal Engineers had recently arrived, leaving England in December 1878 at one day's notice. He proved himself to be a hardworking officer to whom many would owe a great debt ere long had passed. One of his first tasks was to erect a fort for supplies on the Zulu side of the Thukela. It was to be named Fort Tenedos after one of the ships in the area which had supplied a number of men for the Naval Brigade, and it would be surrounded by earthwork ramparts and wire entanglements. HMS *Tenedos* had, in fact, been sailing close offshore for a while but had run aground and had to limp off for repairs.

It was not until 3.30 p.m. on 18 January that the column started to march off. In line with the weather across Zululand that year, it was a damp, rainy start. No doubt there was much grumbling at the prospect of what lay ahead: a march across hard country where even the elements were seemingly against them. Still, the men had taken the queen's shilling and they knew when they signed up that they were at the beck and call of Her Majesty and her appointed representatives.

Pearson had decided to split his forces into two separate divisions for the march. He would lead the first, which would consist of fifty wagons with eight companies of infantrymen, the engineers, part of the naval division, seven companies of NNC and an assortment of cavalry and pioneers. He knew that the road would be in a bad condition after the rains and the second division would therefore follow on twenty-four hours later, which hopefully would help the road to recover (a hopelessly optimistic expectation as it transpired). They were to head first for the Nyoni River and then on to another, the mSundusi. The terrain ahead was better than much of the rest of Zululand: open, rolling hills until later on in the journey. It was also well known to John Dunn whose local knowledge would be invaluable.

The countryside ahead impressed some of the men with its beauty. One of them, Sergeant Norbury in the Naval Brigade, positively waxed lyrical: 'I looked down on what appeared to be a vast green park, gently undulating, thickly studded with mimosas, a flashing stream winding across it, with the distant glittering sea on the one hand, and the lovely blue headland on the other, some twenty miles off ...'[2]

The column stopped for breakfast at St Andrews' mission station just before eight o'clock. They then moved on to the Nyoni. It was only a small stream but it had deep banks which meant that it was not easy to cross. It took several hours of manhandling the wagons to get them over and then the rain started to come down in torrents. It was a miserable first day. Whether or not there were any Zulus in the vicinity to block their progress, this was going to be a tough mission for the soldiers in the column.

Although the roads were known to be bad, Pearson did not yet realise quite how awful. The heavy wagons soon began to churn up the mud tracks into veritable quagmires that sucked the wheels down with each tortured movement. The mud took a vice-like grip on the wagons, making progress agonisingly slow. At the end of the first day's march, everyone was exhausted and frustrated. Pearson changed his mind and decided to let the second division catch him up before continuing.

The second division, led by Lieutenant-Colonel Welman from the 99th Regiment, had eighty wagons but was much weaker, having just two companies of his regiment as the backbone of the escort force with it (though there were a number of NNC companies and some cavalry with it too). This in itself was a risk; a well-organised guerrilla force could easily have attacked the isolated second division separately. Pearson, therefore, decided to transfer three companies of the Buffs to even the two forces up somewhat.

If Pearson's journey had been bad, Welman's was a nightmare. His wagons now had to journey along a road that had just been churned up by the first division. The wagons would not move of their own accord in many places and only brute force served to shift them as the men manhandled the huge vehicles across rutted and potholed roads, foot by agonising foot. Some of them eventually caught up with Pearson and the first division, who had been resting for much of the past day. As soon as they arrived, the fresh first division moved off and the second were ordered to follow them at once. If the men had been grumbling when they first crossed the river, heaven alone knows what comments they must have been making now.

Pearson and his men then reached their second target, the mSundusi, which they crossed successfully. Welman's second division, now close behind, had much the worse of the deal. By nightfall thirty of his wagons had managed to also cross the river, twenty more had reached its banks but had not crossed and the other thirty were spread back down the track, unguarded. It was an appalling situation which almost invited any hostile forces in the vicinity to attack. Pearson seemed unconcerned but it was just as well that the Zulus were not yet ready to go on the offensive. His men were probably more bothered; Welman's troops who did cross over did so without their tents, which were left behind in the wagons. They would spend a most uncomfortable night as a result.

The Zulu strategy had always been to see where the main British threat was likely to materialise and react accordingly. In contradistinction to Chelmsford's approach which was to split his forces, Cetshwayo's was to concentrate his for an attack. He had waited to see where the main threat appeared and had rightly surmised that the main attack would be delivered by the Central Column. Therefore, most of his forces were sent to face that force.

The best that could be done to help the local forces in the way of Pearson's column was to send a body of 3,500 men from Ulundi to irritate the British as much as possible. They had not yet arrived. Pearson, in the meantime, took stock. He decided to change his tactics. An advanced party of engineers and pioneers would be sent out to prepare the route for the wagons and help to ease their progress; this would give the men time to recover their strength.

Yet it was obvious to many that the Zulus were in the area. Harry O'Clery of the Buffs noted that they came across several campfires which were still smouldering, evidencing that someone had been there not long before. Pearson had been noticeably more cautious than Number 3 Column, apparently following Chelmsford's field regulations much more than the commander-in-chief himself did; a laager was erected at every stop.[3]

A scouting party pushed on to the River Tigulu. This, they reported, would be a major obstacle. The rains had swollen it so much that it was now 4½ft deep. This would prove a very difficult barrier to cross so Wynne and a party of engineers were sent ahead to see what could be done to help the column over in safety. This was good news for the rest of the men who could relax and recuperate as a result. However, many of the troops were jumpy. Older officers were dismissive of the raw young soldiers that were with the column, particularly with the 99th. There were regular false alarms of impending Zulu attack at night and sleeping patterns were seriously disturbed as a result, adding to the tiredness of the men.

The march resumed again on the 21st. Pearson had heard that a Zulu force was assembling nearby and a detachment of hundreds of troops was sent to a military homestead off to the east at kwaGingindlovu. When they arrived there, all they found was an old woman. The huts were set ablaze and the men left. This complied with Chelmsford's orders that huts should only be fired with the express orders of the officer in charge and, as this was a military homestead, the action was easily justified. Gratuitous destruction of Zulu dwellings was not yet on the agenda.

By now, a contingent of Zulu warriors from Ulundi had arrived in the area, led by a 70-year-old commander, Godide ka Ndleda. A night attack was considered, which was unusual for the Zulus, and not on this occasion finally launched. Dawn was the favoured time of day, when the enemy was sleeping and the men could be watched and the attack co-ordinated. One morning, guards in the British camp saw that the ground around the wagons had been trodden down as if by hundreds of pairs of feet. In fact, the Zulus had approached very close to the camp but had been discouraged from attacking by the obvious alertness of the sentries, who had been instructed to frequently call out to each other to confirm that all was well.

It was now 22 January, about 4 a.m., and just over 50 miles to the west Chelmsford was galloping to the rescue of Major Dartnell and his men, leaving the camp at Isandlwana exposed to a massive attack from a hidden enemy. As dawn broke above Pearson's camp, scouts were sent ahead to see if there was any sign of Zulus. They found none and so half an hour later the army and the wagons began their tortoise-paced crawl down the track.

The going was as bad as ever, with the roads still in an appalling condition. All the time the engineers and pioneers were forced to go ahead and do what they could to make the track passable. At last, another river was reached, the Nyezane. Here there was a valley which had a good area of flat ground either side of the river but ahead lay a range of hills with one in particular, Wombane, looking down on the river.

It was a fine spot to rest the oxen. There was good water here and the flatness of the surrounding terrain made it a relatively safe place to halt the column. *Vedettes* were posted to ensure that any hostile force was spotted in good time. The men relaxed, happy no doubt to have a break in what was a lovely location.

Some scouts pushed ahead to see what loomed beyond the immediate horizon. Other men, given the opportunity of an unexpected rest, took advantage and dived into the cooling waters of the river for an impromptu bath. The track beyond the Nyezane would not be easy. It climbed steeply up a spur, with large drops on either side into thickly wooded areas, a contrast to the easy-going country (with the exception of the state of the roads) that the men had crossed so far. One of the scouts was riding into the hills ahead when he saw movement in the distance. Looking closely he saw what he believed to be a group of Zulus, not in large number certainly but potentially hostile nevertheless.

He immediately turned his horse about and spurred back to Pearson. The column commander detailed some of the NNC to move forward to drive what was believed to be a small group of the enemy away. It was work that the NNC were well suited for. Although their skills were not highly regarded by many, skirmishing in broken country was believed to be the most appropriate use for them. The men moved forward and soon spotted the Zulus that the scout had seen. They began to climb up the slope towards them.

It was easy, however, for the Zulus to disappear. The thick foliage in the area meant they could quickly hide themselves from view, which they now did. They were soon to reappear on a spur further up Wombane itself. The NNC now moved after them. They were men who knew the ways of the Zulu well. As they moved ahead, they sensed something was wrong. The NNC were much derided by most British soldiers, including their own officers, but the latter would have been well advised to listen to them more often than they did.

The men tried to tell them that they had heard noises from the long grass to their front and they believed that what was concealed in it was more than just a small group of Zulus. Their officers, however, did not listen – many of them did not speak the language anyway – and pushed them on. Yet they did not have long to wait before their fears became reality. Suddenly hundreds of Zulus appeared, shouting their war cry of *uSuthu*. Some of them had firearms and shots rang out.

This was enough for the NNC, who turned and ran. Their officers and NCOs in many cases stayed to fight but were massively outnumbered and quickly eliminated. A story later arose that one of the officers, with a basic knowledge of Zulu, had shouted out orders to his men: '*baleka!*' In this case a little knowledge was fatal for he thought it meant 'charge' when in fact it meant 'run'. The NNC needed no second invitation and began to scamper back down the hill, leaving several of their officers to their fate. Nearby the cavalry saw what was happening and began to fall back in an orderly fashion. Everywhere they looked the hills were swarming with Zulus. They took full advantage of the trees to advance down the hill in surges, hidden from view most of the time and then appearing at a spot further down.

Pearson had a perfect view of all this as near the flat area of ground was a knoll which he quickly ascended. He decided that this would be his command position for the battle that now appeared to be imminent. Two companies of the Buffs, the Naval Brigade and the guns were ordered up there too. They had a good view of what was happening on the slopes of Wombane and soon began to take a toll of the Zulus. The deployment of the British forces was very quick as they were in action even before the Zulus had deployed into their favoured 'horns' formation.

One of the attacking Zulus, Chief Zimema of the uMxhapho, recalled that 'we were still far away from them when the white men began to throw their bullets at us, but we could not shoot at them because our rifles would not shoot so far' – a first-hand insight into the disparity between the weapons available to either side.[4] As they continued to skirmish forward and close the range they also began to take a toll of their enemy. But the technological advantages enjoyed by their foe were already taking effect. Shells exploded amongst the massed ranks, splattering blood and brains over Zimema and his comrades whilst the front ranks were being decimated by the rifles of the infantry. Zimema wistfully remembered later that they all had their assegais to hand but never got close enough to use them.

The attack now developing was from the left horn of a classic Zulu assault formation. The Zulus gamely continued to struggle forward and managed to make it into the bush at the foot of the hill. Then they moved towards some of the wagons, isolated and still attempting to cross the river. Captain Wynne was there, in charge of an engineering company. He could see that the heights above were 'swarming' with Zulus.[5]

Wynne could see that he needed to get his men ready for action. He extended his men in skirmishing order not a moment too soon, as the Zulus suddenly appeared less than 200 yards away. Bullets whizzed around them but did not seem to do much damage. This reference gives an allusion to one of the misconceptions of the war, that the Zulus did not have significant access to firearms. There were, in fact, a number of Zulu warriors armed with them but they were on the whole outdated models and the men using them were not trained or particularly accurate. Victorious trophy-hunters searching the field after the battle found some pieces dating back to 1835.

One man there, Lieutenant Knight of the Buffs, made the astute observation that a misunderstanding of the use of sights on rifles contributed to the Zulus' poor marksmanship – one observer of their sharpshooters in action during the war remarked that 'their fire was all rubbish'.[6] Knight believed that the Zulus used rear sights on rifles in the belief that it would make them more powerful, but these should have only been used when shooting at distance. Nevertheless, many of the Zulus did indeed have guns. White men had been trading them for hunting in Zululand for many years and there was a reasonable supply of them in the country, though the majority of warriors did indeed rely on the assegai as their main weapon.

Fortunately for the British, the straggling wagons made it into camp. Other men rushed into defensive positions and a line of sorts was formed, albeit imperfectly. Amongst them was the Naval Brigade, complete with a Gatling gun. This early version of the machine gun was by no means the finished article, the weapon that turned killing into a form of industry in the trenches of the First World War. It was prone in particular to jamming and other mechanical malfunctions. Nonetheless, it was still formidable, particularly against an enemy armed in the main with close-range stabbing spears. Able to fire off rounds at the rate of 300 per minute, it must have been terrifying to the Zulus when they were first introduced to it.

The *rat-a-tat-tat* of the Gatling sang out as bullets spewed towards the enemy mass. Gaps in their ranks quickly appeared as holes were punched in the Zulu lines. Rifle fire added to the maelstrom of lead. But the British still presented a juicy target and bullets hit home here and there, one shooting Pearson's horse from beneath him. Further to the west, the Zulu right horn was starting to form. However, it did not have the determination of the attacks elsewhere.

Then a much maligned weapon from the Zulu War played an atypically successful part in the battle. The rocket was an ineffective weapon which proved as much use at Isandlwana as a peashooter would. But now, on the very same day that that epic encounter was fought, a rocket fired forth and, tracing an erratic and oscillating trajectory across the bush, screamed through a group of straw huts on the hill, setting them ablaze. Lucky shot it may have been, but it would have done nothing for Zulu confidence.

The rockets' main purpose was as a way of terrifying the enemy by the screech they let out in flight. The Zulus poetically described them as 'lightning from heaven'. Today, at least, they had proved their worth. But even now some saw through the façade created by this fluky strike. Lieutenant Lloyd of the Royal Artillery wrote after the battle that 'the rockets, as I expected, proved of little value; so much has been said of the moral effect on savages but, to my mind, the Zulus displayed the utmost contempt for them … [The rockets] seemed to cause as much anxiety to our own men as to the enemy'.[7]

Already the Zulu attack was petering out. The right horn in particular was struggling, as it had to cross 150 yards of open ground to reach the British lines. In this part of the field many of the men were local volunteers, like Lieutenant Robarts of the Victoria Mounted Rifles, who noted with pride how cool the men kept under pressure. They poured an accurate, debilitating fire into the Zulu ranks, causing the assault to lose its momentum.

Now British infantry started to march forward. Commander Campbell, in charge of the Naval Brigade, asked for and received permission to lead a charge against the enemy. One and a half companies of sailors streamed forward. It must have been a bizarre sight to some seeing sailors storming through the thick bush of Zululand, and Lieutenant Lloyd from the Artillery watched on amazed as 'the Jack Tars seemed mad for blood, for they charged up the hill in any formation banging away right and left, driving the Zulus before them'.[8]

The regular soldiers indeed could not keep up with the sailors. Some of the latter were, however, hit by the odd bullet from the Zulus who were still managing to keep the NNC, who had joined the attack, at a distance. When the Buffs caught the sailors up they too took some casualties. But eventually the Zulus began to crack.

They started to retreat, again using the bush for cover. They were joined by many local Zulus who been spectating from a safe distance and were dejected at the outcome of the battle. Many defeated warriors disappeared behind the protective slopes of Wombane and began to stream away. Some were so exhausted that they threw down their shields and weapons to get away as quickly as they could. Some irregular British troops launched a pursuit of sorts, picking off more men as they sought to get off. It had been a harrowing introduction for them. The dead were thickly clustered, often in tightly packed groups where either a shell had burst amongst them or enemy rifle fire had been thick.

When the inquests began amongst the Zulu high command, there were those who pointed accusing fingers at the right flank and Cetshwayo was unimpressed at Godide's role in the battle; perhaps his age had told against him, though Ntshingwayo at Isandlwana was not much younger than him and had fought very differently. Certainly Godide had had the chance to launch an attack against the enemy when his column was scattered across miles of track, and a guerrilla attack particularly on the exposed rear might have caused chaos. But in some ways he had been unlucky. The prematurely launched attack from Wombane had put his men in action when they were not fully ready.

Things were very different from a British perspective. Pearson had been caught in a dangerous position but had got away with it. The NNC had served an important purpose: their foray up Wombane had triggered a hasty Zulu attack; cynically, their use as bait had proved effective. A more co-ordinated assault from the Zulus might have created a great threat. Yet at the end of it all, Gunner Carroll from HMS *Active*, who was present with the Naval Brigade, was probably not alone when he felt a healthy respect for his enemy now he had encountered him in battle for the first time.[9]

For a number of men, such as Harry O'Clery, this was their first action and it was a trying experience. O'Clery noted with great honesty that:

> we were told by our officers to keep ourselves cool and steady, and fire low; and I tried not to get carried away by the excitement, but it's not so easy when you know that each puff [of gun smoke] may mean a dose of death to you or the man next to you.[10]

It was a long day for the men in other ways; O'Clery noted that they had no time for breakfast before the fight and, as they had to make up the time lost as a result of the action, they did not eat until 9 p.m.

One man, the Rev. Robert Robertson, was despondent at the course of events. He had once been a missionary in Zululand and was a fierce critic of Cetshwayo. Now he was accompanying the army as a kind of chaplain, moving back into a region that he knew well as his mission station had been just a few miles beyond Eshowe. After the battle, Robertson was to be found sitting quietly, reading his Bible and pondering at his lack of success in converting the Zulus to Christianity. One of his servants had walked the field of battle and found his own brother amongst the wounded. He had promptly killed him. To him it no doubt seemed an act of love, as indeed such was the norm amongst Zulu warriors. To Robertson, of course, it seemed very different.

After the battle, named Nyezane by the British after the nearby river (the Zulus called it Wombane), many of the British and irregular soldiers walked around to reflect on their handiwork. A number of them were moved to pity by their wounded enemy; some of them brought them drinks of water carried in their helmets. Others dragged them out of the sun into some shaded spot. It was impossible though to do more for them than this. There were too many of them and the British had to move on with speed towards Eshowe. That said, such displays of humanity were not to be typical of later warfare in Zululand. It is easy to be magnanimous in victory, far less so when heavy defeats have been inflicted on an army.

Even after this triumph, the victors were shocked at the state of the bodies of their own dead. These were literally riddled with assegai wounds. To them, this seemed like deliberate mutilation. However, this was not so. It was a reflection of what happened in a Zulu hunt when a great beast was killed. In such cases, everyone in the hunting party would stab the corpse as a statement of collective participation in the winning of a great prize. This was in effect a badge of honour for the slain, though it was one that was not at all appreciated by the white men with their different paradigms of what was and was not acceptable.

For Pearson the battle had ended with a good result. The main Zulu impi in the region had been bested and the road to Eshowe (if the disintegrating dirt track could be called a road) now lay open. A grave was dug for the dead, twelve men (soon to be followed by two others). In addition, there were another eighteen wounded. The Zulu dead were left where they fell. It was estimated that they numbered 400. But as Colour Sergeant Burnett of the 99th Regiment remarked, it had been 'terribly earnest work, and not child's play', as no doubt some had hopefully thought it might be.[11]

The advance now resumed, after a brief respite, with the men unaware for the time being that more terribly earnest work elsewhere in Zululand that day would fundamentally change the role of Number 1 Column. They rested but briefly after the battle, having buried their dead on the field, being roused at 3 a.m. and on the move at 5 the next morning. It was now just 5 miles to Eshowe, though the going would again not be easy with a steep climb up to the mission station.

At about 10 a.m. the first elements of the column arrived at Eshowe, though it would be five hours before the last part of it reached there. Much to everyone's relief the buildings there were intact. Just as had been the case at Rorke's Drift, the church lent itself to conversion to a stores depot. It also, O'Clery noted, gave the column's best marksmen a fine lookout post.[12]

The location seemed idyllic. There was even an orchard there and a garden, a rare reminder of civilisation in the wildness of Zululand. It was resplendent with, amongst other luxuries, orange trees, peaches, limes and bamboo clumps. There were four main buildings in the mission station, a church built of mud-brick with a corrugated iron roof, a house, a school and a storehouse. This would give good protection to the provisions that needed to be stored there.

There were those, however, who were not impressed by the scenic setting. Captain Wynne of the Royal Engineers was one of the unsung heroes of the war. Indeed, he would lose his life because of it. The work he now started at Eshowe was invaluable. Surveying the ground, he saw that the position was far from satisfactory. It was overlooked from the north and south by higher ground, though given the Zulus' general lack of expertise with firearms that would not necessarily be a fatal weakness. But it did mean that the Zulus would be able to see every movement in the camp.

More worryingly they could approach to within 70 yards of the site up a deep ravine without being spotted. This would give them the chance to rush it before the defenders could prepare themselves. To counteract this, Wynne would supervise the construction of a formidable set of defences, effectively transforming Eshowe from mission station to fortress. He could not abandon the buildings and he had no building materials with him. He would therefore have to make do with what he had.

First of all, an entrenchment was marked out whilst the thick bush around the buildings was cleared by the soldiers. The orchard, much to everyone's dismay (including Wynne's), had to go; it simply offered too much cover to a potential enemy. Then the donkeywork began. Soldiers became navvies, hewing out deep ditches and throwing up the earth to make ramparts. Eventually the ditch was 7ft deep and up to 13ft wide. The ramparts rose 6ft, giving a huge distance of 13ft from the bottom of the ditch.

There were two entrances, a main one at the west which was protected by a drawbridge and a smaller one on the north side where parties of men could venture out and collect water from a nearby stream. Two caponiers were built; these might best be thought of as bunkers jutting out into the ditches with loopholes carved in them that would allow soldiers inside to fire at any enemy who was rash enough to enter the ditch. Two guns were placed either side of the main entrance and a third by the water gate, with the fourth nearby. The Gatling gun was placed on the southern side of the ramparts. It was unlikely that this place was ever going to be successfully attacked by a Zulu impi.

A supply train led by Lieutenant-Colonel Ely was still making its way to Eshowe with more provisions. It had started out from the Thukela on 22 January, that momentous day in the history of the war. It had a relatively small escort, just some 300 men from the regular infantry and a small number of mounted colonials. Pearson was nervous of them travelling through broken country and decided to send out two companies from Eshowe to guide them on in.

He wrote to Chelmsford on the 24th, asking him to move closer to Eshowe so that he could support Pearson's planned next forward moves from the mission station. He also wrote to Durnford on the same day with suggestions for the moves he should make in order to reinforce him. This had been the original plan of action, long since superseded by Chelmsford's orders that he should move in support of Number 3 Column instead. It was curious to say the least that no one seemed to have bothered to tell Pearson that the master plan had changed.

Of course, post-Isandlwana it would change again. Little did Pearson know that when he wrote to Durnford, he had already been dead for two days.

The day after, 25 January, forty-eight empty wagons were sent back to the Lower Drift on the Thukela to pick up more supplies. There were four companies of regular infantry escorting this small convoy, along with two companies of NNC and ten Mounted Infantry. Further work was undertaken when they had left on erecting the ramparts and cutting down the trees and scrub around Eshowe. This returning convoy was led by Brevet Lieutenant-Colonel Coates. After a few hours marching they arrived back on the field of Nyezane.

Lieutenant Backhouse of the Buffs was with the party and kept a diary. In it he described how 'there was an awful stench and the unburied Zulus were something awful to see'. They came across a wounded Zulu whose arm and leg had been shattered by a shell. He had been lying there for three days without food, water or much shade. It was a miracle that he was still alive. The soldiers gave him some biscuits and loaded him on to one of the wagons. They would later have to amputate both of his destroyed limbs, though whether he survived the traumas of Victorian battlefield surgery is sadly not recorded.[13]

The convoy unsurprisingly progressed far more quickly un-laden than it had when burdened with a full stock of supplies, travelling 17 miles in one day. However, it was not all good news; there were no tents and the men on escort duty endured a miserable night under the wagons in the teeth of a heavy thunderstorm. The day after, they met Ely's train on the way to Eshowe, causing the returning convoy to stop for hours to let them pass. It would eventually make it back to the Lower Drift without any alarums.

Everything still appeared to be progressing well at Eshowe until, on 26 January, a strange message was received from Sir Bartle Frere. It told Pearson that Colonel Durnford had been killed and his troops attacked and defeated (interesting that Durnford was already being assigned responsibility for the defeat) but that Chelmsford had fought an action too and been victorious (this was interesting too, for apart from the battle at Sihayo's homestead, which had now been rendered an irrelevance, Chelmsford had not been responsible for any victory).

But it was, in keeping with British communications throughout the war, a confused and generally unhelpful message which provoked further questions rather than offered any answers. Certainly at this stage Pearson was still thinking about a further advance when the time was right. Men were sent forward to scout the way ahead in preparation for this. Interestingly, some of Pearson's sentries had overheard Zulus nearby shouting messages of a great victory for their side on that same day, the 'jungle telegraph' often proving surprisingly effective on the Zulu side during the war.

On 27 January, Pearson decided to pass on the news he had received. It appeared to be mixed tidings; Durnford's loss was unfortunate especially as he was supposed to be acting in concert with Pearson's column. However, the feeling was that Chelmsford's 'victory' more than compensated. Indeed, Lieutenant Robarts noted that 'Colonel Glyn's column with the General have had an encounter on the same day as ours and they utterly routed them'.[14]

The only British victory that this could have referred to was the one at Rorke's Drift (which of course owed nothing to Chelmsford), though the men at Eshowe at this stage had no knowledge of it. It appeared that, even at this early stage, Frere – whose confusing and uninformative dispatch had started the stories – was already hanging on to the battle won there as something of a redeeming feature.

Then, on 28 January, a bombshell dropped. A messenger arrived at the camp with a stark message. It came from Lord Chelmsford and the writer appeared to have been gripped by panic. Without giving too many details, the letter starkly warned that Pearson was to:

> consider all my instructions cancelled and act in whatever manner you think most desirable in the interests of the column under your command. Should you consider the garrison of Ekowe [sic] too far advanced to be fed with safety, you can withdraw it. Hold however if possible the post on the Zulu side of the Lower Thukela. You must be prepared to have the whole Zulu force down upon you. Do away with tents, and let the men take shelter under the wagons, which will then be in position for defence, and hold so many more supplies.[15]

This was quite possibly the most extraordinary communication of the war. With the exception of the orders (or lack of them) left for Durnford at Isandlwana, it was perhaps the least clear item of communication during the whole conflict, and that is no mean achievement. It told Pearson nothing of what had happened, although that it was pretty serious was obvious to everyone who saw it, but worst of all it told Pearson nothing of Chelmsford's plans, probably because he himself did not yet know what they were.

It was perfectly reasonable for Chelmsford to give Pearson an element of choice as he was on the spot and best informed as to what decision to make. However, to ask him to do so without knowing what Chelmsford's plans were was tantamount to asking him to grope his way through the darkest night without the benefit of a torch. How did Pearson now fit with the master strategy – this was the question to be asked. The answer was that there was no master strategy left.

Baffled as to what this confusing message could mean, Pearson held a council of war with his officers. The debate was veering towards deciding to abandon the fort and retreat back to the Thukela. Nevertheless, Captain Wynne – who arrived late – had a decisive impact in resisting this line of argument. He thought that the fort he had built was in an excellent state of repair, that a retreat back to the Thukela would in itself be dangerous and that it would also send the wrong moral message. He was joined by other officers who agreed with his analysis and the decision was made to stay put for now. The arrival of fresh supplies with Ely the next day reinforced this decision.

On 2 February more details of Isandlwana were received, a full week after Frere's initial correspondence. At about the same time a patrol had captured a Zulu in a red jacket, armed with a rifle stamped with the mark of the 24th Regiment on it.[16] They interrogated the captive, who gave a remarkably accurate account of the battle at Isandlwana. There was no time for prevarication in the meantime. Pearson's first step was to send the mounted men – the 'mounted volunteer picnic party' as O'Clery cynically described them[17] – and the NNC back to the Thukela. Many of the men would be of doubtful use in a siege situation, which was already starting to develop, and would only deplete the supplies quicker than they would otherwise.

Some of the men did not even have time to recover their personal possessions from the wagons before starting out. The column set out that same day, at just after 2 p.m., under the command of Major Barrow. He carried a message for Chelmsford with him in which Pearson admitted that he felt the responsibility for what he was doing deeply but explained that 'we are still in the dark as to what has happened'[18] – confirmation, if any was needed, of how inadequate Chelmsford's communication was.

Barrow met Ely on his way up, told him what was happening and advised him to push on to Eshowe as quickly as possible. He also told him to abandon any wagons that he could not get in because they were damaged; seven fully loaded vehicles were abandoned as a result. Then Barrow pushed on with his men back to the Thukela as quickly as possible. Of course, they were on horses whilst the NNC accompanying them were on foot. The sense of panic can be sensed in the time it took to complete the journey back to the Thukela. It had taken well over four days to march up to Eshowe; now Major Graves, in charge of the 2nd Regiment of the NNC, calculated that they made it back (a distance of about 30 miles) in fourteen hours and twenty minutes.[19]

The men of the NNC quickly dropped behind their mounted 'leaders' and were effectively abandoned altogether. They mostly made it safely back to Natal but then promptly, and very sensibly, disappeared back to their homes. It was another appalling example of the lack of leadership that was generally to make the NNC so ineffective during the war. Norris-Newman got hold of a letter in which one returning officer saw in the treatment of the NNC an opportunity missed. After the triumph at the Nyezane, their confidence had been sky-high but the march back completely destroyed it.[20]

At Eshowe the tents were struck and the entire garrison was to sleep under the wagons. This was no small discomfort for the weather was often terrible and the men were frequently soaked to the skin, which was good neither for their morale nor their health. All wagons were brought inside to add to the defences. A new group of them had arrived with Ely from the Lower Thukela. But the rules of engagement had now changed completely. The pace of work accelerated but in the efforts of the troops to bring the wagons inside some of the ramparts were damaged and had to be temporarily reinforced with anything that was to hand – provision boxes, blankets, even valises – there was no time to be choosy.

An initial assessment suggested that there were enough supplies to last for three weeks. There was also a very large stock of ammunition. All in all, there were 1,800 men in the camp, just under 1,500 of them fighting troops, and the majority of these were either regular soldiers or the Naval Brigade, so Pearson could at least take some comfort in their quality. Additionally he had large numbers of oxen to cope with; these were put in laagers, except for a few who would not fit in, and were therefore accommodated in the ditch around the fort.

The mood had now changed. There was panic in the air. That very night the church tower caught fire – someone had tried to burn out a beehive that was in it and had set the whole edifice ablaze as a result. It was dealt with easily enough but reinforced the sense of uneasiness then abroad. From being a second-rate native opponent, the Zulus were now suddenly regarded as supermen. Many a night like that followed: the bowing of the trees in the breeze was seen as a Zulu host approaching, or the rustling of a wild animal in the scrub interpreted as hundreds of native warriors creeping towards the camp. Often in the daytime Zulus would be seen in the distance freely moving around which did nothing to soothe shattered nerves.

Pearson soon calculated that he actually had too many oxen in the camp to cope with. There was limited space and grazing for them all so he decided to drive about 1,000 of them off back to the Thukela, along with twenty-eight mules. The latter had gone barely 5 miles when they were taken by Zulus; all but one which escaped back to the camp were killed. Of the oxen, 500 were also taken by the Zulus whilst the remainder returned to camp with their terrified drivers.

The weather too continued to be bad. One of the sentries, unable to cope with the torrential rain, deserted his post – an offence for which he subsequently received fifty lashes. But the inclement conditions began to take their toll, a problem exacerbated by a shortage of medicines. On 1 February Private Kingston of the Buffs was the first to succumb to the effects of disease. He would not be the last and now another addition to the fort was needed: a cemetery. The men did not move outside the fort unless ordered to. It gradually began to dawn on everyone that a state of siege existed and as a result rationing was introduced to eke out the supplies.

Communication with the outside world was difficult, although it was still possible, if dangerous. The news of Isandlwana when received from two black runners on 2 February just confirmed to Pearson that a dash back to the Thukela was too dangerous. He therefore wrote to Chelmsford asking for reinforcements to be sent. However, the commander-in-chief could not spare anyone from the defence of Natal, which he believed likely to be attacked following the Zulu victory.

Pearson announced the shocking tidings of Isandlwana to everyone the day after. A cloud of gloom descended; many of those encamped at Eshowe knew someone who had been lost. This also led to a strong desire amongst many of the defenders to avenge those who had died.

Chelmsford wrote back, telling Pearson to return to the Thukela with some of his men. Neither Pearson nor his officers believed this to be a viable proposition. Removing some of the garrison would leave a remnant that was too small to defend the extensive perimeter of Eshowe. In addition, an increasing number of Zulus had been spotted in the area and it was felt that they would make a retreat very dangerous. Everyone agreed that they could not comply with Chelmsford's orders. Pearson wrote back to Chelmsford explaining why he was unable to conform but stating that of course he would do so if the commander-in-chief insisted upon it.

Then the siege tightened. More Zulus arrived in the area and any further communication was now impossible. Chelmsford was unable to command Pearson to retreat even if he had wanted to. It was like a bizarre throwback to a former era, the British in their earth-banked castle under siege by their spear-wielding enemies. But Pearson was knowledgeable enough to know that he could do nothing bar wait, so he started to take active measures to improve his position. The defences were assiduously added to. Deep pits were dug in the ground with stakes in them to slow down any Zulu charge. Their position was, against a Zulu attack, impregnable. However, there were other enemies to fight: shortages of food and disease, for example.

Stringent efforts were made in particular to preserve a clean water supply. Men were tasked with making sure the nearby stream was clear of any contamination on a daily basis. Horses and cattle were watered from a different source than the men. Meticulous arrangements were made for toilet facilities too, with latrines dug outside the fort and any overnight detritus carried out and disposed of in the morning, though despite this a frequent memory of those who experienced the siege was the appalling smell inside Eshowe. These arrangements stopped any massive epidemic breaking out, though men continued to fall sick and occasionally expire. Those hospital patients well enough were brought outside to enjoy fresh air during the daytime in what was described as a 'sanatorium' about 400 yards from the camp.[21]

The garrison did what they could to make themselves comfortable. They got into the habit of sleeping soundly under a wagon, for example. O'Clery described how the men did what they could to get some rest 'while creeping things crawled and ran over us while we slept'. The officers at least managed to have more chance of staying dry by sleeping on top of the wagons.[22]

The judicious use of tarpaulins managed to keep some of the elements out. Lieutenant Lloyd, however, experienced a more mundane problem. Night alarms were frequent and had some unfortunate results, 'for on the command going round at night to "stand to arms" one naturally jumped up imagining oneself in a tent, but the real situation was promptly suggested to one by a violent contact of head and wagon'.[23]

Most of the cavalry had gone but some horses were left and an impromptu troop was raised (it was, in retrospect, a mistake to send all the cavalry back to the Thukela as they would have been useful for scouting). The troop was led by Captain Shervinton of the NNC and became known as the 'Uhlans'. They soon proved their worth. Riding out one day they saw a large body of Zulus, several thousands strong, just a couple of miles away. They reported back to Eshowe and the sentries consequently watched extra carefully that night. During the hours of darkness, movement was suddenly seen to the south-west. Nerves frayed, the sentries fired several shots. The artillery was just about to join in when the cease-fire was given as no further movement was obvious. It was only with the onset of daylight that the real threat became apparent. The fort had been in danger of attack by a shirt and a pair of trousers left to dry on a nearby bush.

There were more serious encounters too. Several times during the daytime, Shervinton's patrol came under fire from a bold group of Zulus positioned on a nearby hill. Shervinton therefore set a trap for them, hiding his men away so that they could attack the Zulus as they approached the hill. The Zulus fell for it and were driven off and did not return to that particular spot again.

As time passed, it became increasingly obvious that no major Zulu attack was likely. Cetshwayo was most unhappy that enemy forces were so far inside his lands but correctly reasoned that the threat they were currently posing was minimal. In fact, it was probably better to have 1,500 British troops caught like rats in a barrel than actively fighting elsewhere. He instructed his local commanders to do what they could to lure the enemy out and then attack them in the open. But on no account should they consider attacking them behind the formidable fortifications that they had erected.

Boredom became the biggest challenge for the men under siege. There were two military bands present and they took it in turns to present daily concerts. Inevitably the repertoire was limited and this initially pleasant diversion soon became monotonous. Men read anything they could get hold of regardless of the subject matter.

With morale on a downward spiral but Zulu attacks conspicuous by their absence, a more aggressive stance by the British seemed overdue. Patrols were sent out in the day and came into occasional contact with scattered groups of Zulus, though usually at a distance and with little threat of any loss of life. The defenders were forced to become bolder. Their cattle had denuded the area round the fort of good grazing ground and they therefore had to be taken further away. Large numbers of men were sent to escort them in case of Zulu attack.

Pearson was increasingly encouraged to adopt a more aggressive strategy. It does no good for an enemy to believe that his opponent is in abject fear of him. Besides, supplies were running short and foraging across the local countryside could help address this problem as well as giving a boost to the men's morale. The first such raid took place on 19 February and if the haul was not noticeably exciting, a mixture of mealies and pumpkins, it did help break the monotony of the men's diet.

Four days later came a real treat. The men who had returned to the Thukela had left significant stocks of food behind in their possessions and they were doing no good where they were. An auction was held; that day the men at Eshowe treated themselves from a bizarre menu that included tinned sardines, salmon, pots of jam, a huge ham and several bottles of Worcestershire sauce. One private bought himself a tin of lobster and another of salmon. He then walked straight out of the fort and ate them at once. There was no chance of any of his 'mates' getting a helping.

O'Clery noted that due to the high prices most items went to the officers. The ham was bought by one who offered to share it with a colonel that evening. No doubt to his annoyance the dinner party had to be cancelled, as by the time the meal was due to start someone had stolen the ham.[24]

On 24 February, Pearson himself led a raiding party against a nearby homestead. This provided useful supplies of mealies to supplement the tedious rations enjoyed by those in the fort. Several hundred Zulus watched from a safe distance rather than intervene. As the successful party rode off a shout came over the hills that they had helped themselves to the Zulus' mealies today but they would deprive the British of their coffee tomorrow.

The Zulus did their best, as ordered, to lure the British out of camp into the open. Every day about 500 of them hid close to the fort and did what they could to act as bait. Cattle were attacked when taken out of the fort to graze and English-speaking Zulus freely hurled taunts at the defenders, accusing them of being old women and asking them if they could come and share their coffee with them. They also asked that the cattle be kept well fed as their king would want them back soon.

On 1 March, Pearson launched his biggest raid yet. About 10 miles away from Eshowe was a homestead belonging to Dabulamanzi of Rorke's Drift fame. At 2 a.m. that morning Pearson set off with a force of 500 men. A friendly Zulu guide led them through the night. Everyone was on edge and did their best to stay silent but to Lieutenant Lloyd every gun wheel creaked so loudly that it might have been heard miles away.

They arrived just before dawn, and the surprise seemed to be complete. Pearson, however, wanted to bring up the cannon he had brought with him. This caused a wait of ten minutes, time that made all the difference; for as the sun rose a Zulu meandered out of his hut, outside the homestead but close to Pearson, and looked out over the hills. As his eyes adjusted to the light, he saw the raiding party. He ran like a hare back into the homestead. Although Pearson ordered a party of horsemen to try to cut him off, it was too late and the alarm was raised. Soon all the occupants of the homestead were fleeing into the bush.

There was nothing left to attack. The guns fired but hit nothing whilst the homestead was put to the torch. Pearson, dejected, turned his men around for the long march back. The Zulus, encouraged by this withdrawal, followed them all the way back, taking potshots now and then, though with a limited degree of success. The British soldiers were again impressed at the skirmishing skills of their foe but noted that fortunately they were not matched by their shooting prowess.

No one was hit amongst the British forces but it had been a frustrating foray. If there was a corresponding drop in morale there was soon a boost to it once more. The next day one of the scouts looked into the far distance towards the Thukela, where he saw something flashing. At first he was not sure what it was but others joined him. It eventually dawned on them all that someone was trying to signal to them.

And now, as Captain Pelly Clarke said: 'great was our joy! Faces that had for long borne an anxious and desponding look, assumed a more hopeful aspect; new energy, new life, seemed to be instilled in us, as we found all was not over.'[25] All indeed was not over; there would be more fighting yet to come, more lives yet to be lost on both sides (though mostly on that of the Zulus), but for the men cooped up in Eshowe things were definitely about to improve.

seven

BACK TO THE DRAWING BOARD

Chelmsford Regroups

The defenders in Eshowe had been living in a closed world, cut off from news of the war outside their immediate vicinity. Whilst the siege had been going on there had been a decisive change to the nature of the conflict.

The climactic events at Isandlwana radically altered the conduct of the war. The day after the battle there, Zulus were found snooping around in the vicinity of Rorke's Drift. Before Isandlwana they would probably have been taken prisoner, held for a while, then released. Not now. Smith-Dorrien had assembled a gallows at the drift before the battle for the purpose of cutting bullock hides into strips. He noted that 'the first use I saw the gallows put to was for hanging Zulus who were supposed to have behaved treacherously the day after the Rorke's Drift fight'.[1] Whether any of the Zulus realised that spying was a capital offence is a moot point but in fairness they were not renowned for taking prisoners either.

An air of grimness descended on the British army in southern Africa. Perhaps the reaction of George Howe of the Royal Engineers was typical of many. He was in a party of sappers marching up from Greytown towards the front when stories of a disastrous reverse reached them. This small force, some sixty strong, resolved to dig in close to the border in the abandoned house of a farmer. As they spent the night of 22 January watching out for an expected Zulu attack, Howe kept one bullet aside, ready to use on himself if the need arose.[2]

The news of Isandlwana was taken back to Natal by fleeing refugees, many of whom could not have seen the end of the battle or they would not have survived. The colonists were understandably horrified, expecting an avalanche of

Zulus to descend on them at any moment. At one stage, tensions were so high that colonists threatened to turn on messengers from Zululand who brought bad tidings, accusing them of scaremongering, as if a failure to recognise the Zulu threat would make it go away – a classic psychology for dealing with stressful situations and unwelcome news.[3]

The sense of panic, though, was real. The major towns of Natal, Durban and Pietermaritzburg, were put on alert. Citizens were issued with instructions of what to do if they needed to get into a laager quickly. Church bells would be rung to raise the alarm. Militias were put on standby to come out at short notice in a crisis situation. Chelmsford's arrival in Pietermaritzburg on 26 January, with the news that there was no sign of an imminent Zulu raid into Natal, helped to calm nerves to some extent but it would be a while before confidence was restored.

The colony was on a knife-edge. After all, Frere and Chelmsford had built up the image of the Zulu bogeyman as one of their justifications for the war and the crushing victory for the Zulus at Isandlwana seemed to confirm the view. The rumours had started on the morning of 25 January. They had 'the effect of arousing everyone, and people, in their eagerness to obtain news, devoured the most exaggerated statements with a mixture of avidity and regret. Scarcely any business was transacted; the principal streets were full of groups, discussing the aspects and prospects of the situation.'[4]

There was a delay before official news was released and, in the absence of firm information, people made up their own minds, feeding the sense of panic which seemed to have an insatiable appetite. Many colonists believed that the government was hiding something from them. Then one evening a list of the missing was posted. People stood in large crowds outside the offices where the lists went up, as if awaiting news of some terrible shipping disaster and hoping to see a loved one's name amongst those of the survivors.

When the authorities in Pietermaritzburg started to talk about erecting large laagers for defence the day after, it merely served to feed the panic anew. Instructions were issued to the populace about what to do in the event of an attack. The firing of three guns from the fort in quick succession would be the signal that everyone was to come into the laager for protection. If a fourth was fired it meant 'hurry' for the situation was urgent. In the age-old failed hope of bureaucrats everywhere, the instructions added: 'it cannot be too strongly expressed upon the inhabitants that excitement and flurry should be avoided and suppressed by all possible means'.[5]

This request of 'don't panic' of course merely served to have the opposite effect. Further instructions told the citizens to have food for a family for a week ready in case of emergency. Linen, two buckets, disinfectants, mattresses, plates and cutlery were also to be kept handy. There would, in the event of a crisis, be much expected of the citizen that was beyond the normal call of duty. The orders ended with the statement that 'a display of cheerfulness under the novel and trying circumstances will serve much to lighten the difficulties'.

Cheerfulness was a quality that was conspicuous by its absence in those early days. The streets were filled with the noise of hammering as windows in Pietermaritzburg were boarded over. Convicts were let out to help with the work and Chinese carpenters were much in evidence too. The 26th was a Sunday and the churches were full of congregations praying for deliverance from the threat.

In a foretaste of what was to come from the period of high tension, on the night of 3 February an alarm reached Greytown that the Zulus were on their way. Patrols walked up and down the streets, waking people up in their houses to the terrifying news. The inhabitants made their way to the laager that had been built. It was a false alarm, something troops in the field would suffer terribly from in the months ahead, and when this became clear the tired inhabitants made their way back to their homes.

Even Durban, more distant from the front line, was panicked. The townspeople demanded the erection of bastions and ditches but the Colonial Commandant of Durban, Major Huskisson, thought this an overreaction and proposed instead to fortify key buildings only. It was not only the military authorities who thought that the citizens of Durban had overdone it. The citizens of Escourt were openly dismissive of them; the correspondent of the *Natal Colonist* noted on 20 February that they had prepared themselves 'without any of the excitement and scare which seems to have converted your Durban folks to a set of raving lunatics'.[6]

The sense of depression started to impact on Chelmsford too. He wrote in sombre terms to Wood on 7 February that he was unsure of Pearson's position as all the runners he had sent recently had been killed. He was also worried about Russell who 'appears to have lost heart'. This must have hit home hard as he was one of Chelmsford's appointments. There had also been the first outbreak of horse sickness at Rorke's Drift.[7]

Chelmsford's mood was clearly down, though this was not completely obvious in a report he prepared for Stanley on 8 February. Both Frere and Shepstone had been quick to offer their sympathy for his position.[8] Although he admitted the challenges facing his armies were great, he also noted that the Zulus 'are said to be much disheartened with their losses in their attack on the Rorke's Drift Column'.[9]

But the tension was clearly mounting for on the very next day he prepared another message for Stanley that effectively told him that he wanted help at a senior level, saying that:

> I consider it my duty to lay before you my opinion, that it is very desirable in view of future contingencies that an officer of the rank of Major General should be sent out to South Africa without delay.

In June last I mentioned privately to his Royal Highness the F.M. [Field Marshal] Commander in Chief that the strain of prolonged anxiety and exertion, physical and mental, was even then telling on me – What I felt then, I feel still more now.[10]

This was Chelmsford at his lowest ebb. The debacle of Isandlwana had deprived him of many men and his offensive capacity had been much diminished as a result. Almost as seriously, much of his transport had been taken from him and that left him as powerless as if he had lost every soldier. He could not, if this letter is taken at face value, see a way out of the terrible mess that he had gotten himself into.

Others too were wallowing in a slough of despond. At Helpmekaar Lieutenant Curling spoke of a place where 800 men were crammed into a small space and all inside was a sea of mud. There was not enough room for the men to sleep except in shifts. He could even see the slaughter ground of Isandlwana in the distance. Neither was he enamoured of Chelmsford's leadership, saying in a private letter that 'I think these disasters have quite upset his judgement or rather that of his staff and one does not feel half so comfortable under his command as with a man like Col. Wood'.[11]

There was, though, no Zulu follow-up to the great victory won at Isandlwana. In reality, the cost of their triumph had been high. The losses sustained had been huge, with perhaps 10 per cent of the attacking force dead or mortally wounded. The army went home to lick its wounds and had no great desire for another battle anytime soon. Cetshwayo was as determined as ever to remain on the defensive and there was no tangible impetus to the Zulu cause arising as a result of the stunning outcome of the battle.

Slowly, when a Zulu attack did not come, the feelings of panic in Natal started to subside. Nevertheless, there were still problems to be faced. There were plenty of people willing to volunteer to defend their own homes but not always enough guns to go round for them all. But the colony gradually came to realise that a major Zulu attack was not going to materialise.

In the aftermath of the reverse at Isandlwana, the Natal Native Contingent started to unravel. They had been poorly led and then badly shocked by what they had witnessed at Isandlwana. Many of them now decided to return to their homes. For many officers it was a case of good riddance; the NNC soldiers had not performed well. But the same officers who were so dismissive of their service had themselves been largely responsible for their inadequacies. Lonsdale, previously in command of the 3rd Regiment NNC, which was now defunct, went to the Cape to try and drum up further colonial recruitment.

Whether the 3rd Regiment of the NNC was actually disbanded or merely deserted was a matter of much debate. Chelmsford suggested the latter, but his own instructions to the men after Isandlwana had been far from clear. He asked if the men were still willing to fight, implying they had a choice. A number felt that their place was at home looking after their families, especially if a Zulu attack was imminent, as Chelmsford's own actions in making his way post-haste back to Natal suggested it was. They also had no real understanding of the concept of a continuous period of service; their way, like that of the Zulus across the border, was to take part in a campaign then return home after the battle. Even Harford thought that the NNC had been disbanded at Chelmsford's orders.[12]

Most, in any event, decided not to fight any longer. Their firearms were collected back in from them. Hamilton-Browne was livid at their attitude (with the notable exception of the isiGqoza, battle-hardened Zulus themselves) and suggested that the Great White Queen would soon be sending them aprons when she heard of their lack of valour.[13] Despite this, it seemed as if the regiment disbanded with the full sanction of their officers. It is unclear, given this state of affairs, why Chelmsford later suggested they had deserted – unless, of course, he had changed his mind.

But whatever the true situation, the demise of the 3rd Regiment had a knock-on effect on others. Major Harcourt Bengough, in charge of the 2nd Battalion of the 1st Regiment, was leading his men along the road when they met the departing 3rd Regiment, who advised their fellows to go home too. Men of the 2nd Battalion, terrified as all the white soldiers seemed to have left them to their own devices and the far from tender mercies of the Zulus, needed little encouragement to comply. Bengough, thinking that he was in too weak a position to resist, also gave permission for his men to leave.

Very soon after, Bengough met Chelmsford who was extremely annoyed. Bengough had no right to make any decision to disband his battalion. The men, who had not gone far, were hastily reassembled and addressed by Chelmsford. It was an atypically robust performance; in summary, if the men did not carry on with their designated duties, they would be shot. This seemed to do the trick and the battalion re-materialised and was ordered to journey to Msinga to guard the magistracy there. Arriving at Msinga, they were put to work strengthening the defences, which were far from satisfactory.

The 2nd Regiment was also decimated in the aftermath of the return from Eshowe. This situation could not be allowed to continue; Chelmsford needed the men to free up imperial soldiers and colonial volunteers for other activities. Local magistrates were asked why men had left. They in turn consulted local chiefs and a litany of complaints started to come in.

Chelmsford was forced to go on the defensive. Bulwer, in Natal, had criticised the way the native recruits had been used, being seen as an adjunct to the British army and not a tribal force allowed to fight in their own time-honoured fashion. There were also complaints that the officers did not speak the native language, but Chelmsford was emphatic in resisting the argument, stating that a good officer was more important than a Zulu-speaking one.[14]

However, the evidence is that the native soldiers had been badly led and a number of them were demoralised both by the British defeat and the way in which they had been treated in the field. Lieutenant Harford, who as a regular officer of good standing should be listened to, stated bluntly in a letter home to his mother: 'I can tell you that it has been a most awful time with these people but I will say one thing, the European officer and NCO are a thousand percent worse than the natives.'[15]

Even those who showed some sympathy for their NNC men were affected by their desertion. Bengough was an officer who showed greater understanding than most. At Msinga, they were manning a defensive position on a rocky knoll about 25 miles down the road from Rorke's Drift. He had supervised the construction of a breast-high redoubt here but, owing to the number of desertions then experienced, had to add two flanking bastions. These had walls 6ft high and nearly 4ft thick, a place of last resort in case of an attack.

In mid-February Chelmsford reformed the 2nd Regiment, which was told to support the Natal Border Guard (formed of white colonials) near the drift over the Lower Thukela. Men of the 3rd Regiment were also asked to return. Chelmsford planned to assimilate these into the Natal Border Guard which he decided to reorganise on tribal lines. However, there was not much of a response to these initial summonses. This was perhaps hardly surprising as a large number of the men remained unpaid for the service they had already put in.

In an effort to encourage them, Chelmsford agreed that a larger proportion of them would carry firearms in future. In other ways, Chelmsford too had learned a painful lesson. Most of the native troops would now stay in Natal and perform purely defensive duties. The mounted native troops were an exception though. Their reputation had, alone amongst their brethren, been enhanced by their service previously. Chelmsford wanted them to return to aid his offensive efforts in Zululand itself. But many of them had lost their horses and were hesitant.

Eventually numbers of the NNC returned in dribs and drabs, and it was clear that they would need to be used in a different way, more suited to their traditional warfare. The mounted men were insistent that they wanted a good leader. Theophilus Shepstone the younger, son of the colonial official who had done so much to kick-start the war, was nominated to lead some of them in a troop that became known as 'Shepstone's Horse'. He was widely respected and his appointment seemed to do the trick. The Edendale Horse too came back. All of these men experienced problems: difficulties in obtaining replacement horses for those lost or insufficient carbines to go around, for example. But they were willing and ready to fight.

Chelmsford decided that the NNC would be re-formed into battalions rather than regiments. There would now be five battalions. Some of the officers were removed. Major Graves, who had effectively abandoned his native troops on the way back from Eshowe, was diplomatically moved sideways to what would nowadays be called a 'desk job', following the assertions of a drunken sergeant to his face that he was a 'coward'.[16] Most of the NCOs, the major subject of complaint, were reassigned to other units. In future, at least one officer in each company had to speak the Zulu language. Not everything changed though. The drill process, deeply unpopular with the native troops, was to continue. But on the whole the adjustments were positive and helped to restore morale – eventually.

But this was several months in the future as Chelmsford pondered his next steps in early February. There were ongoing problems with the provisioning of the men faced with the challenge of holding off any Zulu raids. Fort Pine turned out to be a white elephant, with no attacks on it forthcoming. However, it proved to be a particularly unpleasant posting. The fort was manned by colonial troops who were without supplies for fourteen days. They also had no shelter despite the promise that tents were to be provided. It was inevitable perhaps that sickness broke out. It was almost as foreseeable that tensions between colonial soldiers and the British high command would arise.

There were, of course, many opinions as to what had caused the disaster that had overtaken the British army at Isandlwana. Norris-Newman blamed the British government for not sending out reinforcements, in particular cavalry, for 'to carry on a campaign quickly and successfully in Zululand large forces of mounted men are necessary, not only for fighting, but principally for mounted patrol and vedette work, combined with dispatch-carrying and keeping open communications'. There were, the correspondent acknowledged, irregulars who had worked splendidly but there was simply not enough of them to compensate for the lack of regular cavalry.[17] It was a convincing argument, save that when cavalry did eventually arrive no one really seemed to know how to use them.

There was also a quick search for a scapegoat. The victory at Rorke's Drift showed what could be done behind a well-prepared defensive position. Norris-Newman wondered why 900 men at Isandlwana did not enjoy the same outcome. He noted that 'it seems to us here plain that some officer in command of the camp that day not only neglected his duty by not fulfilling the orders given, but also forgot the most simple military rules laid down for warfare against the Zulus'. It would not take long for some to put a name to the man so responsible.[18]

Rorke's Drift proved a useful distraction. The *Illustrated London News* of 22 February was quick to refer to the 'extraordinary bravery displayed by the British troops'. Isandlwana had touched patriotic emotions. The same issue of the publication, whose editor had questioned the motivations for the war, now noted that one of the main reasons for the conflict was the 'savage tyranny of Cetewayo

[sic]' and also remarked that the Zulus were 'the most formidable of all Native African Powers'.

Another contemporary commentator, D.C.F. Moodie, who assembled a history of the war shortly after its ultimate conclusion, came up with the quite ridiculous assertion that:

> if the Zulus had not been severely checked at Rorke's Drift there was certainly a grave probability of their sweeping southward, gathering up the overawed tribes as they went, and devastating South Africa from the Zambezi to Cape Town. We cannot overestimate our debt of gratitude to the defenders of Rorke's Drift.[19]

Chelmsford too saw the merits in talking up the successful defence of Rorke's Drift. In his official report he praised Chard, Bromhead and their men who 'for twelve hours made the most gallant resistance I ever heard of against the determined attacks of some 3,000 Zulus, 370 of whose dead bodies surrounded the post'.[20] The valiant fight that had taken place at the isolated mission station would prove most useful in distracting attention.

Soon after the battle was over, Chelmsford was writing urgent messages to Glyn, in charge of the men at Rorke's Drift, asking him to chase Chard for a report of the action. Glyn was still struggling to come to terms with the dreadful loss of Isandlwana and could not find the energy or interest to speak to Chard. He also felt that the blame for the debacle, when so many of his men had been lost, was subtly being moved towards him by Chelmsford. It was not long before these suspicions appeared to be confirmed, when he was asked by letter for more information about the arrangements made at the camp of Isandlwana. Glyn was overheard in responding caustically: 'odd the general asking me to tell him what he knows more than I do.'[21]

Chard's report eventually reached Chelmsford, a detailed account which gave a very credible summation of the action that had been fought. When the report reached England, Queen Victoria was quick to send a congratulatory message, expressing her pride in the actions of the men. The Duke of Cambridge responded to Chelmsford too, expressing the sentiments that he had the 'fullest confidence in the regiment, and am satisfied that you have done and will continue to do everything that is right'. He closed with the reassuring message that 'strong reinforcements' had already been dispatched.

There then followed a steady flow of decorations for the defenders of Rorke's Drift. This was not a one-off process but rather an ongoing series of awards lasting over many months. Bromhead had also provided a report in which six of his men had been singled out for their bravery. They were awarded VCs for their part. Bromhead and Chard were predictably added to the list too. Others were added later: Surgeon Reynolds in June 1879, Corporal Schiess of the NNC in November of that year and Commissary Dalton in January 1880. Famously, the total medal haul of eleven VCs was, and remains, a record distribution for any single action fought by the British army, given out to about 10 per cent of the total actively involved in the defence.

But not everyone was convinced by the commander-in-chief's attempts at distraction, for the report of Rorke's Drift inevitably went cheek by jowl with that of Isandlwana and the *Illustrated London News* thought Chelmsford's account was 'rather feeble'. It ponderously compared Caesar's famous phrase '*veni, vidi, vici*' to that which applied to Chelmsford, 'I went, I did not see, I suffered a defeat'.

Some saw through what appeared to be a blatant attempt to distract attention from the bigger picture. The Duke of Cambridge later commented that 'we are giving the VC very freely I think'.[22] Garnet Wolseley, soon to be in command in Zululand, was far from happy at the awards given, and was particularly indignant at the suggestion of awards of VCs to Coghill and Melvill, men whom he felt should have died where they were rather than try to escape, whether they were carrying a flag or not.[23]

They were both swimming against the tide. A very Victorian sentimental chord had been struck by the action to save the flag and the queen no less was moved by it. She commanded that a wreath of *immortelles*, dried flowers, be sent to the regiment. She further ordered that from that day on a silver replica of this wreath was always to be carried round the staff of the colours of each battalion of the regiment.

Press interest in these events was not just limited to Britain. American newspapers had paid very little attention to the war up until news of Isandlwana came in. Then everything changed. The *New York Times* had it as its front-page headline story. The following day it offered in its editorial the comment that 'the history of British colonisation in Africa is, like that of its progress in all barbarous and semi-barbarous countries, a history of endless encroachment and bullying invariably ending in conquest'. The disastrous reverse at Isandlwana was entirely the British government's own fault, it opined.

All this might have seemed a trifle odd coming just three years after the American nation's own 'disaster' at the Little Bighorn and decades of broken promises and exploitation in its own backyard. The *Washington Post* was indeed quite conscious of the possibility of such comparisons and explained that the situations were entirely different as America needed Indian lands whereas Britain did not need those of the Zulus. This presumably made the broken promises and decades of exploitation acceptable. But comparisons anyway continued to be made. A later edition of the *Post* would also offer the observation that 'the Zulu are more formidable fighters than the American savages'.[24]

In the aftermath of Isandlwana, Chelmsford was quick to ask for extra resources. On 27 January he had asked Stanley for reinforcements. Huge numbers of native levies had deserted and he feared that the rest would follow suit. He requested a minimum of three infantry regiments and two cavalry, as well as a company of engineers. The cavalry needed to be flexible and had to be prepared to fight as Mounted Infantry because of the exigencies of war in this hostile environment. Some modifications would be required: they needed to have their carbines slung from their shoulders, ready for action, and also had to carry a sword that was shorter than the regulation issue fastened to the saddle.[25]

He also pre-empted Stanley's inevitable response by saying that he had set up a Court of Inquiry to investigate the causes of the defeat. It was in his own interests to take control of the court's composition as he himself might not come out of it too well. Everything had changed because of the defeat. On 28 January, Sir Bartle Frere had written to Chelmsford to say that the awards of the Boundary Commission had been torn up. Indeed, their findings seemed to belong to another epoch even though they had only been announced a few weeks before. There was nothing very enlightened or even remotely legal about any of this.

The inquiry into the loss of the camp at Isandlwana was chaired by Colonel Hassard of the Royal Engineers. He was not held in universally high regard amongst his officer colleagues, some of them thinking him 'rather feeble'. With him sat Lieutenant-Colonel Francis Law of the Royal Artillery and Lieutenant-Colonel Harness, the latter a material witness to Chelmsford's confused responses to the urgent messages received from the camp at Isandlwana whilst he was out looking for elusive Zulus. As a member of the board he could not, of course, give evidence.

It is not clear, however, that he would ever have been called to testify anyway. Chelmsford set very narrow terms of reference, 'to ascertain what orders were given for the defence of the camp, and how these orders were carried out. It was assembled solely for the purpose of assisting the General Commanding in forming an opinion.' These words, penned by Harness, reveal that Chelmsford was not specifically asking for anyone to express an opinion on his actions.

Even in this slimmed-down version of the events of Isandlwana, certain inconsistencies in the command structure emerged. Major Clery, Colonel Glyn's senior staff officer, related the story of how he had first of all written orders to Durnford to bring his forces up but that Crealock had then taken over responsibility for doing so. It was right that Crealock should write the instructions but symptomatic of Chelmsford's style of command that he had not thought this through before deciding on a course of action. Act first, think after, seemed to be the maxim. Glyn's comments were also revealing, basically telling the court that the column had been under the direct control of Chelmsford and implying that he had little to do other than follow direct orders from the commander in the field.

The inquiry barely scratched the surface of what had happened. Chelmsford committed his thoughts on the findings to paper and those points he chose to emphasise were particularly revealing. He was much impressed by the evidence given by Lieutenant Cochrane, that Pulleine had repeated the orders he had received to defend the camp to Durnford on several occasions when the latter encouraged him to commit men to an offensive move against the Zulus.[26]

He also noted his reasons for thinking that the men left in camp were more than enough to cope with any Zulu assault. The ammunition, he noted, was abundant, the soldiers were good shots and everyone was confident of their ability to fight off the enemy. He commented that the ground was too rocky to dig any trenches but that a laager could have been erected by those left behind should they have felt that one was needed.

Major Crealock was recorded as saying that Durnford had been ordered to camp to take command of it. This turned out to be the most controversial statement given in evidence. No copy of the written orders sent to Durnford were ever found; it was later alleged that they had been found on his body and were then conveniently 'lost' when the contents did not appear to bear out Crealock's statement.

Any question of doubt was removed with the discovery of the orders which had been retrieved from Durnford's body and subsequently passed into private ownership. They were found in the archives of the Royal Engineers Museum at Chatham and show, as might have been assumed, that Chelmsford was vagueness personified when the orders were sent off to Durnford. They merely say that Durnford was 'to march to this camp [Isandlwana] at once with all the force you have with you of No. 2 Column'. Just what they were to do when they got there was not mentioned.[27]

Chelmsford was to give a very public airing of his views on the reasons for the loss at Isandlwana. Whilst inspecting the troops near the mouth of the Thukela in February, he gave them an address in which he stated that he believed there had been more than enough troops present at Isandlwana to fight off even 20,000 Zulus. He said that:

> if only they had been kept together, and had not lost their formation, when at a distance from the camp, where they could not renew their ammunition when exhausted; but even then they had their bayonets and knew how to use them. To that alone, he thought, must be attributed the sad loss, and entire slaughter of so many companies of the 1–24th and 2–24th.[28]

In other words, the loss was not his fault.

Others soon became suspicious of the efforts made to make Durnford the scapegoat. Sir Charles Dilke, MP for Chelsea in London, made an extraordinary attack in the House of Commons on 28 March. Dilke presented a question to the House which effectively amounted to a censure on both Frere and Chelmsford. Dilke's statement for debate included the words:

[The House] regrets that the ultimatum which was calculated to produce immediate war should have been presented to the Zulu King without authority from the responsible advisers of the Crown, and that an offensive war should have been commenced without imperative and pressing necessity or adequate preparation; and this House further regrets that after the censure passed upon the High Commissioner by Her Majesty's Government in the Dispatch of the 19th day of March 1879, the conduct of affairs in South Africa should be retained in his hands.

A supplementary statement appended from Colonel Mure added as a point of censure:

and that a war of invasion was undertaken with insufficient forces, notwithstanding the full information in the possession of Her Majesty's Government of the strength of the Zulu Army, and the warnings which they had received from Sir Bartle Frere and Lord Chelmsford that hostilities were unavoidable.

In Dilke's view in the subsequent debate, the loss of all those men at Isandlwana was solely down to the 'gross incompetence' of Chelmsford. In case anyone was left in any doubt, he added:

Lord Chelmsford blames Colonel Durnford for not having fortified the camp. Why, he was there 48 hours himself with the whole of his ammunition for the campaign, and during all those 48 hours he never made the slightest attempts to do what he says Colonel Durnford should have done in 4 hours.[29]

Chelmsford's requests to Stanley for reinforcements had been relatively modest but the response from London was anything but. A reverse of the magnitude that had been suffered was simply unacceptable. Suddenly, the British government found the resources that were previously nowhere to be seen: seven infantry battalions, two cavalry regiments and four artillery batteries, including more Gatling guns. As Norris-Newman postulated, Isandlwana had ironically made an ultimate crushing British victory a certainty; it was 'a mere matter of men, time and money'.[30]

Criticism of Chelmsford quickly started to emerge. The *Spectator* of 8 March was especially critical of the lack of adequate scouting, asking 'how is even one day's work to be arranged, when the country ahead is to the General like the surface of a new planet?' The editor concluded that 'there is a want of grasp of the situation, of everything except sad reflectiveness, which leaves in our minds no other conclusion than the general is by nature unadapted to independent command'.[31] Sir Robert Peel, in the parliamentary debate of 28 March, noted that Chelmsford had been 'out-generalled, out-manoeuvred, surprised, and defeated' and compared him with General Burgoyne in the American War of Independence.[32]

Even if there were those who thought that Chelmsford had been badly out-manoeuvred in the campaign so far, he still had friends in very high places. Much publicity was given to a message from no less a person than the queen to Chelmsford, which stated unambiguously that she 'sympathises most sincerely with him in the dreadful loss which has deprived her of so many gallant officers and men, and that her Majesty places entire confidence in him, and in her troops, to maintain our honour and our good name'.[33]

Horse Guards, army headquarters, were not impressed at the breadth of information gleaned from the inquiry that Chelmsford had commissioned and continued to ask him for more. As time passed and unanswered questions remained, with Chelmsford seemingly unwilling to provide information, even those at Horse Guards who had been allies of the commander-in-chief found their confidence in him diminishing.

It was not until 11 August 1879, long after the fighting in the war was over and Chelmsford had removed himself from the battlefield, that a formal finding on the real reasons for the defeat of Chelmsford's expedition into Zululand was delivered. It was a crucial piece of correspondence as it set out clearly the official view on where responsibility for the Isandlwana debacle actually lay. Written by Adjutant-General Sir Charles Ellice, it was, in reality, expressing the views of the Duke of Cambridge.

In case of any ambiguity, the very first paragraph stated bluntly that 'His Royal Highness [Cambridge] has come to the conclusion that the primary cause of the misfortune, and that which led to all the others, was the under estimate formed of the offensive fighting power of the Zulu army'.

This was a perception which of course came right from the top, from Chelmsford himself. He was further implicitly criticised for dividing his forces as a result of this perception. Other more detailed criticisms followed, six in total, namely:

- the unprepared state of Rorke's Drift to resist a Zulu attack,
- the lack of preparation of a laager at Isandlwana,
- Chelmsford taking half of the men out of the camp at Isandlwana, leaving it in a virtually defenceless state,
- the lack of scouting around the camp,

    – the belief in those leading the army that no serious attack would be made by the Zulus once they had left the camp,

    – the lack of co-ordination in the defence of the camp once the attack came.

Only the last point, that of the unco-ordinated defence, could in any way be attributed to Durnford (or Pulleine), the rest were clearly the responsibility of Chelmsford. Chelmsford's attempts to move the blame elsewhere had failed.[34]

All this, however, was some months away. In February, Chelmsford still had a war to win, regardless of his own future. Morale was low, especially at Rorke's Drift, where the camp had turned into an unhealthy quagmire and there had been plagues of flies. Sickness was rampant and men were starting to die of disease. Spirits were somewhat restored when the lost colour that Coghill and Melvill had tried in vain to save was recovered on 4 February. Major Black of the 2nd/24th led his men out on a mission to find it and also the bodies of Melvill and Coghill. He was accompanied by several survivors of Isandlwana, Raw and Brickhill, as well as Lieutenant Harford.

They followed a path down to a drift across the Buffalo River, the terrain around it being strewn with dead bodies, many of them natives on the British side. Passing down a steep track, the party came across the bodies of Melvill and Coghill. They buried them and held a religious service for them. Various personal items were recovered for their families, Coghill's ring and Melvill's spurs included.

Proceeding carefully along the riverbank, steep-sided and covered in scrubby bush, Harford and a couple of other men came across the colour of the 1st/24th. Although somewhat damaged by immersion in the water, this was still a tremendous fillip for morale. The colour was carried in triumph back to Rorke's Drift where it was gratefully received by Colonel Glyn, who was overcome with emotion. He returned to the gravesite later, where the bodies were disinterred and put in proper coffins. In the process he recovered Melvill's watch, which had stopped at 2.10 p.m., the time he assumed that he had been in the water trying to escape.

There was much debate in Britain about just how the authorities in southern Africa had got themselves in this mess. A vote of censure in the British Parliament against the government was defeated by 306 votes to 246. However, there were a number of critical voices aimed in the direction of Bartle Frere in particular. The *Illustrated London News* noted that:

    he has disregarded the instructions of his superiors; he has taken upon himself to precipitate a war with the Zulu king without adequate means of bringing it to a successful conclusion; he has exposed the colony of Natal, to say nothing of the Transvaal and of the Cape, to serious danger, [an action that] has already brought about an additional 'little war' deemed by the public to be unnecessary, if not unjust.[35]

Bartle Frere did not escape official censure, though for the time being he survived. Sir Michael Hicks-Beach, the colonial secretary, wrote to him that he and his colleagues:

> have been unable to find in the documents you have placed before them that evidence of urgent necessity for immediate action which alone could justify you in taking, without their full knowledge and sanction, a course almost certain to result in a war, which, as I had previously impressed upon you, every effort should have been used to avoid.

In case there was any residual doubt, Frere was further reminded that the desire of the British government was 'that the military operations now proceeding should be directed to the termination, at the earliest moment consistent with the safety of our colonies and the honour of our arms, of the Zulu question'.[36] For now he kept his job, though its importance was soon to be downgraded.

Reinforcements eventually arrived in southern Africa in the middle of March. They continued to arrive throughout the rest of the month. The first task that Chelmsford had in mind for them was the relief of Eshowe, the mission station where Pearson's Number 1 Column was now under siege and had been for nearly two months.

After the despair of early February, Chelmsford's spirits were on the up again. He was now confident enough to face up to one of his greatest inner demons. On 14 March, Major Wilsone Black was given the unenviable task of leading a reconnaissance to Isandlwana. He found provisions scattered all over the ground: tinned fish, meat, jam, milk. Letters, papers and photos were strewn all over the area. The stench of the dead still permeated the air. The bodies were long past the stage of recognition, save remnants of the uniforms which at least allowed Black to work out which units they had belonged to.

They left the field of death without much disturbance from the Zulus, though a few fired shots at them from a safe distance. Black and his men then followed the track that the fugitives from the battle had taken and found a gun carriage minus its gun. At 3 p.m. they arrived safely back at camp having found that a number of serviceable wagons remained on the site.

This was just a first step in restoring morale. Isandlwana would always remain the 'elephant in the room' for the rest of the war. It had given the Zulus a reputation of being invincible and the new recruits already sailing across the sea would be very nervous at the prospect of facing up to them in battle. Chelmsford himself seemed to shudder at the very thought of Isandlwana; a significant part of his future campaign strategy was predicated on the need to avoid a route that crossed over the field of death.

But the war was about to begin anew. It would be very different in character than that which had gone before. There would be no underestimation of the enemy now. On the contrary, it would be a war of careful attrition. It was as if a new commander-in-chief had emerged, an unrecognisable man from he who had existed before the disaster of Isandlwana. Chelmsford's mind was now set on revenge. The gloves were firmly off and this was now a war to the death.

eight

THE TURN OF THE TIDE

Wood's Campaigning in the West

Chelmsford's strategy at the start of the war effectively meant that there were three different stories to be told from the first months of the campaign. Whilst the Central Column was suffering a disastrous reverse and Pearson, as a result, was effectively incarcerated in the mission station at Eshowe, Wood in the north-west of Zululand was left very much to his own devices with, at this stage at least, minimal integration with the other British forces in the country. This was not how it was initially meant to be but, given the dramatic sequence of events at Isandlwana, was how things turned out in practice.

In a frank communication on 3 February 1879, Chelmsford had written to Wood and told him that he and his capable number two, Lieutenant-Colonel Buller, would have to pull him 'out of the mire'. A close examination of Chelmsford's correspondence reveals that he was always close to Wood but this trend became more marked over time. In the aftermath of Isandlwana Chelmsford proposed to send many of his reinforcements up to Wood, who would be the only one of the three column commanders able to operate aggressively for a while.

Chelmsford's mood immediately after the defeat had been one of extreme despondency. He closed his communication to Wood with the wistful words: 'I wish I saw my way with honour out of this beastly country.' But such redemption was a long time off.

The character of the war that Wood was involved in was very different than that fought elsewhere in Zululand. The borders, for one thing, were much more porous for here were the much-disputed lands of the Transvaal. There were also a number of clans whose loyalty to Cetshwayo was suspect and it was hoped that this could be exploited and that some could be persuaded to come over to the

166

British side. Nevertheless, some of the toughest opponents of the British invasion force were to be found here.

Wood had tried to encourage local chiefs to come over to the British side, though more by aggression than persuasion. Even before the ultimatum had officially expired he had been raiding across the border. He was the perfect person for this role, being energetic and prepared to take chances. His men moved swiftly, sweeping down on unsuspecting villages and robbing them of their cattle. They would be returned, he said, if their owners opted to support the British but otherwise they would be sold on.

Wood seemed excessively enthusiastic about his cattle-raiding. Thousands of cattle were seized and sold; some within the British ranks did very well financially out of the situation. He was assisted ably by Buller, a man in many ways cut from the same cloth. In the quest for cattle, Wood and Buller took many chances and in the process exposed themselves to danger. This would ultimately threaten them with a disaster of their own.

Buller led the irregular cavalry with Wood and proved himself to be a very capable officer in this role. His men, armed with carbines, were of course very mobile and well suited to raiding. If, however, they found themselves faced with a large hostile enemy force, they adopted tactics perfectly suited to the threat, probing at the edges, irritating, sniping with the odd shot up close and then retreating rapidly before the Zulus could fight back, until they reached a spot of their own choosing where they had some advantage and then might decide to make a fight of it for a time before moving off again. The tactics they would later use in battle were both highly irritating and effective.

Wood was a widely respected commander in his own right. He was one of 'Wolseley's Ring' – the coterie of officers that frequently found themselves fighting at the side of Sir Garnet Wolseley, Britain's foremost general of his generation. Not that everyone liked Wood; Wolseley thought him too full of himself and over-ambitious. Wood was also perhaps the most accident-prone man ever to command a British army. Alongside the dangers of being wounded in battle and the inevitable exposure to disease, Wood also managed to find some strange ways of injuring himself during his career, the most bizarre of which was falling off the back of a giraffe.

The region in which Wood operated was also one in which the Boers had a strong interest. Wood hoped to encourage them to join his side; excellent horsemen and good shots as they were, they would make first-class irregulars. The Swazis to the north also had ambitions in the region and the whole territory around the borders was, as a result, a hotbed of intrigue. Wood had established his main supply base at Utrecht, a small Boer settlement within the disputed territories. It was not a popular posting; an English officer described it as 'a great swamp, lying in a big hole, surrounded by high hills and a perfect nest of fever'.[1] Along with Luneberg, Utrecht was the main colonial settlement close to the borders of Zululand; both were potentially exposed to attacks from hostile forces.

One man in particular would prove an implacable opponent of Wood. The exiled Swazi chieftain Mbilini had been groomed to be a warrior almost since birth. When he had failed in his bid to gain the Swazi throne for himself he had taken himself off to Zululand (via a stop in the Transvaal), where he had developed a close relationship with Cetshwayo. He would turn out to be a more than capable lieutenant for him in the war with the British.

Mbilini was something of a maverick. He was careful not to overstep the line with Cetshwayo but he certainly acted with almost complete autonomy; he was, after all, not a Zulu. He was a man who was driven most of all by his own personal ambitions, the achievement of which he pursued with ruthless single-mindedness. He was a magnificent guerrilla leader and would prove himself to be a constant thorn in the flesh of the British forces in the region.

Wood had just over 2,000 men available to him. These included regular troops and a battery of guns. However, like Chelmsford, he had no regular cavalry and had recruited a number of local irregulars. Despite their traditional antipathy with the Zulus, there were virtually no Boers included in this number. Following the recent annexation of the Transvaal none of them trusted the British. Chelmsford would write to the Duke of Cambridge, commander-in-chief of the British army, on 1 February that 'from the Transvaal we can expect no assistance. The feeling against us amongst the Boers is very bitter.'[2] The only significant exception to this general rule was Piet Uys, whose father and brother had been killed in the conflict with Dingane forty years before. He had good reason to hate the Zulus more than the British and he came in with the latter.

The border region was mountainous in places and in some of these fastnesses potentially dangerous opponents such as Mbilini were based. Their forces were composed of expert warriors with high morale and fierce determination. Buller found this out early in the war. On 20 January he led a raid against a nearby mountain, Zungwini. He was attacked by 1,000 warriors who almost surrounded him and forced him to retreat.

This raid had been composed of cavalry alone. Two days later Wood led a larger force accompanied by infantry. He managed to catch the Zulus by surprise and they abandoned their cattle and retreated. However, as Wood made off with his prize he saw on another adjacent summit, Hlobane, about 4,000 hostile warriors drilling. He returned on 24 January and a fight ensued, but the results were not decisive. Then the character of the war changed when Wood received news of the stunning reverse at Isandlwana.

It was on 24 January that an exhausted rider from Utrecht caught up with him after travelling 48 miles with a note from Captain Gardner, one of the few survivors from Isandlwana, who had shown the initiative to send a message to Wood telling him what had happened (he had also sent messages to Rorke's Drift and Helpmekaar from the field of Isandlwana before escaping himself). Against the advice of some of his officers, Wood read the message out to the men so that they were fully aware of the disastrous turn of events.

A few days later Chelmsford himself had corresponded with Wood, giving him brief details of Isandlwana and telling him to prepare himself to have the whole Zulu army down on him at any minute. The roles had changed: according to the message, the Central Column, once reconstituted, was to be subordinate to the movements of Wood's force. Wood established a base on a windswept ridge about 15 miles off from Hlobane at Khambula. From this location he was able to keep an eye on both Luneberg and Utrecht whilst also being able to co-ordinate his movements with Rowlands to the north. It also left him well positioned for an offensive move into Zululand itself.

Wood replied to Chelmsford that he was confident the camp he had established at Khambula would be capable of resisting any Zulu attack. It was not mere bluster, as events would prove. Although Wood understood that Chelmsford did not wish him to take any unnecessary risks, he was encouraged to go on to the offensive from time to time. Right on the borders of Zululand he had significant flexibility to manoeuvre. His lines of communication, though extended, were relatively secure. He could move quickly, keep the Zulus on their toes and strike across a wide area. He could also continue to put pressure on the local chiefs to come across to the British side.

Yet the hectic activity this involved came at a personal cost. Wood reckoned that he never slept for more than two or three hours at a time and for the next three months would go round the sentries watching the camp at least twice a night. Over the next couple of months the camp at Khambula would be moved five times, partly for sanitary reasons. Even Divine Service on Sundays, sacred to Victorian sensibilities, was just a brief interruption when the men were allowed to stop digging for a few minutes before starting again.[3]

Wood took great care to deploy scouts, which he put in a screen 20 miles in front of his main force. Patrols were sent 6 miles out before dawn each day. Understanding the ways of the Zulus better than some of his colleagues, Wood watched out for Zulu attacks particularly at the times of new and full moon, considered auspicious times for an attack by his enemy. Conscious of the needs of his men, particularly given the awful weather, sentries outside the camp were allowed tents or blanket shelters.

Wood was not unconscious of the need to keep morale up. In the lull between the raids, with no Zulu attack yet imminent, there was even time to indulge in sports. Wood noted with interest that in a contest to throw an assegai as far as possible, the 'friendly' Zulus with him were easily beaten, reflecting the fact that the close-range stabbing version had now firmly taken over from the throwing version.

Embarrassingly though, the British tug-of-war team was easily defeated by Piet Uys and his Dutchmen. Wood prided himself on having trained a virtually unbeatable tug-of-war outfit that had defeated all comers from the British army before the war, but now found itself annihilated by Uys and his powerfully built comrades. Wood also found time to construct, of all things, both a tennis ground and a polo pitch.

These light-hearted diversions served to keep the men's spirits up. The events at Isandlwana had boosted the morale of the Zulu cause greatly. One of Cetshwayo's close local allies, Manyanyoba, had led an aggressive attack against Luneberg on 26 January and only a vigorous move by the mounted men of the local garrison had forced them off. In the meantime, Zulu forces began to build up in the region of Hlobane, the great, flat-topped mountain that dominated the surrounding countryside and the centre of local resistance to the British.

The local Zulus and in particular Mbilini, who if not a Zulu himself was enthusiastically allied to their cause, had aggressive intentions of their own. They launched a raid towards Luneberg in early February. Their target was not the town itself but the isolated farms around it. They had thought their tactics out well; they carried no guns, just spears, so that there would be no noise to attract the unwelcome attentions of the garrison. Scores of people, mainly black workers on the farms, were slain.

The *Natal Mercury* wrote in graphic detail of the 'atrocious barbarities'. They told how 'they murdered old men, about 50 women, and as many helpless boys and girls'. Little children, the correspondent said, were thrown on fires and one 20-year-old woman was speared thirty-five times. Patrols had been sent out in response and twenty of the raiders killed. The paper ascribed the lack of a more determined response to a shortage of horses.[4]

The raid caused the British intense irritation. They launched counter-attacks, and although these succeeded in recovering some of the cattle that had been taken, they achieved very little in terms of punishing the Zulus or their allies. The local landscape was rocky, the hills were pocked with caves, natural refuges for an aggressive foe and very useful from a defensive perspective. It was like trying to swat a swarm of troublesome flies – as soon as they were swept away from one area they would turn up in another. A long, frustrating campaign beckoned.

But although the military campaign promised to be a difficult one, British spirits were buoyed by a diplomatic coup. The local chief Hamu, who had long been courted as a potential ally, finally decided to collaborate with the British. He was a half-brother of Cetshwayo and it was hoped that his defection would have a crucial effect on the loyalties of other wavering Zulus. It might seem strange for him to change his allegiance so soon after Isandlwana, but he had presumably reasoned that the end result of the war was unavoidable and it would be in his own interests to back the winning horse as soon as possible.

He had not been able to do so before because of the aggressive actions of Mbilini, Manyanyoba and others. His position was exposed, being to the east of Hlobane, and he would need to flee from his lands to join the British as he was not strong enough to stay where he was. A temporary respite after the cross-border raids in early February gave him the chance to do so and he made his move. He went into hiding until he had a chance to flee along with 1,000 of his followers. Word of his planned defection reached Cetshwayo and he sent out a force to stop him. The race was on. Hamu, in the event, managed to make it to Swazi territory from where he would be able to reach the British. However, many of his people were left behind, hiding in caves and forests close to home, dangerously far away from the border and safety.

There were changes in the command structure of the British army at the end of the month. Rowlands, whose leadership had been in the main ineffective, was sent to Pretoria to keep an eye on the Boers who were increasingly restive, no doubt encouraged by the problems caused by the Zulus. His command was then put under the direct control of Wood. The garrison at Luneberg was strengthened as a result, but its lines of communication were vulnerable. Supplies were brought along the road from Derby to the north. It ran very close to the disputed border territories; a perfect position for an ambush.

The ability of a Zulu warrior to move quickly was one of his major assets. Unencumbered by much in the way of equipment, he could move swiftly over ground, making him perfect raw material as a guerrilla fighter. He did not, in practice, often fight this way; a Zulu warrior was very vulnerable when attacking a strongly defended position but this was the way he fought on many occasions during the war with normally disastrous results. It was mainly in the war against Wood that he was used with best effect in guerrilla warfare, which was unfortunate from a Zulu perspective.

At the beginning of March, a British supply column made its way out of Derby towards Luneberg. There were eighteen wagons in it carrying both ammunition and general supplies. Aware that it was on its way, a force of 100 men under Captain David Moriarty of the 80th Regiment set out from Luneberg, sent by the garrison commander Major Charles Tucker, to meet and escort it along the most exposed part of the road.

The weather was again dreadful and heavy rains had swollen the Ntombe River, which the supply train would have to cross. The wagons reached Myers Drift, just a few miles from Luneberg, on 9 March. With enormous difficulty, it was possible to get just a few of the wagons across. However, the river then rose still further making it absolutely impossible to get any others over.

For the next two days the column was effectively cut in two. Moriarty had taken command and erected a laager for defensive purposes. Tucker came out to see the position for himself but rode back, getting drenched in the process as the torrential rains continued to pour down. Erecting a laager was eminently sensible; Mbilini had a stronghold just 3 miles away. What was not so sensible was the way that the laager was organised.

To emphasise the threat, on 10 March a civilian driver recognised Mbilini amongst a group of supposedly 'friendly' natives visiting the camp. This should have put the camp on its guard but it did not. It had rained pretty much non-stop for several days but on 11 March the day dawned fine. Tucker returned to the river to see how things were with his men who had been exposed to awful conditions.

There was a raft on site and Tucker was ferried over to see close up how things were in the laager. He did not like what he saw at all. The water level had started to drop and this meant that there was a gap in the defences which had previously been anchored on the river banks. Perhaps the proximity of Luneberg lulled the defenders into a false sense of security. At any event, they had most certainly taken their eye off the ball.

Neither did Tucker like the way the wagons were attached to one another, leaving gaps in between that a nimble foe could quickly get through. In his own words, the defences looked weak and he could not 'consider this any protection whatever in the event of the Zulus attacking in numbers, as they are sure to do; they can very easily pull themselves over this'.[5] Given this observation, it is surprising that Tucker, the senior officer on the spot, did not try to put things right. But he was prepared, unwisely in retrospect, to make allowances for the lack of diligence in erecting the laager given the trying conditions the men there had had to put up with. He noted, however, that the ammunition inside the laager – there were 90,000 rounds there as this was a supply train – would be hard to get to in an emergency due to the great number of cattle inside. Neither did he think it was particularly sensible to divide the men, yet this was, he later thought with hindsight, a blessing in disguise.

At about 5 a.m. on the morning of 12 March, the sentry watching out from the laager peered through the gloom as the early mists started to break up. There had already been an alarm about ninety minutes earlier when a shot had rung out. Moriarty had decided that this must have been a false alarm and, although he told the sentries to be extra vigilant, the camp settled down to sleep again.

As the eyes of the sentry started to focus, a terrifying sight met his eyes. There were Zulus all around the camp, creeping stealthily down on it. Without bothering to shout an alarm, the lookout fired. So too did the other sentries, waking the camp up with a start. Men rushed into position as quickly as they could but it was already too late. The Zulus fired off a volley, threw down their guns and charged into the camp. They easily scrambled over the gaps that had been left in the laager.

They were inside the defences in a second. The cattle which had been laagered within the wagons were terrified out of their wits, which added to the scene of chaos. Plunging madly around in their vain attempts to run away from the cries of the warriors and the shots that rang out, they made it even more difficult for the defenders to fight back effectively. There was no time for the defenders to organise themselves and the battle quickly became one for individual survival. Vicious hand-to-hand fighting ensued but with the defenders outnumbered over ten to one there was only one possible outcome.

Miraculously, a few men managed to break through the cordon of Zulus surrounding the camp. Private Jones of the 80th was one of them. Using his rifle as a club, he smashed through the ring. Then, throwing his rifle away, he jumped into the swollen river. Diving underwater, he was part-way across when he was attacked by a Zulu. There was a violent hand-to-hand scuffle which ended when Jones stabbed his attacker between the ribs. Jones got out of the river on the other side, ran off and managed to make it to Luneberg. He arrived stark naked and with his feet cut to pieces, having been lacerated by the cross-country run he had endured.[6]

There were a small number of soldiers who had spent the night on the other side of the river, opposite the laager. They had been alerted by the firing nearby. They did their best to organise a counter-attack but they themselves were quickly under threat. A body of Zulus started to cross the river further up with the obvious intention of cutting them off from Luneberg.

These men were under the notional command of Lieutenant Harward. As soon as he saw what was happening, Harward jumped up on his horse and rode off as fast as he could. He later said that this was so he could warn the garrison at Luneberg of the attack, but it was a feeble excuse for abandoning his men when under threat. The soldiers left to fend for themselves could see that the fighting was virtually over on the far side of the river and the large body of perhaps 200 Zulus was already fording the river further up in the attempt to cut them off.

Vastly outnumbered, these thirty-five men encamped across the river from the laager started to make a fighting retreat accompanied by the few who had managed to swim across the river to safety.

Sergeant Booth took command and led the men in exemplary fashion. He was an experienced soldier who had been in the army for fifteen years and would finally retire in 1898 after thirty-three years service. Now, he kept his small band together and from time to time stopped them to fire a disciplined volley at the chasing Zulus, managing to keep them at a safe distance. It was a harrowing experience.

Several times hundreds of Zulus got close and were forced back valiantly. The only break in discipline occurred when four of the retreating British soldiers opted to make their own way back to Luneberg and, isolated from their comrades, were promptly slaughtered. Their bodies were later recovered about

3 miles from the river and brought back to be interred in Luneberg in an atmospheric torch-lit ceremony.

Booth brought the remnant of the escort back to safety. Twelve men of those who were in the laager had also survived by swimming across the river to escape the exultant Zulus. There had apparently been a terrible battle in the river itself as friend and foe fought each other in a desperate attempt to stay alive. One British soldier escaped by grabbing hold of a Zulu who was swimming to safety. Other foes attempted to drown each other in the fast-flowing waters.

Harward had, in the meantime, made it back to Luneberg, where Major Tucker was in command. Tucker was awoken by the sudden emergence in his tent of Harward at 0630. He immediately assembled 150 horsemen when given the shocking news of what was happening at the laager. They rode post-haste towards the site of the camp. About a mile off they saw a swarm of Zulus close by. They were making their escape from the battlefield, expecting that a relieving force would be on them soon.

Tucker and his men completed their journey to the river. When they arrived a horrible sight met their eyes. Scores of dead bodies, many of them naked or half-clothed, were sprawled on the ground. Most of them had been disembowelled in traditional Zulu fashion. Tucker shouted out to see if any were still alive. Incredibly, one British soldier and two friendly natives appeared who had somehow escaped the attentions of the victorious Zulu warriors.

The survival of this British soldier seemed little short of miraculous. He had managed to swim across the river and pull himself out by grabbing hold of a tuft of grass. However, he was exhausted and weaponless, having thrown away his rifle so that he could swim more easily. A Zulu came at him with his assegai. There was a desperate struggle in which the soldier managed to grab hold of his assailant and kill him.

Completely spent by the struggle, the soldier had then fallen back in the water. Here he had managed to hide himself on the edge of the river amongst the reeds. At one point, he heard a voice shout out in very good English 'come out, Jack. They have all gone.' He was about to do so when he saw that the man shouting out was in fact a Zulu with his distinctive shield.

All that was left for the rescue party to do was bury the dead, which was done with all the dignity that could be mustered. Three volleys were fired as a last mark of respect. Then what little was left after the slaughter was recovered, though the Zulus had broken up what they could not take away with them. Even the dogs had been killed, as they had been at Isandlwana. The rescue party left, returning a few days later when the water levels had dropped and ferrying the wagons across was possible.

The disaster did little to discourage the growing impression amongst some British soldiers that their Zulu foe was a terrifying enemy. A few days later a party including Lieutenant-Colonel Redvers Buller came over to enquire into the disaster. Whilst they were present there was a false alarm when some friendly natives approached the camp after dark. Shots rang out, to be followed by others later in the night. Tucker was outspoken in his criticism of the soldiers. In a statement that would certainly resonate with Chelmsford's views, he said that 'these young soldiers are more trouble than they are worth'. The finishing touch was when a sentry had to be talked out of firing at what turned out to be a log of wood.

The British lost seventy-nine men at the massacre on the Ntombe, including some civilian wagon-drivers. Thirty Zulu bodies were also found, though more were no doubt wounded. Harward was court-martialled but, to the incredulity of many, was acquitted. Sir Garnet Wolseley, who would eventually take over from Chelmsford, was so angry at the verdict that he later issued a statement condemning Harward's actions, which was to be read out to all soldiers in Zululand. Booth, in contrast, was eventually awarded the Victoria Cross, although only after some time had passed; it was an award that was, despite this, particularly deserved: he had stepped up to the plate when so badly let down by the officer who was supposed to be in command. He almost lost out on this merited recognition because for a while it seemed that those in authority would prefer that the disaster was forgotten about altogether.

Wood was not of a temperament to let such a reverse go unpunished. He moved into the valley where it had taken place, burning homesteads and scattering hostile warriors as he went. However, the enemy forces did not run away completely but instead made their way to Hlobane, that well-protected fastness that nature had provided so well with defences: steep sides, narrow passes, rocky gorges. Wood reasoned that he would have to attack Mbilini and the abaQulusi people, a Zulu clan living on the mountain, by assaulting Hlobane itself – an extremely ambitious undertaking.

British spirits were cheered when, on 10 March, Hamu arrived in the British camp. He came in on a cart, his huge bulk being so great that it was impossible to find a horse to carry him. His first request was that a force should go and collect his wives. When asked how many of these there were, he said he thought it was about 300. When it was explained that he would have to accompany any force that was sent to rescue the women, he changed his mind and decided to do without them.

It was decided that it would be politically invaluable if the rest of Hamu's tribe could also be brought in, so a force was assembled to do just this. It would be a great challenge as his homestead was only 40 miles away from Ulundi and Cetshwayo would be keeping a close eye on events there. A force, nevertheless, set out and succeeded in collecting about 1,000 refugees.

They had been hiding themselves away awaiting the arrival of a rescuing force. Wood himself was present with those that went to bring them in, witnessing a 'long stream of humanity' that set out at daybreak on 15 March. This collection of the young, women and the elderly covered 30 miles in fifteen hours, accompanied all the way by irregular cavalry. Although the going was not easy, the refugees were spurred on by the terror of being overhauled by Cetshwayo's forces trying to stop them. By 8.30 p.m. it appeared that everyone had left who was going to leave.

It was a perilous undertaking and those who were trying to help spirit them away were caught up in the mood of the occasion. Buller had stated to Wood in typically blunt terms that he would have nothing to do with the 'verminous children', but the latter noted: 'I more than once saw him with six little black bodies in front of and behind his saddle, children under five years of age.'[7]

The column was forced to spend the night out in the open. Time was now of the essence as word would have quickly spread locally that the escape was under way. Wood ensured that they started next morning as soon as it was light. He had also sent out mule wagons from his camp to bring the children in over the last 10 miles. Some of the women in the rear seemed to be going agonisingly slowly up the hills of the Zinguin range. Wood sent Piet Uys down to hurry them up.

The problem was that one of the women was pregnant and on the verge of giving birth. Wood gave firm orders that his interpreter, Llewellyn Lloyd, was not to come into his camp without her. When Wood himself reached camp at 5 p.m. he saw Lloyd having a cup of tea. He started to reprimand him for ignoring his orders and leaving the woman behind until Lloyd told him that the woman was also in camp. Half an hour after Wood had given Lloyd his orders, the woman, having just given birth, was striding past the astonished interpreter at a rate of 5mph, her baby tucked under her arm.

On the way back towards British lines, the ragtag group passed by Hlobane. A few inaccurate shots were fired at the refugees but to no effect. They made their way safely back to the British camp. Chelmsford's hope, however, that the defection of such an important figure might encourage other Zulus to follow suit proved to be over-optimistic. He had miscalculated the loyalty of the majority of Cetshwayo's subjects.

In the aftermath of Isandlwana the Zulu army had been recovering its strength. Their losses had been heavy and a number had returned to their homes. The downside of every male of fighting age in the kingdom being a warrior was that they also had responsibilities at home and it was not possible to keep them permanently in the field, even in times of crisis. And anyway, Zulu custom dictated that after they had slain an enemy, they must take themselves off to perform the requisite purification ceremonies.

Cetshwayo at last managed to assemble another large force. Pearson was safely cooped up at Eshowe and Chelmsford had gone on the defensive. That left Wood as the only British commander who was on the offensive in Zululand.

He therefore offered the greatest threat to Cetshwayo and was the obvious next target for his army. This accorded with his strategy to focus the bulk of his forces against the greatest perceived current source of danger.

The army duly set out from Ulundi towards the west of Zululand. It numbered in the region of 20,000, a substantial threat to Wood. Cetshwayo had earlier given firm orders that on no account were they to attack a prepared position but they were to do what they could to get the British to give battle in the open, where their numbers could be used to best effect. His words were poetic but striking: 'do not put your face into the lair of a wild beast for you are sure to get clawed'.[8] It was excellent advice but unfortunately there were too many hotheads amongst the impi to comply with it.

Wood, in the meantime, had been developing his own plans for an attack on Hlobane. He had received reports that Cetshwayo was sending an army against him but thought it would be some time before it reached the vicinity of his force. He knew that Hlobane would be a tough nut to crack. He had observed it from a distance through a telescope and could see how sheer the sides were. Patrols that had probed the approaches to the mountain had reported how narrow the paths up it were and had also noted that those that were there appeared to be blocked with stone walls.

It was in the early afternoon of 27 March that Wood set out for Hlobane. His plans were not especially well developed, perhaps reflecting the fact that the organisation of such raids was normally left up to Buller. Speed was of the essence and in recognition of this many of the troops used would be mounted, although he would also take along a rocket battery; in all, there were 205 mounted men. The only foot soldiers were 440 native levies, including several hundred of Hamu's warriors. The plan was for the assault on Hlobane to be launched with attacks from either end of the mountain, hoping to catch any hostile forces in a pincer movement. Buller would lead the troops, attacking from the eastern side of the mountain whilst Lieutenant-Colonel Russell would do the same for those coming at Hlobane from the west.

The decision to use mounted troops was a result of the fact that Hlobane was too far away for infantry to march from Khambula and back in a day (the levies were much more mobile than regular soldiers and could therefore move more quickly). However, this move took no account of the awful terrain that would need to be traversed during the attack on the mountain. With its steep, rocky paths and broken boulders strewn across the summit plateau, it might prove very difficult for the horses. In addition, although Buller and his men were very experienced in this kind of warfare, the same could not be generally said for Russell and his contingent.

Many of the men involved in the assault were tired before they started. They had been out raiding for several days before and had had little opportunity to recover from their exertions before they set out again on the 27th. As they made their way across country towards Hlobane, some of the irregular horsemen noticed what looked like campfires in the distance. Either this news was not reported to those in command or little notice was taken of it.

Wood later insisted that he knew that an impi was heading towards him from Ulundi and he had sent out scouts to the south to watch out for them. Their efforts would turn out to be in vain. Wood had, in any case, heard through his spy network that the Zulu army had been delayed in its departure from Ulundi until 27 March. This information turned out to be false; they actually left two days before that.

Russell and his men spent the night at the foot of Zungweni Mountain, close to Hlobane, accompanied by Wood who had decided to join them. Wood did not plan to get involved in the direction of the battle but he took the opportunity to have a long chat with Piet Uys, who had stayed behind to speak with him. Uys and Wood had what proved to be a portentous chat in which Uys asked Wood to look out for his children if he was killed, offering to do the same for the colonel if the roles were reversed.

Buller and his men moved off to the eastern side of the mountain. He tried to confuse any Zulu lookouts that might be in the vicinity by lighting campfires but then riding off and leading his forces to spend the night a few miles off in the cold. The mountain was home to the abaQulusi people, one of the most passionately devoted Zulu clans to Cetshwayo's cause. Mbilini had become closely associated with them and had a homestead on the slopes of Hlobane.

It was a trying night for Buller and his men. At 1 a.m. a heavy thunderstorm began that lasted for four hours. The rays of the sun had not yet started to paint the morning sky when both contingents moved on Hlobane at 3.30 a.m. on 28 March. Buller and his men to the east gingerly started to pick their way up the steep, narrow path. A party of the Border Horse that was with this force, led by Colonel Weatherley, became separated from the rest of the men and fell behind. In the meantime, Buller, at the front, was almost on the summit plateau, struggling on through the heavy thunderstorm. The flashes of lightning illuminated the darkness and Buller was soon seen by abaQulusi lookouts, who started to fire on him. The theatrical setting was an appropriate backdrop for the drama that was about to unfold.

Buller began to lead his men up the final climb to the plateau, where they were soon exposed to a heavy crossfire. Lieutenant Williams, who was with the Frontier Light Horse, was instructed to lead a party of men to return fire and drive the assailants off. He had barely started to carry out his instructions when he was shot through the head. Several other men fell but Buller managed to get the rest of his men up.

Once they were on the plateau, all appeared to be quiet. There were a few knots of cattle around but only a scattering of abaQulusi. However, even now numbers of them were slipping round behind Buller and cutting off his line of retreat. Unperturbed, he instructed his men to round up the cattle.

Meanwhile, Russell had been approaching Hlobane from the other end of the mountain. He had reached a lower hill known as Ntendeka which was joined to Hlobane by a precipitous path up. One look at it and he saw that it would be impossible for mounted men to journey up it so he commanded a party of them to dismount and ascend on foot to meet Buller, who was out of sight but expected to join them later that morning.

Wood had decided to catch up with Buller to the east. He had ridden out of Russell's camp with a small escort. This included a small number of staff officers, amongst whom was Captain Ronald Campbell, a personal favourite. Whilst the others chatted freely, Campbell seemed pensive. When asked what was wrong, he said that he had been thinking of his wife and whether anyone would be writing to her with bad news in the near future.

By the time Wood reached the far end of Hlobane, Buller was long gone but the general path he had taken was obvious both from the trampled grass at the base of the mountain and also from the dead horses that were scattered around. But this did not stop Wood losing the path higher up and taking a more difficult route than Buller had. Weatherley and the Border Horse had not yet made it to the top, unable to do so because of heavy abaQulusi crossfire.

Wood took command of the localised fight and led the men up the track in an attempt to clear the abaQulusi defenders out of the way. They had reached a point about 100ft from the crest of the hill when Wood's interpreter, Lieutenant Lloyd, was shot. Lloyd and Wood had both seen the marksman as he was about to fire but the interpreter was unable to take evasive action and was hit. He fell from his horse and others rushed over to drag him away to safety.

Wood asked Lloyd if his wound was serious and Lloyd replied it was, for his back was broken. The party started to carry him to relative safely to a cattle enclosure a little way below whilst Wood moved a little way further up the hill. Even as he was doing so, a warrior stood up not 20 yards off and aimed a shot at Wood. It missed him but hit his horse, killing it instantly. The horse's head struck Wood on the way down, knocking him over. Wood assured those below that he was alright and made his way down, where he saw to his shock that Lloyd was in a terrible state. As he lay dying, Wood tried to give him a nip of brandy to enervate him but it was already too late. He could no longer speak, his teeth were set and he expired soon afterwards.

The Border Horse, in the interim, were clearly intimidated by the ferocity of the abaQulusi defending the rocks around the path before them. Although Wood urged them forward, they did not respond. Sensing their reticence, Captain Campbell of the Coldstream Guards, who was Wood's staff officer, took the lead. Wood rushed after him with his escort. Campbell had not gone far when he was shot at point-blank range and the top of his head blown off. He had peered into the entrance of a cave where an abaQulusi marksman was so close that his weapon almost touched Campbell's face as he fired. Campbell fell, stone-dead, to the ground, his sombre thoughts on the eve of the battle being fully justified.

His body was recovered and carried back down. Wood, deprived of two of his close confidants in such a short time, lost all sense of proportion. Bugler Walkinshaw was sent back up the rocks to retrieve a prayer book from the saddle of Wood's dead mount. Even as the battle raged about him, Wood ordered that a grave should be dug for both Campbell and Lloyd. The ground was hard and only a shallow trench could be dug. There was a further delay whilst Wood realised the grave was not long enough and ordered it to be extended. Then the bodies of both men were lowered into it and covered with a blanket. With abaQulusi warriors just 30 yards away, he read the burial service over his two staff.

Then he led the remaining escort back down the track and started to ride away. A number of the mules he had with him were killed on the way down. Wood would take no further effective part in the Battle of Hlobane, unable to cope with the enormity of the personal loss he had just suffered, for he was very close to both Lloyd and Campbell.

Weatherley and the Border Horse, in the meantime, began to try and fight their way up to the summit plateau. On top of the mountain, Buller and his men had begun to round up a sizeable number of cattle. However, an increasing number of abaQulusi were moving into action. Those at the rear of Buller's men were becoming more aggressive and others could be seen moving to their aid. The situation was not helped by the topography of the plateau, with frequent dips which hid groups of the enemy from Buller.

In this environment orders became confused and the co-ordination of Buller's troops increasingly fragmented. He was perturbed that he had not recovered the body of Lieutenant Williams who had been killed earlier in the battle and he sent a troop of Frontier Light Horse under Captain Barton back to retrieve it. Barton set off but, before he could complete his task, a rider appeared with fresh orders. He was to abandon the body and get off the mountain as quickly as possible. Buller's orders were, however, unclear and Barton decided to retreat down the track up which Buller's men had originally ascended. As he did so, he met Weatherley and the Border Horse on the way up.

There had been a dramatic and quite terrifying development. Wood had been making his way down from the mountain, devastated by the loss of Campbell and Lloyd but not unduly concerned by the course of the battle. They were driving down some captured sheep and goats when one of his native companions frantically ran up to him and pointed ahead. There was a small rise obscuring the view, which Wood – now on another horse – cantered up to. There, to his shock, he saw a massive force of Zulus, marching in five columns, with a dense centre already deployed in classic Zulu attack formation.

Others had seen it too. Russell and his men further west had been looking on from Ntendeka when what appeared to be a cloud appeared on the hills opposite. It soon dawned on them that this was no cloud but a huge Zulu impi. Cetshwayo's army had arrived and, from a British perspective, it could not have appeared at a worse moment. Russell frantically scribbled a message to be delivered to Wood and then led his men off the plateau to the ground below. This was not easy. They too had captured a huge number of cattle which slowed their progress.

Buller, who could not see very well from his position on the summit, seemed slow to appreciate the looming danger. When the full nature of the threat at last dawned on him, he realised that it would be very risky to retreat the way they had come up. Unfortunately, his attempts to warn Barton of this in his orders went awry. He told him to retreat to 'the right of the mountain', but Barton completely misinterpreted the orders and led his men the wrong way. Despite Buller's efforts, Barton was taking his men back into the position of greatest danger.

The approaching impi had been attracted towards Hlobane by the sound of gunfire and when they saw what was happening they enthusiastically rushed to join the fray. The right wing of the impi rushed towards the very track down which Barton, who had been joined by Weatherley and the Border Horse, was now descending. The horsemen were now effectively surrounded with no option but to fight their way out. They did their best to do so but the odds were stacked enormously against them.

In the bitter fighting that followed, a number of horsemen fell to their deaths over the steep, craggy pinnacles of the cliffs. A few managed to fight their way off down a very narrow and precarious path. Even when they reached the foot of the mountain they were chased by their foe, who were almost as quick across broken country as cavalry. Weatherley died on the mountain but others were killed miles away. Of seventy horsemen involved in this fight, only a fraction escaped.

Buller's command had now fallen apart almost completely and the situation was fast becoming a rout. With only two ways off the mountain, one of which was now effectively closed off to them, a catastrophe loomed. A series of isolated fights was raging, small groups of men firing and stabbing away at each other. In one of them, Captain D'Arcy of the Frontier Light Horse was unhorsed when his mount was hit by a rock the size of a piano plummeting down and taking its leg right off. Some of Buller's men made it to the path down to Ntendeka and began to descend. It was not so much a track as a jumble of boulders across which men and animals had to pick their way with the greatest of care, leaping across gaps in the rocks from time to time in their efforts to escape.

The terrain here was so terrible that it would be given the name 'The Devil's Pass'. Men and horses could only progress slowly, in single file, yet hundreds of the abaQulusi were attacking the fleeing force. Those at the back were frantic to make their escape and man and beast went tumbling over the rocks that festooned the so-called path down the shattered cliff-face as they did their best to hurry down.

The abaQulusi, seeing the precarious position that Buller's men were in, started to pour down fire from both flanks. A stand by a small rearguard temporarily held them up but this was soon overwhelmed. A scene from hell unfolded, with men frantically trying to escape the jubilant enemy. One of them was Piet Uys. As he tried to get down the path, an assegai was thrust deep into his back and he collapsed, mortally wounded.

For some, the sense of imminent death was too much. A Frontier Horseman asked his colleague if there was any chance of escape. His colleague replied that he did not think so, at which point he stuck his carbine in his mouth and pulled the trigger. Another man who was trapped in between rocks was finished off by an abaQulusi woman who had joined the fray. An officer of the irregulars who was renowned for his personal bravery burst into tears when his men refused to follow orders.[9]

Buller himself had made it to the bottom. He did what he could to restore order but even as he did so thousands of Zulus from the impi charged towards the battle. Buller saw that it was now every man for himself and all that could be done was to save as many men as possible, including Captain D'Arcy who he took up behind him. He himself lived up to his reputation for great personal valour by several times charging up the path to rescue isolated soldiers. A number of men escaped on horseback carrying an extra passenger behind them.

With nothing now to be done but to save themselves, Buller and his men retreated as fast as they could from the battlefield. Still slowed by cattle, some were overtaken and slain by Zulu warriors. Russell and his men, with the advantage of spotting the approaching impi earlier, extricated themselves with less difficulty. Nevertheless, it was a battered and bruised force that made its way back to Khambula. Around 100 had died, mostly irregular horsemen, although exact figures are difficult to come by.

Included amongst the dead was Captain Robert Barton, another man whom Wood thought highly of. He had managed to get off the mountain but was chased across the plain for several miles by Zulus on horseback. They eventually caught up with him. Barton was slowed by the fact that he had taken another man aboard his horse. Seeing that the horse was exhausted, the extra man, Lieutenant Poole, got off and was promptly shot.

A Zulu approached Barton and made signs to him to surrender as Cetshwayo had ordered that a prisoner be brought in for questioning; the Zulu, a man named Chicheeli, had already had his fill of killing for the day, claiming to have already slain seven men. Just then, another Zulu shot Barton who fell, wounded, to the ground. Chicheeli was not going to let anyone else claim the kill so he finished Barton off with an assegai. In a remarkable example of the memory skills of some of the Zulus, Chicheeli was able to lead Wood to the exact spot where Barton's body was fourteen months later, after the war was over.

It was a disastrous defeat, second only to Isandlwana, and one brought about by a combination of over-confidence and poor intelligence, not for the first time. The loss of Piet Uys was particularly unfortunate as it ended any chance of Boer involvement in the war. Not only would their fighting skills be missed, but so would their excellent local knowledge which had been of great help to Wood previously. The abaQulusi had also borne some losses in the battle but the main Zulu impi had suffered only minor damage. They were exultant at their victory.

The mood could not be more different in the British camp. Most of the native levies present, already unnerved by the slaughter of Isandlwana, decided to get away almost en bloc as quickly as they could. Only a few mounted horsemen amongst them stayed and they at least had more chance than most of escaping should things go ill with the British once more. Battered British prestige again needed avenging.

As Wood sat down for dinner that night, with an empty chair opposite him, he brooded on the loss of Campbell in particular. He had been a devoted attendant for Wood, watching his back constantly and nursing him back to health when he had been ill; the great exertions he had suffered and the efforts he had made had been taking a great personal toll on Wood. Campbell's loss was a terrible blow and Wood longed for an opportunity to gain his revenge. He would not have long to wait.

In a strange postscript, a patrol was travelling near Zungwini two weeks later when they came across a Border Horse trooper named Grandier. He was exhausted, bruised and stark naked. His story was extraordinary. He said that he had been captured in the battle and first of all taken back to Mbilini's camp, where he was kept tied to a tree whilst a number of warriors debated whether to kill him or not.

It was decided instead to send him to Cetshwayo who wanted a prisoner to interrogate. So Grandier was taken to Ulundi by four mounted Zulus, though he was forced to walk and carry their food. Bizarrely, he was deprived of all his clothes except his hat. When he tried to keep a residue of modesty by tying a handkerchief around his waist, it was quickly taken away from him.

Then he was taken before Cetshwayo, 'a very fat man, not tall, and walks with difficulty. Apparently about 40 years of age.'[10] Whilst in Ulundi, he was shown two spiked cannon that he was asked to repair. He also saw a number of Martini-Henry rifles there. After about ten days, messengers came in with the important news that Mbilini had been killed in an attack on Khambula.[11] Feeling that Grandier had little to tell him, the king decided to send him back for Mbilini's people to kill.

Two warriors were instructed to take him back, one of them armed with an old gun, both with assegais. Whilst they were dozing off in the midday sun, Grandier overpowered the Zulu with the gun and the other ran off. Grandier, travelling at night to avoid detection, was eventually picked up by his own side.

It would later emerge that there were some question marks with this story. It was suggested by Zulus interviewed after the war that Grandier had been taken during the retreat and had been well treated. This alternative version has it that he was released on Cetshwayo's orders, perhaps in an attempt to demonstrate that he was not the savage that British propaganda suggested him to be. In either event, it appears that Grandier was the only prisoner of war taken by the Zulus during the entire conflict.

The Zulus moved on from their victory at Hlobane towards Wood's encampment at Khambula. Many of the regiments had been involved in the triumph at Isandlwana. In addition, although most of the impi had not been involved in the fight at Hlobane, everyone's spirits would have been boosted by the outcome of that battle too. It made the Zulus supremely confident in the decisive battle that now loomed.

Wood himself knew that he would almost certainly be attacked, but it was just possible that the Zulus might slip past and attack the virtually defenceless town of Utrecht instead. He walked round the sentries several times that night although he did not think the Zulus would attack before daybreak. When at last the dawn came, little could be seen. A thick mist enveloped the hills around the camp, putting everyone's nerves even more on edge.

There was no sign of the Zulus, but then again, they could have been nearby and invisible given their skill at taking advantage of cover. Wood, however, decided that the routines of camp life should go on. Foraging parties were sent out to bring back wood so that the men could have some hot food which he thought would be good for morale.

On the morning of 29 March there had been plenty of time for the Zulus to prepare themselves spiritually for the battle. This had not been possible during the frenetic and unexpected build-up to Isandlwana and many Zulus felt that this had contributed to their heavy losses there. There was also an opportunity for the leaders of the Zulu army to provide inspiring oration for their troops, especially from Mnyamana kaNgqengelele of the Buthelezi clan.

Following this, the Zulus moved towards the camp at Khambula, having apparently forgotten the firm instructions of Cetshwayo that they were on no account to attack a prepared position. Wood had been at Khambula for weeks and had constructed a formidable defensive position there. It would be an opportunity for the British to prove themselves against the Zulus and, in particular, to bring their massive superiority in terms of firepower to bear.

Wood had the added advantage that he knew exactly what was coming. It was obvious now that the massive Zulu force, over 20,000 strong, was headed for him and he prepared himself accordingly. His scouts had spotted the Zulus enjoying breakfast along the banks of a stream at about 10 a.m. However, the size of the army facing the British and colonial forces was a shock, most eloquently summed up by the name later given to the stream, amaGoda, which reputedly meant 'Oh my God'.

The scouts spurred their horses back to Khambula as quickly as possible. The camp was atop a ridge which had good visibility over the land round about. Wood had added to its defensive strength by erecting a redoubt on the summit. It was not complex, just earthen walls constructed from the spoil of the ditch that had been dug out around it, but it did not need to be complicated. A laager had been erected nearby in which the cattle could be kept. The wagons in it had been chained together, a ditch had been dug around the edge and earth piled up between the wheels. A palisade led from the laager to the redoubt. A larger laager had also been constructed slightly further to the west.

Visibility was much better to the north, where the ground was open, than to the south, where there was dead ground. But the position was immensely strong and was defended by over 2,000 men, many of them regular British infantry. There were six guns and two rocket troughs and over 500 mounted men. Many of them had lost friends the day before and were burning for revenge, Wood amongst them.

Two of the guns were positioned inside the redoubt but the other four were in the open further forward. They would be covered by the rifle fire of the infantrymen. The main laager was especially strongly defended, with infantry deployed along the walls. By about 11 a.m. the Zulus were reported to be moving towards the camp. However, Wood – calmness personified – refused to contemplate the men missing their lunch and also refused to make them hurry up eating it.[12]

It was at about 1230 that the main Zulu army appeared, 'making the air dark with the dust they raised as they came towards the camp'.[13] It shifted into position to move on Khambula whilst still about 5 miles away. It was obvious that there was about to be a major confrontation. Wood ordered that the tents in the camp be struck – in marked contrast to what had happened at Isandlwana – and the boxes of reserve ammunition were to be opened – also an improvement.

The striking of the tents merely served to enervate the Zulus, who thought that Wood was making ready to try and run off. At about 1300, they were ready to start their advance on the camp. Wood watched on in awe; he reckoned that the Zulu front, when all their men were deployed, was 10 miles long. Their advance was very disciplined and organised. Some of the Zulus spoke English; occasional shouts of 'we are the boys from Isandlwana' rang out. The right horn moved in advance of the rest of the army and waited whilst still about 3 miles off from the camp for the remainder to catch up.

It was the right that started off the attack proper, skirmishing forward until it was only about half a mile away from the British lines. Here were the uVe and iNgombamakhosi regiments, composed of young, headstrong men. Given the length of the line, it is possible that they could not see what was happening on the far side of the army or, alternatively, maybe the competitive rivalry that existed between various regiments had got out of hand. At any event, the right prepared to launch its attack before the rest of the army was ready.

This was exactly what Wood wanted to happen. Seeing the Zulu right ready to strike, he decided to goad them into action. Wood instructed Buller to lead 100 mounted men towards the Zulus and get them to attack. Buller was the ideal man to carry out the instruction. He led his men out and when a few hundred yards off ordered them to loose off a volley.

The plan worked to perfection. Stung by the horsemen, the Zulu right charged as one, their war cry of *uSuthu* filling the skies above Khambula. Buller milked the move admirably. Retreating calmly before the onrush of Zulu warriors, he would order his men to stop occasionally and fire off another round of shots. It was a dangerous manoeuvre and several horses became stuck in boggy ground. At least one of the cavalry was caught and killed.

Another man dismounted from his horse to loose off a shot but could not remount again as his horse was starting to panic. Lieutenant Edward Browne of the 24th Regiment saw his perilous position and came across to help. He steadied the nervous mount, allowing the stranded cavalryman to get back on, thereby saving his life. For this, Browne won the Victoria Cross. The rest of the cavalrymen charged back to the British position. Even as they did so, shells from the guns roared overhead and started to decimate the Zulu ranks.

With the horses safely inside the laager, the Zulus were now close enough for the infantry to fire. Wood gave the order and a tidal wave of sound deafened the men whilst a hailstorm of lead spat forth from the British lines. The volley must have been shattering but it did not halt the Zulu advance. Many of them, oblivious to the bullets, made it to the wooden walls of the laager and started to do their best to get inside.

But it was a strong position and the proximity of hundreds of Zulus meant that the defenders hardly had to aim. The attack was unsustainable and within a few minutes it started to slacken. The Zulus started to back off, a few trying to find inadequate cover behind some anthills about 60 yards off. The rest retreated to the rather more secure protection of some rocks situated about half a mile away.

This was a bad start for the Zulus, for whom the only chance of success lay in overwhelming the defences by a co-ordinated attack from all directions at once. The left flank of the Zulu army had made much slower progress than the right, held up by bad ground, and by the time they were in position to attack, the first assault from the right had already been repulsed. They did have the advantage, though, of dead ground which would prevent the British from firing on them until they were close. However, the last 100 yards were heavily exposed to cross-fire from the main laager and the cattle laager which straddled their line of attack.

The chest, in the centre, was more exposed but the men here came on bravely, under the watchful eye of Ntshingwayo, the victor of Isandlwana, who was again in command. The chest made the most of the scanty cover afforded by huts that had been erected by the native auxiliaries with the British force. Despite heavy shell-fire, the Zulus pushed on valiantly until they were on the edge of the cattle laager.

The decisive point of the battle was about to be reached. The cattle laager was only defended by a single company and this was not enough to keep the Zulus out. Vicious, primeval hand-to-hand fighting followed, spear against bayonet. The defenders were forced back slowly. But unlike Isandlwana, they managed to keep their order and cohesion and although several men were lost, there was to be no full-scale collapse.

The Zulus now had possession of the cattle laager from where their marksmen started to lay down a fire on the main laager and the redoubt. Their actions had also removed the flanking fire that had been coming from the cattle laager and the left Zulu flank was now free to advance more easily. This they started to do, prompting Wood to send out a sortie to break them up. The task was delegated to two companies of the 90th Regiment under Major Robert Hackett.

They were successful in driving back the Zulu skirmishers into the main body. This allowed the British to take control of open ground at the top of the slope up which the Zulus were advancing and a well-aimed volley thudded into their close-packed ranks. The effect was devastating and the Zulus could not stand against it. Instead, they slowly started to retreat back down the slope. Hackett, however, was badly exposed to rifle fire from a position to his right behind some large dunghills, whilst from the other side of the cattle laager more shots were directed at him and his men.

The Zulus were not good shots and many of their weapons were of obsolete vintage but it was still a very dangerous position to be in. Wood also believed that the snipers firing from behind the dunghill were using Martini-Henrys captured at Isandlwana. Now and again a man would go down, such as Lieutenant Arthur Bright, shot in the leg with an apparently minor wound; in fact, it had severed an artery and he would die not long afterwards. Then Hackett himself fell, a bullet through the head. It was a miracle that he was not killed at once but he was completely blind and died a few weeks later.[14]

Seeing that their position was not viable for much longer, Wood recalled the two companies. Two more companies were sent out to escort them back in. The guns were also ordered to start shelling the cattle laager, killing not only the Zulus but some of the cattle trapped inside (of which there were 2,000 at the start of the battle). Buller also ordered his men to start firing into the dunghills, realising that the soft, unpleasant substances that they were made up of would not be much use in stopping a bullet.

The situation now hung in the balance. The Zulus controlled the cattle laager and some parts of the main laager had been abandoned as the fire there was too hot for the British troops to handle. Now the right horn of the Zulu impi returned to the fray. However, they were heavily exposed and fire from both guns and rifles started to extract a heavy toll. It was like running into a maelstrom from which there was no escape. Zulus sought cover wherever they might find it and now and again one would even reach the redoubt, but it was only a matter of time before the Zulus retreated once more.

Then the centre tried again but the trouble was that the attacks were increasingly piecemeal. They had been going on for three hours now and heaps of Zulu dead lay piled across the battlefield. The Zulus were undoubtedly brave but the British position was proving to be a formidable obstacle. By 1730, Wood felt strong enough to order that the cattle laager be reoccupied. A company of the 13th were sent over to drive the Zulus out at the point of a bayonet.

The momentum was going out of the Zulu attack and there was nothing for it but for them to extricate themselves from the battle in as disciplined a fashion as possible. Wood, nevertheless, had no intention of letting them get away without further punishment. It was now time to turn a victory into a rout. The cream of the Zulu army started to break. As they moved off, Wood noticed that 'they were so thick as to blot out all signs of grass on the hillside, which was covered with their black bodies, and for perhaps the only time in anyone's experience it was sound to say "don't wait to aim, fire into the black of them"'.[15]

Whilst bullets and shrapnel from the guns continued to wreak havoc, the cavalry were sent out to finish the job. With Buller in the lead, the horsemen charged out of the laager after the fleeing mass. Captain D'Arcy of the Frontier Light Horse summed up the mood: 'no quarter boys and remember yesterday.'[16] This early opportunity for revenge for the humiliation at Hlobane was gratefully accepted.

A bloodlust descended on the field of battle. Commandant Schermbrucker of the irregulars noted that it would take too long to shoot all the fleeing Zulus; he reckoned a column of about 5,000 of them was trying to escape in front of him. Instead, his men snatched the assegais from dead Zulus and used them to strike down the living. It was a bloodbath.

Wood was later to deny that any atrocities had taken place. A statement appeared in the British press, though it had been directed in the first instance to the Aborigines Protection Society, who had taken an interest in the allegations, saying: 'I believe no Zulus have been killed by white men except in action, and, as I rewarded Wood's Irregulars for every live Zulu brought in, I had many saved.' This was in response to an allegation made by a Private Snook that 500 wounded Zulus had been killed in cold blood after the battle.[17]

Yet it is possible to read an alternative meaning into Wood's account: if a pursuit was perceived as part of an 'action' then those in the way of it might be considered fair game. In any event, it is hard to ignore Schermbrucker's accounts which were consistent with the treatment of Zulu wounded after, for example, Rorke's Drift, and equally difficult not to assume that Wood's words were little more than an attempt to put a positive gloss on what was indeed a slaughter.

The chase went on for 7 miles before the cavalry started to let up. The abaQulusi were particularly cut up and those that survived made their way back to the safety of Hlobane. Only the onset of night saved the rest. As the black blanket of darkness spread across Zululand, it acted as a shield for the shattered impi. Some made their way back despondently to Ulundi where they would give Cetshwayo the awful news. Many just went home.

The effects of the victory were almost immediate. Just a few days later, the mountain fastness of Hlobane was abandoned and those who had, just a week or so before, bloodied the noses of Wood and Buller in its shadow, traipsed away from the British, seeing a terrible retribution coming. British soldiers collected the firearms of their enemy; Captain Woodgate, Wood's staff officer, noted that there were 325 of them, though only fourteen were Martini-Henrys, bearing the stamp of either the 24th or the 80th, the defeated British troops at Isandlwana and Ntombe respectively.[18]

At Khambula, the scene was one of utter carnage. The columnist of the *Natal Colonist* wrote on 11 April from the site that 'we had a heavy shower of rain yesterday, which was very acceptable, as it washed the brains and pools of blood that were saturating the ground down the hill and ravine from Khambula Camp, making the air smell a little sweet'.[19]

Wood had lost twenty-eight officers and men, including those who died of their wounds later. Fifty-five others were wounded. Against this, the British counted 785 Zulu corpses. Many of them made a gruesome sight, blown in half by the shells or with heads taken clean off. The final Zulu losses were, in fact, much greater than this number. Many died several miles away from the camp whilst others would have expired of their wounds later. Estimates, and they must of necessity be speculative, suggest that perhaps 3,000 Zulus died,[20] a truly terrible cost.

But even the victors had their losses. In a touching vignette perhaps more associated with the horrors of the trenches of the First World War, Wood explained that Hackett, blinded when shot through the head, was in shock for some time after the battle. When he later visited him in the hospital tent, Hackett complained of the stinginess of Wood's officers who would not supply proper lighting for him. Not until he was back in Pietermaritzburg was a female visitor prevailed upon to break the news of his blindness to him.[21] He lingered on for several weeks before dying of his terrible injuries.

Buller was instructed to escort the wounded back to the borders of Zululand on the aptly named Blood River. Then Wood commanded his men to bring in any Zulu prisoners that remained in the vicinity for he wished to know more about the regiments that had been involved in the battle. About twenty men were brought in. When their questioning had finished, Wood asked them why he should not kill them when they had shown the whites no mercy. One man proudly replied that 'there is a very good reason why you should not kill us. We kill you because it is the custom of the black men, but it isn't the white man's custom.'[22] Satisfied with the answer, which of course had the merit of accuracy about it, Wood ordered the prisoners to be escorted back to Zungwini Mountain and safety.

The victory at Khambula got Wood off the hook as far as the reverse at Hlobane was concerned. He wrote two official reports, one on each battle. Of Hlobane, it was hard to tell from the report's opening that anything had gone amiss. In a wonderful example of what would now be called 'spin', Wood began with the line: 'I have the honour to report that the Inzhlobana [sic] Mountain was successfully assaulted, and it's summit cleared at daylight on the 28th …'[23] With about 25 per cent of Buller's men lost, this could hardly be counted a successful engagement.

But there was no need to be creative in Wood's report on Khambula, which was indeed the turning point of the war. It was an awful defeat for the Zulus which had reaffirmed the superiority of British arms. It restored confidence at a time when such a fillip was badly needed. The balance of power in the war had shifted inexorably. Cetshwayo was reportedly outraged that his men had ignored his commands and attacked a prepared defensive position and at one stage thought about killing the Zulu commander.[24] However, he may have done better to have led the army himself, as his great and illustrious ancestor Shaka had done in the early years. Regardless, the back of the Zulu army was broken, the cream of the nation's young men cut down in the prime of life. The fate of the war, and of the Zulu nation, had already been decided.

nine

CHELMSFORD TO THE RESCUE

The Relief of Eshowe

Colonel Pearson's isolated position at Eshowe had been giving Chelmsford cause for concern for a while. The defences on the Zulu side of the Thukela at Fort Tenedos, across from the towering heights on which Fort Pearson was perched, were strengthened in case the Zulus should think of an attack across the river. A raid into Natal was inherently unlikely as the river was at its widest point here and getting across would be extremely difficult. That did not preclude an attack on Fort Tenedos though.

The British erected a number of forts in Zululand and Tenedos was in many ways a typical example. It had earthen ramparts with a raised firing step inside. Although the ditch should have been 6ft deep all the way round, it was only 4ft in places because of the existence of rock just below the surface. The banks had been revetted, that is, faced with wooden stakes or sandbags to stop them from crumbling. Holes had been dug around the fort with sharpened stakes at the bottom of them; these uninviting mantraps were known as 'troup-de-loups'. There was also trip wire laid around the camp to impede any attack. Despite the efforts put into its design, not everyone was impressed with it, one staff officer complaining that it was overlooked by hills from which an enemy could fire with impunity.

Chelmsford first thought of going to Pearson's aid in February. With the situation still unclear as far as a Zulu attack on Natal was concerned, this would have been a foolhardy move. Energy was all very well in a commander-in-chief but it had to be focused, otherwise a disaster such as Isandlwana was likely to reoccur. His plan also relied on Pearson meeting him halfway which would again invite a Zulu attack. Chelmsford's place at the time was undoubtedly in Natal, co-ordinating his forces. The fact that he even considered other options was an insight into some of the sketchiness of his strategic thinking.

This plan came to naught, which was perhaps just as well. Sir Bartle Frere was one of those to breathe a sigh of relief. He wrote:

> I was also very glad to hear you had given up the idea of going towards Ekowe [sic] but, till I heard you had abandoned it, I had no idea you thought of anything so rash. It would never do to have YOU shut up, or even out of daily range.[1]

The issue, as ever, was Chelmsford's inability to delegate, though there was not a long list of potential candidates to lead a relief expedition in his stead that sprang to mind.

There was plenty to worry about given Pearson's predicament. It was only a matter of time before the supply situation at Eshowe became desperate. In addition, given the ongoing problems of the weather, disease was also a concern. Although a full-scale epidemic never quite materialised, the cemetery at the mission station was starting to be used more regularly. And the health of most of the garrison visibly deteriorated as the siege progressed.

One of the main problems was that with no communication between the mission station and Natal, Chelmsford had no idea of what was really happening and it was easy to imagine that the situation was even more desperate than it actually was. Then someone thought of using the sun's rays to communicate. A bedroom mirror was commandeered from a hotel and the signalling duly began. The British had already developed heliographs to use elsewhere but no one seemed to have thought about using any in southern Africa which, given the climate and the need, was both a shame and a surprise.

So messages flew across the scrub to Eshowe in Morse code. However, it was far from plain sailing. The cloudy weather meant that the signal was erratic and it was not until 6 March that a message could actually be read. This provided welcome news. It told Pearson that a relief column would be setting off from the Thukela on the 13th, in a week's time.

Captain Wynne was again called into action to manufacture a device to reply with. Various ingenious approaches were tried without success, including a hot-air balloon made of tracing paper with a small paraffin burner to power it. It was not until 14 March that someone else worked out a simpler approach, again using a mirror. This was the breakthrough. From that day on, provided that the sun shone, there could be communication between the Lower Drift and Eshowe.

The news of an imminent relief effort energised the defence. Pearson decided that work should start on a road with which to ease the approach of any rescuing force. The current track was long and winding when it approached Eshowe. It also traversed some thick bush, ideal for launching an ambush. A new route was planned which would be both more direct and also avoid much of the bush. This would, in theory, make Chelmsford's approach markedly safer.

A few days into March, a party of engineers under Captain Wynne set out from Eshowe to begin the work. Three companies of infantry under Lieutenant-Colonel Ely acted as escort. Ely, however, was jumpy. There were parties of Zulus appearing all over the place and he feared an attack. Not everyone was as nervous as him. Captain Wayman of the 99th Regiment was very eager for a scrap but Ely pulled him up, threatening to arrest him if he disobeyed orders. By way of explanation, he said that he had heard a dog bark therefore there must be Zulus in the vicinity. The response from most of the men was one of amusement. From that day on, whenever Ely passed by he was accompanied by sly, discreet barks from wags within the camp.

There were two main obstacles to the construction of the new road. The first was the ubiquitous rain, which constantly created havoc. Several days of potential work were lost as a result of the inclement weather. This also affected the fort; the heavy downpours caused one of the caponiers to collapse and the cooks complained that the wind made it difficult to prepare meals inside Eshowe. The second obstacle was the action of the Zulus, who frequently launched raids on the working parties. This left more men from the garrison guarding the working parties than actually working on the roads, so that progress, such as it was, appeared frustratingly slow.

The Zulus were increasingly bold. On 7 March, Corporal Carson, who had signed up for the Mounted Infantry, had been out on routine patrol. Suddenly, a group of about fifteen Zulus appeared close at hand. Their sudden rush made his horse bolt and Carson hung on desperately. As he tried to spur away, a Zulu speared his horse, though it carried on running. Then several shots were fired. One pierced Carson's thigh, another his hand, the latter virtually amputating two fingers in the process.

Miraculously, a third shot aimed for his back struck his carbine which was hanging over his shoulder. Carrying a carbine in this way was against regulations but on this occasion Carson's disobedience saved his life. Several other mounted men came to his rescue and he trotted back to the fort as if nothing of significance had happened. He was taken to the hospital where the two dangling fingers were removed. He was invalided home soon afterwards.

Even before communication with the Lower Drift was properly established on 14 March, a runner had at last made it through to the fort. Pearson was immediately suspicious. The man was wearing a greatcoat which was normally worn by the 24th, many of whom had of course been slaughtered at Isandlwana. He was also very well oiled in the Zulu fashion. Pearson decided he was a spy who had probably killed the real messenger and clapped him in irons. In fact, it was not until 23 March that the messenger's identity was confirmed by communication with the Lower Drift. Even then Pearson remained suspicious and it seems that the runner was not released until the siege of Eshowe was finally at an end.

The mere threat of an attack on the road-builders for a time seemed to be enough to halt the work. Working parties would be fired on from a distance by Zulus; their aim was not good but it was enough to disrupt construction. On one occasion, hearing the sound of firing from the fort, Pearson recalled the men. The Zulus were elated and kept on firing after they left. Then they went over to the road and did as much damage to it as they could.

A party was later sent out to have another go but again, after they left, the Zulus tried to undo their work. Wynne was most unimpressed at the road's progress and particularly annoyed at Pearson's cautious approach. He had a heart-to-heart with him that evening saying that he would not be able to complete the road unless a much more vigorous mentality was adopted. He was more than likely unusually aggressive; he was not feeling well and suffering from diarrhoea.

When the work parties set out the next day, they had a far stronger escort with them as well as two guns. The Zulus once again fired on them but their shooting was typically erratic. No one was killed or seriously injured as a result. The engineers also came up with a plan to stop their work from being disturbed. They constructed a booby-trap, essentially a landmine or a 'torpedo', as they named it. It was simplicity itself, a charge of dynamite buried beneath a post with a friction tube attached.

Basically, as soon as the post was removed it would explode unless disabled beforehand. The word 'torpedo' was painted on it to warn off any unwary friendly forces. The plan worked to perfection. When the men left that day, they were not even back at the fort before they heard a large explosion. From that day on, no Zulus tried to interfere with the work on the road after the men had left.

On 11 and 12 March, large parties of Zulus, reportedly thousands strong, could be seen near the fort. The timing was suggestive as this was the day before Chelmsford was due to march. It spoke well of the Zulus' spy network. Despite all attempts to interfere with it, the road took shape surprisingly quickly. By the 13th it was ready, though Wynne, perhaps exhausted by his efforts, had reported sick and was not available for duty.

Pearson got 600 men ready to march out to meet the relieving force. They were to take the Gatling gun with them. It was not a move greeted with great enthusiasm by some of the men, who felt that the force was too small and would be very vulnerable if attacked. Then came shattering news: there had been a delay and there would be no march towards Eshowe from the Thukela until 1 April.

This was a big blow for morale. Gunner Carroll of the Royal Marine Artillery complained that:

> our situation is very miserable, not enough to eat, the 8 ounces of biscuit we get daily being maggoty and mouldy. The mealy meal we get we make porridge of. No vegetables. We have been exposed to all weathers for the past seven or eight weeks having had no tents pitched during that time, sleeping under wagons at night, with a wagon cover to protect us from the rain, often having to sit up all night holding it. When raining hard sometimes becomes completely washed out. We wear our accoutrements, with seventy rounds of ammunition in them, night and day, being severely punished if anyone was found with them off at night.[2]

Yet although those under siege did not know the details, Chelmsford was in a much stronger position than he had been a couple of months before. The magnitude of the defeat at Isandlwana had forced the hand of the British government and large numbers of reinforcements had suddenly been found (amongst them Major Charles Bromhead, brother of the hero of Rorke's Drift, who was due to take over the remnants of the 24th). A number of these had been added to the relief column given the objective of going to the aid of Pearson. These included men from the 57th Regiment who had recently arrived from Ceylon (now Sri Lanka) and were at least used to hot and sweaty conditions.

It was a long march up from Durban to the border with Zululand. The days were long and the hours of sleep taken at night short. However, Chelmsford knew he had to move quickly. Pearson had got a message through that supplies would run out by 4 April. In the absence of enough senior officers he would take command of the relief column himself. He would be accompanied by most of the staff that had been with him during the Isandlwana campaign, including the acerbic Crealock and Lieutenant Milne, RN.

Chelmsford got his excuses in early just in case, writing to Stanley back in London that:

> a force moving, however, with a transport through a difficult country is heavily hampered, if attacked determinedly by large numbers, and while feeling every confidence in the ability, courage and determination of those under my command, I trust that, should our efforts fall short of what is no doubt expected of us, circumstances may be duly taken into account.[3]

It was hardly confidence-inspiring stuff. It was also a long way from the bullish Chelmsford of pre-Isandlwana days.

The disaster of Isandlwana indeed had shaken Chelmsford to the core. The standing orders that he issued to his force showed a new-found caution. Companies had to march together in close order. Particular attention was paid to the distribution of ammunition. Chelmsford's orders stated that:

> each wagon and cart with the convoys must have some ammunition boxes placed on it in such a position to be easily got at. The regimental reserve boxes must have the screw of the lid taken out, and each wagon or cart will have a screwdriver attached to one of the boxes so that it may be ready for opening those in which the screw has not been taken out.[4]

The instructions are so detailed it is hard not to speculate that something must have gone wrong in some previous engagement, with Isandlwana being the obvious candidate because of the stories of problems that had arisen there. The impact of Isandlwana on Chelmsford's thinking was also evidenced in the instruction that each night the column must laager and dig a shelter trench around the encampment – very different from the state of affairs on Chelmsford's previous campaign. Great caution was to be taken in the posting of sentries at night. Care was also to be taken that, when sentries ran towards the camp in the event of an attack, they were not fired on. This turned out to be a particularly appropriate injunction.

There were good reasons for the delay as it enabled Chelmsford to build up his force but this could not disguise the sense of letdown in Eshowe. Gunner Carroll went on to explain that nearly half the troops were sick. Men were attacked by a variety of ailments: dysentery, diarrhoea, fever. Indeed there was now a worrying increase in the number of deaths. Midshipman Lewis Coker was in the Naval Brigade and had been in charge of the Gatling gun at the battle of Nyezane/Wombane. He had chosen to sleep in the open rather than protected from the elements so that he could look after the Gatling. It was probably as a result of this that he contracted dysentery. Despite a strong fight, he eventually died on 16 March. Just a lad of 18, he was very popular. Lieutenant Lloyd was at the funeral and noted that there were 'very few dry eyes'.[5]

This was symptomatic of a general downturn in mood around the camp. It was to be followed by more bad tidings. Despite the frequent Zulu aggression against those under siege, actual combat deaths were rare. However, Private Kent of the 99th, who had also volunteered for the Mounted Infantry, was not as lucky as some of his compatriots. On 17 March he was out on patrol, in the very same spot that Corporal Carson had been. As he approached his guard post, five Zulus suddenly appeared and let out a volley.

A bullet struck home. His horse reared and ran off in fright, throwing Kent to the ground. Within an instant the Zulus were on him with their assegais. They stabbed him repeatedly. Two nearby guards rode off for help rather than going to his aid and effectively condemned him to death as a result.

But on the 19th there was an upturn in morale again. A native runner managed to make it through the Zulu cordon with news that the relief column would be setting out on 29 March. Chelmsford had been helped no end by the arrival of reinforcements to bring his depleted forces up to scratch. He now had a large fighting force of 5,500 men available for the relief expedition. The runner also brought other news with him in the shape of a number of letters. These too had a hugely positive impact. It reminded everybody that there was an outside world beyond the siege. Showing a good feel for what would now be called 'communication skills' Pearson had all the general news received posted on a noticeboard for all to see.

The very size of the relief column was a problem for it meant that it moved at a painfully slow pace. They were accompanied by forty-four carts and ninety-four wagons. These carried ten days' supplies for the relief force and a month's worth of provisions for the new garrison that Chelmsford planned to install once he arrived at Eshowe. This was a new Chelmsford: cautious, wary and determined that another disaster must be avoided at all costs. This was also evidenced by the route he had chosen. The first part of the journey had followed in Pearson's footsteps, but then he had moved to the east, closer to the coast, where the ground was more open and cover sparser, making a surprise attack from the Zulus much less likely to succeed.

Chelmsford had arrived at the Thukela on 23 March and there was a buzz about the place. After the former delays, this gave the impression that action was now truly imminent. As the 28th approached, natives from Natal shouted to the Zulus across the river that 'the cow was about to calve'. For several days before the march was due to start, troops were ferried across the river. It was a long-winded process; the pont would take only one wagon and the oxen to haul it at a time so well over a hundred trips were needed for these alone, not even allowing for the thousands of men who also had to get over to Zululand.

The river was over half a mile across and getting everyone over was no mean feat. By the 28th everyone was across. Then the weather broke again. Torrential downpours drenched the soldiers, put out all the campfires and turned the ground into a quagmire. It was certainly not a pleasant welcome to Zululand.

Amongst those with the column were a significant number of journalists, amongst them the ubiquitous and egotistical Charles Norris-Newman. The war was suddenly major news. One journalist who was not there was the war artist Melton Prior, one of the most famous pressmen of his day. He had had a premonition that if he crossed over to Zululand he would not come back alive. Instead Major Crealock offered to provide sketches for him, a suggestion that Prior happily accepted.

Prior's story was a strange one. He had just arrived in Durban when he had a nightmare. He dreamed that he went out with the relief expedition and in his vision saw himself shot and then buried. In the next post that arrived from England, there was a letter from his mother who told Prior that she had had an almost identical dream. She begged him not to go on the expedition. This made his mind up and he stayed behind. Instead, he asked a civilian to go in his stead to supplement the sketches that Crealock was doing on his behalf. The civilian replacement he employed was one of the first to be killed in the march that was about to commence.[6]

The men were up at 0500 on 29 March and on their way an hour later. Chelmsford, in fact, was not with them and only crossed over at 0800, closely followed by John Dunn's men, for most of whom the area of Zululand they were about to enter was home. The column was split into two brigades. With over 3,000 white troops this was a significant force, particularly as on this occasion even the native troops would mostly be armed with modern rifles. The backbone of the imperial troops was provided by the 57th Regiment, 60th Regiment, 91st Regiment, five companies of the 99th, two of the Buffs and a Naval Brigade composed of men from three ships, the *Shah*, the *Boadicea* and the *Tenedos*.

The story of the *Shah* was particularly interesting. She had been sailing the Pacific station and was on her way back to her home port after a three-year mission. She had arrived at St Helena on 6 March, where her captain picked up the news of Isandlwana. After consulting with the governor, it was decided to travel to southern Africa instead along with men from the island's garrison. Chelmsford had been delighted to see them. Not only were the garrison's troops very welcome, so too was the 394-strong Naval Brigade that came ashore from the *Shah*.

The 91st Regiment, on the other hand, represented the first batch of official reinforcements to arrive from England. They had steamed over on the *Pretoria* and were notable most of all for being a Highland regiment, the Princess Louise Argyllshire Highlanders. They made a great impression on all those who saw them, even though they wore tartan 'trews' rather than kilts; the regiment had for a time, at the beginning of the nineteenth century, lost its Highland status. Their pipers, understandably, made a particular impression.

Orders for those elements of the NNC that had disbanded were given in February. Only a few headmen objected, the major problem being that they said they did not want to be led by 'Germans' whose language they did not understand – an insight into the cosmopolitan composition of the NCOs, most of whom had been got rid of in light of the many complaints that had been received about them in the early months of the war.[7]

As well as being issued with rifles, they were given training in marksmanship. The despised drilling remained though. The 2nd Regiment was formally dissolved on 10 March and two independent battalions set up in its stead. Much has been said about the ineffective use of the NNC previously and, in fairness, it does seem that a number of lessons had been learned and many of the mistakes that had initially existed had now been eliminated.

Chelmsford had decided to travel, in relative terms, light. There would be no tents for the men, who would have to make do as well as they could without them. There would only be ten days' rations too, biscuits, tinned meat and tea in the main. Despite these efforts, 122 wagons and carts would still be required.[8]

By the time the first day's march was over, this large, cumbersome force had crawled its way to the Nyoni River. Still the rains continued, drenching those without tents to the skin, making them thoroughly miserable. The tot of rum they were issued probably made little difference. They were also required to make a laager in line with the revised mentality that now existed. It was not a success. The laager was supposed to allow enough room inside for the oxen but when it was completed only a third of them would fit.

There was also insufficient room for many of the men to even grab a token piece of protection from the rain under the wagons. Most of them resorted to using their greatcoats in a futile attempt to stay dry. The only benefit, such as it was, of the rain was that it caused the next day's start to be delayed until 7 a.m. The Nyoni was swollen from the downpours and each wagon had to be man-handled across with the aid of branches pulled down from the nearby trees in an attempt to aid the process.

Although the sun thankfully soon dried out sodden clothes, there was not enough to eat. Despite this, on the second day the column managed to move 8 miles, and the process of the night before was painstakingly repeated. A laager was prepared with the wagons formed into a square. A trench was dug around this and used to form a rampart; almost a return to the tactics of Roman legionaries on the march two millennia before. It was a big improvement on the previous day's effort but it was not long before the inside of the square was a mess, churned up by the heavy tread of oxen and no doubt with a very unsavoury aroma too.

Even then, not everyone thought much of the efforts made. John Dunn looked on with a critical eye, thinking that the men needed to shape up a lot if they were to face a Zulu impi. This was not surprising as most of them were new to Africa and had heard fearsome things of the warriors they were about to face. Now Dunn was more firmly committed to the British cause than ever. There could be no going back to his previous life as a resident of Zululand and a confidant of Cetshwayo. For him more than anyone, this was a war that generated confused emotions. By the time it was over he and his former friend Cetshwayo would be bitter enemies.

The morning of 30 March was typically misty. As a result of their advance that day, the column was now faced with another river to cross. This one, the amaTigulu, would provide a major challenge. It was 40 yards wide and 4ft deep. The evening brought rain yet again. The laager was formed in a rough square and a trench put up around it. The oxen were housed in the laager and the men slept on a mattress of mud between it and the trench. It was a truly awful experience but typical of every other night so far.

And so on the 31st the major challenge of crossing the amaTigulu was faced. Mounted men crossed first to see if there were any Zulus waiting on the other side to launch an attack. There were not. Then the infantry started to cross, up to their chests in water in places, their rifles raised above their heads to keep them dry. Thirty-two oxen, twice the normal number, were needed to drag each wagon across. It took six hours for the column to reach the other side.

As a result, only 2 miles were covered that day. Some Zulus were spotted during the march but they had not threatened the column at all. However, the march was clearly being closely watched. A raiding party had been sent out by Chelmsford to burn a nearby homestead. The garrison of Eshowe had actually seen this in progress and therefore knew that relief was rumbling closer. It was a gratifying feeling.

For Eshowe, that assistance was not coming a moment too soon. Food stocks were running low. On the 29th, the day the march was planned to commence, a message was received from the Lower Drift from Chelmsford. The commander-in-chief wanted help from Pearson and requested that he send out a force of 500 men to meet him. Pearson was reluctant to do so. He explained by return that the health of the men in the fort had been badly affected by their deprivations – a process accelerated by underfeeding. Chelmsford accepted this but said that he would fire two cannon when on the march if he felt he was in trouble and needed help. In such circumstances he expected Pearson to do what he could. He might well have been concerned at the siege mentality that had apparently taken hold of Pearson.

By 30 March, Chelmsford's advanced guard could be seen approaching the amaTigulu River. That night the position of his camp was betrayed by a plethora of campfires. The men in Eshowe waited for rescue, for news from home and for everyday items such as tobacco. In fact, much better communication had already materialised and the garrison were treated that day to the reading out of a newspaper which brought them up to date with events in the outside world. The next morning mounted scouts from Chelmsford's army were seen just 10 miles out from Eshowe. Pearson prepared to send out the best men he had available to provide assistance to Chelmsford if required.

If the Zulus were going to intervene before Chelmsford arrived at Eshowe then they would have to do so quickly. Despite the change of route from that previously taken, the new ground that the column was entering was still less open than that through which they had journeyed so far. There was plenty of scrub now for any hostile force to conceal itself in. Because of this more care was taken with the scouting, making sure that there was no hidden threat ahead. Again, Chelmsford had learned the lessons of Isandlwana.

The Naval Brigade was sent off in front along with the 57th Regiment. The change in terrain was soon noted by Norris-Newman who commented that whereas before the column had passed through gentle hills and wooded knolls, now there were many more trees, long grass and treacherous bogs. Apart from anything else, this caused the column to fragment and from time to time a halt was required to allow the wagons to close up again.

By 1 April, the daily routine of constructing a laager for the overnight camp had developed into a finer art and a position was established near Gingindhlovu. Firearms, rockets and Gatling guns were arranged at the corners. The horses and oxen were placed inside the wagons which were now positioned with slightly more precision as the men were more practised in the art of assembling a laager. Captain Molyneux of the 22nd (Staffordshire) Regiment, who was out in Zululand as a special service officer, went to reconnoitre along with John Dunn, a man with vast local knowledge.

That evening was misty, thick enough to conceal any smoke from Zulu fires. Molyneux and Dunn were on their own and made their way to the waters of the Nyezane River. If there were any Zulus, they were on the far side of it. Dunn prepared for an act of derring-do. Before he did so, he confessed that he had never been in a situation like this with an English officer before and he did not know if he could rely on Molyneux. The two men agreed to a code of conduct: if one was attacked then the other would help whilst the man in trouble was still alive. If, however, he was dead then the other could save himself. The two men agreed to the arrangement.

It was raining hard, which was good for it provided cover. They trod the banks carefully for a couple of miles and then Dunn approached the river through some thick scrub. He listened, with the trained ear of a man who knew this country intimately. Save for the splash of the raindrops in the river there was nothing. Dunn handed his rifle to Molyneux and stripped. With the aid of a fallen tree whose trunk acted as a kind of bridge across the river, he lowered himself into the water and pulled himself across.

A crane, startled by Molyneux's presence, broke the muffled stillness of the evening with a startled cry, causing the captain's heart to skip a beat as he waited for Dunn to return. After what seemed an eternity, his eyes pierced the gloom and he saw a man lowering himself into the river on the other side. It was Dunn and he had electrifying information. He had seen an impi and many fires not far off. However, he was almost spotted, a scout advancing to within a few yards of him when the noisy crane had soared into the air. He had been obliged to lay deadly still for what seemed like forever until the scout had moved off.

Dunn dressed, his body frozen with the numbness of the night. They galloped back to the laager, which was itself filling with water. Molyneux's description of it is revealing:

> when 5,000 human beings, 2,000 oxen and 300 horses have been churning up five acres of very sodden ground for 2 or 3 hours it makes a compost neither pretty to look at, easy to move about in, nor nice to smell. There were unpleasant reptiles about also, for two puff adders had been killed close to our wagon.[9]

So many Zulus had been seen in the vicinity that it was clear that something was brewing. As night fell, the sky darkened and the air grew heavy. Soon rumbles of thunder reverberated across the sky and lightning flashes provided vivid illumination to the scene. It seemed almost as if it were an omen of a storm of another kind about to break. There was, not for the first or last time in this war, a false alarm when a sentry thought he saw something in the night. The men stood to for an hour but it was clear that there was no enemy in the vicinity. Yet most people in the camp felt that they were not very far away.

Cetshwayo hoped that the stunning victory at Isandlwana would make the British more amenable to peace overtures. However, nothing could be further from the truth. Like a wounded lion, the British Empire sought to strike back. So the Zulu king had reluctantly prepared for war once more. Although he still thought that the main threat to his kingdom did not come from this region, an army of up to 12,000 men had still been assembled, many of them local warriors.

They had been gathering for several days but only now were they ready to go on to the attack under the command of Somopho kaZikhale, chief of the Thembu clan. Alongside him was Prince Dabulamanzi, whose warriors had suffered defeat at Rorke's Drift. Much has been made of the Zulus' scouting network, but on this occasion it cannot have been working too effectively, for when the relief column started out on 29 March, the Zulus were not yet in a position to face it. Only on the late evening of 1 April had the last elements been put in place.

Night falls quickly in Africa. Swiftly too does the day come, without the extended ritual of half-light that most Europeans are used to. At the crack of dawn on 2 April, mounted scouts were sent out from Chelmsford's camp. Sentries had been keeping an anxious watch during the night. There was tangible tension in the air. There was also, as usual, heavy rain around to dampen the spirits. The darkness was followed by a typical Zululand morning, damp and misty, adding an ethereal touch to proceedings.

About an hour after these sentries went out, there were shots heard from the river. At first it was not clear what was happening. Then the scouts were seen spurring towards the camp for dear life. One, slower than the others, had been out fetching water when he was overwhelmed. From across the river a terrifying sight emerged, thousands of Zulus charging towards the camp. They seemed to be coming on in four separate columns. Bugles trumpeted out their alarms. The weary soldiers charged with defending the laager shook the stiffness from their joints after the uncomfortable night in the open and prepared for the serious business of staying alive.

The defenders took up their positions, with firm instructions ringing in their ears not to fire until ordered to do so. There would be no independent firing. Instead they were to fire in volleys, setting up a screen of lead which would, it was hoped, prove impenetrable. The infantry assembled in their square whilst the Gatling guns prepared to unleash havoc on the Zulus advancing fearlessly towards them.

The Zulus split into two columns and crossed at several drifts about a mile away from each other. Then they re-formed and adopted their traditional battle formation. They were coming from the north of the laager; the left horn moved to attack the north-east corner and the chest advanced towards the north face of it. The right formed up further to the west.

When they were about 800 yards off, a few straggly shots rang out from the Zulu ranks. Again their opponents watched in admiration as they skirmished their way towards the lines, taking advantage of every hollow that pierced the ground and every bush that grew up from the sodden earth to try and find protection against the withering fire that awaited them. They would weave in and out, almost seeming to disappear only to emerge again that much closer to the British lines. Rather than coming on in a solid mass, the Zulu ranks split up into small knots of five or six and made their way through the long grass.

Now the Gatling guns of the Naval Brigades began to play their symphony of death. One of the gunners had measured out the distance the night before as being 800 yards and asked permission to give his Gatling a trial run. Chelmsford, nearby, overheard the conversation and assented provided it was just a brief burst. With a chilling, monotonous rhythm, the bullets spat out and started to bring down Zulus armed with spears and protected by cow-hide shields. But this was nothing compared to what was to come.

The British army had known its share of ups and downs over the years but the British infantryman had become renowned for his ability to fire his rifle as part of a co-ordinated volley. The discipline of the British troops held firm, despite the sight of the Zulus swarming towards them. Then, when they were about 400 yards off, the order was given. The sound of the volley that followed made an indelible impression on everyone who was there as a sheet of flame shot out. One of those present, Guy Dawnay, attached to the NNC, was in action for the first time. He had 'never imagined even such a crash of sound as the whole thing'.[10]

Some were less impressed. Adjutant Wilkinson of the 60th noted that some of the young riflemen were not sticking to orders and were firing independently. Apart from anything else, this created clouds of smoke which helped obscure the Zulus and make them a more difficult target. John Dunn was playing his part too, sat atop a wagon and firing at the enemy. He noticed that much of the British fire was inaccurate because the men were using long-range sights when the Zulus were moving closer.[11] Informed of this, Chelmsford gave the order for the men to drop the sights, which they did. For a time the firing became more accurate but then, with the Zulus still closer, they had to be ordered to drop them again. This was not a ringing endorsement of the training of the new recruits.

Still the Zulus came on, seeking more cover as they did so. Unfortunately for them, the grass around the camp had been trampled flat by soldiers, horses, wagons and oxen and for 100 yards around it there was no cover to be had. Desperately the Zulus sought for a weakness as they had found at Isandlwana. However, here there was no break in the line to be found. As the war went on, the Zulus would be confused by the British square with no back to it, just men facing them on every side.

This was the battle that Chelmsford wanted, his men in proper position, their Martini-Henrys and Gatling guns able to take their toll of the enemy to maximum effect. The Zulus tried everywhere to break the line but could not get closer than 30 yards. Piles of dead were accumulating all around the square. But despite the losses they sustained, the Zulus came on gamely. One of them, no more than a boy, one of the mat-carriers who accompanied the impis as they went to war and carried provisions for the warriors, got too close to the laager. He was immediately grabbed by one of the sailors on the other side of the wagons and pulled in. His captor kept him quiet by sitting on him throughout the rest of the battle. After it was over, the young Zulu would be recruited as a mascot on the ship HMS *Boadicea* and later entered the Royal Navy, a remarkable if little-known survivor of the conflict.

Norris-Newman was inside the laager. He was enjoying himself, freely taking part in the shooting. The war correspondent in Victorian Britain was no independent observer and Norris-Newman's sensibilities had been neutralised by the bodies of slaughtered friends on the field of Isandlwana. He and a companion, a driver named Palmer who was a crack-shot, spotted three Zulu snipers in a bush 100 yards off. Between the two of them, they managed to shoot them down. After the battle the two men went to see what had become of their targets 'and Palmer and I took and divided the trophies of war, including their native dress, arms, and accoutrements; and we keep them yet, as most prized and hardly won trophies'.[12]

A *donga* just a few yards away from the north-east corner of the British square gave some respite to the Zulus. From here they made a rush for some bushes just 10 yards off from the British lines. They of course provided no protection at all and large numbers of dead were later found piled up there. There was no doubting the determination of the attackers but the battle was turning into a massacre.

Some of the Zulus' rifle fire occasionally had an effect. Lieutenant-Colonel Francis Northey of the 60th was in the lines when he was hit in the arm. He handed over command to his number two and then went off for treatment. This seemed to unnerve his men; Hamilton-Browne thought that for a time they were distinctly 'wobbly'. Their firing became more erratic and the officers had to make great efforts to keep their nerve so that their men were inspired to emulate their example.

Northey was still concerned about his men and when the attack intensified he sat up to shout his encouragement. His wound was worse than first thought as the bullet had lodged near his spine. His enthusiastic shouting did him no favours for it caused a haemorrhage and he collapsed in a pool of blood. Meanwhile, on the western side of the laager, a youthful-looking officer, Lieutenant George Johnson, was recklessly exposing himself to fire to encourage his men. He was struck in the heart by a Zulu bullet and died soon afterwards.

It took just a quarter of an hour for the Zulu attack to begin to tail off. But some of them still pushed on, skirmishing through the bush, trying to get close. As they were repulsed by one part of the square, they moved on to the next but with identical results. The right horn began its attack on the rear (south side) of the square possibly led by Dabulamanzi himself. The 91st Regiment were here and for whatever reason – they were no more experienced than many of the other British soldiers present – they stayed much calmer than some of their colleagues elsewhere in the square, whose firing had been erratic if still deadly.

Despite this, the Zulus pushed home their attack vigorously and Chelmsford put several companies on standby as a reserve in case help was needed. Rockets and cannon added to the cacophony but were not always of much use; Dawnay noticed one rocket strike the ground a quarter of a mile off and then head back towards the laager. Molyneux, meanwhile, looked on in wonder as Zulu riflemen fired at the rockets as they passed over their heads.

By 7 a.m. Chelmsford noticed a significant loss of impetus in the Zulu advance. He ordered the cavalry under Brevet Major Barrow to prepare to go on the offensive. Barrow was a fine leader of cavalry; the First World War general Sir John French would meet him a few years later and describe him as 'the finest and best character I ever met'.[13] Barrow led his men out of the square. The Zulus were not normally particularly happy when faced with cavalry and they were now demoralised. Despite this, they did not break.

Barrow and his men had been unleashed too early and were in danger of being cut off. Molyneux was sent out to help. He ended up in a scrap for his life. His horse was shot by a Zulu; it managed to stagger back to the square but then collapsed in a heap after spinning in a somersault. Molyneux was forced to administer the *coup de grâce*. Barrow himself was injured in the retreat back to the square.

Next it was the turn of the right (eastern) side of the square to be attacked. The Zulus here were more exposed to heavy fire than anywhere else, with several hundred yards of open ground between them and the British lines. The main body of troops here was the 57th and, despite the loss of several men to Zulu marksmen, they held firmer than most. It quickly became apparent that the Zulus would get little change out of this assault either.

Two of Chelmsford's staff had close shaves. Crealock was hit on the arm by a spent bullet whilst Lieutenant Milne from the *Active* had a bullet pass through his sleeve but merely graze his arm. But even in the heat of battle there were moments of light relief. John Dunn noticed a man from the NNC sitting underneath a cask of rum that a bullet had pierced. He had helped himself to some of the contents, clearly disturbed at thinking they might be wasted, and was lying in a stupor even as the battle raged.

The attack, though, was definitely slackening. It was time for the cavalry to have another go. Barrow was fit enough to lead them. The Zulus resisted half-heartedly at first. Then they began to retreat. This merely egged the cavalry on, joined by bodies of NNC who were anxious to get in on the act. The cavalrymen hacked at the flanks of the Zulus, who now started to flee. Soon flight turned into rout and the Zulus streamed away from the field of battle as fast as they could.

Despite the repulse of the Zulu army, not everyone had been impressed by the performance of the troops. Hamilton-Browne was involved in the battle, joining the column after having had a short break at the Cape recruiting new troops. He was only at Gingindhlovu by chance. Whilst he was most impressed by the performance of the naval recruits to the army, and was particularly fascinated by the ruthless efficiency of the Gatling guns, he was not encouraged by the performance of the new young soldiers who made up most of the reinforcements. Others noted that the men needed more training in how to fire in sections; the firing had been so erratic at times that an almost impenetrable smokescreen had shrouded the battlefield on occasions, making it impossible to see the Zulu army to shoot at.

Hamilton-Browne had also taken part in the pursuit after the battle. He witnessed first hand some of the inadequacies of the Imperial Mounted Infantry, who were after all a scratch unit composed of men who were used to fighting on foot. In particular, they were not trained to use a sword, especially when on horseback. In one incident he had seen a cavalryman ride down a fleeing Zulu. When he went to strike him with his sword, the cut had missed and instead removed an ear from his horse. In another incident, a rider who went to the aid of an unseated comrade who was in hand-to-hand combat with a Zulu almost succeeded in amputating the hand of his friend rather than slaying his enemy.[14]

The pursuit was vigorous. Dawnay stated that it was impossible to spare wounded Zulus for they insisted on fighting on whilst there was a breath of life in them. His NNC men were firing at anything that moved – including him – and he was forced to confiscate several rifles for the safety of friend as much as foe. Lieutenant Hutton of the 60th Rifles admitted that 'all those that were desperately wounded and unable to get away with their retiring friends were doubtless assegaied by our native troops, and the proportion of killed to wounded was very large'.[15] But it was not just black soldiers who were finishing off the wounded. Private Powis of the Mounted Infantry happily admitted to playing a part in decapitating three wounded Zulus who were trying to escape.[16]

With the battle now effectively over, a few of the men were given permission to go and inspect the column's handiwork. The long grass around the laager concealed a stack of bodies. One of those delegated to supervise burial parties, Lieutenant Hutton, reckoned that 520 Zulus were buried and estimated that in all there were 1,000 enemy dead. Although numbers vary, an estimate of 1,000–1,200 dead is the most common, which again amounts to something like a 10 per cent casualty rate (in terms of mortality alone; there would be walking wounded who escaped).

In the aftermath of battle, 453 Zulu guns were collected. Few of them were Martini-Henrys so if the Zulus had helped themselves to large stocks of these at Isandlwana, not many found their way to the impi here; 425 of them were outdated models of little effective use. In comparison to Zulu losses, reports suggest that four British/colonial troops were killed and twelve wounded, though some thought that NNC losses were higher than this. Amongst the unfortunate few was Porter, the unfortunate civilian artist who Melton Prior had sent in his place because of his pre-campaign premonition. Interestingly, about 11,000 rounds of ammunition were recorded as having been fired in the battle – not a large number if there were over 3,000 white troops in action.

Far off, the garrison at Eshowe had been watching the fight at Gingindhlovu with an interest that became ever more enthusiastic as the course of the battle became clear. When it was obvious it was over, Pearson flashed his congratulations to Chelmsford. Chelmsford responded with something even more useful: fifty-eight carts laden with supplies for the garrison, whose provisions were supposedly on the point of running out.

The path along which this convoy travelled was exposed to further attack from the Zulus but it is indicative of their state of mind that the supply chain was unopposed. The slaughter at Gingindhlovu had broken the spirit of the impi sent to destroy the redcoats. The convoy passed the battlefield of Nyezane of which fight much evidence still remained. It was a reminder of another era, when Pearson's column had moved on Eshowe, its spirits high, its confidence soaring. Isandlwana had changed that and the Zulu enemy, despite the recent reverse they had suffered, was a much more intimidating adversary than it had been back then.

A number of those on the march commented on the fact that it was one of the toughest they had ever been on. But after hours of toil, they at last came upon Pearson's new road which would lead them straight to Eshowe. Norris-Newman was in a race to be the first to make contact with the garrison. He won it. At around 5 p.m. the defenders of Eshowe saw a horseman appear in the distance. Norris-Newman rode up and began to shake hands with everyone he came across. 'Proud to shake hands with an Ekowian' was his rather ostentatious greeting. One of the recipients of his pompous salutation dryly responded that he was three months late.

In the meantime, Pearson was on his way down the track with 500 men in case Chelmsford and the main force needed help. The two men met a few miles away from Eshowe. They shook hands and exchanged formal greetings in a rather stiff-upper-lipped Victorian way. Then they rode on their way towards the mission station together.

It was dark when the haunting sound of distant bagpipes from the pipers of the 91st Highlanders announced the imminent arrival of the relief force to the garrison. It was a surreal sound in this humid African landscape but it was the final affirmation of rescue for those inside the mission station. A number of the garrison had turned in for the night, tired of waiting for the relief column, but the walls were soon lined with an excited, relieved and expectant throng. The night air was rent by cheers of joy piercing the stillness and tears ran freely down the faces of some of those present.

It was an irony that the column was in more need of provisions than the garrison was. Supplies had been carefully garnered inside Eshowe but now, with relief at hand, these were freely consumed and a veritable feast, certainly by recent standards, was enjoyed by all. Norris-Newman happily commented that it was the best food he had enjoyed since he left Fort Tenedos. With their liberation, a number of the garrison partook of their first proper 'smoke' for a while. This at least was in good supply within the relief column. A wagonload of letters also arrived, much to the delight of those who had been deprived of news from the outside world for three months.

Chelmsford had seen enough on his march up to the mission station to convince him that the risks involved in garrisoning it were too great. Further, it was questionable whether a continued occupation of Eshowe had sufficient strategic merit to make it sensible. It had originally been envisioned as an advanced base from which to support a three-pronged attack on Ulundi. Now that strategic plan had changed and Chelmsford was forced to develop a new one instead.

Eshowe would be difficult to keep supplied in its exposed forward position and Chelmsford's plan, when finally developed, would make it much less strategically important. Therefore, it would be abandoned.

At 5 a.m. the next morning, 4 April, the bugles sounded to wake the men from their heavy sleep. Chelmsford had decided on one last flamboyant gesture. He decided that he would send a force to wipe out Dabulamanzi's homestead which was a few miles off. However, his mounted men failed to catch the Zulus there by surprise with the result that when they arrived they found it deserted. Those there had made their way to safety in some nearby hills and they aimed a few hopeful shots at the British. The shooting on this occasion was more accurate than was typically the case, causing some discomfort to those who were targeted. But none were hit and the homestead was set ablaze.

The garrison now started to leave Eshowe. They had mixed emotions, for the men had put a lot of work into fortifying it and their labours were effectively in vain. Wagons were hauled out from the positions in which they had temporarily been deployed for defensive purposes, whilst anything that could not be taken but might be of use to the Zulus was destroyed. The pipers sounded forth again as the retreat from Eshowe began. Over 100 wagons, some of them carrying a number of sick members of the garrison, started to move south. By the time of departure, nine officers and over 100 men were on the sick list.[17]

Not all of them were leaving Eshowe, though. The cemetery was now the permanent home of twenty-eight men. The funerals that had taken place had initially been performed with full military honours but deaths became too frequent and this practice was dropped. The wet weather had flooded a number of the graves; one witness recalled one soldier being buried literally floating in his grave in a pool of water.

It was a long, drawn-out, straggling column that now set out for Natal – a state of affairs that was a worry for Chelmsford. When the head of it reached the appointed campsite for the day at 5 p.m., the tail had still not left Eshowe. However, no attack came and the column continued unhindered. Remarkably, on their way they stumbled across a badly wounded Zulu, who had been shot through the foot at Gingindhlovu and had been crawling for miles. On this occasion it was a sight that inspired pity and he was taken onboard a wagon for treatment.

Despite the sense of relief, or perhaps because of it, nerves were frayed. When a camp was set up near the Nyezane River, an entrenchment was erected around it. At 3.30 a.m., one of the sentries saw something moving in the shadows. When his challenge went unanswered, he fired into the darkness. Men woke hastily from their heavy sleep and stood to. In the meantime, John Dunn's natives were outside the camp and understandably started to make their way back into it. In the darkness, they were indistinguishable from hostile Zulus.

The soldiers in the camp had fixed bayonets and, seeing a number of black men coming towards them, started to attack. In the confusion two of Dunn's natives were killed and a number wounded. Those under attack frantically tried to tell their assailants in broken English that they were a 'fiend' and Dunn was incensed, shouting out 'they are killing my people'. Chelmsford was livid. He noted that it was a dark night with excellent visibility and the state of 'funk' could only be ascribed to the youthfulness of the soldiers.[18] It was yet another commentary on the ineptitude, as he saw it, of the army reforms that had been a feature of the previous few years.

By 6 April, a camp had been established close to the battlefield of Gingindhlovu. In the aftermath of the slaughter there, the air was now noxious with the stench of decaying bodies, some of which were found in the water supply used by those in the camp. There were also still wounded Zulus in the vicinity and some were treated with humanity and brought into the camp for treatment.

But not all. A young soldier, Jack Royston, found two wounded Zulus, shot in the chest, lying in a *donga*. They were able to walk and he led them back towards the camp. As he was doing so, a colonial officer came up, turned on him for his softness and shot both men dead. This was, by today's standards, a war crime. It was the same back then, particularly when such behaviour was judged against Chelmsford's initial campaign injunction that any wounded enemy was to be treated with compassion.

As the column continued its journey, Dunn passed several of his homesteads. They had been wrecked by Zulus intent on revenge for his perceived treachery. Particularly upsetting for him was the destruction of his journals which he had painstakingly assembled over many years. It was as if part of him had died. He muttered as he moved dejectedly past, 'I have not done with the Zulus yet'.

It was 11 a.m. on the 7th when the garrison at last reached the Natal border and safety. On 9 April, Corporal Licence of the Royal Engineers noted that the night before he had slept with his boots off for the first time in three months.[19] The returnees were enthusiastically welcomed back. The fortifications at Eshowe had not long survived their departure. Some of those in the column could still see the mission station when the Zulus set fire to it once it had been abandoned. Thick smoke weaved its way into the sky, a funeral pyre for Chelmsford's original plan and the men who had given their lives for it.

The cost borne by the Zulus was, as always in this war, massively greater than that suffered by the British, but they had at least seen the back of the white man in Eshowe for now. They had succeeded for a while in conducting a flexible guerrilla war against the entrapped Pearson and his men, and these had been good tactics; there may have been no major victory but hundreds of British soldiers were kept inactive and out of the war for three months. In contrast, the attack against a prepared British position at Gingindhlovu had been a great tactical error and the Zulus' chances would have been much greater if they had attacked the relief column whilst it was stretched out.

On the other hand, Gingindhlovu vindicated Chelmsford's tactics. He had been right all along to think that in a fight against a compact British position the Zulus would be fighting a lost cause. Yet this also served to emphasise the sloppiness that had led to the catastrophe of Isandlwana. He had plenty of time to think on this as he made the four-day journey back to the Thukela along with the men who had been rescued. A new plan of campaign needed to be formulated, one that was helped no end by the stream of reinforcements that were starting to flow into southern Africa in a move to restore the tarnished prestige of a world superpower.

But there were dissentient voices in southern Africa as well as Britain, who were increasingly critical of the conduct of the war. The Cape Town correspondent of the *Daily News* noted that almost nothing had been gained by the war so far. Further, 'every day makes it more apparent that the expenditure on account of this war will be something enormous'. He noted that southern Africa had been ransacked for horses and mules and that 800 of the latter were being fetched from as far afield as Montevideo in Uruguay. He thundered, in terms that would touch the heart of any self-respecting accountant, that the projected cost of the war was likely to be in the region of £200 per Zulu. All this for what the correspondent called 'the bugbear which Sir Bartle Frere has so carefully raised'.[20]

Not for everyone did the relief of Eshowe end their suffering. The death toll of Eshowe was not yet complete. In the wagons were men who were suffering from diseases contracted during the siege. Norris-Newman noted that there were ninety-three people on the sick list. There was fever, dysentery, colic and diarrhoea to cope with. Saddest of all perhaps, Captain Warren Wynne, who had been indefatigable in his efforts to protect the besieged Eshowe, died on 19 April, the day of his thirty-sixth birthday. The officer who led his funeral service, Lieutenant Courtney of the Royal Engineers, who was the only officer in the vicinity at the time, could barely get through it without breaking down.

For the majority of the several thousand Zulus who had died in the Eshowe campaign, there were no names recorded for posterity, yet their loss would have been greatly felt by their loved ones. There is no roll of honour for them, little historical memory even; no records of poignant last rites as they were interred. Indeed, many of them lay where they fell; if they were lucky their bodies were covered over with a shield by a friend who had fought with them at Wombane or Gingindhlovu. For most, they lay undisturbed where they had died, to rot and bleach in the desiccating sun. Sometimes their comrades would be too worried about saving their own lives to pay any last respects. All too often their comrades would themselves be dead.

The headcount of the Zulu dead in the war was starting to reach frightening proportions: Isandlwana, Khambula, Wombane, Gingindhlovu – the resources of the Zulu nation were being bled dry. But the killing was not yet over. Britain needed a crushing victory to restore its prestige, but so too did Lord Chelmsford. The garrison at Eshowe had been rescued and brought back to safety and the pieces on the chessboard were more or less back where they had started. What was effectively the first Zulu war was over, and the second was about to begin.

ten

THE SETTING SUN OF THE BONAPARTES

The Death of the Prince Imperial

Disaster had not quite finished with Chelmsford yet. As he began to implement his plans for the second invasion, he would soon have another distraction on his hands. Even as he pushed his way towards Ulundi and triumph, the attention of the world would be gripped by another dramatic interlude.

A hard-nosed assessment of the death of the French Prince Imperial, Louis Napoleon, would inevitably arrive at the conclusion that it had very little impact whatsoever on the progress of the war. Yet this is one occasion when a cold, objective view would distort an accurate understanding of events. For the British public, this was the news story of the year. It far outshone Isandlwana in terms of its impact on the popular consciousness. It was no less the case in the prince's own country, even though he was in exile with no prospect of a return to his homeland. It also provided Chelmsford with yet another terrible turn of events to explain away.

Even at the time it was recognised that the death of the Prince Imperial was a minor incident in the war, but the unique circumstances of his status 'combined to invest it with a special pathos and interest, almost worldwide'.[1] In terms of pathos it was hard to come up with a storyline that would outdo it. Louis' great-uncle was one of the greatest names in history: Napoleon Bonaparte. He was always the ghost in the room as far as the prince was concerned, an idol to live up to. For the press the story of Louis' untimely death was a godsend; the home correspondent of the *South Australian Courier* captured the mood when he wrote that 'since the death of the Prince Consort I doubt whether any event has excited a greater sensation'.[2]

The great Napoleon I, the first Emperor of France, left what proved to be an impossible legacy to live up to. Bonaparte was a clinical thinker, a strategist *par excellence* who had an ability to reason and think through a problem with all the hallmarks of genius. His great-nephew, on the other hand, was a rash, impetuous youth whose bravery was never in doubt but whose judgement certainly was. From the moment that he was first given permission to participate in the Anglo-Zulu War he gave every indication that his recklessness would get him into trouble. In short, his untimely death was a disaster waiting to happen.

The pathos of Louis' story was not only connected to his illustrious heritage, it also arose from the fact that he died in a war that was nothing to do with him, fighting for a country that was a traditional enemy of his beloved France. If France had not been a republic, then by the rights of inheritance he would have been her emperor and more likely to be scheming against Britain than fighting for her.

But France was a republic. Unfortunately, the great Bonaparte's military genius was an aberration, one that was not inherited by his descendants. Louis' father, Emperor Napoleon III, had been completely out-generalled during the Franco-Prussian War of 1870. The genius then was not a Bonaparte but the 'Iron Chancellor', Otto von Bismarck, of Prussia. Bismarck once famously said that history was just a piece of paper covered with print; for him the main thing was to make history, not to write it. It was an aspiration that Louis also held.

At the end of the Franco-Prussian War Napoleon III had lost not only the conflict but also his imperial crown. Forced to flee to Britain, he lived out his life in relative obscurity. Although he longed for his people to summon him back, they never did. France remained a republic, as she has stayed until this day. The old emperor died in 1873, leaving his claim to the crown to his son. However, there was little realistic prospect that he would ever be able to fulfil it.

Louis was an only child, doted on by his mother the Empress Eugenie, a proud, independent woman of Spanish origin with some Scottish blood flowing in her veins from a couple of generations back. She had nearly died giving birth to her son and this had a dramatic effect on her health. The end result was that her physicians advised against giving birth to any further children as it would be highly dangerous for her. This helps to explain why Eugenie was a particularly protective mother.

Once in England, at the quiet country house, Camden Place in Chislehurst, where he lived in exile with his mother, Louis sat around and moped for a time. He was not a good student and he found little to entertain or divert him. Then, his life was changed forever when someone suggested to his parents that a course at the Royal Military Academy might be the solution. It seemed to be an inspired choice; here he would be taught how to become either an engineer or an artilleryman; the latter, of course, would give him a direct link with his great-uncle.

Louis jumped at the chance. He did not have the appropriate qualifications to enter so he was required to take an exam. Few expected him to pass it given his academic record but he surprised them all. The thought of a military career had inspired him to make up for his former lethargy and he worked exceptionally hard to make up for his deficiencies. He found himself accepted for the academy at Woolwich.

It was whilst at Woolwich that he received the news of the death of his father. A massive crowd turned out to witness his funeral. Queen Victoria herself travelled down to Chislehurst to see the coffin along with her daughter, Princess Beatrice, who was very fond of Louis; there would be frequent speculation in the British press that an engagement was imminent, though the queen was very close to her daughter and would be reluctant to let her go. On the day of the funeral, Louis played his part manfully but as a 16-year-old it was a terrible strain on him.

With a Herculean effort, Louis then finished his studies at Woolwich as the seventh highest member of his class. He was given the honour of leading the passing-out parade which marked his graduation, a gesture which moved his proud mother to tears. The top ten in the class were allowed to join the Engineers if they so wished but Louis turned the honour down. A Bonaparte could only ever become an artilleryman.

Louis was an excellent horseman who typically got on his horse by vaulting into the saddle. But boredom and a sense of drifting was what most characterised his life and after leaving the academy he had nothing to do. He searched desperately for an opportunity to see real action. War broke out in the Balkans between Russia and Turkey in 1878. Louis tried to join in on the side of the Austrians who seemed about to intervene against the Russians. Eugenie, his mother, was shocked when she heard of the idea: 'you will spend your time in an Austrian garrison playing billiards and making love to an Italian singer.'[3] But the realities of European politics meant that a would-be emperor of France, even one in exile, could not realistically hope to embroil himself in a European war on behalf of another nation.

Then came the Anglo-Zulu War. The news of Isandlwana sent shockwaves across Britain. It raised the profile of what would have seemed just another minor colonial spat to something far more significant. It was not just the public that was spurred into action. With reinforcements desperately needed, a number of volunteers rushed to join up. Some of them were no doubt inspired by what they saw as a sense of patriotic duty, regardless of the rights and wrongs of the war. Others joined to satisfy their thirst for adventure. Louis decided to volunteer his services too, his main reason being a longing for action. He therefore wrote to the Duke of Cambridge, the commander-in-chief of the British army, asking for permission to join the forces involved in the war in Zululand.

The decision to put himself forward was, typically for the prince, entirely impulsive and made without reference to anyone else. It made no sense at all, other than the fact that it would give him the chance for military adventure that he craved. As he himself put it with a characteristic sense of self-importance: 'when one belongs to a race of soldiers it is only with sword in hand that one gains recognition.'[4]

The reaction of Eugenie was also typical. She had convinced herself that she walked hand-in-hand with tragedy, a perception that her own fate and that of her husband merely served to confirm. She had always cosseted Louis and, since the emperor's death, this trait had become even more marked. She refused to contemplate Louis' departure on what she perceived as a foolhardy and dangerous adventure.

Yet it seemed for a time that the empress had little to worry about. In a military sense there was little a raw, inexperienced artilleryman could bring to the campaign. On the other hand, his presence could be both an embarrassment and a distraction for the British military authorities. Louis was still a potential would-be Emperor of France, despite being unlikely to return as such to his homeland. However, regardless of his current situation in exile, the French would be quick to turn on their traditional rivals should anything go wrong.

For this reason, great care would need to be taken to ensure that nothing happened to him. This would be a most unwelcome distraction for Lord Chelmsford. The best way to avoid the problem was simply to stop him from travelling to southern Africa in the first place. There was no advantage to be gained from Louis' offer, and the Duke of Cambridge had little hesitation in rebuffing him.

Louis' response, however, showed a rare sense of how to influence people. Rather than reacting aggressively, his reply was couched in such courteous and polite terms that it disarmed Cambridge. Although he admitted that the rejection letter he had received had distressed him, Louis was quick to realise that he could offer little in a military sense. He explained that he 'looked on this war as an opportunity of showing my gratitude towards the Queen and the nation in a way that would be very much to my mind'. Reaffirming his disappointment, he concluded charmingly that 'I remain nonetheless deeply devoted to the Queen and deeply grateful to your Royal Highness for the interest you have always displayed in me'.[5]

Cambridge showed the letter to Queen Victoria, as Louis probably hoped he would. The queen was very moved by the prince's eloquence and charming sentiments. The wall of resistance against Louis' participation started to crumble, though Prime Minister Benjamin Disraeli refused to have anything to do with it, his politically experienced nose sensing trouble ahead.

Eugenie's resistance had also softened. Cambridge finally relented, although he could not be perceived to give the Prince an 'official' position. Louis would be allowed to go but only as a private visitor with no official status. If, however, he wished to offer his services to the British army in an unofficial capacity when he arrived in southern Africa, then there would be little anyone could do to stop him.

Disraeli was bemused by this stance and by the royal audiences Louis was later granted before leaving for southern Africa. His instinct was to steer well clear but he had effectively been ignored. The queen had seen Louis' appeal as directed to her personally, in gratitude for the kindness shown by the country who had accepted him into exile, and her support for his involvement was crucial.

The idea that Louis was going out as a private observer was a sham. He would go with a letter in his pocket addressed to Chelmsford from Cambridge asking him to look after the prince. Yet even the queen was nervous. Louis had acquired a taste for exhibitionist and sometimes dangerous gestures, and Victoria mused that she hoped he would not expose himself to unnecessary risk, 'for we know he is very venturesome'.[6]

Louis intended to sail for southern Africa on the *Danube* which was scheduled to leave on 28 February. He would take a valet with him but no other servants. He was exhilarated at the prospect before him but nevertheless took the precaution of writing out a will in true soldier fashion before his departure. The greatest ordeal for the young prince was his last breakfast with Eugenie before leaving for Southampton. The empress travelled down with him on the train though she seemed inwardly distraught at his imminent departure. She saw him on to the ship, then watched as the gangplank was hoisted up and his ship sailed away into the unknown. It would later stop at Plymouth before leaving England accompanied by the strains of a band playing *Auld Lang Syne*.

The crossing did not get off to the best of starts. The trip across the Bay of Biscay was awful and Louis, along with everyone else, was violently ill. Following this, there was a lull in both a meteorological and an emotional sense. Boredom set in and there was little to do to disturb the monotony before bad weather struck again. Louis hoped that the ship might put in to St Helena, a place of sacred memory for the Bonapartes, but he was disappointed as they sailed close to the island but did not stop there.

It was on 26 March, nearly a month after leaving Southampton, that Louis arrived at Cape Town. Here he was invited by a messenger from Lady Frere to visit Government House. Although a long way from the front line in Zululand, it was here that he got his first glimpse of the other, non-glorious side of war. He met about fifty widows, bereaved by the defeat at Isandlwana and clearly devastated as a result.

His stop in Cape Town was brief, for the day after arriving the *Danube* set out on the last leg of her voyage to Durban. It was the most dangerous part of the journey. The coast of Natal was notorious for its reefs and sandbanks and over the years had become the graveyard for many ships. But on arrival at Durban, after a trouble-free trip, Louis' ambitions were again frustrated. Lord Chelmsford, whom he was keen to be introduced to, was away on his relief expedition to Eshowe. Louis would have to wait for his return before seeing him.

Chelmsford eventually returned to Durban on 9 March and Louis arranged to see him the next day. With Chelmsford was the staff officer, Captain Molyneux, who had shared John Dunn's adventures on the night before Gingindhlovu. He made a telling observation that the prince was anxious to gain recognition and was a good swordsman and horseman, 'but of course like all high-spirited young men is a little difficult to manage'.[7]

Louis presented Cambridge's letter to Chelmsford. This explained that it was out of the question to take Louis on in an official capacity. However, the government had 'sanctioned my writing to you and to Sir Bartle Frere that you show him kindness and render him assistance to see as much as he can with the columns in the field. I hope you will do so.'

This was being somewhat economical with the truth. Whoever in the government had sanctioned the letter, it was not Benjamin Disraeli, though he suspected all along that such a letter existed. But even Cambridge was not without his doubts; he concluded his letter to Chelmsford with the ominous words that 'my only anxiety on his account would be that he is too plucky and go ahead'.[8]

It is clear from this correspondence and also Queen Victoria's pensive thoughts that even thousands of miles away they were afraid the prince's personality and lack of maturity might lead to problems. Given these *ex ante* comments, it is amazing that Cambridge and others colluded in his participation in the war. It was also grossly unfair on Chelmsford who, whatever faults he may have had, did nothing to encourage these moves and would, if given the chance, probably have done everything he could to discourage them.

Yet, if Chelmsford did see the arrival of the prince as something tantamount to a poisoned chalice, he was both a product of his class and a victim of the circumstances he found himself in. Chelmsford was renowned for his civility and politeness, and these were qualities that made it difficult for him both to rebuff the highest-ranking member of the French imperial dynasty and also the Duke of Cambridge, who was the first cousin of Queen Victoria as well as his commander-in-chief. In addition, Chelmsford desperately needed allies in the aftermath of Isandlwana and Cambridge had so far been rock solid in his support. He could not afford to antagonise him.

Chelmsford was publicly gracious in the extreme in response to the prince's arrival. He proposed to Cambridge to make Louis an aide-de-camp, a member of his headquarters staff. It had privately been hinted that it would not be appropriate to attach Louis to a native corps and a staff appointment seemed to be the perfect solution. It meant that Chelmsford could theoretically keep an eye on him. However, in practice Chelmsford had a war to win, one which had started extremely badly for him, and he would never have the time or the opportunity to act as nursemaid to a headstrong prince.

Nevertheless, he wrote to the Duke of Cambridge that 'I should feel much obliged if Your Royal Highness would assure the Empress that I will look after the Prince to the best of my ability, and that I am convinced I shall find him a very valuable addition to my staff'.[9] These were words that would come back to haunt him.

Quite what to do with Louis in practice remained very unclear to everyone, not least Chelmsford himself. Louis had also contracted a fever. His state of health was not improved when he vaulted on to the back of an unruly horse at Pietermaritzburg on his way to the front, hoping to show off his skills in calming it down. Instead the horse threw him off, injuring him. This meant that he had to rest for a short time to recuperate. It also cast some doubts on the prince's skills as a supposedly excellent horseman.

But at last he arrived on the borders of Zululand and the prospect of action loomed tantalisingly close. Here he was in a position to witness the preparations for the second invasion of Zululand. In the light of the earlier disaster at Isandlwana, Chelmsford had revised his plans. Wood was to be allowed to carry on with a good deal of flexibility with what was now termed a Flying Column. Chelmsford would accompany another column from the border to the south. It would be nominally led by Major-General Edward Newdigate but again, with Chelmsford accompanying the column, his role in reality was going to be largely a supporting one; as Captain Montague of the 94th Regiment put it, the men were 'only sorry that Lord Chelmsford's presence with the Division allowed [Newdigate] no opportunity of proving his soldier-like qualities'.[10] This column would be made up of troops who were part of the old Central Column, half wiped out earlier in the war, accompanied by a large batch of reinforcements from England. Once they had crossed the Zulu border, Wood and Chelmsford would join up.

In the meantime, another column further to the east would advance, this time closer to the coast than previously. But the defeat at Isandlwana had certainly succeeded in involving the British government in the war. This second invasion force was massive: 22,545 men, of whom over 15,000 were regular soldiers or members of the colonial militia, the rest being native troops.[11]

Exactly what route the main force was to take proved to be a conundrum. It was decided that the Rorke's Drift road did not after all provide the best option. It ran close to the border with Zululand where supply lines were vulnerable. It also led directly past Isandlwana and nothing so far had been done to bury the British dead left there. Marching past the sun-blanched skeletons of hundreds of fallen comrades was hardly likely to boost morale.

Instead, Chelmsford decided to follow a route about 25 miles to the north-west, through Dundee. He did not have good intelligence and more scouting needed to be done to fill this significant knowledge gap. His forces started to assemble at Dundee in mid-April. It was a tiny settlement but it was soon lost amongst the sprawling encampment that started to grow around it. Chelmsford also decided to set up an advance supply depot at Conference Hill, halfway between Dundee and Khambula, where Wood was still in camp.

This was too far north for an invading army. If he followed a route from there, he would leave Natal badly exposed to Zulu raids – a constant worry for both him and the government of Natal. So he needed to find a route further south which would enable him to reach the road to Ulundi, past Isandlwana, which would be conveniently bypassed as a result.

Louis recovered his strength sufficiently to join up with Chelmsford again at Dundee. On 2 May they rode together to Wood's camp at Khambula. Here he not only enjoyed touring the battlefield, where much evidence of the fierce fighting must still have been obvious, but also meeting up with old friends such as artillerymen Arthur Bigge and Frederick Slade, whom he had spent time with at Aldershot in manoeuvres a few years before. He was also presumably delighted when Wood laid on a show for his edification, showing him how every man in the camp could get to their assigned battle position within three minutes of the alarm being given.[12]

Louis was delighted to meet up with several Frenchmen serving with Wood's irregulars. But unfortunately he was still not fully recovered from his illness and had a relapse. A few days after arriving at Khambula, Chelmsford moved to Utrecht, further from the front, where Louis was billeted in a house. This would no doubt have been a welcome change from staying in a tent, except the whole experience of outdoor life had apparently caused Louis' spirits to soar. He was, it was reported, delighted with it, as it 'made him feel that he was really doing soldiers' work such as he had never done before'.[13]

Chelmsford now had the opportunity to appoint more men to his staff. He was a poor delegator and would never willingly let go of many tasks. On 8 May, however, he did appoint Colonel Richard Harrison as his quartermaster-general. Although Harrison did not want the job – he was an engineer who would rather have been in the field with his company – he dutifully poured his energies into the task. He pondered his role and considered it was threefold: the organisation of the forces, the collection of supplies and the reconnoitring of Zulu territory through which the army was to advance.

Harrison had with him a young officer, Lieutenant Jahleel Brenton Carey, of the 98th Regiment, whose duties were to produce sketches of the territory ahead to inform the planning of the invasion. Chelmsford asked Louis to assist Harrison in the collection of information regarding the distribution of troops and depots. Carey had proved himself of considerable use on several occasions during the current campaign. He had been onboard a troopship, the *Clyde*, that foundered on the Natal coast, though fortunately all the men onboard had got off safely. Stranded for a while on the Natal coast, Carey had quickly taken charge of assembling temporary accommodation for the troops with virtually no raw materials to use other than those he found in the wild.

Carey spoke reasonable French and had seen something of the Franco-Prussian War. He and Louis, therefore, had several things in common. It seems the two men became good acquaintances, though friendship was too strong a word to apply to their relationship. Louis came from quite another circle; even on campaign he would dine with Chelmsford's staff whilst Carey would take his meals with Harrison.

Scouting for the invasion now began in earnest. It was necessary not just to confirm an appropriate route but also to probe Zulu defences in the border regions. The first major advance, led by the 2nd Battalion of the reformed Natal Native Contingent under Major Bengough, set out on 13 May. They encountered small parties of Zulus but only minor skirmishes ensued. Bengough's men enthusiastically burned down any Zulu hut they came across; the pretence that this was just a war against Cetshwayo and not his people had now been abandoned once and for all. The only major problem occurred when Bengough and his men returned to Natal. Being in the main natives, they were mistaken for Zulus and almost fired on by 'friendly' forces.

Harrison, in charge of scouting operations, was not impressed at the regular cavalry units that had arrived from England. Their horses had still not recovered from the journey – a problem with horses accompanying armies on long sea voyages throughout the ages – and the men seemed unaware of the realities of warfare in southern Africa. Instead, reliance continued to be placed on the irregular cavalry who were much more attuned to what was required. The regular cavalry were most put out at being deprived of what they saw as their rightful place and there was barely concealed resentment as a result.

In the meantime, Wood had started pushing forward, aiming to clear the land in front of him of any hostile elements so that he could rendezvous with Chelmsford's column. Redvers Buller was with him. The party, about 150 strong, was ambushed but the Zulu attack was successfully repulsed. However, the fact that an ambush had been launched was suggestive. The land ahead of the British in the border region appeared to be largely deserted yet there were enough Zulus to launch a dangerous attack without warning. It should have put the invaders on their guard.

Harrison himself took part in some of the patrols. On 15 May he was on one with Buller. They advanced a number of miles into Zululand through open country. At Thelezeni Hill they split into two groups. In one of them was a very gung-ho Prince Imperial. They stopped in a deserted homestead for breakfast; here it was obvious that Zulus had been present not long before. Then they moved on again, towards the northern side of the Nqutu plateau, on the far side of which, a few miles off, was Isandlwana.

As they entered more broken country, a small party of Zulus was spotted on a hill. Then a larger group appeared of about fifty men. Some of the cavalry were spoiling for a fight. More experienced men, such as Lieutenant Raw, who had been one of the first men to spot the main Zulu impi at Isandlwana, thought that the Zulus would scatter before they were close enough to attack. Sure enough, when they reached the top of the hill there were no Zulus to be seen.

But then a solitary figure appeared on another summit. Spotting him, Louis dug his spurs into his horse and charged recklessly towards him. Raw and six mounted natives chased after him, not to help him catch the Zulu but to protect the prince from himself. No one knew how many Zulus might be concealed or whether a trap was being laid. On this occasion the Zulu escaped and there was no ambush. But there were several other similar instances on the patrol where Louis charged off and men had to be dispatched to bring him back.

One trooper later recalled that the prince was a 'real terror'. It seems many of the men were genuinely fond of the tearaway prince but more experienced campaigners saw his actions for what they were: seriously irresponsible and juvenile acts that threatened not only his own life but also those of the men with him. Louis, it seemed, had no sense of judgement. By acting fearless, he was in danger of acting foolish.

The reconnaissance returned to camp without major incident after bivouacking out under the stars. It was no doubt a great adventure but it had failed in its main purpose. No viable route towards Ulundi had been identified and so another patrol was required. It set out on 18 May, led by Harrison. Louis was again with him and they would be given a strong escort led by Buller. They took three days' rations, tinned meat and biscuits, with them.

The party advanced into Zululand to the Thelezeni ridge, near which they were to meet Buller. However, there was no sign of him. They moved on into difficult country and still there was no Buller. Somewhat exposed, they were forced to bivouac under the stars again. No fires were lit for fear of alerting Zulus to their presence. There was absolute silence, though there was still the odd alarm, reputedly as a result of Carey's nervousness.

Dawn still brought no sign of Buller. Harrison decided to continue his patrol without the escort. A party of sixty Zulus was seen in the distance, apparently trailing them. Sensing a threat, Harrison decided to drive them off. It was entirely predictable that Louis was at the head of the charge. The Zulus scattered and on top of a hill they found a homestead with several items of loot that had been plundered from the captured camp at Isandlwana. It was named

'Napoleon Kraal' in Louis' honour, which must have been a massive boost to his ego.

By the time they returned to Thelezeni it was beginning to get dark. There was still no sign of Buller and Harrison was on his guard after seeing a number of Zulus around during the day, so they decided to push on through the night rather than risk camping out in the open. They reached Conference Hill at dawn, in itself a dangerous time of day as the sentries around British camps were becoming well known for their nervousness which had often led to friendly forces being fired at in error. Fortunately, Harrison expected this and went to great lengths to ensure that the sentries did not mistake them for the enemy.

Back in camp, Louis renewed acquaintances with a French journalist, Paul Deleage of *Le Figaro*. Although a republican, Deleage had quickly fallen under the prince's spell. Louis spoke to him enthusiastically about his recent adventures but offered the opinion that 'if I had to be killed, I should be in despair at the thought of falling in [a minor action]. In a great battle, very well; it's for Providence to decide; but in an obscure skirmish – ah, no, that would never do.'[14]

It turned out that Harrison had been unlucky in several respects. There had been confusion over the rendezvous point which was why he had missed Buller. To compound the situation, Buller had then set out on his own reconnaissance. He had discovered his own route into Zululand and had recommended it to Chelmsford. Although more northerly than Chelmsford ideally wanted, it would avoid the Nqutu hills altogether and allow a very early joining of forces between Wood and Chelmsford's columns, so it was adopted.

Louis' reckless actions had clearly been noticed. Word had reached Chelmsford and he decided to take action. The prince's status demanded politeness so instructions were given to Harrison rather than Louis. Harrison noted that 'by direction of Lord Chelmsford I gave the Prince written instructions that he was never to leave the camp without a proper escort. His ordinary work was to sketch the camps occupied by Headquarters, and the roads they traversed when on the march.'[15]

It seemed like the perfect solution. Louis was, by definition of his role, either to be close to headquarters or near large parties of marching soldiers. Chelmsford's motives for the move were perfectly clear as he himself noted: 'The Prince Imperial went on a reconnaissance and very nearly came to grief. I shall not let him out of my sight again if I can help it.'[16] Harrison responded with confirmation that 'the Prince was not to go out without a proper escort and that he was to apply to him for one when it was wanted'. He reinforced the message by giving it to Louis in writing.[17]

Louis did his best to be enthusiastic about his new role but did not enjoy it. He chafed to see action again. He did not do his new job well, with Carey who was working with him forced to burn the midnight oil to correct his frequent errors. It would not have helped that in his absence others were starting to push deeper into Zululand, though the full invasion had not yet begun, increasing his sense of frustration at missing out on the action.

On 21 May the Cavalry Brigade crossed the river at Rorke's Drift and into Zululand. Their mission was a sombre one: to make for the battlefield at Isandlwana. It was a large force, too big for the Zulus then in the area to take on. When they made it through to the sphinx-like hill of Isandlwana, the sight that met the British forces was sobering indeed. Bodies, now mostly little more than skeletons, littered the grass, bleached dry by the scorching sun. Some still had dried-out bits of skin attached to them, making their appearance even more grotesque. Some of the remains were hurriedly buried, though the fallen of the 24th were left where they were – Colonel Glyn had asked that the task of burial be left to their surviving comrades from the regiment.

Despite the importance of burying the dead, this was not the main purpose of the foray. The far more practical objective was to recover as many service-able wagons as possible. Surprisingly, the brigade found forty of them which it returned with to Rorke's Drift in the afternoon. Quite why the Zulus had not used the four months since the battle to permanently put them out of action is not clear.

As much as anything, this reflected the fact that the Zulu army, though large, was not a standing one. Men would turn up for a campaign, fight and then go home again – a model that a medieval feudal warrior would understand in concept if not detail. They needed to return to their homesteads not just to help with domestic tasks but also to purify themselves in a series of complex rituals that had to be performed if they had killed an enemy in battle.

This visit to the sombre field of Isandlwana understandably made a great impact on those there. For some it was quite trivial details that made an impression; one man noticed a four of diamonds playing card close to the body of Lieutenant-Colonel Pulleine.[18] Another man present was the journalist Archibald Forbes. He traced the path that some of the fleeing British and colonial soldiers had tried in vain to escape down. What he saw shocked him to the core, in particular a ravine that he came across which was strewn with the detritus of death. His description of the scene, a masterpiece of journalism, would have done credit to an Edgar Allan Poe short story:

In this ravine dead men lay thick, mere bones, with toughened discoloured skin like leather covering them, and clinging tight to them, the flesh all wasted away. Some were almost wholly dismembered, heaps of yellow clammy bones. I forebear to describe the faces, with their blackened features and beards bleached by rain and sun. Every man had been disembowelled. Some were scalped, and others subject to yet ghastlier mutilations. The clothes had lasted better than the poor bodies they covered, and helped to keep the skeletons together.[19]

It was a moving description of the field of battle. Forbes remarked on the sense of calm and of surprisingly poignant details, such as the fact that wheat was growing freely where it had fallen from torn sacks and had been fertilised, he mused, by the blood of the slain. There were terrifying details too, of skeletons with a bayonet thrust through the mouth so deeply that the skull was forced into the ground, of ambulance wagons with dead bodies strewn around, presumably some of them invalided soldiers who had been pulled out and massacred as someone made a vain attempt to take them to safety. The party had come across the body of Durnford who had 'died hard' in the midst of a knot of men. His body was wrapped in a tarpaulin and buried beneath a cairn. It must have been a sombre patrol that returned to camp and it is safe to say that none there would ever forget it.

But the war had to go on. Further probing into the border regions followed which made it clear that there was no large Zulu army waiting to oppose a new invasion force. On 29 May Chelmsford, accompanied by, amongst others, Louis, rode over the border to judge for himself how things stood. There were many British patrols out but no sign of any hostile Zulus. Chelmsford moved as far forward as Thelezeni, from where he sent Carey and some dragoons to push still further ahead.

Although nothing happened which at the time appeared to be significant, there were several minor incidents that with retrospect gave warning of problems ahead. Whilst Molyneux was riding with Louis, they heard a gunshot to their left. Quickly turning to see what was happening, there appeared to be no obvious sign of any trouble – one of the cavalry might even have been shooting at some of the local wildlife to add to his food supply. This did not stop Louis drawing his sword and charging hell-for-leather towards the general direction that the shot had come from. Leopards, as they say, do not change their spots, and at the first sign of an incident the Prince Imperial had recklessly reverted to type.

Another man present on the foray, Sir William Beresford, Buller's aide-de-camp, was with the prince when he was trying to mount his horse. Despite his reputation for horsemanship, he had trouble doing so. Beresford remarked to Louis that the horse, which he had picked up on arrival in Natal, was too big for him. Perhaps affronted – the prince, in true Bonaparte tradition, was not a tall man – Louis replied that this was not the problem. His difficulty in getting on his horse was explained by the fact that his trousers were too tight. Whatever the truth of this incident, it would, above all others, assume massive significance within the next forty-eight hours.

In another of those incidents which, whilst seeming trivial at the time, was in retrospect far from being so, Carey had been out sketching. Chelmsford had sent him on with his escort of dragoons. Soon after he was seen by Brigade Major Herbert Stewart from the Cavalry Brigade. Still smarting at the perceived underuse of his cavalry, Stewart was angered that dragoons were, in his view, being used for such inappropriate and menial work. He castigated Carey for this, which was completely unfair. The men were there under Chelmsford's orders and the commander-in-chief would have been well within his rights to put Stewart, his subordinate officer, firmly in his place. But there is no sign that this was ever done. Instead, Carey was left with a flea in his ear and a firm warning from a senior officer that he was not to use regular cavalry for escort duty again.

Stewart, in fact, knew Carey well and the rebuke was probably not directed at him personally but reflected a general dissatisfaction and growing sense of frustration in the way that the cavalry were being used. Remarkably, a few days earlier, Chelmsford had even considered sending the brigade to the Transvaal to perform garrison duty. This gave a deep and worrying insight into Chelmsford's uncertainty as to how best to use them; this given a war in Zululand where the terrain was in some parts, if not all, well suited to cavalry and where the Zulus had a healthy dislike of fighting men on horseback. Regular cavalry tactics, it is true, would have to be adapted against a non-European enemy and that would not happen overnight, but no real effort was made to even attempt this. This approach called into question the wisdom of the oft-repeated remarks that more cavalry were needed in southern Africa. No one now seemed to know what to do with them.

The time for a final showdown had been reached. A decision was made to launch the invasion on 1 June. When this news spread around the camp, no doubt the men felt a variety of emotions, not least fear. For one man, though, it seemed like the start of a glorious adventure. On the eve of the invasion Louis, exhilarated once more, approached Harrison and asked if he could undertake an extra reconnaissance of the road ahead the following day.

Harrison considered the request. The ground that the prince was proposing to cover had been well scouted on a number of occasions and there had been no sign of any significant concentration of Zulus. Harrison therefore agreed. Soon after, Carey approached Harrison and asked if he could join Louis. Harrison, knowing that Carey was an experienced officer, assented.

The small party was ready to set off just after 9 a.m. on 1 June, Whit Sunday. Carey, almost as an afterthought, asked Harrison about an escort party and was told to go to the Cavalry Brigade to request one. Perhaps because of the recent incident with Stewart, Harrison suggested that a small escort of irregulars and native cavalry might be appropriate. Carey approached Stewart who gave him six men from Bettington's Horse. He said that he would also order some Basuto cavalry for him.

Carey duly approached the headquarters of Captain Shepstone, who was in charge of the Basutos, and he sent out orders for a party to be assembled. There was, however, confusion as to where the Basutos should assemble, with the result that there was a delay in them reaching Carey. In the meantime, the prince was champing at the bit to get on. The party therefore set off without the Basutos, presuming that they would catch them up. As they rode out, the prince bade a cheery 'goodbye' to Melton Prior, the war artist, who was camped nearby. Prior wished him a 'jolly morning'.[20]

This first decision on that fateful day was hugely significant. The Basutos were locals, who were more attuned to spotting danger than anyone else, so their absence was important. But the prince was impatient, so the party left without them. In reality it was the prince who was making the key decisions. Carey, who had not been specifically charged to command the expedition, seemingly went along with this. In most cases, with a minor foray such as this, an unclear chain of command would have gone largely unnoticed. Now it was a situation that would soon become a matter of life and death.

The party set off, the prince in particular enjoying himself. Around them on all sides were small groups of horsemen moving out in advance of the main column. The grass was particularly long and thick – a result of the recent torrential rains – but there was no sign of a hostile Zulu anywhere. The party soon reached the stopping point planned for the column later that day. Here Harrison caught up with them.

Harrison was surprised that the Basuto horsemen that were supposed to be accompanying the prince in his escort were not there. He suggested that Louis and his party should not venture any further forward until the Basutos caught up with them. Then he rode off to attend to other duties. Carey suggested that they wait for the Basutos but Louis replied 'oh no, we are quite strong enough'.[21] Louis may have written in his pocketbook the phrase 'escort under Captain Carey'[22] as his very last entry, but his actions suggested that something rather different was taking place.

This was another moment of truth. A senior officer, Harrison, had suggested that they stay where they were but his advice had been ignored. A more junior officer had suggested the same but had been effectively overruled. Carey did not feel strong or perhaps worried enough to argue, but in fairness to him it is far from clear that Harrison himself was any more able to keep the headstrong prince in check. The prince was not a man used to being ordered about and ignored these suggestions as if they had come from servants in his household. Again, it was clear who was actually in charge of the party.

Major Grenfell of the 60th Rifles, on the headquarters staff, had come across the party and decided to move forward with them (he also, of course, outranked Lieutenant Carey). The command structure of the group was further reinforced by the fact that Grenfell and Louis rode at the front with Carey behind them. Grenfell had not been present when Harrison had ordered the party to stay where they were until the Basutos arrived and it would have been interesting to see what he would have done to prevent them from moving off if he had been.

Grenfell had already met the prince earlier in the campaign. He noted in a letter to his sister soon after that 'He is a very plucky little chap, and will, I think, get himself shot before the campaign is over'.[23] Now they were reunited. They rode on for some miles, becoming more isolated from the other British patrols. Again, there was no sign of any hostile Zulus. Grenfell then decided that he would return to camp. He had a short word with Louis and rode off with the injunction 'Take care of yourself and don't get shot'. Louis pointed to Carey and replied 'Oh no, he will take very good care that nothing happens to me'.[24]

The small party rode steadily on until they reached a ridge. Below this they could see the gently meandering waters of the Nondweni River. The brooding spurs of the Nqutu range lay to the south – territory that Louis had ridden through just over a week before. It was a boiling hot day with a draining heat that sapped all energy from the body and slowed the thinking process. Carey suggested that they should off-saddle here on the ridge. Once again, he was overruled by the prince who wished to move nearer the river.

Carey did not argue and the party moved towards the river. Getting closer, they saw a small village of six huts. The Zulu guide went ahead to explore and returned, confirming that it was empty. The scouting party therefore moved in. They failed to notice that dense mealie fields hugged the edge of the village, providing perfect cover for any stealthy enemy. Although they carried their carbines with them, these were always unloaded whilst on patrol to avoid accidents, but they made no attempt to load them now they had stopped. As one contemporary writer later noted, they were acting 'as if they were in Hyde Park'.[25]

It was around 2.40 p.m. and, tired by their long ride and the blistering heat, some of the men sat down in the shade of the huts and began to doze off. Louis was still trying to shake off the effects of the fever that had attacked him and was perhaps more tired than anyone. Some of the patrol wanted coffee and the Zulu guide went off to the river for water. Carey strolled around the area and looked around the surrounding hills. Then, about forty minutes later, he returned to the prince who spoke to him enthusiastically about some of the great Napoleon's finest battles.

It was about 3.35 p.m. when Carey suggested they should move off. Louis again asserted his unofficial authority by suggesting they delay for ten minutes, but then changed his mind and they prepared to move off. Some of the horses had wandered off and Carey and Trooper Le Tocq went towards the river to fetch them and started to saddle up. Just as they were doing so, their native guide said that he had just seen a Zulu down by the river.

This increased the sense of urgency but there was no sign of anything akin to panic or even concern. It was about 4 p.m. when they were ready to move off. Louis, significantly, gave the order to 'prepare to mount'. The men started to climb up on their saddles. Suddenly, the dreamy stillness of the heavy afternoon air was rent asunder by the shattering staccato of gunfire.

Carey, who had already managed to mount his horse, turned around and saw 'the black faces of Zulus about twenty yards off, rushing towards us through the mealie-fields'.[26] It was one of those slow-motion moments when everything seemed to happen in a parallel universe, where each man's actions assumed an exaggerated significance and perhaps each man's life flashed before his eyes. What had been an afternoon reverie, a peaceful passage through the countryside of Zululand, had suddenly become a frantic, individual fight for survival. Unknown to them, the patrol had been watched ever since they arrived and there were perhaps forty Zulus now attacking them.

So sudden was the fusillade that Corporal Grubb at first thought that one of the patrol had accidentally discharged his weapon. But then the war cries of *uSuthu*, followed by what were described as 'perfect volleys', shattered this hopeful illusion. The Zulus, shouting '*nanga amagwala amangisi*' ('kill the English cowards'),[27] could be seen running through the mealies, sensing the vulnerability of their prey.

Carey was quickly away towards safety, accompanied by two troopers. Sergeant Willis had his foot in the stirrups but had not mounted, and his horse charged wildly off with him clinging on at its side for dear life. Corporal Grubb was mounted but struggled to keep his horse under control as he had not managed to get its bit in properly. Le Tocq had been thrown off his steed. He managed to get back on but he was not properly seated and it was all he could do to stop himself falling again.

A few hundred yards from the village was a *donga* where Carey stopped along with Troopers Cochrane and Le Tocq. It now dawned on them that Louis was not with them. Louis had not been mounted when the first shot was fired. He had tried to vault on to Tommy, his horse, but had failed to do so. Le Tocq, himself riding for his life, had charged past and told the prince in French to hurry up and mount his horse.

Louis tried but failed. About a dozen Zulus were running at him now. Grubb had been desperately riding off when he looked back and saw the prince struggling to hang on to his horse as it galloped off. He stopped and tried to let off a shot at the Zulus rapidly approaching Louis but at that very moment his horse jumped into the *donga* and he was nearly thrown off. Louis had been hanging on to a pistol holster in front of the saddle but the strain on it was too much and it broke, throwing him to the ground and leaving him to await his fate.

Despite what the prince had wished, he was after all to die in a minor skirmish, not in a great battle. For him there was no Marengo, no Austerlitz, not even an epochal defeat on the scale of Waterloo. He was about to die in the shadow of six huts in an unknown corner of Zululand in a tawdry little ambush.

Louis had played out his death many times in his mind. He noted disdainfully how the officers in Zululand carried revolvers, not swords, to defend themselves. This was no way to die. A hero must perish with his sword in his hand. In a final, bitter irony he had lost his sword in his desperate attempt to mount his horse. He had taken the precaution of carrying a revolver with him but the symbolism of the lost sword was bitingly apt. In this war, the sword was redundant, obsolete, an anachronism. So too, harsh though it is to say given his poignant end, was this emperor without an empire, this Bonaparte without a role.

Louis turned to face his attackers. Several shots from his revolver all missed. Then a thrown spear struck him in the chest. It fell out and Louis rushed at one of his attackers. A Zulu in turn fired at him but also missed. Then another spear hit home. Louis turned and ran towards the *donga*. He turned again and fired more shots, which also missed; an assailant later commented on the look of shock on his face as he realised that not one of the shots he had fired had found a target. There was now a small crowd of Zulus after him and gaining on him. Louis was defending himself with an assegai in his right hand and a pistol in his left. As he moved back, he tripped in a hole in the ground and fell.

This was the end. The Zulus moved in and, in a final flurry of stabbing assegai blows, snuffed out the life of the Prince Imperial. Probably when he was already dead, he was stabbed in the right eye. Two other troopers had died, along with the Zulu guide. But there was only one death that mattered to the world.

Louis' demise had gone unseen by his escaped colleagues. Carey and the small group with him, now joined by the other escaped cavalrymen, stayed at a distance. They could not see down into the village but one of them had seen Louis' horse, rider-less, galloping off. There was no attempt to go back, with Carey no doubt thinking that it was too late in any case. This may well have been true but his honour was fatally besmirched by the fact that he did not even try.

Carey's torment would not be long in beginning. He rode back as fast as he could towards the main column. His route took him towards the Flying Column. His bad luck continued for out in advance of this was Redvers Buller, someone whose personal bravery could not be doubted as it bordered on suicidal at times. If there was one man who, in Carey's situation, would have charged back into the fray, it was Buller.

Buller saw a distant rider galloping towards them as if chased by a thousand Zulus. He was clearly frantic. It was Carey and when he approached he was asked immediately what was wrong. Breathlessly Carey spluttered out the unbelievable words: 'The Prince – the Prince is killed.' Buller asked, straight to the point, where he had died and where was his body. Carey pointed into the distance where, a few miles off, some Zulus could be seen moving up a hill dragging several horses away.

Clearly incredulous that he had left the prince where he was, Buller asked Carey how many others he had lost. Carey replied that he did not know. Buller glared at him and uttered words that must have hit home as hard as any assegai: 'Then you should be shot and I hope you will be. I could shoot you myself.' At which the fuming Buller turned his back on the disconsolate Carey. It was a sentiment that other soldiers shared; Bettington later noted in his diary that 'if I had been there, I should have saved him or I should have stayed there with him'.[28]

Carey moved on to camp, where Harrison was dining with Grenfell. They had noticed that the prince's party was late for dinner but did not think too much of it. When Carey arrived, he was greatly agitated. He told them why and they sent him to Chelmsford's tent at once. Harrison was quick to question Carey on whether he had left the prince. When he said he had, Harrison replied that he should at least have tried to bring home his body. Ironically, Tommy, the hard-to-control horse, had survived and had been brought back to the camp.

The news was a hammer-blow to Chelmsford. Everyone's worst fears had been confirmed. No less a person than Queen Victoria had feared that Louis' recklessness would end in disaster. Yet they had passed their responsibilities on to Chelmsford. Now it was his neck that was on the chopping block. It was certainly most unfair. But Chelmsford had been taught many times in the past few months that life was far from fair. He wrote a short dispatch to Stanley on 2 June briefly outlining the tragic events and ending significantly that 'I myself was not aware that the Prince had been detailed for this duty'.[29]

Carey poured out his soul in a letter to his wife written that night. It was the epistle of a desperate man in a situation where he was out of his depth. It was, of course, a private letter written to his closest confidante in circumstances which would tax the strongest of men, but in its way it gives a sharp insight into his character. In his view, he could have acted no differently than he did. He explained that he thought the prince was with him when he galloped out of the village. He turned to his Christian religion in the hope of redemption, confessing himself a 'wicked man' for not saying his prayers as regularly as he should and for not attending Sunday services because of his duties.

Chelmsford, he said, was of course very cut up about Louis' death. It was an understandably disjointed letter with frequent interjections of self-pity: 'Oh! For some Christian sympathy! I do feel so miserable and dejected! I know not what to do!'[30] What he had to do in practical terms was guide a strong force early next morning back to the site of Louis' death. All of a sudden there were no problems in finding regular cavalry for an escort. No less than two squadrons of lancers and another of dragoons were there, along with a large party of irregulars. Chelmsford could not bring himself to go. Given his usual bravery and energy, he can only have stayed behind because the blow was personally shattering.

A few Zulus were seen in the distance but they melted away when they saw the size of the approaching force. As they finally neared the village, those local harbingers of death, vultures, were seen to fly off. They found the bodies of the two dead troopers and then that of the man whom they had really come for. Louis, staring blankly at the sky, was riddled with assegai wounds, most of them, men noted approvingly, in the front. Round about him was all that was left of his personal possessions: most poignantly a sock with the letter 'N' stitched in it. While most of the party looked on in a sense of awed silence, a few pulled up handfuls of grass with the prince's blood on it as if it were some sort of holy relic.

A fellow Frenchman, Deleage the newspaperman, was present. The French republican looked down with almost unbearable pain on the still, lifeless and bloodied corpse:

> The Prince was lying on his back; his arms, stiffened by death, crossed a little above the chest; the features showed no signs of pain, or any contraction whatever; the left eye was half closed; the right eye had been destroyed by an assegai stab. The chest was pierced by seventeen wounds, and according to their custom, the Zulus had cut open the stomach, but the incision was only a small one and the viscera had been spared.[31]

It was a bitter moment as he knelt by the fallen prince and kissed his cold hand.

The bitterness was clearly tinged with anger. He noted that 'that was a true Frenchman, who alone, deserted by all, had known how to die like a Frenchman, with his face to the foe'.[32] In a heartbreakingly poignant moment, Melton Prior of the *Illustrated London News* watched on as Deleage, tears streaming down his face, took out an English penny and symbolically placed it over the eye that had been pierced by a spear.

If the British army might have been seen as letting Louis down on campaign – and Frenchmen everywhere were quick to assert as much, with their 'prince' much more popular in death than he had been in life – they made up for it now. The body would be taken back to England for burial but no expense or effort was spared in the funeral arrangements that would take place in southern Africa. As the sombre cortege bringing back Louis' body moved towards the camp, regiment after regiment was assembled to meet it. His body was carried on a gun carriage. A Catholic priest read out the service over the mortal remains of the heir of France whilst overhead a strange sky loomed, dark and leaden.

The makeshift shroud, a common blanket, was draped in a tricolour with Chelmsford and his staff walking behind the gun carriage, drawn by six black horses, whilst the mournful dirge of the pipes of the 21st played the prince on his way. Surrounded as they were by the mist-draped mountains of Africa in the distance, it was a strangely affecting scene. Chelmsford stood by the body, leaning on a cane, looking to bystanders a broken man, his eyes red and his heart heavy. After this ceremony – the first of a number – the body was embalmed by a surgeon to protect it on its long journey back to Europe.

Those watching had their own thoughts. Crealock commented poignantly: 'Thus sets the sun of the Bonapartes.' Melton Prior, ever the professional, worked through the night making sketches for the *Illustrated London News* so that he could trump his rivals. Chelmsford ensured that further ceremony would be arranged for the prince as his body was taken to the coast and from there onboard ship back to England.

Carey would be court-martialled for his part in the prince's death. His crime, such as it was, had not been Louis' demise, rather his failure to try and do anything about it. Carey could muster a range of legitimate defences. The command structure was unclear and the actions of others, such as Harrison and Grenfell, had played their part. The attack had been so sudden that the initial confusion that followed was entirely justifiable. By the time they had re-formed it was already too late.

It was indeed not an open and shut case. Norris-Newman noted that Louis' death 'was to some extent influenced by the anomalous position held by the Prince, and the independence of his peculiar non-official connection with the expedition'. It was a situation worsened, the correspondent noted, by Louis' rashness and unwillingness to act in a disciplined fashion.[33] Carey did his best to defend himself, markedly saying in his evidence that Harrison had 'stated that I was not in [any] way to interfere with the Prince, as he wished him to have the entire credit for choosing the camp'.[34]

The court martial was initially held in southern Africa, with Colonel Glyn acting as president of the court, and Carey was found guilty of having misbehaved before the enemy and in failing to attempt to rally the escort and go to the prince's defence (the charge did not specify anything about the other two soldiers or the Zulu guide who were killed, confirming who the court martial was really all about). However, the panel noted a number of extenuating circumstances which it hoped would be taken into account when a sentence was decided upon.

The verdict was sent to England for confirmation. It was here that the court martial's proceedings started to unravel. The findings were passed to the deputy judge advocate general, Judge James O'Dowd. He dropped a bombshell. He thought, for one thing, that the evidence against Carey was highly doubtful; indeed, he was of the opinion that it demonstrated how Carey was never in charge of the patrol, rather Louis was. But crucially he also doubted that the court martial had the right legal authority to sit at all. He therefore refused to confirm the findings and Carey was reprieved.

The court of public opinion – or more accurately army opinion – was less forgiving. Carey's career would probably have gone nowhere far, though in the event it is hard to know, for Carey, by then a captain, would die in India in 1883. He did not help himself. Following his acquittal he became increasingly self-opinionated, alienating a number of allies in the process. Chelmsford was sympathetic to Carey, understanding better than most what an impossible position they had all been put in by the presence of this brave but reckless young prince. He did not doubt that Carey had panicked, but understood why, in the circumstances, he had done so.

When the overturned court martial verdict came through, attention turned to Harrison. He had been oblivious to the debate concerning Carey in England. Though many soldiers in southern Africa found fault with Carey for his actions, back home there was much more public sympathy for him. Harrison was informed of Carey's acquittal on 16 August. With it was a letter from Horse Guards, which made various observations on Harrison's part based on what Carey had said in his court martial.

They were not complimentary. Harrison, it was suggested, should have cleared the mission in advance with Chelmsford (who was considered blameless). His instructions to both Carey and Louis should also have been clearer (which at least seems fair comment). Harrison protested his innocence and appealed to clear his name. The response to this was a suggestion that it was now time to let the matter rest. Harrison then acted in the same way that many a good soldier over the years has when faced with such a response: he shut up. It did him no harm. He would end his career as a general.

The dramatic tale of Louis' death took some time to reach Europe. He died on 1 June; the news of it would not reach Britain until the 19th. Queen Victoria was at her retreat in Balmoral when there was a knock on her door at 10.40 p.m. It was her trusted confidant John Brown. He told her the awful news. She was shocked to the core. Soon after she was joined by her daughter Princess Beatrice, who could not stop the tears from flooding down her face. The queen wept too. It was dawn before they got back to bed.

Everyone, including John Brown, was deeply distressed. There was no doubting that the prince was a charming young man; he had, after all, reduced a republican like Deleage to tears by his demise. But there was something else, a sense of pathos; it was a sentimental melodrama of the type so beloved of the Victorian age. The Bonaparte legacy was no more and they were mourning the passing of history.

When Disraeli learned the news he too was moved; it may be uncharitable to suggest that it was the political fallout that worried him most, but it is probably also true. However, the reactions of outsiders were nothing compared to the reaction of she who loved him most. The awful task of telling Eugenie fell to her oldest adviser and companion, the Duc de Bassano. It was 21 June by the time he was informed (the delay suggesting how worried everyone was at breaking the news to the empress).

De Bassano knocked on the empress' bedroom door and, when he entered, his grim demeanour instantly revealed that something terrible had happened. As if in an effort to deny her deepest fears, Eugenie asked if Louis had been injured. There was no response. She moved towards Bassano but he averted his gaze, unable to speak. It was a gesture more eloquent and telling than any words. She knew in the depths of her being what the unsaid message meant. Eugenie promptly fainted.

The effect across Britain was sensational. The court went into mourning. Fears were expressed for the life of the empress, who remained in a state of shock for days. The dreams of Queen Victoria, she noted in her journal, were haunted by Zulus.[35] A special supplement of the *Illustrated London News* was completely devoted to the death of the prince. Paris, which in life had done nothing much to welcome his presence, mourned him too. Some Frenchmen pointed fingers at their own government; many more pointed them to the one on the other side of La Manche.

Louis' body arrived off Plymouth on 9 July. Even in death he caused controversy. Queen Victoria wanted to provide a state funeral; Disraeli would not hear of it. However, the supposedly private funeral would be about as elaborate as it was possible to be. The final leg of Louis' journey by sea was appropriately to Woolwich. Here the coffin was greeted by high-ranking representatives, both British and French. Amongst the former was the Duke of Cambridge, as culpable as most for the death of Louis.

And yet the ultimate responsibility for his death rests with Louis himself, in his lack of judgement which had not before been seriously put to the test and was found wanting in his most trying hour. The plate on his coffin was marked with the simple legend: 'Eugene Louis-Jean-Joseph-Napoleon, Prince Imperial, Born at the Tuileries, March 16, 1856, Slain by the Enemy, in Zululand, June 1, 1879.' Nothing could have been more wrong. Louis was killed fighting in a war that was dubious in the first place for a country that was not his own. How could the Zulus possibly be his enemy?

The last remains of Louis Napoleon, hope of the Bonapartes, were delivered back to his mother at Camden Place. They were taken from there to the nearby Roman Catholic church at Chislehurst where they were given their final rites. A huge crowd turned out to watch the final journey whilst in the church itself were representatives of the top levels of the British establishment and from royal families around Europe. It was a dull day but that did not stop an estimated 40,000 people turning up, helped by the railway companies who laid on thirty-two special trains to Chislehurst.[36]

Pride of place was given to a wreath laid on the coffin by Queen Victoria herself. She saw Eugenie. It was a short meeting – it lasted a minute, the Bonapartes' close adviser Augustin Filon reckoned – and little was said, but there was little need to say anything. If there was one thing that Victoria understood it was the premature death of a loved one. Her critics would say that mourning was what Victoria did best.

She was very satisfied with the way the ceremony went. Disraeli, though, predictably poured a dampener on the whole thing, noting: 'I have just got a telegram from the Queen who has returned to Windsor and seems highly pleased at all that has occurred at Chislehurst this morning. I hope the French government will be as joyful. In my view, nothing could be more injudicious than the whole affair.'[37]

For Disraeli, politics always took precedence over pathos and these comments might seem jarringly sour. Yet if applied to the whole business of the Prince Imperial's involvement in the Anglo-Zulu War, as opposed to just his last rites, the last sentence is about as good a critique of the whole sorry affair as one could come up with. Disraeli would surely argue that his political instincts had been right all along – he told the House of Lords on 23 June that the prince had been 'needlessly sacrificed'. By implication, everyone else's instincts, including those of his sovereign and the leader of his country's armed forces, had been wrong.

Whilst Chelmsford attempted to work around yet another blow to his plans for the final conquest of Zululand, the empress tried her best to cope with her loss. Louis' death was tragic confirmation of what she had known all along, that the hand of fate had turned against her.

She could at least do her part in erecting a suitable memorial for her family. She built a house at Farnborough in 1880 and erected there a Benedictine abbey, and beneath its beautiful church was a crypt, a small and intimate echo of the great Bonaparte's vast memorial edifice in Les Invalides in Paris. It is still a peaceful, tranquil spot. Although the last of the French monks has long gone, and the brothers are now English, there is no doubt about the origins of this haven of tranquillity. Here even now lies Napoleon III, the Last Emperor, his wife Eugenie who, outliving them all, died in 1920, and her beloved son, a victim of his own legacy and his desperate desire to live up to a history of greatness. It is, to misquote some words penned in a later tragic conflict, a corner of a foreign field that is forever France.

eleven

RACE FOR VICTORY

Chelmsford's Vindication

Reinforcements were pouring into southern Africa. There had been a rush of volunteers, including of course the Prince Imperial. Another, less well known but an eyewitness to many events concerning the Coastal Column, was Major Bindon Blood of the Royal Engineers. Blood had been disappointed not to be involved in the Afghan War but was quickly accepted for service in Zululand, along with his company of engineers. Blood believed that a shortage of engineers at the beginning of the war had been partly responsible for the disastrous start to the campaign. He particularly regretted the poorly defended positions at Isandlwana and Rorke's Drift, where impromptu measures had had to be taken.[1]

Blood had travelled out with Major-General Marshall, who would be in charge of the Cavalry Brigade. His ship was packed to the gunwales with fellow officers and troops. Whilst he was confident in his own men, he was less sanguine about many of the infantrymen. There had been a scramble to rustle up trained soldiers to fill the gaps in many of the infantry battalions destined for southern Africa. Blood gave the distinct impression that the bottom of the barrel had been scraped in the process: 'it came about that our battalions landed in Zululand full of incompletely trained men, a great proportion of whom had never fired a round of ball cartridge, while many had never fired a round of blank before they embarked.'[2]

Blood considered the process unsatisfactory in other ways too. Ships had left short of coal, a situation that could have been remedied by a delay of twelve hours. Instead, they had rushed out of port with the result that they were delayed for up to six days when they arrived off the Cape, as they needed to restock and there were insufficient supplies locally available. But at last, Blood and his men arrived at Durban and prepared to do their bit.

The Coastal Column was designated the 1st Column, Chelmsford's – nominally under Newdigate – was the 2nd Column, and Wood's the Flying Column. The latter two would effectively merge just over the border, staying separate but only a few miles apart. The 1st Column, under the newly arrived General H. Crealock, brother of the waspish and unpopular Crealock on Chelmsford's staff, was to advance very deliberately, so much so that it was to attract critical comment from some quarters.

Following the coastal route were 7,500 troops, largely composed of the men who had previously marched with Pearson, along with those who had been in the relief column that lifted the siege of Eshowe. Chelmsford correctly reasoned that it would meet with little opposition as the Zulus would be forced to concentrate their forces elsewhere. The 2nd Column, once it affected a junction with Wood's Flying Column, represented a force of over 8,000 men.

The 1st Column was to advance slowly up the coastal road, stopping frequently to build forts en route. A large pontoon bridge was assembled across the Lower Thukela as a way of speeding up supplies. The forts would serve as secure supply bases. It undoubtedly seemed a good idea on paper but the practice was somewhat more of a challenge. The frequent halts that ensued slowed progress to a snail's pace. The bad weather continued, frequently turning the roads into mud which were made worse by the heavy traffic that journeyed up and down them. There was, however, next to no resistance from any local Zulus who had long resigned themselves to their fate.

It was not a happy experience for the troops, who were awarded the sarcastic sobriquet of 'Crealock's Crawlers'. Crealock, according to Bindon Blood, suffered poor health and that cannot have aided the speed of the advance. Discipline became a problem, no doubt aggravated by boredom. On one occasion, Blood was present when there was a mad rush from some soldiers towards the camp. It turned out to be a party of men from Ireland who had rather unwisely been given the job of looking after the rum supply.

One of the kegs had disappeared and had done sterling service for the Connaught boys who were guarding it. Now they were running wild through the camp. Flogging was still allowed in the army though strangely no longer in the navy. The guilty men were tried by a court martial and, in Blood's words, 'got a couple of dozen apiece well laid on, which I have no doubt did a lot of good to them and to others like them who had to see it'.[3]

Blood was presumably rather disappointed when it later transpired that 1879 was the last year in which flogging was used in the British army (it was officially abolished in 1881), though he made a point of avoiding seeing the floggings being administered. Lieutenant Henry Curling certainly was against the abolition, writing that 'it will be quite impossible to keep up discipline now that flogging is done away with. However, it will soon be established again as men will now occasionally have to be shot and then what an outcry there will be.'[4] During the Anglo-Zulu War, 545 British soldiers were flogged. When the law barring it as a punishment was passed, Chelmsford was one of those in the House of Lords speaking against it.[5]

Blood also met John Dunn who was with the column. He noted that around him were his 'flocks and herds and followers, many of them ladies and children of various ages'.[6] Presumably he either did not know or did not wish to shock his readers with the fact that many of the women were probably Dunn's wives and the children were in the main his too.

The journey was tough on the oxen, dozens of whom collapsed and died on the track from exhaustion. There was no time to dispose of the cadavers carefully and they were just dragged out of the way to the side of the road and left to rot. This, of course, did nothing for hygiene and added to the ever-present danger of disease. Fort Pearson was converted to a hospital where there were sometimes up to 400 patients in residence.[7]

The main fighting would be the responsibility of Number 2 Column in conjunction with Wood. Before the war Chelmsford had attempted to present himself as a man who believed that war should be fought in a civilised manner, though this was perhaps a sop to his own conscience as he, after all, had helped to manufacture a war that his enemy did not want. Now, after the trauma of Isandlwana and the death of the Prince Imperial, the gloves were off.

The character of the war had changed. Chelmsford had clearly reasoned that the will of the Zulu people needed to be broken. It was amazing how defeat had changed the rules of engagement, almost as if the war had become personal. Now huts were burned without compunction by his men whenever they came across any. Food was commandeered, cattle or grain, whenever they stumbled across it. A pall of misery hung over the land.

There was, nevertheless, still danger for the invaders. On 5 June Buller was scouting ahead of the Flying Column. He came across a party of Zulus apparently intent on blocking his progress. Never one to shirk a fight, Buller led his men in a charge against them. A vicious scrap followed. A party of the 17th Lancers (a regiment most famous for its suicidal involvement in the Charge of the Light Brigade) came to help him but, as they did so, a bullet struck a young adjutant, Lieutenant Frith, through the heart. Killed instantaneously, his body was taken back to camp. It reflects the rather one-sided nature of the war that the death of this one individual was greeted with much melancholy and mourning whilst no one batted an eyelid at the deaths of hundreds of Zulus.

There was still fight left in some of the Zulus. Even as the British were advancing, sizeable raids were launched in the region of Luneberg, causing considerable damage and giving a timely reminder that the war was not quite over. Worryingly for the British, the Zulus received some support locally from Boer dissidents, clearly unhappy at what they saw as the usurpation of their country in the recent past. It did not presage well for the future and an Anglo-Boer War was just a couple of years away.

Chelmsford's attitude was now hardened. Convinced that the outcome of the war was a foregone conclusion, he was already thinking ahead to the terms of any final settlement. Whatever the specifics, he was certain that Cetshwayo must be deposed, for:

> so long moreover as he remains on the throne, so long the military system will be, by some means or other, maintained, in spite of any promises he may make to the contrary; and I believe on this point he will have the Zulu nation on his side, as it is so deeply imbued with military instinct, and so proud of its military traditions.

He completed his thoughts stating, without a hint of irony, that if Zululand was 'parcelled out amongst some of the principal Zulu chiefs, ruling independently, but under the control of the British Government, I foresee a bright future not only for Natal and the Transvaal, but also for Zululand itself'.[8]

There was an inevitability about the advance: slow, determined and relentless. Caution was the watchword now. Every night laagers were formed around the juggernaut as it rumbled ever deeper into the hinterland of Cetshwayo's kingdom. The troops were often nervous, especially those recently arrived from England. There were many false alarms as hallucinating sentries imagined thousands of Zulus creeping up on the camps at night.

Incidents such as the death of Frith and the Prince Imperial played on the nerves of the new arrivals. On the bright, moonlit night of 6 June, there were some allied native troops outside the laager, one of whom let off a bullet accidentally. The camp was up in a flash. Strange shapes were seen outside the perimeter and these were shot at repeatedly.

Inside the laager the horses and cattle were panic-stricken by the sound of firing. Eventually, calmer heads prevailed and stopped the shooting. Two or three friendly natives had been hit. However, the main 'threat' came from two sources. The first was a couple of stray oxen outside the camp who would surely have been deeply embarrassed if they had known the trouble they had caused. The second was a party of very inanimate cooking kettles which had been positioned outside. Sadly for them, the incident was fatal as they were riddled with holes, which made any ongoing use as a cooking utensil impossible.

The fort that was being erected on the spot was to be called Fort Newdigate after the column commander, but to most of the army it was henceforward christened 'Fort Funk'. Amongst those being shot at that night was Chard, the hero of Rorke's Drift, who was with a detachment of engineers constructing the fort.

The embarrassment that would have been caused if the man who had survived 4,000 Zulus had been shot by his own side does not bear thinking about.[9] It was at the time said that 50,000 rounds had been expended, a tale that undoubtedly lost nothing in the telling.[10]

Chelmsford was under immense pressure from Britain now to bring the war to a speedy conclusion. In response to a message from Stanley, he had replied, 'I cannot understand what you mean by considerable anxiety existing as to the indefinite prolongation of the war', explaining that the Zulus were a tough and well-organised enemy and that, despite the reverses at Isandlwana, the Ntombe and Hlobane, his forces had made good progress.

He had also been informed that it was possible a senior officer would be sent out to complete the war, something which he openly regarded as a 'threat'. In fact, Sir Garnet Wolseley was already en route to replace him. Chelmsford further defended himself against concerns expressed by the Duke of Cambridge about the distance between the columns in Zululand, explaining that this was unavoid-able given the nature of the country. He was also annoyed by the presence of a large number of journalists and felt that they were giving a sensationalist and jaundiced view of the campaign, which he believed was having an impact on both Stanley and Cambridge to his detriment.[11]

Chelmsford needed to ensure that the war was won before Wolseley arrived. Only if he did so would he achieve a vindication of sorts. The invasion was now progressing at full tilt and the momentum was firmly back with the British and their local allies. Cetshwayo sent increasingly desperate messages to Chelmsford trying to find a peaceful solution, but the events at Isandlwana had meant that anything less than outright victory was unacceptable.

A message received by Chelmsford on 16 May via Crealock was typical of the tone of these communications: 'white man has made me king, and I am their son. So they kill the man in the afternoon whom they have made king in the morn-ing? What have I done? I want peace; I ask for peace.'[12]

It was sometime in the middle of June that Chelmsford heard of Wolseley's imminent arrival. The decision to replace him was for several reasons. There was increasing dissatisfaction in Britain, certainly in the government, at both how long the war was taking and how costly it was; by now the army with Chelmsford was bigger than that which had been led by Wellington at Waterloo and included no less than ten generals. Chelmsford had also fallen out with the government of Natal and, in particular, Sir Henry Bulwer. Wolseley was now to assume responsibility for both the military and political conclusion to the war.

The telegram announcing Wolseley's dispatch came as a shock to Chelmsford. The message said: 'the appointment of a senior officer is not intended as a censure on yourself, but you will, as in ordinary course of service, submit and subordinate your plans to his control.' Experience would show that Chelmsford had no intention of doing any such thing. But he would not have much time to finish off the war, as Wolseley 'leaves the country by next mail'.[13]

Wolseley was the golden boy of his generation – Britain's only general, as he was widely known. He was, nevertheless, an unbearable egotist and a reformer to boot which meant that he was not trusted or liked by the establishment. Renowned for his personal bravery, he had become associated with a number of officers whose careers had dovetailed with his, the famous 'Wolseley Ring'. Included amongst them were both Wood and Buller.

He had an unerring ability to be a divisive influence amongst the establishment. This was well demonstrated when he was appointed. Queen Victoria, who was a firm supporter of Chelmsford, noted that although she would sanction the appointment, she would not approve of it. On the other hand, Disraeli – again at odds with his sovereign on the issue of the war – conceded that 'it is quite true that Wolseley is an egotist and a braggart. So was Nelson.'[14]

But he was the obvious choice to finish the war off quickly and he jumped at the chance to do so, having been in southern Africa just a few years previously. He was the ideal man for a crisis situation, as was emphasised a few years later when General Gordon was trapped in Khartoum; it was Wolseley who was sent too late to the rescue. Wolseley would indeed finish the Anglo-Zulu War off but not in the way expected. When he knew Wolseley was on his way out to southern Africa, Chelmsford determined to finish the fighting before Wolseley could take over.

On 21 June, Harrison was out with some of Buller's men when he got a good view of Ulundi, the ultimate target for the column. For him, his job was almost at an end. His role was to bring the men safely to a place where they were in sight of the enemy and ready for battle, and that had been achieved. His timing was impeccable for a more senior officer, Lieutenant-Colonel East, had arrived from England and would take over Harrison's duties. Chelmsford asked Harrison to stay on as East's assistant which he did, though he was frustrated at the limitations placed on him in his new role. Harrison had done a fine job but his part in the war would always be clouded by the unfortunate death of the Prince Imperial.

The column moved pass Isipesi, beyond the fateful lion-hill (as Chard, the hero of Rorke's Drift, had described it) of Isandlwana. It then joined up with the initial planned route of the first invasion. It moved into the emeKhosini Valley, the place of the kings, the most sacred spot in Zululand. Here were the graves of the Royal House of Zululand. On 26 June they were ruthlessly burned. It was a cruel act of total war, equivalent to the Zulus marching into London and setting Westminster Abbey on fire. It was no doubt effective in helping to break the will of the Zulu people, but it is doubtful if it could be described as civilised.

This was destruction on a huge scale. By the end of the day, 2,000 huts lay in ashes. The most revered article in all Zululand was there, the *inkatha yezwe yakwa-*

Zulu. This was a python skin stuffed with some of the sacred objects of Zululand, including the body dirt of Cetshwayo and his ancestors. Every year in the First Fruits ceremony a huge bull would be slain after an extended tussle which often left a trail of dead and wounded Zulus in its wake. The bull's corpse would be burned to ashes which would be added to the sacred but unappetising cocktail in the *inkatha*. It was the embodiment of the soul of Zululand and its destruction would have a shattering effect on the morale of the Zulu people.

There was little attempt by the Zulus to stop the advance and it is hard to avoid the conclusion that the effect of the great losses they had suffered had sapped their morale. Harrison, who accompanied Buller on some of his scouting expeditions, left some detailed accounts of their progress. Marches were typically short but the organisation of them did not impress Harrison. He noted in his journal that he took more care over organising a parade back in Aldershot than the general staff seemed to be doing here in the backyard of a dangerous foe. He was quick, nonetheless, to exonerate Chelmsford himself from this imputation, noting that he showed great energy in trying to sort things out.

The advance was very slow, to some painfully so. The life was slowly crushed out of Zululand across the areas through which the army passed, plumes of smoke marking its progress from any homesteads that were on its route. Although the lot of the British soldier was much better, this was still no picnic for them. Men slept on the ground with a blanket and, if they were lucky, a waterproof sheet. The terrain on which they slept was rock hard. Each night a laager had to be constructed, a painstaking process that took a great deal of time and often had to be subtly corrected because it was rarely a case of getting it right first time. Trenches also had to be hacked out of the rock-hard ground.

By 27 June, the army was in a position where it was overlooking the White Mfolosi River, on the far side of which was Ulundi. Here they erected a laager where any men who were below par in terms of health could stay, along with some of the stores. This would effectively be an advanced camp for the final push on Ulundi.

From here, the rest of the army moved out with ten days' rations, determined to force a decisive battle to bring the war to an end. Cetshwayo sent out a number of gifts in an effort to buy them off, but Chelmsford was not going to forego what he saw as his vindication for the sake of a few elephant tusks or oxen. But the men were still nervous. There were frequent reports of imminent attacks on the column over the course of a number of days, but they were all unfounded.

In a final attempt to buy Chelmsford off, a particularly poignant gift was offered. The Zulus who killed the Prince Imperial may not have been aware at the time of the importance of the man they had slain, but it had subsequently become obvious that someone of great significance was involved. Now Cetshwayo sent Chelmsford Louis' sword, that much-prized and very personal possession. Chelmsford was no doubt pleased to get it but was not swayed from his resolve.

It is ironic that, despite concerns that Natal would be exposed to raids from the Zulus, no attack had been made of any great significance after Rorke's Drift until the last week of June. Then, a party of 1,000 Zulus crossed over the Middle Drift to unleash chaos on the immediate area. They were in two parties and attacked up the Thukela Valley, burning seventy-four settlements, killing nearly thirty people and taking 1,000 head of cattle and goats as a prize. However, on their way back to Zululand they were attacked by the local Border Guard and many of the cattle were recaptured.[15]

Relations between Chelmsford and Bulwer in Natal had reached breaking point because of the commander-in-chief's decision to launch cross-border raids to unsettle the Zulus. Bulwer was dead against this strategy as he believed it would lead to damaging raids being launched in retaliation. He had intervened as a result, leading to Chelmsford complaining to the Duke of Cambridge that 'I have been much annoyed by the action of the Lieutenant Governor of Natal who when I ordered the Native forces along the border to make demonstrations and if possible raids into Zululand actually sent orders without consulting me or my Staff forbidding any native to cross the border'.[16] He went on to state that 'Sir H. Bulwer from my first arrival in Natal has thrown every obstacle in my way'.[17]

It is true that the two men had rarely seen eye to eye, and it is hard to avoid the conclusion that the British were sometimes their own greatest enemy. The NNC had regrouped and had played an important part in guarding the borders yet, despite improvements to their conditions, they were still being let down far too often. Many of them were not happy. In June some were complaining that although they had worked for five months, they had only been paid for one. It must have been annoying to those at the Middle Drift that they had to take time out to go and pay the annual hut tax they owed – there presumably being no chance of that particular payment being delayed, unlike their salaries.[18]

By this time, Sir Garnet Wolseley was in southern Africa. He held an early interview with Sir Henry Bulwer, who expressed to him in outspoken terms the view that 'Bartle Frere had forced on this war which was quite unnecessary'. He further stated that he had been pressurised by Frere to sign the ultimatum in the first place and that the annexation of the Transvaal was a great mistake. He also felt that responsibility for Chelmsford's military disasters could be put firmly at the feet of his aide, Crealock, on whom he had relied too heavily for advice.[19]

The new commander in the field was faced with a quandary. The main action was clearly going to be with Number 2 Column and Chelmsford. However, Wolseley doubted that he had time to reach it before any conclusive action was fought. Wolseley's agenda, though unspoken, was clear: he wished to be the man in charge when the final battle was fought, making him the general who brought the war to a successful conclusion. Chelmsford's agenda was equally transparent: he must win the war before Wolseley took over and as a result achieve his vindication.

Wolseley, who had landed at Durban on 27 June, had decided he had no option but to join the Coastal Column. It is true that they would not be involved in any final battle but this was the best position from which to communicate with Chelmsford and tell him to wait for him. 'Crealock's Crawlers' had established a beachhead on the coast of Zululand itself, at Port Durnford, and he sailed up the coast to here.

A landing on this part of the southern African coastline was no easy matter. The 'port' was unapproachable by large ships and landings could only be made by the men being brought ashore on surfboats, which would be dangerously exposed to the strong currents in the process. A flat-bottomed boat had been put into service for the purpose, attached to a wire tied to a point on the land at one end and a sea-anchor at the other.

Passengers would be battened down below whilst this happened. It was an arrangement that worked well when the seas were light but must have been absolutely terrifying when they were rough. Being down below was like being entombed and the boat must have felt like a coffin in such circumstances. Unfortunately for Wolseley, he arrived off Port Durnford when the weather was most unkind. For nearly three hours they tried without success to land.

Ironically, not long before they had arrived the seas had been calm but now they became unmanageable. Wolseley (who had arrived on HMS *Shah)* and his entourage endured a terrifying couple of hours before giving up. Bindon Blood, who was on shore at the time, noted that:

> [Wolseley] and his staff undoubtedly had a shocking time for two hours or so whilst battened down in the landing-boat, in a rather rough sea, and they would not hear of trying again, but were off to Durban at once! Of course next morning there was a flat calm, and they could have landed in row-boats if they had stayed.[20]

Wolseley must have been beside himself with frustration and his mood would not have been helped by Chelmsford's correspondence which showed that he had no intention of putting off a final decisive battle before the new commander-in-chief arrived to steal the glory from him. He did say that he was prepared to delay for a couple of days, knowing that the Zulu commissariat would be stretched to the limit and beyond if they had to feed a large army for any length of time. But regular correspondence from Wolseley, telling Chelmsford to stop and reunite with Crealock's Coastal Column, was ignored.

The gods of war had at last smiled on Chelmsford. By 30 June Chelmsford's expanded column, with Wood's troops now effectively an integral part of it, was camped on the southern banks of the White Mfolosi, on the threshold of Ulundi itself. Although Chelmsford had anticipated that the Zulus would attack him as he advanced down the hills that led to the final approach, they did not do so. They were saving themselves from one great final effort in defence of Cetshwayo's capital.

Cetshwayo was desperate to avoid the inevitable. Chelmsford responded to his peace overtures cynically, saying that he must advance to the Mfolosi River, just in front of Ulundi, as his men needed water. The king must return the two cannon he had taken from the field of Isandlwana as well as a heavy cattle fine. Chelmsford undertook not to launch any offensive action until 3 July – just enough time to ensure that his men were ready for the final assault. However, if there was any firing on his army then he would consider the temporary truce to be at an end.[21]

On 1 July, Harrison again went scouting and chose a site for the army to camp at later that day. From where he was, he could clearly see a large Zulu impi manoeuvring in Ulundi. For a time it looked as if they might attack, but experienced observers assured him this was not the case. He had been making preparations for about an hour when a message was received from Chelmsford. It informed him that the Zulus were advancing and were only 3 miles off. He had thirty minutes to finish laagering the camp. He knew that he could not do this in the position where he was but had noted another place about three-quarters of a mile back to which he hurriedly returned. The laager was completed in the time allowed but the feared attack did not materialise.

Cetshwayo's pride and joy were his white cattle. These were traditionally kept by the king of Zululand. Now, on 2 July, he sent 140 of them to Chelmsford in a final attempt to forestall him. But they did not arrive. Some of the young Zulu soldiers were so enflamed by this final humiliation that they would not let the cattle pass out of Ulundi. Better by far to fight and die than bend the knee in this embarrassing fashion. Strangely, Chelmsford saw this incident being played out in the distance, spotting the cattle first of all being driven towards him and then being taken back again.[22]

That night the British erected two laagers near Ulundi. The troops in them were understandably more jumpy than ever given the proximity of a huge Zulu impi. A sentry outside one of the laagers shouted a challenge during the night, as a result of which a number of 'friendly' native troops, also outside, tried to run in.

Harrison was one of those inside the laager. He awoke from his slumbers under a wagon to find a Zulu, armed with an assegai and bleeding, standing over him. It must have seemed like a nightmare but Harrison was composed enough to realise that the 'Zulu' was in fact a 'friendly' and the blood had resulted from him charging through the 'abattis' (thorn-bush barricade) that had been erected around the camp. Fortunately, on this occasion at least, although there was a considerable amount of panic, no one was hurt.[23]

It was perhaps as well that there were other experienced hands in camp to realise what was happening. Sir Harcourt Bengough was attached to Chelmsford's column but had held a command position with the Natal Native Contingent and had been particularly active in the Isandlwana campaign, though his troops were at a distance from the actual fighting and had fortunately survived unscathed as a result. He was awoken around midnight and, trying to stand up, was at once knocked over. Frantically but futilely he searched for his revolver. However, he quickly worked out that it was yet another false alarm.

Molyneux was there too and gave a wry account of what was happening, noting particularly Chelmsford's response to it. There was a stampede into the camp, a 'black avalanche', as he called it. Then:

> a burly native landed full on the adjutant-general's prostrate form, who at once forgot all about his published work on *The Treatment of Natives*. He forgot to call them '*abantu*' (people), '*amadoda*' (men), or '*amabuti*' (soldiers); he did not recollect to them they were acting like '*amalufula*' (common blacks); but called them [---] {with the addition of an adjective} and other things; and he beat them till we regained our good temper, which had been temporarily lost with the disturbance of our beauty sleep.[24]

Next day, a fort was built between the two laagers, a rough structure formed of the boulders that were strewn around the slopes. Cetshwayo continued to send out emissaries to plead for a peaceful solution and a temporary truce was agreed. Chelmsford was happy to entertain these overtures, a cynical move which gave him more time to prepare for the final battle. Both sides now watched each other closely. Occasionally a Zulu sniper would take a pot-shot at a British soldier coming down to the river to collect water, but there was a short space of relative calm whilst both armies steeled themselves for the battle that loomed.

The pot-shots, as it turned out – which would certainly have resulted from a lack of discipline in the Zulu ranks and not from any order from Cetshwayo – gave the British an excuse to advance. In a symbolic gesture, cattle that had previously been sent out by Cetshwayo as a peace offering were driven back across the river to him by the British as a sign that his peace overtures had been rejected. Buller was sent out to perform his usual activity of aggressive harassment, which he did with enthusiasm.

The Zulus' decision to fight one final battle was a brave one but was, in the end, both tragic and futile. Buller, Wood's trusted lieutenant, led 500 of his men across the river. The fording point was overlooked by bluffs on either side but the crossing was successfully made. Buller's objectives were both to make sure the crossing was undefended and also to scout the land beyond. The first was positively achieved. There were a few Zulus there when he crossed but they quickly scampered into the long grass behind.

Buller now spotted a few Zulu horsemen a little way off. They too started to ride away from him. Leaving a reserve to watch the crossing, Buller led the rest of his men in a determined chase after them. They had gone about a mile when Buller sensed that something was wrong – not a moment too soon. Just 50 yards in front were masses of Zulus waiting to spring a trap.

A ragged volley rang out from the Zulu ranks; fortunately for their enemy most of them fired high. But now other Zulus appeared, racing to cut off Buller's line of retreat. It was touch and go for a while whether the cavalry would make it, but they did at last manage to outpace the chasing pack. Buller was saved by the reserve he had posted who caused the Zulus to halt their chase. It had been close to a disaster, although the losses were light compared to what they might have been: three dead, four wounded and thirteen horses lost.

One man in the British ranks in particular distinguished himself in the engagement. This was Captain William Beresford, on the staff of Colonel Wood. When the Zulu trap had been launched, a volley rang out which brought down several men. One rider was shot but not killed. He fell from his horse and sat, stunned, on the ground. Beresford saw what was happening and, in an instant, turned around to go and pick him up.

The Zulus were now charging forward. The man that Beresford was trying to rescue told him to leave him or they would both die. It might be expected that, in true Victorian tradition, Beresford came up with some flowery speech concerning the relative merits of 'death or glory', but his response was instead to say that he would punch him in the face if he did not climb up on his horse. This did the trick and the overloaded horse did its best to run off.

A race for life then followed, the horse lumbering up a slope chased by a horde of fleet-footed Zulus. When they threatened to catch them, the accurate revolver marksmanship of a third man, Sergeant O'Toole (all three British soldiers involved were Irish), kept them back. Eventually the race was won and all of them escaped.

Beresford would later win a Victoria Cross for his gallantry which, it must be said, evidenced a very different reaction to a crisis than that displayed by Jahleel Brenton Carey the month before. The wounded man, Sergeant Fitzmaurice, was bleeding so profusely over Beresford that when they arrived back at the laager 'you could not tell whether it was rescuer or rescued who was the wounded man, so smeared was Beresford with borrowed blood'.[25]

There was an almost comical postscript. Charles Fripp of the *Graphic* had been sketching events on the far side of the river from the British camp and was therefore in great danger. Buller, not renowned for his tact, peremptorily ordered him to cross back to the British lines. Fripp, a man with a short fuse, was angered at his tone of voice and, crossing back to the main force, soon got into an argument with Beresford, who stuck up for Buller. Tensions escalated and, before anyone could intervene, Fripp and Beresford had come to blows. Fripp had to be restrained and almost had his clothes torn off in the process. It was incredible to see that, just minutes after escaping the Zulus, Beresford – still covered in blood from the incident – was indulging in fisticuffs with one of his own side.[26]

Despite Buller's near-disaster, the scouting mission had served its purposes. It had located a good spot for Chelmsford to aim for – a low rise in the plain beyond the river – and it had also teased out some useful information about the position of the Zulu army. That night, the great war songs of the Zulu impi could be heard in the British camp but, rather than being harbingers of triumph and a confirmation of Zulu greatness, they were rather the last laments of a way of life that was about to disappear.[27]

Nevertheless, the noise was unsettling. Molyneux wrote that:

> we could gather from the volume of sound that there was a goodly host assembled and between the roars of the men came the shrill cries of the women, which told the old hands that they had got hold of the three bodies of the troopers killed that day and were mutilating them.[28]

He also theorised that they rather overdid the celebrations, which meant that they were late getting ready for the battle next day.

And so it was that at 5 a.m. on 4 July Chelmsford led his men into battle for one final time. He left his baggage train on the south side of the river and took with him over 4,000 white troops, including the 17th Lancers, nearly 1,000 black troops, twelve guns and two Gatling guns as well as a detachment of Dragoon Guards – according to Molyneux this came to a rather precise total of 5,142 men.[29] They also, on this occasion, carried plenty of spare ammunition with them. This was the strongest force that Chelmsford had had at his disposal during the entire war. They crossed over the shallow water, barely up to their knees, unopposed and headed towards Ulundi.

Chelmsford's battle formation involved arranging the men in a gigantic square with the NNC safely kept in the centre; whatever faults he may have had strategically, it was hard to fault his tactics on this occasion. Cavalry rode up and down to protect the flanks whilst the army advanced intently across the plain. They would retreat inside the square if and when battle commenced. Buller was in the lead with his irregular cavalry. All was set fair for a climactic confrontation.

The early morning mists started to lift. The British advanced slowly across the plain, stopping several times to ensure that their formation stayed intact. Then they halted, daring the Zulus to come on and attack. Five companies of the 80th Regiment held the front of the square with the two Gatling guns in the middle of their line. Artillery was positioned at three of the four corners.

Chelmsford's actions at this time, witnessed up close by Molyneux, were interesting. Wood came across and proposed that the force should entrench. Chelmsford, who would probably take advice from Wood sooner than anyone else, would not hear of it. The Zulus had often taunted the British for hiding behind their fortifications. It was time for that to stop. 'No', he bluntly replied, 'they will be satisfied if we beat them fairly in the open. We have been called ant-bears long enough.'[30]

He also insisted on remaining on horseback, which of course meant that he was more at risk of being shot, as even allowing for the Zulus' widely reported bad marksmanship they tended to shoot high. His personal courage was never in doubt and his action now merely confirmed what was already known. Yet taken together these decisions also point to a desire for vindication, to demonstrate that he had bested the Zulus fair-and-square in a fight using the tactics he had always advocated.

The ranks were four deep, the front two kneeling, the rear standing. Here, about a mile off from Ulundi, the British army prepared for battle in an African version of the squares that had been seen at Waterloo sixty-four years earlier. In many ways, it was a throwback to a bygone era. Against modern armies, even irregulars like the Boers, these tactics would have been disastrous, but against a native enemy they were perfectly suited.

It was just after 8 a.m. when the first Zulu was sighted. Cetshwayo had summoned all available men to Ulundi to fight the final battle, although as it had loomed close he changed his mind and told his men that they should not fight as they would be slaughtered.[31] But they would not hear of it. Here were the veterans of Isandlwana and the survivors of Khambula, men with very different tales to tell. The impis started to assemble slowly, without any sense of urgency, until perhaps 25,000 Zulus were prepared for battle.

As they started to get closer, Chelmsford sent out his irregular cavalry to goad them into action. An attack was exactly what he wanted; it gave him the opportunity to immolate their ranks in the teeth of a Martini-Henry hurricane. It worked to perfection. With the horsemen firing into them from a distance of only 100 yards, the Zulus started to break into a trot. The irregulars, acting effectively as bait, lured them on until they were in range of the artillery. As soon as they were, the cannon flamed forth, lobbing their lethal shot into the packed Zulu ranks.

The square opened to let the horsemen in and then, like the doors of a vault, slammed shut again. Within minutes the square was surrounded and the battle began in earnest. At 200 yards, the rifles of the infantry opened up. The British formation confused the Zulus who looked for a weakness at the rear, just as they had found at Isandlwana. However, it was not to be. Each side they attacked was as solid as the last.

The rifle fire was devastating. So thick were the clouds of smoke that on several occasions Chelmsford had to call a halt to the firing to allow it to clear. Those on the receiving end spoke of it in awe: of the impact of the bullets as they thudded into flesh, of the smoke which choked their lungs, of the noise which seemed to make the very earth shake as if it were alive.

One man who was in those ranks, a warrior from the iNgombamakhosi named Sofikasho Zungu, said later:

> there was such a roar of guns that we were utterly bewildered. One shot went close to my head and I fell down and thought I was dead. I saw one whose head was struck off right next to me and his body stood up quivering with hands clenched until he fell.[32]

Although the Zulus tried as usual to skirmish through the grass their position was hopeless. The Gatling guns did great execution although from time to time they would jam providing merciful if short-lived relief. Still the odd Zulu got within a few feet of the lines, almost at stabbing distance, but was inevitably shot down before managing to launch himself into an attack.

The closest the Zulus came to anything like a breakthrough was an attack launched on one of the corners, under the cover of smoke that was billowing from a nearby homestead that the British had set ablaze. The war artist Melton Prior was there and reckoned that the Zulus were 6,000 strong and came on in ranks thirty deep. Chelmsford, aware of the threat, urged his men to fire as fast as they could, almost begging them to increase the rate at which they loaded the bullets and pulled the trigger.

A wall of bullets met the Zulus, 'a sleet of death', as the incomparable war correspondent Archibald Forbes called it.[33] At this range there was no need to aim. Shoulders started to ache as the brutal recoil of the Martini-Henrys bit back into the soldiers firing them. Barrels became hot at the constant firing. But if it was an ordeal for the British, what then for the Zulus? They fell in their hundreds, their twitching corpses piled in heaps on the ground into which their blood flowed. Bravely they still came on but were unable to penetrate the screen of lead that emanated from the British lines.

The Zulus resorted to taking cover in the grass and using their firearms to attack the British. Against a trained enemy the square formation would have been quickly decimated, but the marksmanship of most of the Zulus was poor. Bullets typically shot over the heads of the British lines. Occasionally one would strike home but the cavalry, in their elevated position, were most at risk. Here and there one or two Zulus, 'the boldest and the bravest', tried to push on but it was useless.[34]

A party of several thousand Zulus started to make their way out of Ulundi itself and towards the battlefield. These were older men, who had duties to perform in Ulundi itself, and it was a desperate last attempt to make a difference. It did not. As they advanced down the slope from the homestead towards the British lines, the artillery, now warmed to their task, started to extract a devastating toll and the advance faltered and then stopped. The Gatling guns quickly jammed and became inoperative but it made little difference to the course of the battle.

Ironically, the British were almost in as great a danger from their own ranks as they were from the Zulus. Melton Prior watched as a rocket screeched forth from one of the tubes in the square:

[He] watched its triumphal progress amongst the enemy, until, catching a corner of a hut, it suddenly altered its direction, then, striking the ground, it once more deviated from its proper course and came straight back at us, luckily missing our square by a quarter of a yard. My faith in rockets and tubes has sufficiently weakened since that occasion.[35]

After ninety minutes of one-sided slaughter, the intensity of the Zulu attacks slackened. This was noticed by many, including Chelmsford. The infantry were ordered to stand to one side. It was time to unleash the Lancers. They levelled their lances towards the breaking enemy, an anachronism from another age in most wars but perfect for this one. Yet these were not warriors from the age of chivalry but horsemen tasked with applying the *coup de grâce* to the Zulu nation.

There was an almost hypnotic motion to their killing. They skewered their target and then, in an upward movement, removed the lance, ready to strike forward again against the next target, though occasionally their weapons stuck awkwardly in the shields of their opponents.[36] The irregular cavalry followed up in their wake, picking off Zulus who had managed to avoid the needle-sharp spears of the Lancers. It was a matter of minutes before the Zulu retreat became a rout. Very rarely, a knot of Zulus would turn and make a stand. In one such instance, a volley brought down and killed Captain Wyatt-Edgell of the Lancers.

With the scent of victory in their nostrils, those in pursuit became enflamed with thoughts of revenge for those lost in the war. Chelmsford's chivalric pretensions about being merciful to the wounded now evaporated completely. Any sense of moral superiority that the British might have had (which of course is a debatable point as they were primarily responsible for the war in the first place) was exposed as being nothing more than a hypocritical charade. The NNC enthusiastically joined in the chastisement of a beaten enemy, killing off the wounded that littered the area around the square and along the line of retreat. All wounded Zulus within 300 yards of the square were massacred.

The cavalry chasing the demoralised Zulus were equally cold-blooded. One found a Zulu shot through both legs lying helpless on the ground. He calmly asked him a number of questions in a matter-of-fact fashion, then, when he was satisfied that no more information could be had, finished him off. Another came across a Zulu in great pain, asking to be taken to a doctor. The horseman tapped his carbine and told him 'this is all the medicine you must expect'.

A few prisoners, however, were taken. They were demoralised and beaten, aware that any further fighting against the white man's bullets was futile; Wood thought that 'the Zulu attack was conducted in a hurried, disorderly manner, contrasting strongly with the methodical systems pursued at Kambula [sic]'.[37] A Zulu survivor later admitted that 'we had not much heart in the fight'.[38] Their hopes had died along with a way of life. The fight was all over before 10 a.m. Chelmsford had lost two officers and ten men with a further sixty-nine wounded. The dead were buried at the heart of the square and the march then resumed on towards a now defenceless Ulundi. The men were allowed to stop at a stream and fill up their water bottles. It had been thirsty work.

Chelmsford had been coolness personified during the battle, fought in the open, exactly where the Zulus had wanted it to be fought, and confirming what he had argued all along, that properly organised the British forces in Zululand would overwhelm their foe. Even Forbes, no friend of the now ex-commander-in-chief, admitted that 'Lord Chelmsford's soldierly coolness and decisive clear-headedness in action go far to redeem the passiveness and peevish vacillation which are his characteristics when no battle is raging. One might wish him a military Rip Van Winkle, only wakening to direct a battle.'[39]

A few men rode ahead into Ulundi, from which smoke was already starting to cloak the sky. They were curiosity-hunters and treasure-seekers but there were no precious jewels for them to help themselves to. The Zulus did not have such trinkets, exotic bird feathers or leopard or otter skins in the main being all the decorative adornment they needed. Zululand's real treasure was its cattle, a surrogate form of currency in the region, and the British and their colonial allies had already helped themselves to most of those.

By the afternoon it was over. Zululand was a thing of the past. Around the battlefield perhaps 1,500 Zulu corpses were already starting to decompose beneath the searing sun. Friends and family would come for some of them and offer them what dignity in death they could. Most, though, were left to rot where they were, carrion for the wildlife that gorged itself on the bounty that had been left for them.

That afternoon the sky was thick with clouds of smoke from burning Zulu homesteads. Men like Captain Molyneux were disappointed in their efforts to find loot as a souvenir of the war. He had gone into Ulundi, an enormous place he noted, 700 yards long and 500 across, 'but the heat was so intense from the burning mass that little looting could be done before it was all destroyed'.[40] He had to content himself with some shields he had found that had somehow managed to escape destruction. Cetshwayo's residence, a surprisingly western building – a bungalow plastered on the outside and papered in, replete with glass windows – also went up in smoke.[41]

Melton Prior, the artist, had a very close brush with death as Ulundi burned. He had made his way into Ulundi and thought it was now time to leave as the flames took hold. As he made his way back towards the entrance to the settlement he saw, to his horror, he was being stalked by a Zulu on the other side of a fence. There were no friendly troops around and Prior started to run. It was a race to reach his horse before the Zulu caught him. With the hostile warrior in close pursuit, he managed to mount his horse and, digging his spurs in, escaped to safety. Only when he returned to camp did someone tell him that they had witnessed the event from a distance and he was in fact chased by five Zulus and several thrown assegais had just missed him.[42]

Others were not so fortunate. The Honourable William Drummond was head of Chelmsford's intelligence department. He had, in a cavalier fashion, been in a race to be the first to Ulundi, a challenge which incidentally he lost. However, he did not return to camp and was feared dead. His body was found shortly afterwards in the charred remnants of the royal capital.

Meanwhile, news was taken to the outside world. The correspondent of the *Daily News*, Alexander Forbes, asked Chelmsford if he could send his dispatch back with one of the army's couriers. Chelmsford, who disliked Forbes intensely, which was unsurprising as he was often scathing in his criticism of the campaign, said no. Angered, Forbes decided to take the dispatch himself. It was an incident that reflected on the difficult relationship between Chelmsford and the news media. He had introduced a precedent of issuing military passes to correspondents, previously unnecessary – something which did not go down well with some of them.[43]

Forbes therefore set out on what he called a 'ride of death'. Local newspapermen pointed out that it was the same ride that colonial couriers made every day, unescorted, without ever hitting the headlines because of it. This was perhaps a bit harsh; Forbes rode 110 miles in twenty hours using six horses. Chelmsford not unusually changed his mind and decided to send his own courier an hour after Forbes had left, but it would take him six hours longer to complete the ride. The first bit of the journey was particularly dangerous; two mounted NCOs had traversed the same ground a few days previously and had not completed their mission; their multiply speared bodies were found a fortnight later.[44]

Chelmsford had completed his vindication as far as he was able. Cetshwayo was defeated and on the run (he had left before the final battle, probably fully aware of its final outcome). As far as it was within his power to do so, Chelmsford had started to wipe the stain of Isandlwana from his record. However, he would never achieve complete vindication. For the triumph at Ulundi was only what was ever anticipated of him, whilst the catastrophe he had suffered earlier was a shock that none expected.

Sir Garnet Wolseley was in the region now. Let him have the challenge of picking up the pieces and finishing off the war. He had been quick enough to accept the 'honour' of commanding the forces in this God-forsaken land; now let him understand the cost of doing so. Chelmsford's prospective appointment as Resident in Zululand was off the table anyway, but he did not care. He wanted to get away from Zululand as quickly as possible.

And so he moved back, away from the fleeing Cetshwayo. The army was glad to go. Their spirits were lifted still further when, on the very next day, a group of entrepreneurial traders appeared selling a gratifyingly wide range of goods for the soldiers; these included jam, tobacco, tinned meat and Normandy butter. They understandably did a roaring trade.[45]

Looked at from many perspectives, Chelmsford's retreat was strange. The war was not yet over. Ulundi had been taken and the Zulu army badly beaten but there were still thousands of warriors left to fight should they have the will. And Cetshwayo had not been captured. Even some of those with him at Ulundi were mystified. Years after the event, Blood remarked that 'the Zulus made no visible attempt at a rally, although thanks to Lord Chelmsford's arrangements, or rather to his neglect of obviously advisable precautions, there was nothing to prevent such an attempt'.[46]

But for Chelmsford this was enough; within a few days of the Battle of Ulundi he would resign his post. And indeed there would be no Zulu fight-back. The war, despite Blood's comments, was indeed effectively over with just mopping-up arrangements to see to. Chelmsford would now return home, to be feted by some, castigated by others. His friends in the British establishment, including one in the highest place of all, made sure that his dignity was protected as far as they were able.

On 9 July, Chelmsford, who had already tendered his resignation, sent a terse message to Stanley in London. He enclosed a copy of a General Order from Wolseley, saying: 'you will see that I have been deprived by this General Order of the position given to me by Her Majesty of Lieutenant General commanding the Forces in S. Africa.' He protested at his demotion and the way in which it had been done. He now, as he put it, proposed to 'extricate himself from a false position'.[47]

But the truth could not be hidden. Chelmsford was the one in ultimate command when his men at Isandlwana were overwhelmed. His attempts to pass the buck were rejected out of hand by many. He would be awarded several more honours by a grateful queen, even if to some her gratitude appeared badly misplaced. But Frederic Thesiger, Second Baron Chelmsford, would never command an army in the field again.

Chelmsford has been judged differently by different historians, perhaps reflecting in part the era in which they lived. The Honourable Gerald French, who wrote in the 1930s, was a strong supporter of his strategy, but in recent times the commander has become criticised much more for the incompetence of the expedition and the disasters that it suffered.

Perhaps now we are far enough away to strike a balance. A critical examination of the campaign as a whole will show that it was militarily ill-conceived. The fatal mistake all along was the flawed assumption that the Zulus would be an easy target which led to the mortal sin of over-confidence. This was backed up by inadequate intelligence-gathering and desperately bad communications, not just as a result of technological limitations. For this Chelmsford can rightly be criticised. It was recognised as such even at the time; Norris-Newman remarked of the Isandlwana campaign that 'we were proceeding with too much confidence and with greater celerity than was consistent with safety'.[48]

Chelmsford did at least learn from his mistakes. His second invasion was methodical and, in the main, free of alarms. Responsibility for the death of the Prince Imperial, which in its own way was a personal disaster for Chelmsford, should be laid with, primarily, the reckless prince himself but, secondarily, those who unwisely let him go to southern Africa in the first place.

Chelmsford's tactics had been thorough and had been totally vindicated at Ulundi, a crushing victory for both his army and him personally. The government back home in London might moan that it had taken too long and had been too costly but the second campaign was not costly in one respect: the lives of British soldiers. On reflection, for this most of his men would have surely been profoundly grateful. That said, as soon as Wolseley took over he made strenuous efforts to 'reduce the excessive rate of expenditure which had so far been maintained in connection with this war'.[49]

Lord Chelmsford himself was profoundly affected by the conflict. At least three different Chelmsfords can be identified during its course. The first of them, pre-Isandlwana, was excessively confident. This Chelmsford took extreme risks because of the low regard he had for his foe, making him appear reckless, even foolhardy. But he was not alone; many others felt the same way. The *Natal Mercury* noted on 16 January 1879 that 'so far, every incident goes to show that the Zulu military qualities have been greatly overrated'.[50] The editor of that august publication, like Chelmsford, was forced to revise his opinion.

Then, immediately post-Isandlwana, the pendulum swung to the opposite extreme. This Chelmsford was full of self-doubt, his morale at the lowest imaginable ebb. It was understandable given the personal disaster he had suffered. At this low point, Chelmsford had decided that he had had enough and wished someone else to take the strain of command.

But then there was something of a resurgence. A new Chelmsford emerged, as if from a cocoon, one characterised by steely resolve. This Chelmsford was in many ways the alter ego of the first one; cautious (too cautious his critics would say), calculating, still of course with some of the same faults – limited communication skills, poor delegation, a worrying ability to change his mind, for example – but in other ways a totally different animal than the one who had begun the war.

Chelmsford certainly managed to divide opinion. Disraeli was scathing in his criticism of him. In a letter to the queen, he wondered why Chelmsford needed so many troops to subdue a country the size of Yorkshire. The queen, replying on 1 September 1879, wrote that his critical comments both 'grieved and astonished her'. The biggest criticism she could make of Disraeli was to suggest that recalling a commander when he was unsuccessful was 'to act as the French used to do'.[51] Disraeli, in any event, refused to meet Chelmsford at Hughenden Manor, the prime minister's country seat, when he returned to England, despite the queen's desire that he do so. Chelmsford was, however, invited to Balmoral.

Even some of those who it might be thought suffered because of his short-comings as a commander stood by him. Sergeant Evan Jones of the 24th wrote in a private letter home that 'there is not a man in the 24th that would not fight and most willingly die for him'.[52] Supporters of Chelmsford, at the time and subsequently, aver that Chelmsford succeeded in his mission, in their words terminating 'the reign of terror hitherto maintained by Cetywayo [sic]'.[53] Therein, of course, lies the weakness in the argument, for there never was a reign of terror save in the fevered imaginations of some of the administrators, soldiers, missionaries and colonists in southern Africa.

Others, though, had little time for him. An unnamed artilleryman wrote home that 'Lord Chelmsford is most unpopular amongst the men, who look on him as a very inferior general – and so he is, for now he is over-cautious as he was before over-rash, and the delays in advancing are most vexatious'.[54] The major criticism of Chelmsford, which could never be vindicated, was the flawed political decision to invade Zululand in the first place which he was party to. Apart from the doubtful moral dimensions of it, Confederation also failed as a policy. As soon as the war was over, it was abandoned. Zululand would have its own special solution imposed on it, which would be awful in terms of its consequences.

Moral considerations of the political dimensions of the war are dangerous from a modern, post-colonial perspective. Inevitably, if colonialism is considered per se to be wrong, then any colonial intervention must be wrong too. Therefore, from this perspective, it must be taken as a given that the invasion of Zululand was morally indefensible.

Yet many European nations at the time were colonial powers. The French might condemn the British for their actions but they were busy carving out their own African empires as were, or soon would be, others such as the Germans and Belgians. The Americans might pontificate about the evils of colonialism in Africa but they themselves were busy breaking treaty after treaty with 'Indians' in their own backyard. Russia too was on its own colonial mission, albeit one that did not extend to Africa. Contemporary criticisms of colonialism from most quarters should be taken for what they are: hypocritical point-scoring.

Yet it cannot be denied that the final solution to the problem of Zululand was to be particularly disastrous. Wolseley was to impose a settlement that effectively carved up Zululand into thirteen different states, each with its own ruler. One of them would be John Dunn, landing on his feet yet again. He at least would be fully compensated for his dubious part in the war.

On 8 July, just four days after the crushing British victory at Ulundi, Wolseley was accepting the surrender of local chiefs on the coast. He made a great show of it; bands and pipers were ordered to be present to generate a real sense of military occasion. The surrendering Zulus were given passes by John Dunn which gave them the right to move around freely without any interference from those who were now, for the time being at least, an occupying power. On 19 July, Wolseley further announced the break-up of the Zulu kingdom.

In the meantime, the hunt for the fugitive Zulu king went on. By this stage, no holds were barred in the search for the fleeing ruler. Huts were burned, women and children taken captive, cattle confiscated. It was reported that so many prisoners were taken that the numbers held captive were finally reduced not through any moral consideration, but because it proved impossible to look after them all. Some Zulus produced safe-conduct papers given to them by the British, but they proved worthless. Prisoners were allegedly flogged in the search for information on Cetshwayo's whereabouts.[55]

On 28 August, Major Marter of the 1st Dragoon Guards was leading a troop in a remote part of Zululand. He had received a tip that Cetshwayo was hiding in a homestead in the Ngome forest. The area was quite mountainous and some locals had guided Marter to the edge of a precipice overlooking a valley far below. They could see a small settlement with about twenty huts in it. This, their guides said, was where Cetshwayo was.

There was only the narrowest of paths down, covered with suffocating creepers. It was a dangerous descent but a hill on the plain shielded them. This enabled them to completely surround the settlement and then pounce. There was no resistance. In a hut at the far end of the homestead was the king. He refused to come out at first and asked to be shot. He would not budge until Marter's men prepared to set fire to the hut.

Only then did he emerge, proudly defiant until the end. He would be taken towards the coast and then, by ship, to Cape Town along with some of his wives and servants. On the journey, he evinced a particular fondness for 'Holland's Gin'. He blamed Shepstone for the war, saying that 'he was the man that set light to the fire that burned up Zululand'.[56]

Some of those who saw him were surprised at what they witnessed. Walter Dunne, a survivor of the epic at Rorke's Drift, was one of those who witnessed Cetshwayo on this sad journey, and he remarked:

> from what I had heard I expected to see an obese, ill looking savage, but on the contrary, he was a fine looking, intelligent man with good features. He descended slowly from the ambulance, and walked with natural dignity to the tent provided for him, raising his head to cast a steady glance on those who were in front of him; a glance which seemed to shew that as a king he felt his altered position, but bore up against it. His demeanour was manly and digni-fied, and not unworthy of a captive king.[57]

On his way to the coast, Cetshwayo saw sights that must have devastated him. At Ulundi only ten huts were left unburned. It was a scene repeated throughout Zululand. Shortly before leaving for exile, the king asked for John Dunn to come and see him. Dunn would not, though whether this was a matter of unjustified bitterness or merely a guilty conscience was not clear.

It did not take long for the British troops who had flooded into Zululand to start moving back out again. Amongst those leaving were the heroic defenders of Rorke's Drift. They marched through Pietermaritzburg to tumultuous acclaim. As they did so, they saw Commissary Dalton in the crowd. Spontaneously, the men of the 24th stopped and made him march with them. He too was a hero.[58] For others, there was only a temporary halt to their campaigning; some like Bindon Blood now made their way out to Afghanistan to fight another foe on another continent.

On 1 September, Wolseley announced to the people of Zululand how their country was to be governed in the future. The new commander-in-chief proudly wrote that 'I now feel, therefore, in a position to report that the Zulu War has been satisfactorily concluded'. In a statement that may have stuck in the throat a bit, Wolseley graciously noted that the final victory at Ulundi, the only major battle fought since he arrived in southern Africa, had been fought under the command of Chelmsford and to him all the credit rightfully belonged.[59]

Contradicting these fine words were his private feelings. On 30 June he had written in his journal of Chelmsford: 'it is too dreadful to feel that the honour of HM Army and the national welfare should be in such hands.'[60] Chelmsford's behaviour in the build-up to the decisive battle of Ulundi and his perceived petulance afterwards led Wolseley to write that 'his contumacious disobedience of my orders to correspond only through my Chief of Staff [a sideswipe by Chelmsford at his demotion to a status below that of Wolseley] does not recommend him to me as a soldier'.[61] It would not probably have upset Chelmsford to know this, as he and Wolseley did not see eye to eye. More upsetting perhaps would be Wolseley's journal note that both Wood and Buller, highly regarded by Chelmsford, did not regard him as fit to be a corporal.[62] This did not reflect well on either of them as, for all his faults, Chelmsford had been quick to direct credit their way in the highest quarters.

On the surface all was sweetness and light. Wolseley went out of his way to be polite to Chelmsford until he left. But this was just a public face. Privately, he noted that he was 'hoping at the same time that I shall never again meet him on duty'.[63] Wolseley was frustrated at his failure to arrive in time to snatch the glorious victory he craved in the campaign. In the journal he kept of his experiences, the very last entry, dated 25 May 1880, reveals just how caustic he had become about the whole campaign by then:

> So ends my second mission to South Africa, I have been successful but it will be amusing to watch how my enemies at the Horse Guards will endeavour to denigrate my services & prevent their being recognised in any way by the Authorities. I never expect anything from any Government, so I shall not be surprised if I do not receive from the present Ministry any expression of thanks even. When there is anything serious to be done anywhere, I shall probably be sent for. Until then I must be content to bide my time.[64]

And so Wolseley returned to his homeland to await the call, which would come when he was asked to rescue the besieged General Gordon at Khartoum, though again he would arrive just too late. He never, in his view, received the thanks he was due and it is especially unlikely that many of the Zulu people thanked him for his efforts on their behalf. The war was not quite over. A few days after Cetshwayo's capture, British forces in the north-west of the country were blowing up the entrances to caves with Zulus (including women and children) who would not surrender still inside them – even then, two men of the 2nd/24th were killed in these last skirmishes.[65] But there would be no more pitched battles or organised resistance. The end was indeed nigh.

The peace terms Wolseley imposed incorporated all the conditions that the British had sought at the start of the war: the disbandment of the regimental system in Zululand, an injunction against taking life without just cause and the abolition of the witch doctors' arts. Each new sub-state created would be under the watchful eye of a British Resident who had great powers; for example, any succession to the chieftainship of a territory was subject to the Resident's approval.[66]

Those who really suffered were the Zulu people. Their lot immediately after the war was grim; crops were destroyed, badly affected anyway after several years of drought (the recent heavy rains had merely exacerbated the damage already done). The new structure was unsustainable. In an attempt to divide and conquer, Wolseley was all too successful. Great tensions were exposed and exacerbated as a result. Just a few years after the Anglo-Zulu War was over, the country was at war again. This time, Zulu would be fighting Zulu in a war far more destructive than that against the British.

The notions of colonial power as a civilising influence were quickly abandoned as a sham as the Anglo-Zulu War progressed. In a nation that prided itself on its Christian morals and ethics, some rather hypocritical and patronising attitudes soon revealed themselves. Apparently, fighting 'savages' required different rules.

Certainly Norris-Newman thought so, writing that:

> the fallacy of fighting with an uncivilized race with the same feelings of humanity that dictate our wars with civilized races was thoroughly proved; and it thus was shown that in Zululand neither men, kraals, cattle, nor crops should be spared on any pretence whatever, except on the complete submission and disarmament of the whole nation.[67]

Wherever this attitude came from, it had little to do with the Christian ethics espoused by the majority of the British nation. Chelmsford's original argument – however sincerely it might have been held at the beginning of the war – that the war was not against the Zulu people but their king, was shown to be utter nonsense.

A brief note sent by Chelmsford to Wood on 20 June summed up the mood. It instructed Wood to take care not to burn settlements that were too near his camp, as he had been forced to send men to put the fire out as it was endangering his own position. There was no humanitarian aspect to this stance, as the concluding sentence proved: 'if you leave the kraals near this camp, we will do the burning before we leave.'[68]

Yet even those who had sided with the victors were not happy with the outcome. The colonists in Natal were particularly disgruntled at the lack of any compensation for the losses and damage they had suffered as a result of the war. Nor were natives who had sided with the British any happier.

Chief Maqwe of the amaQadi people was one such complainant. He was quoted by the *Natal Witness* as saying that 'never more will I fight for the white man'. He had experienced the extremes of climate that the campaign had offered, had seen men who were loyal retainers shot dead by his side. In return, he had received nothing. In conclusion, he told the reporter that 'my heart is angry and never again will I respond to the call of your Government'.[69]

Their lot was at least better than that of Cetshwayo. He never came to terms with the war or its outcome. In 1881, he wrote: 'Mpande did you no wrong, and I have done you no wrong, therefore you must have some other object in view in invading my land.'[70] He was later given permission to travel to England where, resplendent in western-style suit, he even had an audience with Queen Victoria.

She must have had very mixed feelings at meeting a man whose armies had slaughtered so many British officers and helped destroy Chelmsford's career, but on the surface she acted in a dignified and courteous manner. Cetshwayo was later given back a small part of his land to rule, but it was a token gesture and only caused him pain as he watched at close hand Zululand ripping itself apart in civil war.

The war, in the long run, solved little. The British were forced to intervene again in later years in an attempt to restore order but wounds resulted from the war which, in their own way, contributed to the terrible era of apartheid. Zulu soldiers served with expeditions sent from South Africa to the trenches of the Western Front in the First World War; the white elements of the army received medals for their gallantry, the Zulus did not.

The Anglo-Zulu War was an inglorious episode in British colonial history yet, like all wars, it exposes contradictions, even hypocrisies, in all of us. For much as we might condemn the morality of war, many of us are still in awe of the bravery it demonstrates from soldiers on both sides, whatever the rights and the wrongs of the conflict. But it would also be the hardest of hearts that is not, in the end, touched too by its tragedy and pathos. In these emotions most of all perhaps lie the reasons for our continuing fascination with the ill-advised and ultimately heartbreaking tragedy of the Anglo-Zulu War.

One of those there, Corporal George Howe of the Royal Engineers, noted in his letters how his army burned so many of the homesteads they came across. He wondered what would happen after the war, through the winter of 1879, thinking: 'how the Zulus will manage I don't know, we burnt about 20,000 huts. I feel for the poor women and children.'[71] The war, in the end, cost over a thousand British lives and over £5 million.[72] The accountants did not prepare a similar profit and loss account for the Zulus. Many acknowledged them as a gallant and brave enemy. Even Smith-Dorrien, later a First World War general, refuted the allegation that they were 'savage' after he saw the horror scenes that so-called civilised nations produced some thirty-five years later, remarking that the Zulus appeared as comparative angels after the beastly nature of that global conflict.[73]

Perhaps it is most appropriate to end with the words of one of the victors. Charles Fripp was a war artist who was present at Ulundi and watched as Zululand went up in flames. As he looked on he remarked:

the smoke of Cetywayo's [sic] burning kraal hung like a pall over the plain to conceal hundreds of dead warriors from the great moon which stood calmly and gloriously in the eternal heaven above. Whatever the rights or wrongs which brought on the war, these same brave Zulu died resisting an invasion of their country and their homes. Naked savages as they were, let us honour them.[74]

Savages they were not, but brave warriors they were, fighting in defence of a way of life against an invader they did not understand. Let us honour them too.

NOTES

1. A Clash of Empires

1 Taylor, p. 102.
2 Hallam Parr, p. 108, described him as a man 'preferring a quiet life, with the society of his wives and good living'.
3 Colenso and Durnford, p. 17.
4 Shepstone's comments were widely reproduced at the time. The source used here is *The Cape Monthly Magazine* of May 1875.
5 Colenso and Durnford, p. 21.
6 *The Cape Monthly Magazine*, May 1875.
7 See, for example, Hallam Parr, p. 148.

2. The Scene is Set

1 Molyneux, p. 99, puts the sum at 12s 6d.
2 Cited in Greaves, *Rorke's Drift*, p. 29.
3 Moodie, p. 20.
4 Thompson, p. 1.
5 Ibid., p. 3.
6 'Assegai' is not a Zulu word but is derived from Arabic. The Zulus called the spear an *iklwa*, an onomatopoeia based on the sound that the weapon was supposed to make when withdrawn from an enemy's abdomen.
7 Molyneux, p. 105.
8 Laband and Thompson, *The Illustrated Guide to the Anglo-Zulu War*, p. 14.
9 Dated 6 June 1878; referenced in *The War Correspondents*, p. 2.
10 Colenso and Durnford, p. 285.
11 See Hallam Parr, p. 121.
12 *The War Correspondents*, 3 August 1878, p. 7.

13 Sir Theophilus Shepstone Papers, Natal Archives Depot, Pietermaritzburg, cited in Laband, *Lord Chelmsford's Zululand Campaign, 1878–1879*, p. 3.
14 Ibid., cited in Laband, *Lord Chelmsford*, p. 5; also in French, p. 42.
15 CP 10/5, cited in Laband, *Lord Chelmsford*, p. 6.
16 WO 32/7699, cited in Laband, *Lord Chelmsford*, p. 12.
17 WO 32/7702.
18 Molyneux, p. 20.
19 CP 26/20, cited in Thompson, p. 6.
20 From 'The Natal Mercury' in *The War Correspondents*, p. 15.
21 Greaves, *Rorke's Drift*, p. 52.
22 WO 32/7699, cited in Laband, *Lord Chelmsford*, p. 12.
23 Although christened Henry Evelyn Wood, he was always known as Evelyn Wood.
24 CP 10/17, reproduced in Laband, *Lord Chelmsford*, p. 22.
25 Sir Evelyn Wood Papers, Killie Campbell Africana Library, Durban 26/11, referenced in Laband, *Lord Chelmsford*, p. 27.
26 Ibid., 26/12, in Laband, *Lord Chelmsford*, p. 30.
27 Wood, p. 22. This was an insight suggesting that the policy of Confederation was already in trouble. It was no surprise when, just a few years later, the Boers in Transvaal too were up in arms against the British.
28 Norris-Newman, p. 31.
29 WO 32/7702.
30 WO 32/7704, letter to Stanley from Chelmsford, 25 November. See Laband, *Lord Chelmsford*, p. 33.
31 Letter from Pietermaritzburg, 7 December, in Sir Theophilus Shepstone, see Laband, *Lord Chelmsford*, p. 37.
32 Emery, *Marching Over Africa*, p. 58.
33 See Moodie, pp. 13–6.
34 See French, p. 38, who noted in 1939 that 'no one owning to the scantiest knowledge of the Zulu people or their history could have been sanguine of a peaceful issue' after this announcement.
35 Moodie, p. 17.

3. A Moral Victory?

1 Cited in Lock and Quantrill, *Zulu Victory*, p. 67.
2 WO 32/7704.
3 Letter from Chelmsford to Pearson, 15 December 1878, PP, in Laband, *Lord Chelmsford*, p. 41.
4 Letter from Chelmsford to Wood, 16 December 1878, in Sir Evelyn Wood collection, Pietermaritzburg; see Laband, *Lord Chelmsford*, p. 44.
5 CP 27.

6 Letter from Chelmsford to Pearson, 31 December, PP, see Laband, *Lord Chelmsford*, p. 49.

7 Norris-Newman, p. 32.

8 From *My Recollections of a Famous Campaign*, cited in Lock and Quantrill, *Zulu Victory*, p. 76.

9 Norris-Newman, p. 109.

10 Cited in Lock and Quantrill, *Zulu Victory*, p. 72.

11 Norris-Newman, p. 36.

12 Hamilton-Browne, p. 101.

13 See *The War Correspondents*, p. 28.

14 *Curling Letters*, p. 46.

15 Quoted in Lock and Quantrill, *Zulu Victory*, p. 77.

16 Hallam Parr, p. 181.

17 Hamilton-Browne, p. 102; Norris-Newman, p. 38.

18 *The Red Soldier*, p. 66. Ellis would die at Isandlwana.

19 Thompson, p. 37.

20 Hamilton-Browne, p. 105. This is a picturesque tale but unfortunately Norris-Newman, who was also present, heard the challenge from the Zulu but recorded that there was no reply to it. See Norris-Newman, p. 39.

21 Harford is usually referred to as a lieutenant though he noted that he was an honorary captain whilst he was in the NNC. See Harford, p. 143.

22 Hamilton-Browne, p. 108. Harford, however, did not mention the anecdote in his own memoirs so this may be another example of Hamilton-Browne's vivid imagination at work.

23 Ibid., p. 111.

24 Norris-Newman, p. 42.

25 WO 32/7712.

26 Harford, p. 120.

27 Hamilton-Browne, p. 107.

28 Norris-Newman, p. 42.

29 Letter from Chelmsford to Frere, 12 January, CP 27, in Laband, p. 60 and French, p. 73.

30 Ibid., Chelmsford to Commissary-General Strickland, 13 January, in Laband, p. 67. This is a superficially strange comment which reflects on the hierarchical attitudes of the British army of the time. Dalton was in his mid-forties.

31 See Colenso and Durnford, p. 29.

32 CP 27, in Laband, p. 68 and French, p. 77.

33 Ibid., letter to Frere, 16 January, in Laband, p. 68 and French, p. 78.

34 Letter, 16 January, in Sir Evelyn Wood Collection, WC II/2/2. See Laband, p. 70.

35 A.H. Swiss, *Records of the 24th Regiment* (London, 1894), cited in Greaves, *Rorke's Drift*, p. 84.

36 Norris-Newman, p. 43.

37 For further information on the Edendale Horse, see Thompson, p. 11.

38 Quoted in Greaves, *Rorke's Drift*, p. 79.

39 Letter to Frere from 'Insalwana Hill', 21 January, CP 27, in Laband, p. 74 and French p. 81.

40 Quoted in Lock and Quantrill, *Zulu Victory*, p. 134.

41 Norris-Newman, p. 46.

42 Harford, p. 121.

43 Hamilton-Browne, p. 119.

44 Quoted in Lock and Quantrill, *Zulu Victory*, p. 138.

45 Norris-Newman, p. 51.

4. The Day of the Dead Moon

1 Private McNulty of B Company 1st/24th who, fortunately for them, had been sent to face the Pondos rather than fight the Zulus, otherwise they too would probably have died with the rest of their battalion. In *Marching Over Africa*, p. 80.

2 CP 8/29 in Laband, p. 81. The message appeared widely in the press, for example in *The Times* of 12 February 1879.

3 CP 8/15 in Laband, p. 76.

4 Both references in CP 27.

5 See Greaves, *Rorke's Drift*, p. 227.

6 Norris-Newman, p. 46.

7 Hallam Parr, p. 190.

8 Lock and Quantrill, *Zulu Victory*, p. 151.

9 Hallam Parr, p. 192.

10 CP 27.

11 Lock and Quantrill, *Zulu Victory*, p. 160.

12 This is what Major Spalding, in charge at Rorke's Drift, had told him, though Chard had received no orders directly. See his report to Queen Victoria in, for example, Greaves, *Rorke's Drift*, where both his initial official report and later more detailed account for the queen are both reproduced in full. They also appear in *The Noble 24th*.

13 *Curling Letters*, p. 92.

14 Ibid., p. 50.

15 From *Times of Natal*, in Moodie, p. 69.

16 Moodie, p. 72.

17 Colenso and Durnford, p. 218.

18 The version of events portrayed in the movie *Zulu Dawn*.

19 WO 33/34 63908, cited in Lock and Quantrill, *Zulu Victory*, p. 186.

20 Ibid., p. 186.

21 Ibid., p. 188.

22 Colenso and Durnford, p. 219.

23 Letter in *The Times*, 2 April 1879.

24 Gardner's statement in WO 32/7711.

25 Quoted in Snook, p. 213.

26 Smith-Dorrien, p. 27.

27 See, for example, Lock and Quantrill, *Zulu Victory*, p. 326. See also Ian Knight in *By the Orders of the Great White Queen*, p. 85 and Lieutenant Colonel Mike Snook.

28 Quoted in Knight and Castle, *Isandlwana*, p. 42.

29 Colenso and Durnford, p. 221.

30 Bickley's statement on ammunition shortages can be found in *The Noble 24th*, p. 192.

31 Norris-Newman, p. 82.

32 Ibid., p. 78.

33 *Curling Letters*, p. 94.

34 Snook, p. 303; Appendix 1 lists the number of British/colonial participants and casualties in the battle.

35 *Curling Letters*, p. 109.

36 See Knight and Castle, *Isandlwana*, p. 44.

37 Colenso and Durnford, p. 321.

38 Reported, for example, by Richard Stevens of the Natal Mounted Police. See Greaves, *Rorke's Drift*, p. 95.

39 Care must be taken in interpreting such accounts literally. Stories of similar barbarities were features of other Victorian-era conflicts such as the Indian Mutiny and were no doubt on occasion exaggerated. But they were widely believed and encouraged a ferocious response. Intriguingly, a Mr Jamieson of Durban wrote of the 'Meerut spirit', the desire for revenge which related to a massacre at Meerut that had taken place in the Mutiny. See Harford, p. 147.

40 Gunner Carroll, a shipmate from HMS *Active*, noted his demise in his journal from Eshowe on 2 February, showing that the story had become established surprisingly quickly.

41 Hallam Parr, p. 224.

42 Moodie, p. 38.

43 Laband and Thompson, *The Illustrated Guide*, p. 108.

44 Ibid., p. 106.

45 The letter to his father describing his escape is reproduced in French, pp. 98–101. Also reproduced in *The Red Soldier*, p. 88.

46 Essex's letter, published in *The Times*, 2 April 1879.

47 Smith-Dorrien, p. 13.

48 Reproduced in *Curling Letters*, p. 97.

49 Smith-Dorrien, p. 28.

50 Ibid., p. 29. Private John Williams, Colonel Glyn's groom who survived the massacre, noted in his report (reproduced in *The Noble 24th*, p. 195) that Coghill left the camp very soon after Melvill. In the melee he had overtaken him.

51 From the article 'Welsh Soldiers in the Zulu War' by Alan Conway, *National Library of Wales Journal*, Summer 1959, reprinted and accessible at www.genuki.org.uk/big/wal/Zulu.html. Originally printed in *North Wales Express*, 11 April 1879.

52 Russell's subsequent report, dated 1 April, WO 32/7731.

53 Harford, p. 126.

54 WO 32/7711.

55 Hamilton-Browne, p. 132. A similar message was recalled by Major H.G. Mainwaring of the 24th who was near to Black at the time. See *The Noble 24th*, p. 199.

56 Thompson, p. 44.

57 Colenso and Durnford, p. 225.

58 Norris-Newman, p. 57.

59 Hallam Parr, p. 194, says that it was about 3.30 p.m. when those in camp, some way behind the general, heard of the message that Lonsdale delivered.

60 Reproduced in French, p. 157.

61 Gosset gave evidence at the subsequent inquiry and his account is quoted in French, pp. 103–5.

62 Moodie, p. 73.

63 Greaves, *Rorke's Drift*, p. 97, quoting the 24th Regiment Official History.

64 Moodie, p. 45.

5. Nowhere to Go

1 Quoted in Greaves, *Rorke's Drift*, p. 102.

2 This is the widely held view, though one Zulu witness was described by Hallam Parr, p. 185, as having received orders from Cetshwayo to cross into Natal and push the invaders back to the Drakensberg, many miles away across Natal.

3 WO 32/7711.

4 *Marching Over Africa*, p. 84.

5 See research by Greaves which identifies that Lieutenant Harford had seen it entrenched when the column crossed on 11 January. In 'The Pre-Defence of Rorke's Drift', Journal of the Anglo-Zulu War Historical Society, No 24.

6 Harford, p. 129.

7 I am grateful for this information from Dr Adrian Greaves, which has been obtained from researching through the journals of Hammar in 2008. Interestingly, a letter from Trooper Harry Lugg mentioned at the time that

there were two Swedish missionaries at the mission station in the build-up to the battle. See *The Red Soldier*, p. 132.

8 Hallam Parr, p. 237.

9 Quoted in Chard's report to Queen Victoria. Witt's reports are ambiguous as to how much he witnessed and it is not clear exactly when he escaped from the mission station to safety.

10 Quoted in Knight, *Nothing Remains But to Fight*, p. 102.

11 Chard's report to the queen.

12 Mentioned in *North Wales Express*, 18 April 1879. From Alan Conway, 'Welsh Soldiers in the Zulu War' in *National Library of Wales Journal*, Summer 1959.

13 Russell, quoted in Lock and Quantrill, *Zulu Victory*, p. 226.

14 Norris-Newman, p. 61.

15 Harford, p. 130.

16 *The Red Soldier*, p. 94.

17 Wood, p. 31 (footnote 1).

18 Alan Conway, 'Welsh Soldiers in the Zulu War' in *National Library of Wales Journal*, Summer 1959.

19 Hallam Parr, p. 232.

20 Hamilton-Browne, p. 141.

21 Harford, p. 131.

22 Norris-Newman, p. 69.

23 See research by Greaves in Journal No 24 of the Anglo-Zulu War Historical Society.

24 Printed first in 1880, *Cetshwayo's Dutchman* was re-released in 1989.

25 Hallam Parr, p. 249.

26 *Curling Letters*, p. 122.

27 Cited in Knight, *Nothing Remains But to Fight*, p. 77.

6. Under Siege

1 From the account of Harry O'Clery of the Buffs in *Told From The Ranks*. Much of his account appears in *By the Orders of the Great White Queen*. It is also reproduced in full in *Zulu: 1879* (D.C.F. Moodie and the Leonaur Editors).

2 Quoted in Knight and Castle, *Fearful Hard Times*, p. 49.

3 See *Told from the Ranks*, p. 165.

4 Quoted in Knight and Castle, *Isandlwana*, p. 64.

5 The description of Zulus 'swarming' into action or appearing to be 'like a lot of bees' appears so frequently in accounts of the war from both sides that it is worth noting. It gives an idea of the mass of the Zulu forces and also the noise; frequent analogies to 'murmuring' in accounts underline the general impression.

6 Montague, p. 60.
7 Quoted in Knight and Castle, *Fearful Hard Times*, p. 70.
8 Quoted in Knight and Castle, *Isandlwana*, p. 71.
9 In Gunner Carroll's journal, 22 January.
10 *Told from the Ranks*, p. 166.
11 *The Red Soldier*, p. 186.
12 *Told from the Ranks*, p. 168.
13 Quoted in Knight, *Nothing Remains But to Fight*, p. 77.
14 Quoted in Knight and Castle, *Fearful Hard Times*, p. 79.
15 Quoted in Knight and Castle, *Isandlwana*, p. 75.
16 O'Clery in *Told from the Ranks*, p. 168.
17 Ibid.
18 Quoted in *Fearful Hard Times*, p. 83.
19 Thompson, p. 83.
20 Norris-Newman, p. 92.
21 Shervinton, p. 38.
22 *Told from the Ranks*, p. 170.
23 *Fearful Hard Times*, p. 92.
24 *Told from the Ranks*, p. 170.
25 Knight and Castle, *Isandlwana*, p. 89.

7. Back to the Drawing Board

1 Smith-Dorrien, p. 32.
2 Emery, *Marching Over Africa*, p. 60.
3 Norris-Newman, p. 74.
4 *Natal Witness*, 28 January in *The War Correspondents*, p. 64.
5 Ibid., p. 65.
6 *The War Correspondents*, p. 72.
7 Sir Evelyn Wood Collection in Laband, p. 99.
8 Frere wrote to Chelmsford in encouraging tones on 25 January and to Shepstone on the same day. Both quoted in French, pp. 115, 118.
9 CP 8/48 in Laband, p. 102.
10 WO 32/7709 in Laband, p. 102.
11 Curling, p. 126.
12 Harford, p. 133.
13 Thompson, p. 74.
14 Government House Natal Papers in Laband, p. 113.
15 Harford, p. 118.
16 Thompson, p. 89.
17 Norris-Newman, p. 87.
18 Ibid., p. 88.
19 Moodie, p. 56.

20 *Illustrated London News*, 8 March 1879, quoting from Chelmsford's report.
21 Quoted in Greaves, *Rorke's Drift*, p. 177.
22 Ibid., p. 187.
23 In the event, there was no provision to award the VC posthumously. Coghill and Melvill would receive the award several decades later when the rules were changed.
24 See an article by Matthew Annis, *No Sort of Parallel* in Journal of Anglo-Zulu War Historical Society, No 25.
25 Sir Evelyn Wood Collection in Laband, p. 82.
26 CP 8/31. Chelmsford's notes on the inquest are referenced in full in Laband, p. 92 and French, p. 144.
27 See Journal of Anglo-Zulu War Historical Society, No 4, cited in *Crossing the Buffalo*, p. 217.
28 Norris-Newman, p. 107.
29 Hansard, 28 March 1879.
30 Norris-Newman, p. 47.
31 Reproduced in Journal of Anglo-Zulu War Historical Society, No 15.
32 Hansard, 28 March 1879.
33 *Illustrated London News*, 1 March 1879.
34 The report is reproduced in full in Lock and Quantrill, *Zulu Victory*, pp. 280–1.
35 *Illustrated London News*, 5 April 1879.
36 Colenso and Durnford, pp. 281–4.

8. The Turn of the Tide

1 John, p. 448.
2 CP 28 in Laband, p. 87.
3 Wood, p. 34.
4 Reported in *The War Correspondents*, 27 February 1879, p. 69.
5 Letter by Major Tucker to his father in Emery, *The Red Soldier*, pp. 157–62.
6 Emery, *Marching Over Africa*, pp. 75–6.
7 Wood, p. 42.
8 Quoted in *With his Face to the Foe*, p. 152.
9 Article by Wood in *Pearson's Magazine*, reproduced in Moodie, p. 140.
10 Quoted in *By the Orders of the Great White Queen*, p. 199. A Zulu survivor of the later battle at Ulundi confirmed part of the story: see WO 32/7763.
11 This news was inaccurate. Mbilini had indeed been killed but in a minor skirmish with irregular cavalry on 4 April.
12 Wood, p. 58.
13 Letter from Private Fowler VC of the 90th Light Infantry in Emery, *Marching Over Africa*, p. 78.
14 Prior, p. 94.
15 Quoted in Knight, *Great Zulu Battles*, p. 160.

16 *The Red Soldier*, p. 169.
17 *The Times*, 1 September 1879. Snook's letter home, which caused such a storm, is reproduced in *The Red Soldier*, p. 173.
18 *The Red Soldier*, p. 175.
19 Quoted in Laband and Thompson, *The Illustrated Guide*, p. 54.
20 See Knight, *Great Zulu Battles*, p. 161.
21 Wood, p. 65.
22 Ibid., p. 68.
23 Norris-Newman, p. 156.
24 Ibid., p. 86.

9. Chelmsford to the Rescue

1 Quoted in Knight and Castle, *Isandlwana*, p. 95.
2 From Gunner Carroll's journal of 13 March.
3 WO 32/7722 in Laband, p. 130 and French, p. 171.
4 CP 7/37: Memorandum in Laband, p. 132 and French, p. 172.
5 Quoted in Knight and Castle, *Fearful Hard Times*, p. 142.
6 Prior, pp. 90–1.
7 Thompson, p. 91.
8 Norris-Newman, p. 130.
9 Molyneux, p. 130.
10 Quoted in *Fearful Hard Times*, p. 197.
11 *The Red Soldier*, p. 202.
12 Norris-Newman, p. 139.
13 Quoted in Knight and Castle, *Fearful Hard Times*, p. 39.
14 Hamilton-Browne, p. 212.
15 *The Red Soldier*, p. 202.
16 Ibid., p. 205.
17 Colenso and Durnford, p. 293.
18 WO 32/7727: Report to Stanley in Laband, p. 139.
19 *The Red Soldier*, p. 213.
20 *Illustrated London News*, 10 May 1879.

10. The Setting Sun of the Bonapartes

1 Norris-Newman, p. 192.
2 Moodie, p. 181.
3 Filon, *Recollections of the Empress Eugenie*, p. 285.
4 Filon, *Memoirs of the Prince Imperial*, p. 188.
5 Ibid., p. 187.
6 Ibid., p. 111.
7 Molyneux, p. 149.

8 Private letter from the Duke of Cambridge, which he read out to the House of Lords on 23 June 1879. The duke also read out a private note he had sent to Sir Bartle Frere. Quoted in Filon, *Memoirs of the Prince Imperial*, p. 197 (though the exact wording is slightly different).

9 CP 28: in Laband, p. 146 and French, p. 181.

10 Montague, p. 59.

11 Colenso and Durnford, p. 306.

12 Ibid., p. 325.

13 Ibid., p. 326.

14 Cited in John, p. 457.

15 Harrison, *Recollections* in *With His Face to the Foe*, p. 178.

16 Ibid.

17 Colenso and Durnford, p. 328.

18 Emery, *Marching Over Africa*, p. 64.

19 *Daily News*, 21 May 1879, in *The War Correspondents*, p. 102.

20 Prior, p. 105.

21 From Carey's initial report. This was quoted along with the comments of other witnesses in the *Illustrated London News*, 5 July 1879.

22 Filon, *Recollections of the Empress Eugenie*, p. 294.

23 Grenfell, *Memoirs of Lord Grenfell*, p. 59.

24 Ibid., p. 55.

25 Blood, p. 194.

26 *Illustrated London News*, 5 July 1879.

27 Trooper Grubb in Moodie, p. 176.

28 Cited in Filon, *Memoirs of the Prince Imperial*, p. 220.

29 CP 11/8: in Laband, p. 183 and French, p. 242.

30 Reproduced in *The Washing of the Spears*, pp. 532–4. Interestingly, many men in the camp freely expressed their sympathy for Chelmsford given the position he had been placed in. See Montague, p. 56, for example.

31 *Illustrated London News*, 16 July 1879.

32 *The Times*, 14 July 1879, cited in *With His Face to the Foe*, p. 217.

33 Norris-Newman, p. 193.

34 *Illustrated London News*, 5 July 1879.

35 *Queen Victoria's Highland Journals*, p. 206 – entry for Friday 20 June.

36 *Illustrated London News*, 19 July 1879.

37 Letter to Anne, Countess of Chesterfield, cited in *With His Face to the Foe*, p. 256.

11. Race for Victory

1 Blood, p. 185.

2 Ibid., p. 175.

3 Ibid., p. 192.

4 Curling, p. 139.

5   Emery, *Marching Over Africa*, p. 63.
6   Blood, p. 193.
7   Colenso and Durnford, p. 336.
8   Memorandum, 8 June, in Laband, p. 189.
9   Emery, *Marching Over Africa*, p. 62.
10 Smith-Dorrien, p. 38.
11 CP 28: Letter to Stanley, 10 June, in Laband, pp. 190–4.
12 Colenso and Durnford, p. 309.
13 Ibid., p. 352 (see also WO 32/7733). The message was sent via St Vincent on 29 May but took several weeks to arrive at Chelmsford's camp.
14 Farwell, p. 219.
15 Norris-Newman, p. 217.
16 CP 28: 11 April 1879, in Laband, p. 147 and French, p. 180.
17 Ibid.
18 Thompson, p. 112.
19 In Wolseley's journal, Monday 30 June.
20 Blood, p. 198.
21 WO 32/7771: in Laband, p. 203 and French, p. 277.
22 WO 32/7763: Chelmsford's detailed report on the battle, in Laband, p. 208; also in WO 32/7763 there is a statement from one of the Zulus present in Ulundi confirming the events surrounding the cattle.
23 Molyneux, p. 181.
24 Ibid., p. 182.
25 The words of the war correspondent Archibald Forbes, in *By the Orders of the Great White Queen*, p. 247.
26 Prior, pp. 114–5.
27 Ibid., p. 115.
28 Molyneux, p. 184.
29 Ibid., p. 185.
30 Ibid., p. 186.
31 From an interview with the then captured king in *The Natal Mercury*, 18 September 1879.
32 Quoted in Knight and Castle, *Isandlwana*, p. 126.
33 From the *Daily News* in Moodie, p. 208.
34 Norris-Newman, p. 212.
35 Prior, *Campaigns of a War Correspondent*, p. 118.
36 Grenfell, p. 62.
37 Norris-Newman, p. 214. See also Wood, p. 81.
38 WO 32/7763.
39 Moodie, p. 209.
40 Molyneux, p. 189.
41 Norris-Newman, p. 214.
42 Prior, p. 122.

43 Ibid., p. 92.

44 They were Lieutenant Scott-Douglas and Corporal Cotter, the latter of the 17th Lancers. See Montague, p. 146.

45 Molyneux, p. 191.

46 Blood, p. 190.

47 CP 21/7: In Laband, p. 218.

48 Norris-Newman, p. 46.

49 Colenso and Durnford, p. 357.

50 Quoted in *The War Correspondents*, p. 37.

51 French, p. 351.

52 *The Red Soldier*, p. 253.

53 Ibid., p. 357.

54 Ibid., p. 223.

55 Colenso and Durnford, p. 361.

56 *The War Correspondents*, p. 163.

57 Bennett, p. 107.

58 Molyneux, p. 207.

59 Norris-Newman, p. 341.

60 Preston, p. 49.

61 Ibid., p. 55, journal entry dated 12 July.

62 Ibid., 15 July.

63 Ibid., 25 July.

64 Ibid., p. 298.

65 Montague, p. 181, suggests that the party of Zulus involved were little more than bandits.

66 Colenso and Durnford, pp. 369–71.

67 Norris-Newman, p. 47.

68 Sir Evelyn Wood Collection, in Laband, p. 199.

69 *The War Correspondents*, p. 166.

70 Quoted in Laband and Thompson, *The Illustrated Guide*, p. 5.

71 Emery, *Marching Over Africa*, p. 63.

72 See French, pp. 426, 428.

73 Smith-Dorrien, p. 32.

74 From 'Reminiscences of the Zulu War' in *Pall Mall* magazine, p. 20 (1900).

BIBLIOGRAPHY

Primary sources in this book have been abbreviated in the following fashion:
  CP, Chelmsford Papers, National Army Museum, London
  PP, Pearson Papers, National Army Museum, London
  WO, War Office Papers, Public Records Office, London (now The National Archives)

What follows does not purport to be a comprehensive bibliography. It is rather a record of the major sources that I have relied on in the preparation of this book. In addition to the sources quoted below, I have also made extensive use of all the *Illustrated London News* journals published between November 1878 and November 1879. Note that we are fortunate to have a substantial amount of Chelmsford's documents easily available thanks to the efforts of both the Honourable Gerald French and Professor John Laband. When documents appear in both books, I have provided references for each of them. I have also referenced articles from the Anglo–Zulu War Historical Society; these are duly credited when used within the book.

Bancroft, James W., *Rorke's Drift*, Spellmount, Tunbridge Wells, 1990
Bengough, Sir Harcourt M., *Memories of a Soldier's Life*, Edward Arnold, London, 1913
Bennett, Ian, *Eyewitness in Zululand*, Greenhill, London, 1989
Blood, General Sir Bindon, *Four Score Years and Ten*, J. Bell and Sons, London, 1933
Colenso, Frances E. and Durnford, Edward, *Colenso & Durnford's Zulu War*, Leonaur Ltd, 2008 (originally published 1879)
David, Saul, *Zulu: The Heroism and Tragedy of the Zulu War*, Viking, London, 2004
Duff, David (ed.), *Queen Victoria's Highland Journals*, Webb & Bower, Exeter, 1980

Emery, Frank, *Marching over Africa*, Hodder and Stoughton, London, 1986

Farwell, Byron, *Eminent Victorian Soldiers – Seekers of Glory*, Norton, Ontario, 1988

Filon, Augustin, *Memoirs of the Prince Imperial*, Heinemann, London, 1913

———, *Recollections of the Empress Eugenie*, Cassell, London, 1920

French, Major G., *Lord Chelmsford and the Zulu War*, John Lane, The Bodley Head, London, 1939

Greaves, Adrian, *Crossing the Buffalo: The Zulu War of 1879*, Weidenfeld & Nicolson, London, 2005

———, *Rorke's Drift*, Cassell, London, 2002

Greaves, Adrian and Best, Brian (eds), *The Curling Letters of the Zulu War*, Leo Cooper, Barnsley, 2001

Grenfell, Field-Marshal, Lord, *Memoirs of Lord Grenfell*, Hodder and Stoughton, London, 1925

Guide to St Michael's Abbey Farnborough, Pitkin, Andover

Hamilton-Browne, G., *A Lost Legionary in South Africa*, BiblioLife, Charleston (undated)

Harrison, Sir Richard, *Recollections of a Life in the British Army*, Smith, Elder & Co., London, 1908

John, Katherine, *The Prince Imperial*, Putnam, London, 1939

Knight, Ian, *British Fortifications in Zululand 1879*, Osprey, Oxford, 2005

——— (compiled), *By the Orders of the Great White Queen*, Greenhill, London, 1992

———, *Great Zulu Commanders*, Arms & Armour, London, 1999

———, *Essential Histories: The Zulu War 1879*, Osprey, Oxford, 2003

———, *Go to your God Like a Soldier*, Greenhill, London, 1996

———, *Great Zulu Battles 1838–1906*, Arms & Armour Press, London, 1998

———, *The National Army Museum Book of the Zulu War*, Pan Books, London, 2004

———, *Nothing Remains but to Fight*, Greenhill, London, 1993

———, *The Zulus*, Osprey, Oxford, 2004

———, *With his Face to the Foe*, Spellmount, Staplehurst, 2001

Knight, Ian and Castle, Ian: *Fearful Hard Times – the Siege and Relief of Eshowe, 1879*, Greenhill, London, 1994

———, *Isandlwana*, Pen & Sword, Barnsley, 2000

Laband, John and Knight, Ian, *The War Correspondents: The Anglo-Zulu War*, Sutton, Stroud, 1996

Laband, John and Thompson, Paul, *The Illustrated Guide to the Anglo-Zulu War*, University of Natal Press, Pietermaritzburg, 2000

Laband, John P.C., *Lord Chelmsford's Zululand Campaign 1878–1879*, Sutton, Stroud, 1994

Lock, Ron and Quantrill, Peter, *Zulu Vanquished*, Greenhill, London, 2005
———, *Zulu Victory*, Greenhill, London, 2002

Molyneux, Major General W.C.F., *Campaigning in South Africa and Egypt*, Macmillan, London, 1896, reprinted Bibliolife (undated)

Montague, Captain W.E., *Campaigning in South Africa – Reminiscences of an Officer*, William Blackwood and Sons, Edinburgh and London, 1880, reprinted as *Campaigning in Zululand*, Leonaur, 2006 (the latter is the source of references used here)

Moodie, D.C.F. and the Leonaur (eds), *Zulu 1879 (Eyewitness to War Series)*, Leonaur, 2006

Morris, Donald, *The Washing of the Spears*, Pimlico, London (1994 edition)

Norris-Newman, Charles L., *In Zululand with the British throughout the War of 1879*, Greenhill, London, 1990 (first printed 1880)

Parr, Captain Henry Hallam, *A Sketch of the Kafir and Zulu Wars*, Kegan Paul and Co., London, 1880

Payne, David and Emily (ed. Dr Adrian Greaves), *Harford – The Writings, Photographs and Sketches*, Ultimatum Tree Limited, 2008

Phillips, William Peter, *The Death of the Prince Imperial in Zululand, 1879*, Hampshire County Council Museum Services Publication, Winchester, 1998

Preston, Adrian (ed.), *The SA Journal of Sir Garnet Wolseley*, Balkema, Cape Town, 1973

Prior, Melton, *Campaigns of a War Correspondent*, London, 1912

Ransford, Oliver, *The Great Trek*, Cardinal, London, 1972

Shervinton, Kathleen, *The Shervintons – Soldiers of Fortune*, Usher Unwin, London, 1899

Small, E. Milton, *Told from the Ranks*, Andrew Melrose, London, 1897

Smith-Dorrien, Horace, *Smith-Dorrien, Isandlwana to the Great War*, Leonaur, 2009 (this is a reprint of Smith-Dorrien's *Memories of Forty-Eight Years Service*, first published in 1925)

Snook, Lieutenant Colonel Mike, *How Can Men Die Better*, Greenhill, London, 2005

Taylor, Stephen, *Shaka's Children – A History of the Zulu People*, HarperCollins, London, 1994

Thompson, P.S., *Black Soldiers of the Queen*, University of Alabama Press, Tuscaloosa, 2006

Vijn, Cornelius, *Cetshwayo's Dutchman*, Greenhill, London, 1988

Wood, Evelyn, *From Midshipman to Field Marshal*, Methuen and Co., London, 1906 (2 volumes)

INDEX